The Writings of
Henry D. Thoreau

Journal

Volume 2: 1842-1848

HENRY D. THOREAU

Journal

VOLUME 2: 1842-1848

JOHN C. BRODERICK, *GENERAL EDITOR*

EDITED BY
ROBERT SATTELMEYER

PRINCETON, NEW JERSEY

PRINCETON UNIVERSITY PRESS

MCMLXXXIV

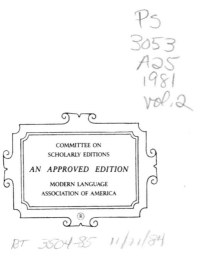
*The Committee emblem means that one of a panel of textual experts
serving the Committee has reviewed the text and textual apparatus of
the original volume by thorough and scrupulous sampling, and has
approved them for sound and consistent editorial principles employed
and maximum accuracy attained. The accuracy of the text has been
guarded by careful and repeated proofreading of printer's copy according
to standards set by the Committee.*

*The editorial preparation of this volume, and costs associated with its
publication, were supported by grants from the Editing and Publication
Programs of the National Endowment for the Humanities, an
independent federal agency. During the early stages of editing, support
was provided through the Center for Editions of American Authors of the
Modern Language Association.*

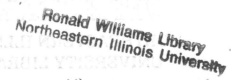

Contents

Long Book

[FALL 1842]–MARCH 1846

While we ascended the stream, plying the oars, or shoving our way along, with might and main, the current of our dreams also was somewhat ruffled and impetuous; but when we turned the prow down stream, rock, tree, kine, knoll, silently assuming new and varying position, as wind and tide shifted the scene, we yielded ourselves to the liquid undulating lapse of thought.

> Where'er thou sail'st who sailed with me,
> Though now thou climbest loftier mounts
> And fairer rivers dost ascend
> Be thou my muse, my Brother.

{*Two-fifths page blank*}

The land seemed to grow fairer as we withdrew from it– Far away to the south west lay the quiet village left alone, under its elms and button woods in mid-afternoon – And the hills notwithstanding their blue etherial face –seemed to cast a saddened eye on their old playfellows.

As we swept slowly down the stream we passed the large and conspicuous flowers of the hibiscus–covering the dwarf willows, and peering through the leaves of the grape– Nature seemed to have attired herself for our departure, with a profusion of fringes and curls, reflected in the water.

This flower is not very common or accessible in our vicinity– And we wished to send word of its locality to a friend we had left behind before it was too late– We were just gliding out of sight of the village spire when it occurred to us that the farmer–in the adjacent meadow will wend to church on the morrow and carry the news

for us—and by the monday at least while we shall be
floating over the bosom of the Merrimack the flower's
friend will be reaching to pluck the blossom on the water
of the Concord.

Only the deeper souls are reserved for the high tragedy
of life. The rill whose

> "siluer sands and pebbles sing
> Eternall ditties with the spring"

is silenced by the first frosts of winter—but the stern and
sad Dantean souls, on whose bottom the sun never
shines, clogged with sunken rocks and the ruins of
forests, from whose surface comes up no murmur, are
strangers to the icy fetters which bind a thousand
contributory rills.

> "Pulsae referunt ad sidera valles"

> , "et invito processit Vesper Olympo."

I should read Virgil if only to be reminded of the
identity of human nature in all ages. I am pleased even
with such still lines as

> —"jam laeto turgent in palmite gemmae,

or

> "strata jacent passim sua quaeque sub arbore poma."

{One-third page blank}

These Indian relics in our fields which have preserved
their rugged forms so long are evidence of the vital
energy of the people who made them.

{One-fourth page blank}

The village of Concord is situated on Concord
river—about 15 miles from where it empties into the
Merrimack—

A river—a huge volume of matter ceaselessly rolling
through the fields and meadows of the substantial

earth—making haste from the high places by the stable dwellings of men and Egyptian pyramids, to its famous reservoir. By a natural impulse the dwellers on its banks would at length accompany its waters into the lowlands of the globe. Rivers must have been the guides which conducted the footsteps of the first travellers. The constant lure, where they flow by our door, to distant adventure and exploration.

> I was born upon thy bank river
> My blood flows in thy stream
> And thou meanderest forever
> At the bottom of my dream

Many a time had I stood on the bank of the stream watching the lapse of the current—an apt emblem of all progress—following the same law with the system, with time—with all that is made. The weeds at the bottom gently bending down the stream, shaken by the watery wind, though still firmly planted where their seeds had sunk—but anon to die and go down the stream. The shining pebbles at the bottom not anxious to better their condition.

The chips and weeds and occasional logs and stems of trees that floated past—fulfilling their fate—these were objects of singular interest to me— And at length I had determined to launch myself on its current and float like them whither it might bear me.

This great but silent traveller which had so long journeyed past my door—at three miles an hour—might I not put myself under its escort?

{*One-fourth page blank*}

There are moments when all anxiety and stated toil must cease in presence of the infinite expanded leisure of nature. In a sultry day—stretched on the deck of his craft, the boatman drifts upon the sluggish waters, and the very mood of nature compels him to reflection.

{One-half page missing}

Friends are the ancient and honorable of the earth. The oldest men did not begin this league. It is older than Hindostan and the Chinese empire– So long has it been cultivated and still is a staple article– It is a natural and durable league– Warm serene days like this only bring it out to the surface. There is a friendliness between the sun & the earth in pleasant weather–the grey content of the land is its color.

{One-half page missing}

In friendship we worship moral beauty without the formality of religion.

There is one principle at the bottom of all affinities. The magnet cultivates a steady friendship with the pole, and all bodies with all others. The friendliness of nature is the goddess Ceres, who presides over every sowing and harvest–and we bless the same in sun and rain. The seed in the ground tarries for a season with its genial friends there. All the earths and grasses and minerals are its hosts who entertain it hospitably, and plenteous crops are the result.

This principle is at the bottom of all romance and chivelry all rural–pastoral–poetical life– The moon shines for some Endymion. Smooth pastures and mild airs, are for some Coridon and Phyllis. Plato's republic is the scene of Platonic love–and Paradise belongs to Adam & Eve.

consider how much the sun and the summer–the buds of spring and the sered leaves of autumn are related to

the cabins of the settlers which we discover on the
shore–how all the rays which paint the landscape radiate
from them. The flight of the crow and the gyrations of
the hawk have reference to their roofs.

Friends do not interchange their common wealth but
each puts his finger into the private coffer of the other.
They will be most familiar, they will be most unfamiliar,
for they will be so one and single that common themes
will not have to be bandied between them, but in silence
they will digest them as one mind; but they will at the
same time be so two and double, that each will be to the
other as admirable and as inaccessible as a star. He will
view him as it were through "optic glass"–"At evening
from the top of Fesolé" And after, the longest period he
will still be in apogee to him.

Fare well Etiquette! My neighbor inhabits a hollow
sycamore, and I a beech tree–no 2 p 60 {1:122}

{One-fourth page blank}

Sat. Aug 31st 1839.

A warm drizzling rain obscured the morning and
threatened to delay our voyage, but at length the leaves
and grass were dried, and it came out a mild afternoon,
as serene and fresh as if nature were maturing some
greater scheme of her own– After this long dripping and
oozing from every pore, she began to respire again more
healthily than ever. So with a vigorous shove we launched
our boat from the bank, while the flags and bullrushes
curtsey'd a Good-speed, and dropped silently down the
stream.

It had been loaded at the door the evening before, half
a mile from the river–and provided with wheels against
emergencies but with the bulky cargo which we stevedores
had stowed in it–it proved but an indifferent land

carriage— For water and water casks there was a
plentiful supply of muskmelons from our patch which
had just begun to be ripe—and chests and spare spars
and sails and tent and guns and munitions for the
galleon— And as we pushed it through the meadows to
the river's bank we stepped as lightly about it as if a
portion of our own bulk and burden was stowed in its
hold—we were amazed to find ourselves outside still

Some of our neighbors stood in a recess of the
shore—the last inhabitants of Ithaca—to whom we fired
a parting salute, and conferred the welfare of the state.

{*One-fifth page blank*}

Gradually the village murmur subsided, and we
seemed to be embarked upon the placid current of our
dreams, and floating from past to future, over billows
of fresh morning or evening thoughts.

{*Four-fifths page blank*}

Our boat which had cost us a week's labor in the
spring was what the Lynn fishermen call a dory—15 feet
long by 3 in breadth at the widest part—a little forward
of the centre. It was green below with a border of blue,
out of courtesy to the green sea and the blue heavens.
Stout and servicable but consequently heavy and difficult
to be dragged over shallow places or carried around falls.

A boat, when rightly made and once launched upon
its element has a sort of life of its own— It is a kind of
amphibious animal—a creature of two elements—a fish
to swim and a bird to fly—related by one half of its
structure to some swift and shapely fish, and by the
other to a strong-winged and graceful bird. The fins of

the fish direct where to set the oars, and the tail gives
some hints for the form and position of the rudder. So
also we learn where should be the greatest breadth of
beam and depth in the hold. The bird shows how to rig
and trim the sails, and what form to give to the prow
that it may best balance the boat and divide the air
and water.

In the present case our boat took readily to the water,
since from of old there had been a tacit league struck
between them, and now it gladly availed itself of the old
law that the heavier shall float the lighter.

One of our masts served for a tent pole at night, and
we had other long and slender poles for shoving in
shallow places. A buffalo-skin was our bed at night and
a tent of twilled cotton our roof–a snow white house
8 feet in height and as many in diameter.

Sep 12 –42
The dead limbs of the willow are rounded and adorned
with the climbing Mikania (Mikania scandens) which
fills every crevice in the leafy bank, contrasting agreeably
with the gray bark of its supporter–and the now brownish
balls of the button bush. While the nature of each plant
is satisfied the general effect is enhanced to him who
sails by.

The rose-colored polygonum raises its head proudly
above the water on either side. Flowering at this season
and in these localities its little streak of red looks very
rare and precious– The white polygonum too in dense
masses and fields skirts the sides of the stream
The cardinal flowers and pickerel weed are now nearly
out of blossom

The bright blue (purple) flowers of the soap wort gentian, sprinkled here and there in the meadow–startle the passer like flowers which Proserpine might have dropped.

The snake-head grows close to the shore–and in the adjacent low grounds the Virginia Rhexia and Drooping Neottia, or Ladies' Tresses. A kind of coreopsis or sun flower now blooms above the river– And a tall dull red flower like milkweed.

Tansy in its prime–and tobacco pipes

There were a few berries still left on the hills, hanging by very slender threads.

As the night stole over, a new freshness was wafted across the meadow, and every blade of cut grass seemed to teem with life.

We glided noiselessly down the stream occasionally driving a pickerel from the covert of the pads, or a bream from her nest, and the small green bittern now and then sailed away on sluggish wings from some recess in the shore. We wondered if by its patient study by rocks and sandy capes it had wrested the whole of her secret from nature yet. What a rich experience must be its–standing on one leg, and looking out from its dull eye for so long on sunshine and river–moon and stars. What knowledge of stagnant pools–and reeds–and fogs. It would be worth while to look with the eye which has been open and seeing at such hours and in such solitudes. I would fain lay my eye side by side with its. When I behold its dull yellowish green–I wonder if my own soul is not a bright invisible green.

July 28 –42

The banks of the river are in the height of their beauty at this season– They are like the mossy brink of some cool well, the narrow leaved-willow lies along the surface of the water, in masses of light green foliage; nor should I forget the button-bush, spotted with its large white balls.

The pure white blossoms of the arrow head flower stood in the shallow parts of the river—and a few cardinals on the margin proudly surveyed themselves reflected in the water.

The robin is seen flying directly and high in the air at this season, especially over rivers, where in the morning they are constantly passing and repassing in company with the black bird.

The reflection in still water shows that for every oak and birch too growing on the hill-top, as well as for elms and willows, there is a graceful etherial tree making down from the roots—an ideal for that actual.— It suggests the mystery of all picture— What is that which is satisfied with this equally with the substance?

Faint purple clouds began to be reflected in the water, and the cow-bells tinkled louder along the banks. Like sly water rats we stole along nearer the shore—looking out for a place to pitch our camp.

It seemed insensibly to grow lighter as the night shut in, and the farthest hamlet began to be revealed which before lurked in the shadows of the noon.

{*One-fourth page blank*}

To-day the air was as elastic and crystalline as if it were a glass to the picture of this world— It explained the artifice of the picture-dealer who does not regard his picture as finished until it is glassed.

It was like the landscape seen through the bottom of
a tumbler, clothed in a mild quiet light, in which the
barns & fences chequer and partition it with new
regularity, and rough and uneven fields stretch away
with lawn-like smoothness to the horizon. The clouds
(in such a case) are finely distinct and picturesque– The
light blue of the sky contrasting with their feathery
whiteness.– They are a light etherial Persian draperry–fit
to hang over the Persia of our imaginations– The Smith's
shop resting in this Greek light seemed worthy to stand
beside the Parthenon. The potato and grain fields are
such as he imagines who has schemes of ornamental
husbandry. So may you see the true dignity of the
farmer's life.

A little bread and sugar and Cocoa boiled in river
water made our repast– As we had drank in the fluvial
prospect all day so now we took a draught of the water
with our evening meal, to propitiate the river gods, & whet
our vision for the sights it was to behold.

The building a fire and spreading our buffalo skins
was too frank an advance to be resisted. The fire and
smoke seemed to tame the scene– The rocks consented
to be our walls and the pines our roof.

{*One-third page blank*}

I have never insisted enough on the nakedness and
simplicity of friendship–the result of all emotions–their
subsidence a fruit of the temperate zone. The friend is an
unrelated man, solitary and of distinct outline. On this
same river a young maiden once saild in my boat–thus
solitary and unattended but by invisble spirits– As she
sat in the prow there was nothing but herself between
me and the sky–so that her form and life itself was
picturesque as rocks and trees– She was not child to any

mortal, and had no protector   she called no mortal
father. No priest was keeper of her soul no guardian of
her free thoughts. She dared ever to stand exposed on the
side of heaven.

Our life must be seen upon a proper back ground– For
the most part only the life of the anchorite will bear to
be considered. Our motions should be as impressive as
objects in the desert, a broken shaft or crumbling mound
against a limitless horizon.

I shall not soon forget the sounds which I heard when
falling asleep this night on the banks of the Merrimack.
Far into night I hear some tyro beating a drum
incessantly, preparing for a country muster–in Campton
as we have heard–and think of the line
   "When the drum beat at dead of night"

I am thrilled as by an infinite sweetness, and could
have exclaimed–
Cease not thou drummer of the night–thou too shalt
have thy reward– The stars hear thee, and the firmament
shall echo thy beat, till it is answerd, and the forces are
mustered. Fear not, I too will be there. While this
darkness lasts heroism will not be deferred.
But still he drums on alone in the silence & the dark.

{*One-fifth page blank*}

We had made 7 miles, and moored our boat on the
west side of a little rising ground which in the spring
forms an island in the river. The sun was setting on the
one hand while the shadow of our little eminence was
rapidly stretching over the fields on the other. Here we
found huckleberries still hanging on the bushes and
palatable, which seemed to have slowly ripened for our

especial use, and partook of this unlooked for repast with
even a devout feeling.

When we had pitched our tent on the hill side a few
rods from the shore, we sat looking through its triangular
door in the twilight at our lonely mast on the shore, just
seen above the alders, the first encroachments of
commerce on this land– Here was the incipient city and
there the port–it was Rome & Ostia– That straight
geometrical line against the water–stood for the last
refinements of civilized life. Whatever of sublimity there
is in history was there symbolized. It was the founding
of Tyre and Carthage.

For the most part there seemed to be no recognition of
human life in the night– No human breathing was
heard. Only the wind was alive and stirring. And as we
sat up awakened by the novelty of the situation, we heard
at intervals foxes stepping about over the dead leaves and
brushing the dewy grass close to our tent; and once the
the musquash fumbling among the potatoes and melons
in our boat, but when we hastened to the shore to
reconnoitre, we could see only the stars reflected in the
water scarcely disturbed by a distant ripple on its surface.
After each sound which near at hand broke the stillness
of the night each crackling of the twigs or rustling of
leaves there seemed to be a sudden pause and deeper
silence, as if the intruder were aware that no life was
rightfully abroad at that hour.

But as if to be reminded of the presence of man in
nature as well as of the inferior orders–we heard the
sound of distant alarm bells come to these woods not far
from mid night probably from the town of Lowel But a
most constant and characteristic sound of a summer
night, which we did not fail to hear every night
afterwards though at no time so incessantly and
musically as now–was the barking of the house dog– I

thought of Shakspeare's line "I had rather be a dog and bay the moon" Every variety of tone and time nearer and more remote from the patient but anxious mastiff to the timid and wakeful terrier—even in a country like this where the farm houses were few and far between —was a sufficiency of sound to lull the ears of night

wow-wow-wow-wow—wo—w

I have heard the voice of a hound just before dawn while the stars were still shining from over the woods & river far off in the horizon when it sounded sweet & melodious like an instrument

The night is almost equally indebted to a less constant and more musical interruption from the cock—who at intervals from the very shutting of night—prematurely ushers in the day.

The hounding of a dog pursuing a fox in the horizon seems naturally to have first suggested the harmonious notes of the hunting horn, to alternate with and relieve the lungs of the dog. How long this natural bugle must have rung in the woods of Attica and Latium before the horn was invented.

—

Sunday sep 1st 1839

We passed the noon under an oak on the banks of the canal in chelmsford. From Ball's hill which is the St Anne's of Concord voyageurs to Billerica meeting house the river is twice or three times as broad as in Concord— A deep and dark stream, flowing between gentle hills and occasional cliffs, and well wooded all the way It is one long lake bordered with willows. The boatmen call it a dead stream. For long reaches you can see but few traces of any village.

It seemed a natural sabbath today—a stillness so intense that it could not be heightened. There was not

breeze enough to ruffle the water. The cattle stood up to
their bellies in the river and made you think of
Rembrandt.

we encamped under some oaks in Tyngsboro, on the
east bank of the Merrimack, just below the ferry.

Sept 2nd Camped in Merrimack on the west bank by a
deep ravine.

Sept 3d in Bedford, on the west bank, opposite a large
rock, above Coos falls."

Sept 4th Wednesday. Hooksett east bank 2 or 3 miles
below the village, opposite mr. Mitchels.

sept 5th walked to Concord 10 miles

sept 12th Thursday Rowed to the northern part of
Merrimack near the ferry, to a large island near which
we camped.

sept. 13 Rowed and sailed to Concord about 50 miles.

{One-fifth page blank}

Must not our whole lives go unexplained without regard
to us, notwithstanding a few flourishes of ours, which
themselves need explanation?

Yet a friend does not afford us cheap contrasts or
encounters– He forbears to ask explanations but doubts
and surmises with full fates, as we silently ponder
our fates.

Sept 13th we sailed along as gently and steadily as the
clouds through the atmosphere over our heads–watching
the receding shores and the motions of our sails. The
north wind stepped readily into the harness we had
provided for it–and pulled us along with good will– We
were not tired of watching the motions of our sail–so
thin and yet so full of life, now bending to some generous

impulse of the breeze. And then fluttering and flapping
with a kind of human suspense. We watched the play of
its pulse as if it were our own blood beating there.

It was a scale on which the varying temperature of
distant atmospheres was graduated. It was some
attraction that the breeze it played with had been out of
doors so long. Our lives are much like a sail alternately
steady and fluttering–and always at the mercy of the
breeze.

There are many skilful apprentices, but few
master-workmen– On every hand we observe a truly wise
practice–in education–in morals–and in the arts of
life–the embodied wisdom of many an ancient philosopher
but unless we do more than simply learn our trade–are
more than apprentices–the world will have been little
benefitted by our life.

{One-third page blank}

The celestial phenomena answer to the poetical or ideal
in man– The stars are distant and unobtrusive, but
bright and enduring, answering to our aspirations.

Just before sunset the light in the west is purer deeper
and more memorable than at noon.

All day the dark-blue outline of Crotched mountain in
Goffstown skirted the horizon

"Plato gives science sublime counsels, directs her
toward the regions of the ideal; Aristotle gives her
positive and severe laws, and directs her toward a
practical end."

Degerando.

We took pleasure in beholding its outline, because at this distance our vision could so easily grasp the design of the founder– It was a pretty victory to conquer the distance and dimensions so easily with our eyes–which it would take our feet so long to traverse.

Notwithstanding the unexplained mystery of nature, man still pursues his studies with confidence, ever ready to grasp the secret, as if the truth were only contained, not withheld–as one of the three circles on the cocoanut is always so soft that it may be pierced with a thorn, and the traveller is grateful for the thick shell which held the liquor so faithfully.

Gracefulness is undulatory like these waves–and perhaps the sailor acquires a superior suppleness and grace through the planks of his ship from the element on which he lives

A sentence that was written while the world went round–while grass grew and water ran.

{One-fifth page blank}

Sometimes this routine which is in the sunshine and the finest days–as that which has conquered and prevailed–by its antiquity and apparent solidity and necessity–seems respectable. Our weakness needs it and our strength uses it. We cannot draw on our boots without bracing ourselves against it. Many hours we spend in this waking sleep, during which the hand stands still on the face of the clock, and we grow like corn in the night.

Men are as busy as flowers or bees, and postpone every thing to their business, as carpenters discuss politics between the strokes of the hammer, while they are shingling a roof.

Who sleeps by day and walks by night,
Will meet no spirit but some sprite.

music no 8-257– {1:446}

Spring in Virgil–near end of 3d v. {1:212}
v. 8 p 239– {*missing*}
v. 9th p 11. {1:469}
v 9th 18 {*missing*}
red bird v 8 39 {*missing*}

Style–Carlyle–&c middle of 2nd and end of 2nd or third.
no 4 p 144 {*missing*}
V. no 6–
v 7. p 98-129 {*missing*}
v. 8– 296-7– {*missing*}
This B. p 77 {40}

Sometimes we exult in stark inanity–leering on nature
and the soul. Do the gods reveal themselves only to sedate
and musing gentlemen, and does not the buffoon in the
midst of his antics catch an unobserved glimpse which
he treasures for his lonely hours?

By the game of tom fool we learn a more catholic
philosophy.

But if ye cannot be my most serene and mighty
friends–then I pray ye use me–as in no 4 p 14
{1:234-235}

Friends will have to be introduced each time they
meet, for they are eternally strange to one another, and
when they have appropriated each others value for the
last hour, they go and gather a new measure of
strangeness for the next. Like two boughs which creak
upon one another in the wood, the sap of the one never

flows into the pores of the other, for then the wind could no more draw from them the strains which enchanted the wood.

All those abuses which are the subject of reform with the philanthropist the statesman and the house keeper—are unconsciously amended in the intercourse of friends.

All exhibition of emotion or affection seems premature, like the buds which push out and unfold themselves in warm days near the end of winter, before the frosts are gone.

Well, so I shall go home to help on the revolution of the seasons— Perhaps I may find some Autumnal work to do. I feel complimented when nature condescends to make use of me even without my knowledge as when I help scatter her seeds in my walk, or carry burrs and cockles on my clothes from field to field— I feel such pride as the boy who holds a horse for the circus company whom all the spectators envy.

In the wildest nature there is the raw material for the most refined life—a sort of anticipation of the last result and greater refinement already than will ever be attained. No doubt there is papyrus by this river's side, and here are the rushes for light—and the goose only flies over head. Here is the bast for shoes or for matting—

The song sparrow whose voice is one of the first heard in the spring sings throughout the season—from a greater depth in the summer—as it were behind the notes of other birds.

{*One-fourth page blank*}

As the temperature and density of the atmosphere so
the aspects of our life vary– In this bright and chaste
light the world seemed like a pavilion made for holidays,
and washed in light. The ocean was a summer's lake, and
the land a smooth lawn for disport–while in the horizon
the sunshine seemed to fall on walled towns and villas.
And the course of our lives was seen winding on like a
country road over the plain.

The sun setting presumes all men at leisure and in
contemplative mood.

All these sounds–the hum of insects at noon–the
crowing of cocks in the morning–the baying of dogs at
night–are the evidence of natures health or soundness.

{*One-fifth page blank*}

Away up among the hills here I learn that nature is
very catholic and impartial– Strawberries and tomatos
grow as well in one man's garden as anothers, and the
sun lodges kindly under his hill side.

Given pleasant weather and scenery and any simple
employment is alluring, because it detains us in the
neighborhood

It was a cloudy drizzling day with occasional
brightenings in the mist when the trill of the tree sparrow
seemed to be ushering in sunny hours

{*Two-fifths page blank*}

There is all the refinement of civilized life in the
woods, under a sylvan garb. The wildest scenes even have

an air of domesticity and homeliness to the citizen— And
when the flicker's cackle is heard in the clearings he is
reminded that civilization has imported nothing into
them. Science is welcome to their deepest recesses for
there too nature obeys the same old civil laws.—

The little red bug on the stump of a pine for him the
wind shifts and the sun breaks through the clouds.

{One-fifth page blank}

The country has not much changed since the days of
the pilgrims. "For summer being ended, all things," said
they, stand in appearance with a weather beaten face,
and the whole country full of woods and thickets
represented a wild and savage hue."

{One-fifth page blank}

As for farming, I am convinced it is too tame for
me—and my genius dates from an older era than the
agricultural. I would strike my spade into the earth with
such careless freedom, but accuracy, as the woodpecker
his bill into a tree.

{Three-fourths page blank}

This town too (Concord) lies under the skies—a port
of entry and departure for human souls

Occasionally we rise above the necessity of virtue into
an unchangeable morning light— And find ourselves on
a level with surrounding nature. Such should be the
average life of man.

When we looked out from under our tent—the trees
were seen dimly through the mist, and a cool dew hung

upon the grass. And in the damp air we seemed to inhale
a solid fragrance.

{*One-third page blank*}

The poets exhibit but a tame and civil side of nature.
They have not gone west of the mountains. There are
sterner savager—and more primeval aspects than they
have sung. It is only the white man's poetry— If we could
get a clear report from the Indian it would be different—for
he is more conversant with pure nature. We should do
him more justice and understand better why he will not
exchange his savageness for civilization. I cannot think
him wilful—for steel hatchets, and rifles are a great
temptation.

{*One-half page blank*}

What an impartial and instructed teacher is
nature— Spreading no crude opinions—flattering none.
The moon-light so civil yet so savage—because equally
above and indifferent to all sublunary conditions.

The moon shines with a paler, more historical light,
than the sun—and hence is best suited to ruins.

The moonlight is the best restorer of antiquity. Of a
mild night when the moon shines full—the houses in our
village have a classical elegance— And our half finished
wooden church has at such an hour reminded me of
whatever is most famous and excellent in art. So serene
it stood like a living creature, under the dews of night,
intercepting the stars with its rafters.— Whatever
architect it may have had by day—it acknowledged only
Vitruvius at night— The architectural beauty of its bare
rafters—and its irregular staging built around it—told of
an old master It had an unintentional flowing grace.
The stageing which the workmen erect for their

convenience is for the most our only genuine native
architecture. and deserves to stand longer than the
building it surrounds.

In this light there are no fresh colors–but only light &
shade–and the new is confounded with the old.

I never tire of the beauty of certain epithets which the
ages have slowly bestowed as the Harvest and Hunters
moon– There is something pleasing in the fact that the
irregularity in the rising of these two moons, and their
continuing to rise nearly at the same time for several
nights should have been observed by the husbandman,
before it attracted the attention of Science.

All great laws are really known to the simple necessities
of men before they become the subject of science.

{*One-third page blank*}

The painter to avoid difficulty makes ripples on the
surface where nature suggests innumerable and deep
reflections.

As I pass along the streets of our village on the day of
our annual Cattleshow, when it frequently happens that
the leaves begin first to strew the ground under the breath
of the October wind, the lively spirits of their sap seems
to mount higher in the trees than any plow-boys let loose
that day. It invites me away to the rustling woods where
they are preparing for the winter campaign.

The men in yonder skiff floating so boyantly without
a ripple amid the reflections of the trees, like a feather
in mid air, or a leaf wafted to the surface of the water
without over turning over or wetting its upper side, seem
still in their element–so silently and delicately have they
followed their instinct without ever interrogating the
natural laws–or the noise of invention and experiment

– As birds fly and fishes swim–men walk and sail.
It reminds me how noble and natural the whole life
of man might be.– As fair as at this distance it seems

When I hear any musical sound in nature, as if it were
a bell ringing I feel then that I am not belated, but in
season wholly, and enjoy a prime and leisure hour.

{One-fifth page blank}

It takes a valor to open the hearts of men superior to
that which opens the gates of cities.

When I go into the Museum and see the mummies
wrapped in their linen bandages–I see that the times
began to need reform as long ago as when they walked
the earth. I go out into the streets and meet men who
declare that the time is near at hand for the redemption
of the race–
Let us know that as man stood in Nineveh–so he
stands in New York today

Sunday Sep 1st
We glided over the broad bosom of the merrimack
between Middlesex and Tyngsboro at noon, here a quarter
of a mile wide, while the rattling of our oars was echoed
over the water to those villages, and their slight sounds
to us. Their harbors lay as smooth and fairy like as the
Lido, or Syracuse or Rhodes in our imaginations. Like a
strange piratical craft we flitted past the dwellings of
noble home-staying men–seeming to float upon a tide
which came up to every villager's breast, as conspicuous
as if we were on an eminence. Communicating with the
villas and hills and forests on either hand by the glances
we sent to them, or the echoes we awakened. We glanced
up many a pleasant ravine with its farm house in the
distance, where some contributory stream came in, Again

the site of a saw-mill, and a few forsaken eel pots were all
that greeted us.

{*One-third page blank*}

Our thoughts reverted to Arabia Persia and
Hindostan–the lands of contemplation–and dwelling
place of the ruminant nations. And in the experience of
those noon tides we found an apology and an instinct for
the opium–betel–and tobacco chewers. Mount Sabér,
according to the French traveller and naturalist Botta is
celebrated for producing the Kát tree. Of which "The soft
tops of the twigs and tender leaves are eaten," says his
reviewer, "and produce an agreeable soothing excitement,
restoring from fatigue, banishing sleep, and disposing to
the enjoyment of conversation."

What a dignified oriental life might be lived along this
stream, browsing the tree tops–and chewing mallows and
apple tree buds like the camelopards–rabbits and
partridges.

Salmon Brook runs under the rail-way–but we sailed
up far enough into the meadows which border it, to learn
its piscatorial history from a haymaker on its banks. He
told us that silver eel was formerly abundant here, and
pointed to some sinker creels at its mouth.

Salmon Brook	Silver eels
Pennichook	Wooden creels
Ye sweet waters of my brain	These the baits that still allure
When shall I look	And dragon fly
Or cast the hook	That floated by
In thy waves again?	May they still endure?

Monday 2nd

At noon we rested under the shade of a willow or maple
which hung over the water, and drew forth a melon from
our repast–and contemplated at our leisure the lapse of
the river and of human life. The still unravelled fate of

men ministered to the entertainment of our chance hours. As that current with its floating twigs and leaves so did all things pass in review before us– Far away in cities and marts and on this very stream the old routine was proceeding still– At length we would throw our rinds into the water for the fishes to nibble–and add our breath to the life of living men.

Our melons lay at home on the sands of the merrimack, and our potatoes in the sun and water on the bottom of the boat–looked like a fruit of the country.

Monday Sep 2nd

Now & then we scared up a king-fisher or a summer duck.

Sunday 1st

At a 3d of a mile over the water we heard distinctly children repeating their catechism in a cottage by the river side– While in the broad shallows between a herd of cows were cooling their hides and waging war with the mosquitoes.

While we sail here we can remember unreservedly those friends who dwell far away on the banks and by the sources of this very river and people this world for us–without any harsh and unfriendly interruptions.

{*One-third page blank*}

Tuesday

The banks of the Merrimack are steep and clayey for the most part and trickling with water–and where a spring oozes out a few feet above the level of the river, the boatmen cut a trough out of a slab with their axes and place it so as to receive the water, and fill their jugs conveniently. Bursting out from under the root of a pine or a rock, sometimes this purer and cooler water is

collected into a little basin close to the edge of and level
with the river–a fountain head of the Merrimack.–

so near along lifes stream lie the fountains of innocence
and youth–making fertile the margin of its turbid stream.
Let the voyageur replenish his vessel at these
uncontaminated sources.– Some youthful spring
perchance still empties with tinkling music into the oldest
river, even when it is falling into the sea. I imagine that
its music is distinguished by the river gods from the
general lapse of the stream and falls sweeter upon their
ears in proportion as it is nearer the sea.

As thus the evaporations of the river feed these
unsuspected springs which filter through its banks so our
aspirations fall back again in springs upon the margin
of our life's stream to refresh and purify it.

The routine of these boatmen's lives suggests to me
how indifferent all employments are, and how any may
be infinitely noble and poetic in the eyes of men, if
pursued with sufficient boyancy and freedom. For the
most part they carry down wood and bring back stores
for the country, piling the wood so as to leave a little
shelter in one part where they may sleep, or retire from
the rain if they choose.

I can hardly imagine a more healthy employment, or
more favorable to contemplation, or the observation of
nature.– In no weather subject to great exposure–as the
lumberers of Maine–and in summer inhaling the
healthfullest breezes. But slightly encumbered with
clothing–frequently with the head and feet bare.

From morning till night the boatman walks backwards
and forwards on the side of his boat, now stooping with
his shoulder to the pole, then drawing it back slowly to set
it again–meanwhile moving steadily and majestically
forward through an endless valley, amid an ever changing
scenery,–now distinguishing his course for a mile or

two—and now finding himself shut in by a sudden turn
of the river, in a small woodland lake.

All the phenomena which surround him are simple
and grand— The graceful majestic motion of his craft,
must communicate something of the same to his
character. So will he move forward to his objects on land.
There is something impressive and stately in this motion
which he assists. He feels the slow irresistible motion
under him with pride as if it were the impetus of his
own energy.

At noon his horn is heard echoing from shore to shore
to give notice of his approach—to the farmer's wife with
whom he is to take his dinner—frequently in such retired
scenes that only muskrats and king fisher's seem to hear.

{*One-fourth page blank*}

Tuesday

We passed a boat before sunrise, and though we could
not distinguish it for the fog, the few dull sounds we
heard, carried with them a sense of weight and
irresistible motion which was impressive.

{*Four-fifths page blank*}

If ever our idea of a friend is realised it will be in some
broad and generous natural person—as frank as the
daylight—in whose presence our behavior will be as simple
and unconstrained, as the wanderer amid the recesses of
the hills.

The language of excitement is picturesque merely—but
not so with enthusiasm You must be calm before you can
utter oracles— What was the excitement of the Delphic
priestess compared with the calm wisdom of Socrates!
God is calm

Enthusiasm is a supernatural serenity.

{*Two-fifths page blank*}

Rivers are the natural highways of all nations, not
only levelling and removing obstacles from the path of
the traveller–quenching his thirst–and bearing him on
their bosom, but conducting him through the most
interesting scenery of a country most rich in natural
phenomena, through the most populous portions of the
globe where the animal and vegetable kingdoms attain
the greatest perfection.

{*Three-fifths page blank*}

We passed a man on the shore fishing with a long birch
pole and a dog at his side–standing like caryatides under
the cope of heaven– We passed so near as to agitate his
float with our oars, and drive luck away for an indefinite
term–but when we had rowed a mile as straight as an
arrow with our faces toward him, he still stood with the
proverbial patience of a fisherman the only object to
relieve the eye in the extended meadow–under the other
side of heaven–and there would stand abiding his
luck–till he took his way home at evening with his
fish– – He and his dog! (it was a superior contemplative
dog) may they fare well. I trust we shall meet again. He
was no chimera or vision to me.

When we had passed the bridge we saw men haying
far off in the meadows, their heads moving like the herds
grass. In the distance the wind seemed to bend all alike.

Friday
We skimmed lightly over the water before a smacking
breeze with all sails set– The wind in the horizon seemed
to roll in a flood over valley and plain–and every tree
bent to the blast, and the mountains–like school-boys
turned their cheeks to the blast.

{*One-fifth page blank*}

We lay listening to the sound of the current   We
already knew–before we had looked abroad–by the fresh
wind that was blowing, the rustling of the leaves and
the rippling of the water that there was a change in the
weather.

The mist gradually rolled away, and we were relieved
from the trouble of watching for rocks. We soon passed
the mouth of the Souhegan with a fair wind, and the
village of Merrimack.

Friday
When we awoke the face of nature seemed to have
undergone a change– We heard the sigh of the first
autumnal wind, and saw the first tinge of russet on the
hills–even the water seemed to have got a grayer hue.

We saw by the flitting clouds, by the rushing river, and
the lights in the cottages on shore– We saw by the faces
of men that the fall had commenced. The grape vine–the
goldfinch in the willow–the flickers flying in flocks, and
the piping of the plover–all repeated the tale. Cottages
looked more snug and comfortable, and their tapers told
more tales– We looked in vain for the south wind.

It proved a cool and breezy autumn day, and by the
time we reached Nashua we were obliged to sit muffled
in our cloaks, while the wind and current carried us
along. The inhabitants left their houses to gaze at us from
the banks.

I who sail now in a boat, have I not sailed in a
thought? V chaucer

Shad Salmon and bass are still taken in this river as
well as at the mouth of the Concord.

{*Nine-tenths page blank*}

Tuesday sep 3d

About noon we passed the village of Merrimac where some carpenters were at work mending a scow on the shore. The strokes of their mallets echoed from shore to shore and up and down the river, and their tools gleamed in the sun a quarter of a mile from us, which made boat building seem as ancient and honorable as agriculture, and we realized how there might be a naval as well as pastoral life— We thought of the traveller building his boat on the banks of the stream under the heavens— As we glided past at a distance these out-door workmen seemed to have added some dignity to their labor by its publickness—it seemed a part of the industry of nature like the work of hornets and mud wasps

The whole history of commerce was made plain in this scow turned bottom upward on the shore. Thus men begin to go down upon the sea in ships. There was Iolchos and the launching of the Argo.

—

> The waves slowly beat
> Just to keep the noon sweet
> And no sound is floated oer
> Save the mallet on shore
> Which echoing on high
> Seems a caulking the sky

We passed some shag-bark trees on the opposite shore skirting the waters edge. The first I had ever seen

On the sandy shore of the Merrimack opposite to Tyngsboro, we first discovered the blue bell— A pleasant sight it must be to the Scotchman in Lowell mills.

> The moon now rises to her absolute rule,
> And the husbandman and hunter

Acknowledge her for their mistress.
Asters and golden reign in the fields
And the life everlasting withers not.
The fields are reaped and shorn of their pride
But an inward verdure still crowns them
The thistle scatters its down on the pool
And yellow leaves clothe the vine—
And nought disturbs the serious life of men.
But behind the sheaves and under the sod
There lurks a ripe fruit which the reapers have
    not gathered
The true harvest of the year
Which it bears forever.
With fondness annually watering and maturing it.
But man never severs the stalk
Which bears this palatable fruit.

The hardest material obeys the same law with the most fluid. Trees are but rivers of sap and woody fibre flowing from the atmosphere and emptying in to the earth by their trunks—as their roots flow upward to the surface. And in the heavens there are rivers of stars and milky ways— There are rivers of rock on the surface and rivers of ore in the bowels of the earth.

From this point the river runs perfectly straight for a mile or more to Carlisle bridge—which consists of 20 piers—and in the distance its surface looks like a cobweb gleaming in the sun.

{Two-fifths page blank}

In the morning the whole river and adjacent country was covered by a dense fog—through which the smoke of our fire curled up like a subtler mist. But before we had rowed many rods the fog dispersed as by magic and only a slight steam curled up from the surface of the water.—
We reached the falls in Billerica before noon, where we left the river for the canal, which runs six miles through

the woods to the Merrimack at Middlesex. As we did not
care to loitre in this part of our voyage while one ran
along the tow path drawing the boat by a cord, the other
kept it off from the shore with a pole, so that we
accomplished the whole distance in little more than an
hour.

There is some abruptness and want of harmony in this
scenery since the canal is not of equal date with the
forests and meadows it runs through.

You miss the conciliatory influence of time on land
and water.

In the lapse of ages no doubt nature will recover and
indemnify herself. Gradually fit shrubs and flowers will
be planted along the borders Already the king-fisher sits
on a pine over the water, and the dace and pickerel swim
below. All works pass directly out of the hands of the
architect. and though he has bungled she will perfect
them at last.

Her own fish-hawks hover over our fish-ponds

were pleased to find that our boat would float in
M. water

By noon we were fairly launched upon the bosom of
the merrimack–having passed through the locks at
Middlesex–and felt as if we were on the ocean stream
itself.

Beaver river comes in a little lower down draining the
meadows of Pelham, Windham, and Londonderry, the
Irish settlers of which latter town were the first to
introduce the potatoe into N.E.

{*One-fourth page blank*}

Two men called out from the steep and wooded banks
to be taken as far as Nashua but we were too deeply

laden– As we glided away from them with even sweeps
while the fates scattered oil in our course–as the sun was
sinking behind the willows of the distant shore,–we
could see them far off over the water–running along the
shore and climbing over the rocks and fallen trees like
ants till they reached a spot where a broad stream poured
its placid tribute into the Merrimack– When a mile
distant we could see them preparing to ford the
stream– But whether they got safely through or went
round by the source, we never learned.

Thus nature puts the busiest merchant to pilgrim's
shifts. She soon drives us to staff and scrip and scallop
shell.

The Mississippi the Nile the Ganges can their
personality be denied? have they not a personal history
in the annals of the world– These journeying atoms
from the andes and ural and mountains of the moon–by
villas–villages–and mists–with the moccasined tread of
an Indian warrior. Their sources not yet drained. The
mountains of the moon send their tribute to the pasha as
they did to Pharaoh without fail. though he must collect
the rest of his revenue at the point of the bayonnette

Consider the phenomena of morn–or eve–and you will
say that Nature has perfected herself by an eternity of
practice– Evening stealing over the fields– The stars
come to bathe in retired waters The shadows of the trees
creeping farther and farther into the meadows. And a
myriad phenomena beside.

Occasionally a canal boat with its large white sail
glided round a promontory a quarter of a mile before us
and changed the scene in an instant– Occasionally
attaching ourselves to its side we would float back in
company awhile–interchanging a word with the voyageurs
and obtaining a draught of cooler water from their stores.

Occasionally we had to muster all our energy to get round a point where the river broke rippling over rocks and the maples trailed their branches in the stream.

The rain had pattered all night And now the whole country wept, the drops falling in the river, and on the alder, and in the pastures, but instead of any bow in the heavens there was the trill of the tree sparrow all the morning. The cheery faith of this little bird atoned for the silence of the whole woodland quire.

Nothing is so attractive and unceasingly curious as character. There is no plant that needs such tender treatment, there is none that will endure so rough. It is at once the violet and the oak.– It has no acquaintance or companion, but goes silent and unobserved longer than any planet in space, and when at length it does show itself, it is like the flowering of all the world, and its before unseen orbit is lit up like the path of a meteor.

It is what we mean let us say what we will. We hear no good news but some trait of noble character. After years of vain familiarity some distant gesture some unconscious behavior of my friends speaks to me with more emphasis than all his kind and wise words. It is planetary.

It goes hence with averted face to make itself more known by distance– The world may be very busy while the bud is unfolding but when the flower is seen all this forwardness is late and as it were defeated retrospective.

{One-fifth page blank}

The wind in the woods sounds like an incessant waterfal dashing and roaring among rocks

I cannot help being encouraged by this blithe activity in the elements in these degenerate days– Who hears the rippling of the rivers will not utterly despair.

A forest is in all Mythologies a sacred place, as the oaks among the Druids, and the grove of Egeria– And what is Robin Hood–without his Barnsdale and Sherwood– It is the life that is lived in the unexplored scenery of the wood that charms us.

I wish to go away and live by the pond, and when my friends inquire I have no better reason to give–than that I shall hear the wind whispering among the reeds.

{One-fourth page blank}

Whole weeks and months of my Summer life slide away in thin volumes like mist and smoke–till at length some warm morning perchance I see a sheet of mist blown down the brook to the swamp and I float as high above the fields with it.

We wend not asunder–our courses do not diverge. But as the web of destiny is woven it is fulled and we are cast more and more into the centre. Our fates at leasst are social

I can recall to mind the stillest summer hours, in which the grasshopper sings over the mulleins, and there is a valor in that time the bare memory of which is armor that can laugh at any blow of fortune.

For our life time the strains of an harp are heard to swell and die alternately. And Death is but the pause when the blast is recollecting itself.

The flowing sail–the running stream–the waving tree–the roving wind–are all great and current motions.

Character is Genius settled or established.

The death of friends will inspire us as much as their lives. If they are great and rich enough–they will leave consolation to the mourners as well as money to defray the expenses of their funerals

The real history of anything is only the true account of it which is always the same.–

Their memory is incrusted over with sublime and pleasing thoughts as the monuments of others are overgrown with moss.

Nature is a greater and more perfect art. When the overhanging pine drops into the water by the action of the sun and wind, rubbing it against the shore, its boughs are worn white and smooth, and take fantastic forms, as if turned by a lathe.

Everywhere in our corn and grain fields the earth is strewn with the relics of a race, which has vanished as completely as if trodden in with the earth– When I meditate on the destiny of this prosperous branch of the Saxon family, and the unexhausted energies of this new country–I forget that what is now Concord was once Musketaquid, And that the American race has had its history– The future reader of history will associate this generation with the red man in his thoughts, and give it credit for some sympathy with that race– Our history will have some copper tints at least and be read as through an Indian summer haze– But such were not our reflections

But the Indian is absolutely forgotten but by some persevering poets. By an evident fate the White man has commenced a new era. What do our anniversaries commemorate but white men's exploits? For Indian deeds there must be an Indian memory–the white man will remember his own only– We have forgotten their hostility as well as friendship. Who can realize that within the memory of this generation in our last war–the remnant of an ancient and dusky race of warriors the stockbridge Indians within the limits of this very state–furnished a company for the war–on condition only that they should not be expected to fight white man's fashion–or to train–but Indian fashion still– And occasionally their wigwams are seen on the banks of this very stream still, like the cabins of the muskrats in the meadow.

They seem like a race who have exhausted the secrets of nature–tanned with age–while this young and still fair saxon race–on whom the sun has not long shined, is but commencing its career.

Wherever I go I am still on the trail of the Indian.– The light and sandy soils which the first settlers cultivated were the Indian corn fields–and with every fresh ploughing their surface is strewn with the relics of their race–

Arrow heads–spear heads tomahawks, axes–gouges –pestles–mortars–hoes pipes of soap-stone, ornaments for the neck and breast–and other implements of war and of the chace attract the transient curiosity of the farmer– We have some hundreds which we have ourselves collected.

And one is as surely guided in this search by the locality and nature of the soil as to the berries in autumn– Unlike the modern farmer they selected the light and sandy plains and rising grounds near to ponds and streams of water– –which the squaws could easily cultivate with their stone hoes. And where these fields have been harrowed and rolled for grain in the fall–their surface yields its annual crop arrow heads and other relics as of grain.– And the burnt stones on which their

fires were built are seen dispersed by the plow on every
hand.

   Their memory is in harmony with the russet hue of
the fall of the year
   Instead of Philip and Paugus on the plains here are
Webster & Crockett. Instead of the council house is the
legislature.

{One-fourth page blank}

   It is always singular but encouraging to meet with
common sense in very old books as the Veeshnoo
Sarma– It asserts their independence on the experience
of later times.– A playful wisdom which has eyes behind
as well as before, and oversees itself. This pledge of
sanity cannot be spared in a book–that it sometimes
reflect upon itself–that it pleasantly behold itself–that it
hold the scales over itself.

   In the present instance, the story and fabulous portion
winds loosely from sentence to sentence as barrows and
oases in a desert– It is as indistinct as a camel track
between Mourzuk to Darfour.

   Science knows that the isolated mountains in the
horizon are but portions of an unseen range.

   The stream of the story rushes past unregarded–while
the reader leaps from sentence to sentence as stepping
stones.

{Two-fifths page blank}

   There may be curtesy–there may be good will, & even
temper & wit–and talent, and sparkling conversation–and

yet the the higher faculties pine for exercise. Ignorance and bungling with love are better than wisdom and skill without, our life without love is like coke and ashes–

Men may be pure as alabaster–and Parian marble –elegant as Tuscan villas–sublime as Terni, and yet if there is no milk mingled with the wine at their entertainments–better is the hospitality of of Goths and Vandals.

In a promiscuous company we always address ourselves to that person who alone can understand us, and cannot get him out of our mind even when conversing with another.

{One-third page blank}

Are setting hens troubled with ennui? These long march days–setting on and on in the crevice of a hay-loft–with no active employment.–?

Friendship is a perennial spring time.

Though nature's laws are more immutable than any despots, yet to our daily life they rarely seem rigid, but permit us to relax with license in summer weather. We are not often nor harshly reminded of the things we may not do. I am often astonished to see how long and after what manifold infringements of the natural laws, some men whom I meet in the highway maintain life. She certainly does not deny them quarter–they do not die without priest.– – In any case they are sure not to depart out of her demesnes.– It would seem as if consistency were the secret of health.– How many a poor man striving to live a pure life pines and dies after a life of sickness.– and his friends wonder if nature is not pitiless. While the confirmed & consistent sinner, who is content

with the rank life he leads, a mass of corruption still
dozes comfortably under a hedge. Nature is very kind
and liberal to all persons of vicious habits—and does not
exhaust them with many excesses.

The sap of all noble schemes drieth up, and the
schemers return again and again in despair to "common
sense and labor." But to return is not the right way—nor
will it be the last.

Nature supplies inexhaustible means to the most
frugal methods. Having carefully determined the extent
of her charity, she establishes it forever; her almsgiving
is an annuity.— She supplies to the bee only so much
wax as is necessary for its cell, so that no poverty could
stint it more—but the little economist which fed the
evangelist in the desert, still keeps in advance of the
immigrant, and fills the cavities of the forest for his
repast.

{One-fifth page blank}

When I behold an infant I am impressed with a sense
of antiquity, and reminded of the sphinx or Sybil. It
seems older than Nestor or Jove himself, and wears the
wrinkles of Saturn.

Why should the present impose upon us so much! I
sit now upon a stump whose rings number centuries of
growth— If I look around me I see that the very soil is
composed of just such stumps—ancestors to this. I thrust
this stick many aeons deep into the surface—and with my
heel scratch a deeper furrow than the elements have
ploughed here for a thousand years— If I listen I hear
the peep of frogs which is older than the slime of
Egypt—or a distant partridge drumming on a log—as if it
were the pulse-beat of the summer air.

I raise my fairest and freshest flowers in the old mould.

–Why, what we call new is not skin deep–the earth is not yet stained by it. It is not the fertile ground we walk upon but the leaves that flutter over our head

The newest is but the oldest made visible to our eyes. We dig up the soil from a thousand feet below the surface and call it new, and the plants which spring from it.

In whatever moment we awake to life, as now I this evening after walking along the bank, and hearing the same evening sounds (that were heard of yore) it seems to have slumbered just below the surface–as in the spring the new verdure which covers the fields has never retreated far from the winter.

All actions and objects and events lose their *distinct* importance in this hour–in the brightness of the vision– As when sometimes the pure light that attends the setting sun, falls on the trees & houses, the light itself is the phenomenon–and no single object is so distinct to our admiration as the light itself.

For the most part we think there are but few degrees of sublimity, that the highest is but little higher than that we now behold But we are always deceived–sublimer visions appear–and the former pale and fade away. I read tonight the well known lines of Shakspeare which were selected out of his own works, when Pope had wisely declined to write one, and it *did* make the world fade–so serenely so sublimely true.

If criticism is liable to abuse–it has yet a great and humane apology. When my sentiments aspire to be universal then my neighbor has an equal interest to see that the expression be just, with myself.

We are often prompted to speak our thoughts to our neighbors or the single travellers we meet, but poetry is a communication addressed to all mankind, and may therefore as well be written at home and in solitude, as uttered abroad in society.

The relations and contemporaries of the old poet did not hear these fine thoughts of his any better, perhaps not so well, as we. He was not inspired with any eloquence to reach private ears—or particular times

{*One-fourth page blank*}

My friends, why should we live?
Life is an idle war a toilsome peace;
　　To-day I would not give
A mere consent for its securest ease.

　　Shall we out-wear the year
In our pavilions on its dusty plain
　　And yet no signal hear
To strike our tents and take the road again?

　　Or else drag up the slope
The heavy ordinance of virtue's train?
　　Useless but in the hope,
Some far remote and heavenward hill to gain.

The tortoises rapidly dropt into the water as our boat ruffled the surface amid the willows—

We glided along through the transparent water breaking the reflections of the trees.

{*One-fourth page blank*}

Not only are we late to find our friends—but mankind are late—and the is no record of a great success in history.

My friend is not chiefly wise or beautiful or noble– At least it is not for me to know it. He has no visible form nor appreciable character. I can never praise him nor esteem him praiseworthy–for I should sunder him from myself–and put a bar between us.– Let him not think he can please me by any behavior or ever treat me well enough. When he treats I retreat.

{One-half page blank}

I know of no rule which holds so true as that we are always paid for our suspicions by finding what we suspect. There can be no fairer recompense than this. Our suspicions exercise a demoniacal power over the subject of them. By some obscure law of influence when we are perhaps unconsciously the subject of another's suspicion, we feel a strong impulse, even when it is contrary to our nature to do that which he expects but reprobates.

No man seems to be aware that his influence is the result of his entire character–both that which is subject and that which is superior to his understanding– And what he really means or intends it is not in his power to explain or offer an apology for.

As it waxed late in the afternoon and we rowed leisurely up the gentle stream shut in between fragrant and blooming banks where we had passed our first night, and drew nearer to the fields where our lives had passed, we seemed to detect the hues of our native sky in the south west horizon. The sun was just setting with warm purple colors behind the fringed edge of a wooded hill.– So rich a sunset as would never have ended but for some mysterious reason unknown to men. and surely

to be marked with brighter colors than ordinary in the
scroll of time   the evenings have no principle of decay
in them. Though the shadows of the hills were beginning
to steal over the stream, the whole river valley undulated
with mild light purer–deeper and more memorable than
the noon– So does day bid farewell to solitary vales
where no men reside.

There are objects in nature which represent all the
differences and degrees which are familiar to our
thoughts. Nature is civilized as well as savage–forever
and unalterably. After sitting in my chamber many days
reading the poets–I went out early one foggy morning in
July, and heard a screech owl in a neighboring wood.
Thus sound–proclaimed another dynasty to me.

Two blue herons with their long and slender limbs
relieved against the sky were seen travelling high over
our heads– The lofty and silent flight of these birds
wending their way at evening surely not to alight in any
marsh on the earth's surface, but perchance on the other
side of our atmosphere, was a symbol for the ages to
study–whether impressed upon the sky–or sculptured
amid the hyeroglyphics of Egypt. Bound to some northern
meadow–they held on their stately stationary flight like
the storks in the picture, and disappeared at length
behind the clouds. It was like a vision of Styria or
Cayster. And dense flocks of black birds were winging
their way along the river course, as it were on a short
evening pilgrimage to some shrine of theirs–or to
celebrate so fair a sunset.– And after the night had set
in our boat awakend the clamors of some geese which
had settled in this part of the river.

The sun setting presumes all men at leisure and in a
contemplative mood.

Here were several masons employed in repairing the
locks–in a wild and solitary part of the river–who
expressed an interest in our adventures. Especially one
young man of our own age who had inquired if we were
bound up to 'Skieg–who when he had heard our story and
examined our outfit–still asked us other questions
reluctantly–and always turning to his work again as if
it had become his duty–

When we were ready he left his work and hellpt us
through the locks with quiet enthusiasm–telling us that
we were at Coos falls–and we could still distinguish the
strokes of his chisel for some sweeps after we had
left him.

We wished to camp this night on a large flat rock in the
midst of the stream just above these falls–but the want
of fuel, and the difficulty of fixing our tent firmly
prevented us. So we withdrew as we supposed to a
retired part of the shore–but we discovered the next
morning that we had pitched our tent directly in the path
of the masons whom we had seen crossing the river in
their boat the evening before– And now going to their
work again they came upon us as we were rolling up our
tent– And taried awhile to examine our furniture–and
handle our guns which were leaning against a tree.

We soon after passed a large and densely wooded
island which would have been an addition to a nobleman's
estate.

Tuesday–

At intervals when there was a suitable reach in the
river–we caught sight of the Goffstown mountain–the
Indian Un-can-nu-nuc rising before us, on the left of the
river– "The far blue mountain."

{*One-fourth page blank*}

We soon after saw the Piscataquoag emptying in on our left–and heard the falls of Amoskieg above.

It was here according to tradition that the sachem Wonolanset resided, and when at war with the mohawks his tribe are said to have concealed their provisions in the cavities of the rocks in the upper part of the falls.

The descent is 54 feet in half a mile.

The manchester manufacturing company have constructed a canal here–through which we passed.

Above the falls the river spreads out into a lake –stretching up toward Hooksett– We could see several canal boats at intervals of a mile or more standing up to Hooksett with a light breeze. With their broad sails set they moved slowly up the stream in the sluggish and fitful breeze–as if impelled by some mysterious counter current–like Antediluvian birds. A grand motion so slow and steady. For the most part they were returning empty, or at most with a few passengers aboard. As we rowed near to one which was just getting under way, the steers man offered to take us in tow–but when we came along side we found that he intended to take us on board, as otherwise we should retard his own voyage too much–but as we were too heavy to be lifted aboard–we left him and proceeded up the stream a half a mile to the shade of some maples to spend our noon

In the course of half an hour several boats passed up the river at intervals of half a mile–and among them came the boat we have mentioned, keeping the middle of the stream and when within speaking distance the steers man called out if we would come along side now he would take us in tow. But not heeding their taunts we made no haste to give chase until our preparations were made–by which time they were a quarter of a mile ahead.

Then with our own sails set—and plying our four oars,
we were soon along side of them—and as we glided close
under their side, we quietly promised if they would throw
us a rope that we would take them in tow.

And then we gradually overhauled each boat in
succession untill we had the river to ourselves again.

No man was ever party to a secure and settled
friendship—it is no more a constant phenomenon than
meteors and lightning— It is a war of positions of
silent tactics.

With a fair wind and the current in our favor we
commenced our return voyage, sitting at ease in our boat
and conversing, or in silence watching, for the last sign
of each reach in the river, as a bend concealed it from
view. The lumbermen who were throwing down wood
from the top of the high bank, 30 or 40 feet above the
water, that it might be sent down the river—paused in
their work to watch our retreating sail.

{One-fifth page blank}

In summer I live out of doors and have only impulses
and feelings which are all for action— And must wait for
the quiet & stillness and longer nights of Autumn and
Winter, before any thought will subside.

—

I mark the summer's swift decline
The springing sward its grave clothes weaves

Oh could I catch the sounds remote
Could I but tell to human ear
The strains which on the breezes float
And sing the requiem of the dying year.

None of the feathered race have yet realized my conception of the woodland depths. I had fancied that their plumage would assume stronger and more dazzling colors, like the brighter tints of evening, in proportion as I advanced farther into the darkness and solitude of the forest. The red election, brought from their depth, did in some degree answer my expectation–gleaming like a coal of fire amid the pines.

In Autumn what may be termed the dry colors preponderate in Summer the moist. The Asters and golden rod are the livery which nature wears at present. The golden rod alone seems to express all the ripeness of the autumn, and sheds its mellow lustre on the fields as if the now declining summer sun had bequeathed its hues to it. Asters everywhere spot the fields like so many fallen stars.

Sept 29–42

To-day the lark sings again down in the meadow and the robin peeps, and the blue birds old and young have revisited their box–as if they would fain repeat the summer–without the intervention of winter–if nature would let them.

The forms of beauty fall around our path like ringlets from the head of a child–as ripples in the wake of the boat, or curled shavings from the plane– While we go serenely on our way.– Beauty is a finer utility whose end we do not see.

Oct 7th –42

A little girl has just brought me a purple finch–or American linnet. These birds are now moving south. It reminds me of the Pine and spruce–and the Juniper and cedar on whose berries it feeds– It has the crimson hues of the October evenings and its plumage still shines as if it

had caught and preserved some of their tints. (beams?).
We know it chiefly as a traveller.

It reminds me of many things I had forgotten. many
a serene evening lies snugly packed under its wing.

There is a depth in Autumn which no poetry has
fathomed– Behind the rustling leaves–and the stacks of
grain–and the bare clusters of the grape–I am sensible of
a wholly new life–which no man has lived. My faith is
fed by the yellow leaf. Who can hear the wind in October
rustling the wood without believing that this earth has
more mysterious and nobler inhabitants than Fauns and
Satyrs Elves and Fairies– In the fading hues of sunset
we see the portal to other mansions of our Father's house.

> I am the Autumnal sun,
> With Autumn gales my race is run.
> When will the hazle put forth its flowers,
> And the grape ripen under my bowers?
> When will the harvest and the hunter's moon
> Turn my midnight into mid noon?
>   I am all sere & yellow,
>   And to my core mellow.
> The mast is dropping within my woods
> The winter is lurking within my moods
> And the rustling of the withered leaf
> Is the constant music of my grief,
>   My gay colored grief,
>   My autumnal relief.

We do not learn much from learned books but from
true–sincere–human books–from frank and friendly
biographies– Let me know how any man thought–and
wavered and resolved, succeeded and failed, what he did
and refrained from doing– I only want to know more of
the life of man–of any man. In a true biography–any
would be great–and any small.

The life of a good man, does not improve me any more
than the life of a freebooter, for the inevitable laws
appear as plain in the infringement, as in the observance.

And perhaps all life is maintained to the end by an equal expense of virtue of some kind. We all know what children we are sometimes in our virtues–what men in our vices. The decaying tree while yet it lives asks for sun wind and rain as well as the green one. It secretes sap and performs the functions of health.

Gower writes like a man of common sense and good parts who has undertaken with steady rather than high purpose to do narrative with rhyme. With little or no invention following in the track of the old fablers, he employs his leisure and his pen-craft, to entertain his readers, and speak a good word for the right. He has no fire or rather blaze–though occasionally some brand's end peeps out from the ashes, especially if in a dark day you approach the heap–and if you extend your hands over it you experience a slight warmth, more than elsewhere – And even in fair weather you may see a slight smoke go up–here and there.

He narrates what Chaucer some times sings. He tells his story with a fair understanding of the original and sometimes it gains a little in blunt plainness and directness in his hands.

Unlike the early Saxon and later English his poetry is but a plainer and directer speech than other men's prose. He might have been a teamster and written his rhymes on his wagon seat as he went to mill with a load of plaster.

The woods begin to assume the brighter tints of autumn about the middle of September. The Sumack –grape and maple are among the first to change. The milk-weed turns to a very deep rich yellow.

The banks by retired roadsides are covered with asters–hazles–brakes–and huckleberry bushes–emitting a dry ripe scent.

Facts must be learned directly and personally–but principles may be deduced from information. The collector of facts possesses a perfect physical organization–the philosopher a perfect intellectual one. One can walk–the other sit–one acts, the other thinks. But the poet in some degree does both and uses and generalizes the results of both–he generalizes the widest deductions of philosophy.

{*One-third page blank*}

Oct 21st 42

The atmosphere is so dry and transparent, and as it were inflammable at this season–that a candle in the grass shines white and dazzling, and purer and brighter the farther off it is. Its heat seems to have been extracted and only its harmless refulgent light left. It is a star dropt down. The ancients were more than poetically true when they called fire Vulcan's flower. Light is somewhat almost moral– The most intense–as the fixed stars and our own sun–has an unquestionable preeminence among the elements. At a certain stage in the generation of all life, no doubt, light as well as heat is developed– It guides to the first rudiments of life. There is a vitality in heat and light

{*One-third page blank*}

I never tire of the beauty of certain epithets which the ages have slowly bestowed, as the–Hunters moon and the Harvest moon. There is something pleasing in the fact that the irregularity in the rising of these two moons, and their continuing to rise nearly at the same time for several nights should have been observed by the husbandman before it attracted the attention of Science.

All great laws are really known to the necessities men, before they become the subject of study to the intellect.

Oct 26th 42

The maples stripped of their leaves so early, stand like a wreathe of smoke along the edge of the meadow.

Kindness which has so good a reputation elsewhere, can least of all consist with friendship– No such affront can be offered as a conscious good will–a friendliness which is not a necessity of the friends' character. Its foundations must be surer than those of the globe itself–secure from whim or passion, and the laws of truth and magnanimity have their root and abiding place in our friend. He seeking a friend walks on and on through the crowds of men as if in a straight line without stopping.

Oct 30th –42

There is something witch-like in the appearance of the witch-hazel which is now in bloom, Its irregular–angular stem, and petals like Furies' hair, or small ribbon streamers. Its blossoming too at this irregular period, when other shrubs have lost their leaves even, looks a little like witches' craft. surely it blooms in no garden of man's There is a whole fairy land on the hillside where they grow.

Every little flower that grows by some remote dingle or pond side, has virtues medicinal to heal our spirits which do not have to be distilled from its roots, but by its simply growing and blooming thus our lives are constantly related to the healthy and true. No crede or theory can be true which will not bear to be contrasted with these simple and cheerful aspects of nature. No greatness can afford to bustle past the humblest flower or blade under its feet. Even the tiny blossoms of the cryptogamous plants bloom yet in silent reproach to the

imposing theories of the philosopher–which have
(overlooked their existence)

I feel that I draw nearest to understanding the great
secret of my life in my closest intercourse with nature.
There is a reality and health in (present) nature; which
is not to be found in any religion–and cannot be
contemplated in antiquity– I suppose that what in other
men is religion is in me love of nature.

{One-fourth page blank}

I love to hear some men speak though I hear not what
they say– They are great natures, and it takes a good
deal to support their life. Theirs is no thin diet. The very
air they breathe seems rich and perfumed, and the sound
of their voices falls on the ear, as naturally as the
rustling of leaves or the crackling of fire.

The distinctions of right and wrong–of sense and
nonsense–seem petty–when such great and healthy
indifference comes along. They have the heavens for
their abettors, as if they had never stood from under
them. They look at the stars with an answering ray. Their
words are rich and voluminous for they proceed out of a
deep though unconscious sympathy with the nature of
things. They are earth-born–γηγενη–as was said of the
giants & Titans of old time. Their eyes are like glow-worms
– Their motions graceful and flowing as if a place
were already found for them–like rivers flowing through
vallies.

Those indicate slightly what might be the life of men
on earth.

an immortal life should not be destitute of an
immortal abode.

The difference between the severe beauty of Greek art
and the luxury of modern taste–is felt in the contrast

presented by the expressions which respectively designate
them.– Tό καλον and *beau idéal.*

The former is a chaste and reserved beauty–the ideal
beau idéal–a pure core of light, which reminds us of
the line
"Her beauty twinkleth like a star within the frosty night."
It leaves our grosser duller conceptions, as the nucleus
of a comet its lurid train, behind.

The latter is more like the lurid flitting light of a
will-o'-the wisp a meadowy boggey light–not a
Ροδοδακτυλος εως

Men who are felt rather than understood–are being
most rapidly developed. They stand many deep.

In many parts the merrimack is as wild and natural as
ever and the shore and surrounding scenery exhibit only
the revolutions of nature The pine stands up erect on its
brink and the alders and willows fringe its edge–only
the beaver & the red man have departed.– They are the
primeval and natural echoes that are awakened. The
sound of this timber rolled down the steep banks–or the
distant scow just heaving in sight round a distant
headland enhance the majestic silence and vastness of
nature.

Through the din and desultoriness even of a Byzantium
noon–is seen the fresh & primitive and savage nature in
which Scythians and AEthiopians dwell. What is echo,
what are light and shade–day and night–ocean and
stars–earthquake and eclipse there? The works of man
are swallowed up in the immensity.

We learned afterward that we had pitched our camp
upon the very spot which a few summers before had been

ocupied by a roving party of Penobscots.– as if we had
been led by an Indian instinct. We could see rising a few
miles before us a dark conical eminence–called Hooksett
pinnacle a landmark–for boatmen.

Some stray sound from a far off sphere comes to my
ear from time to time to remind me of the fabulous notes
I had almost forgotten. It is as if my shoulder jogged
the stars.

My friend knows me face to face–but many only
venture to meet me under the shield of another's
authority–backed by an invisible corps du reserve of wise
friends and relations. To such I say farewell we cannot
dwell alone in the world.

Sometimes by a pleasing sad wisdom we find ourselves
carried beyond all counsel and sympathy. Our friend's
words do not reach us.

The truly noble and settld character of a man is not
put forward, as the king or conqueror does not march
foremost in a procession.

In the shallow parts of the river where the current is
rapid and the bottom pebbly you may see the curious
circular nests of the lamprey eel–some of them as large
as a cartwheel half a foot high and dishing within. The
eels are said to collect these stones and form them in to
circles with their tails. they are called Petromyzon
stone sucker
The nests of the bream are somewhat similar though
much smaller and more indistinct. The fish may be seen
at all times poised over the centre and attending to its
spawn. These things look more like art than anything

else in the river. And many a nest is successively emptied
by the cunning fisherman who knows where to cast
his bait.

Among others I have picked up a curious spherical
stone–probably an implement of war–like a small paving
stone–about the size of a goose egg–with a groove worn
quite round it–by which it was probably fastened to a
thong or a withe–and answered to strike a severe blow
like a shotted colt.

I have since seen larger ones of the same description

The arrow heads are of every color and of various
forms–and materials–though they are commonly made of
a stone which has a conchoidal fracture. Many small ones
are found made of white quartz which are simple
equilateral triangles–with one side slightly convex.
– These were probably small shot for birds and
squirrels. Where the arrow heads are found the chips
which were made in manufacturing them are much more
numerous– Wherever a lodge stood for any length of
time. And these slivers are the surest indication of Indian
ground–since the geologists tell us that this stone is not
to be found in this vicinity.

The spear heads are of the same form and material
only larger.

Some are found as perfect and sharp as ever for time
has not the effect of blunting this stone And when it
breaks it has a ragged edge which makes a worse cut
than steel– Yet they are so brittle that they can hardly
be carried in the pocket without being broken.

It is a matter of astonishment how the Indians ever
made them with no iron or steel tools to work with– And
I doubt whether one of our mechanics with all the aids
of Yankee ingenuity could soon learn to copy one of the
thousands under our feet. It is well known that the art of
making flints which is best understood in Germany is
only acquired after long practice and then requires

some unusual knack in the operator they being struck out
with a hardened steel chisel–but the arrow-head is of
much more irregular form, and like the flint such is the
nature of the stone, must be struck out by skilful
blows– A blow of a hammer cracks them into a hundred
pieces.

An Indian to whom I exhibited some–but who like
myself regarded them only as relics of antiquity–suggested
that as white man has one blacksmith who did all the
work for many families– So Indian had one arrow head
maker– But the number of chips (or to keep up the
analogy–the cinder heaps) imply too many forges–and
that there must have been as many artists, unless like
the cobblers of old times, the Indian blacksmith–went
round from wigwam to wigwam–and supplied the wants
of the warrior.

I have seen some from the south seas which were
precisely similar– So necessary–so little whimsical–and
so important in the history of the human race is this
little tool.

So has the steel hatchet its prototype in the stone one
of the Indian–and the stone hatchet–in the necessities of
man.

Venerable are these ancient arts whose early history is
lost in that of the race itself.

Here too is the pestle and mortar these–ancient forms
and symbols older than the plow or the spade.

The invention of that plow which now turns them up
to the surface marks the era of their burial.

An era which can never have its history–which is
older than the invention of history.

These are relics of an era older than–modern
civilization–compared with which–Greece and Rome–and
Egypt are modern. And the savage retreats and the white
man advances.

I have the following account of some relics in my
possession which were brought from Taunton in Bristol
County. Many a field which had been planted with corn
for many years The sod being broken the wind began to
blow away the soil and then the sand–for several years
until at length it was blown away to the depth of several
feet–where it ceased– And the ground appeared strewed
with the remains of an Indian village–with regular
circles of stones which formed the foundation of their
wigwams–and numerous implements beside.

{*One-fourth page blank*}

Commonly we use life sparingly, we husband it as if it
were scarce, and admit the right of prudence, but
occasionally we see how ample and inexhaustible is the
stock from which we so scantily draw– And learn that
we need not be prudent–that we may be prodigal, and
all expenses will be met.

Am I not as far from those scenes though I have
wandered a different rout, as my companion who has
finished the voyage of life.? Am I not most dead who
have not life to die, and cast off my sere leaves?

Such was the sabbath of the land and the placidness
of the water that the sailor was in suspense whether the
water floated the land or the land held the water in its
bosom.

It seemed the only right way to enter this country
borne on the bosom of the flood which receives the tribute
of its innumerable vales– The river was the only key
adequate to unlock its maze. We beheld the hills and
vallies–the lakes and streams in their natural orders
and position.

A state should be a complete epitome of the earth—a natural principality and by the gradations of its surface and soil conduct the traveller to its principal marts.

Nature is stronger than law. And the sure but slow influence of wind and water, will balk the efforts of restricting legislatures. Man cannot set up bounds with safety but where the revolutions of nature will confirm and strengthen not obliterate them.

Every man's success is in proportion to his *average* ability. The meadow flowers spring and bloom where the waters annually deposit their slime, and not where they reach in some freshet only. We seem to do ourselves little credit in our own eyes but we do not disappoint our neighbors. For our performance which all know must ever fall short of our aspiration and promise which only we can know entirely. As a stick will avail to reach further than it will strike effectually, since its greatest momentum is a little short of its extreme end. A man is not his hope nor his despair—nor his past deed.

But it is in the order of destiny that whatever is remote shall be near, whatever the eyes see the hands shall touch. The sentinels upon the turret and at the window—and on the wall—behold successively the approaching traveller —whom the host will soon welcome at the gate.

It is not to be forgotten that the poet is innocent, but he is young—he is not yet a parent or a brother to his race. There are a thousand degrees of grace and beauty before absolute humanity and disinterestedness.—

The meanest man can easily test the noblest. Is he embraced— Does he find him a brother.

{*One-fifth page blank*}

I am sometimes made aware of a kindness which may have long since been shown, which surely memory cannot

retain. Which reflects its light long after its heat. I
realize my friend that there have been times when thy
thoughts of me have been of such lofty kindness that they
passed over me like the winds of heaven unnoticed–so
pure that they presented no object to my eyes, so generous
and universal that I did not detect them. Thou hast loved
me for what I wast not–but for what I aspired to be. We
shudder to think of the kindness of our friend which has
fallen on us cold–though in some true but tardy hour we
have awakened– There has just reached me the kindness
of some acts–not to be forgotten–not to be–remembered.
I wipe off these scores at midnight at rare intervals in
moment of insight and gratitude.

{*One-third page blank*}

Far oer the bow
Amid the drowsy noon
Souhegan creeping slow
Appeareth soon.

Where gleaming fields of haze
Meet the voyageur's gaze,
And above the heated air
Seems to make a river there.

The pines stand up with pride
By the Souhegan's side,
And the hemlock and the larch
With their triumphal arch
Have accompanied its march
    To the sea.

No wind stirs its waves
But the spirits of the braves
    Hov'ring o'er
Whose antiquated graves
Its still water laves
    On the shore.

But with an Indian's stealthy tread
It goes sleeping in its bed
Without joy or grief
Or the rustle of a leaf
From the Lyndeboro' hills
To the merrimack mills
Without a ripple or a billow
Or the sigh of a willow
Which trails in its stream
The mid current of its dream.

Not a sound is floated o'er
save the mallet on shore
Which echoing on high
Seems a caulking the sky.
experienced river
Hast thou flown for ever?
Souhegan soundeth old
But the half is not told.
What names hast thou borne
In the ages far gone?
When the Xanthus and Meander
Commenced to wander–
Eer the brown bear haunted
On thy forest floor
Or nature had planted
The pines by thy shore.

With a louder din
Did thy current begin
When melted the snow
On the far mountain's brow
And the drops came together
In that rainy weather.

—

Methinks that by a strict behavior
I could elicit back the brightest star
That lurks behind a cloud.

—

I have rolled near some other spirits path
And with a pleased anxiety have felt
Its purer influence on my opaque mass
But always was I doomed to learn, alas!
I had scarse changed its siderial time.

There is something indescribably wild and beautiful
in the aspect of the forest skirting and occasionally
jutting into the midst of new towns—which like the
sand-heaps of fresh fox boroughs have sprung up in its
midst. The uprightness of the pines and maples assert the
ancient rectitude and vigor of nature. And our lives have
such a back ground where the pine flourishes and the jay
still screams.

Gray sedulously cultivated poetry but the plant would
not thrive. His life seems to have needed some more
sincere and ruder experience

Occasionally we rowed near enough to a cottage to see
the sunflowers before the door—and the seed vessels of the
poppy like small goblets filled with the waters of
Lethe.— but without disturbing the sluggish household.
Driving the small Sand-piper before us.

This village was once famous for the manufacture of
straw bonnets— The Dunstable braid was known far and
wide— And occasionally some industrious damsel tripped
down to the waters edge to put her straw asoak—and
stood awhile to watch the retreating voyageurs.

Fog.
Thou drifting meadow of the air
Where bloom the dasied banks & violets
And in whose fenny labyrinths
The bittern booms, and curlew peeps
The heron wades and boding rain crow clucks;

Low anchored cloud,
Newfoundland air,
Fountain head and source of rivers,
Ocean branch that flowest to the sun,
Diluvian spirit, or Deucaleon shroud,
Dew cloth dream drapery
And napkin spread by fays—
Spirit of lakes and seas and rivers—
Sea fowl that with the east wind
Seek'st the shore— Groping thy way inland
By which ever name I please to call thee
Bear only perfumes and the scent
Of healing herbs to just men's fields.

—

From this place the valiant Capt. Lovewell marched in pursuit of Paugus—the 18 day of May—whom he overtook at Pigwacket.

{One-third page blank}

I am amused with the manner in which Quarles and his contemporary poets speak of nature—with a sort of gallantry, as a knight of his lady—not as lovers—but as having a thorough respect for her—and some title to her acquaintance.

They speak manfully and their lips are not closed by affection
"The pale faced lady of the blackeyed night"
Nature seems to have held her court then and all authors were her gentlemen and esquires—and had ready an abundance of courtly expressions.

Quarles is never weak or shallow though coarse and untasteful. He presses ablebodied and strong backed words into his service—which have a certain rustic fragrance—and force—as if now first devoted to literature—after having served sincere and stern uses.

He has the pronounciation of a poet though he stutters.
He certainly speaks the English tongue with a right
manly accent. To be sure his poems have the—musty odor
of a confessional.

{One-fourth page blank}

When we made our fire on the banks of the Merrimack
at noon to boil some rice for our dinner, the fine grey
smoke went silently up and sealed the treaty we had made
with nature. The flames of our fire spreading amid the
dry grass, and its smoke casting grotesque shadows on
the ground, seemed a phenomenon of the yellow noon.
And we sat like Indians on the banks, bound upward
through the summer. Our adventure seemed in harmony
with the operations of nature, and we progressed up the
stream (without effort or haste) as naturally as the
wind and tide went down—not outraging the calm days by
unworthy bustle or impatience.

Great prose perhaps commands my respect more than
great verse—since it implies a practical elevation and
level height—and a life pervaded with the grandeur of the
thought.

It proves an actual conquest and retention of territory.
The poet often only makes an irruption like the cossack,
or Parthian horse—and are off again firing while they
retreat but—the Prose writer has conquered like a Roman
and settld colonies.

> How little curious is man
> Who hath not searched his mystery a span
> But dreams of mines of treasure
> Which he neglects to measure
> For three score years and ten
> Walks to and fro amid his fellow men
> Oer this fine tract of continental land
> His fancy bearing no divining wand.

Our uninquiring corpses lie more low
Than our lifes curiosity doth go
Our most ambitious steps ne'er climb so high
As in their daily sport the sparrows fly.
And yonder cloud's borne farther in a day
Than our most vagrant steps may ever stray.
Surely O Lord he hath not greatly erred
Who hath so little from his birth place stirred.
He wanders through this low and shallow world
Scarcely his bolder thoughts and hopes unfurled
Through this low walled world which his huge sin
Hath hardly room to rest and harbor in.
Bearing his head just oer some fallow ground
Some cowslip'd meadows where the bitterns sound.
He wanders round until his end draws nigh
And then lays down his aged head to die.
And this is life—this is that famous strife.

His head doth coast a fathom from the land
Six feet from where his grovelling feet do stand.

{One-fourth page blank}

Talking is very singular— The most constant
phenomenon when men or women come together is
talking— A chemist might try this experiment in his
laboratory with certainty—and set down the fact in his
journal— This characteristic of the race may be
considered as established— No doubt every one can call
to mind numerous conclusive instances.— Some nations
it is true are said to articulate more distinctly than
others— Yet the rule holds with those who have the
fewest letters in their alphabet.— Men cannot stay long
together without talking, according to the rules of polite
society— (As all men have two ears and but one
tongue—they must spend the extra & unavoidable hours of
silence in listening to the whisperings of genius and this
fact it is that makes silence always respectable in my
eyes.) Not that they have any thing to communicate—or

do any thing quite natural or important to be done–so–but by common consent they fall to using the invention of speech–and make a conversation good or bad. They say things–first this one and then that. They express their opinions as they are called.

By a well directed silence I have sometimes seen threatening and troublesome people routed. You sit musing as if you were in broad nature again– They cannot stand it–their position becomes more and more uncomfortable every moment. So much humanity over against one without any disguise–not even the disguise of speech!

Not only must men talk–but for the most part must talk about talk–even about books or dead and buried talk. Sometimes my friend expects a few periods from me– Is he exorbitant? He thinks he has delivered his opinions and now it is my turn. Sometimes my companion thinks he has said a good thing, but I dont see the difference. He looks just as he did before. Well it is no loss I suppose he has plenty more

Then I have seen very near and intimate very old friends, introduced by very old strangers, with liberty given to talk. The stranger who knows only the countersign says Jonas–Eldrad. giving those names which will make a title good in a court of law (It may be presumed that God does not know the christian names of men.) Then Jonas like a ready soldier makes a remark–a benediction on the weather it may be–and Eldrad swiftly responds, and unburdens his breast–and so the action begins. They bless god and nature many times gratuitously, and part mutually well pleased, leaving their cards– They did not happen to be present at each other's christening.

Sometimes I have listened so attentively and with so much interest to the whole expression of a man that

I did not hear one word he was saying—and saying too
with the more vivacity observing my attention.

But a man may be an object of interest to me though
his tongue is pulled out by the roots.

Men sometimes do as if they could eject themselves
like bits of packthread from the end of the tongue.

Scholars have for the most part a diseased way of
looking at the world. They mean by it a few cities and
importunate assemblies of men and women—who might
all be concealed in the grass of the prairie.

They describe their world as old or new—healthy or
diseased—according to the state of their libraries—a little
dust more or less on their shelves. When I go abroad
from under this shingle or slate roof—I find several things
which they have not considered— Their conclusions seem
imperfect.

Marlowe p 397 & 413 no 8 {1:457}

As with two eyes we see and with two ears we hear—if
our bodies are not mutilated—with the like advantage
does man meet man.— He makes no complaint—he offers
no encouragement—but one human being is made aware
of the neighboring and contemporaneous existence of
another. Such is the tenderness of friendship. Friends
never recognize each other as finite and imperfect beings,
but with a smile and as strangers. My intercourse with
men is governed by the same laws with my intercourse
with nature.

> As oceans ebb and flow
> Our spirits go.

> All things are current found
> Oer the uneven ground.

Spirits and elements
Have their descents.

Night and day—year on year,
High and low far and near,
These are our own aspects
These are our own regrets.

Ye gods of the shore
Who abide evermore,
I see your far headland
Stretching on either hand.

I hear the sweet evening sounds
From your undecaying grounds
Cheat me no more with time
Take me to your clime.

This first sabbath morning as we dipt our way along
between fresh masses of foliage overrun with the grape
and a smaller flowering vine, the surface was so calm
and both air and water so transparent that the swift flight
of a kingfisher or robin over the river—was as distinctly
seen reflected in the water below as in the air above. The
air was of so pure and vivid a blue that we saw how vain
it would be for the painter to copy it— Only nature may
exaggerate herself.

There was a high wind this night which we afterwards
learned had been still more violent elsewhere—and had
done much injury to the corn fields far and near, but we
only heard it sigh (occasionally) that it could not shake
the foundations of our tent. and laid our ears closer to
the ground with a sense of security—while the blast swept
on to alarm other men.

The pines murmured—the water rippled and the tent
rocked a little—and before sunrise we were ready to pursue
our voyage as usual.

Buonaparte said that the three o clock in the morning courage was the rarest but I cannot agree with him. Fear does not awake so early. Few men are so degenerate as to baulk nature by not beginning the day well.

I hold in my hands a volume of essays and poems–in its outward aspect like the thousands which the press sends forth– And if the Gods permitted their own inspiration to be breathed in vain it might be forgotten in the mass–but the accents of truth are as sure to be heard on earth as in heaven. The more I read it the more I am impressed by its sincerity its depth–and grandeur– It already seems ancient–and has lost the traces of its modern birth. It is a silent evidence of many virtues in the writer. More serenely and humbly confident this man has listened to the voice which all may hear–and with greater fidelity reported it. It is therefore a true prophecy, and shall at length come to pass. It has the earnest grandeur of the Greek tragedy–or rather its Hebrew origins– Yet it is not necessarily referred to any form of faith. The solid slumbering–heavy depth of the sentences–is without recent parallel. It lies like the sward in its native pasture with its roots undisturbed–and not spread over a sandy embankment.

{One-fifth page blank}

We made our way slowly up the river, through the fog–till at length the sun's rays began to struggle through the mist–and showed the pines dripping with dew.

The small green bittern–the genius of the shore–stood probing the mud for its food, a melancholy contemplative bird, with ever an eye upon us though so demurely at work, or was running along over the wet stones like a wrecker in his storm coat, looking out for wrecks of snails and cockles. Then away it goes with a limping flight

uncertain where it will alight, until a rod of clear sand
amid the alders invites its feet. But now our steady
approach compels it to seek a new retreat. It is a bird of
the oldest Thalesian school and no doubt believes in the
priority of water to the other elements. When the world
was made from water was he made—when the earth
subsided from the waters was he left on the shore. A relic
perhaps of some slimy antediluvian age, which yet
inhabits these bright American rivers with us Yankees.
He is of my kindred after all then—and I have a lingering
respect for my unreclaimed brother. There is something
venerable in this race of birds, which might have trodden
the earth while yet in a slimy and imperfect state. What
second advent does he look forward to—meanwhile bravely
supporting his fate—without sympathy from proud man.

The bass wood grows on the shore—the lime or linden
the white wood of the mechanics—with a broad green
leaf—the inner bark of which genus furnishes the material
for the fisherman's matting of which Russia makes so
much use— The peasants using the same material for
shoes.

The neighboring wood was alive with pigeons which
were now moving south looking for mast—like ourselves
spending their noon in the shade. It is pleasant to stand
in the oak or white pine woods and hear the slight
wiry winnowing sound of their wings—and their gentle
tremulous cooing. You will frequently discover a single
pair in the depths of the wood, sitting upon the lower
branches of the white pine, at noon— So silent and
motionless and with such a hermit-like appearance as if
they had never strayed beyond the skirts of the
forest—while the acorn which was gathered in the woods
of Maine is not yet digested in their crops.

Men nowhere east or west live as yet a natural
life,—around which the vine clings—and which the elm
willingly shadows a life of equal simplicity and sincerity
with nature—and in harmony with her grandeur and
beauty. The natural world has no inhabitant.

Men make a perpetual mistake with respect to respect
to travelling. Who ever got nearer to Rome by aid of the
most favorable winds—or the most industrious diligence?
But all travelling grows out of a wish to return home and
stay at home—if the traveller can find it.

Nought was familiar but the heavens from under
whose roof the traveller never passes.

Dense flocks of bobolinks rise before us russett &
rustling as if they were the seeds of the meadow grass
threshed out by the wind. Each tuft gives up its bird—

{One-fourth page blank}

These modern ingenious—but disingennuous arts and
sciences do not affect me as do those more venerable arts
of hunting and fishing and perhaps of husbandry As
ancient and honorable trades as those which the sun and
moon and winds pursue—coeval with the faculties of
man—and invented when hands were invented.— We do
not know their John Gutenberg and Richard Arkwright.
Though the poet would make them to have been gradually
learned and taught—

According to Gower

And Iadahel as saith the boke,
Firste made nette, and fishes toke.
  Of huntyng eke he fonde the chace,
Whiche nowe is knowe in many place.

> A tent of clothe with corde and stake
> He sette up first, and did it make.
>   also Lydgate says
> Jason first sayled, in story it is tolde,
> Toward Colchos to wynne the flees of golde.
> Ceres the Goddes fond first the tilthe of londe;
>
> *   *   *
>
> Also Aristeus, fonde first the usage
> Of mylke, and cruddis, and of hony swote;
> Peryodes, for grete avauntage,
> From flyntes smote fuyre, darying in the roote;

This carries us back indeed to those days—or rather that morning twilight, when men went groping about to find the simple gifts which the gods had dropt—and one found this and another that. May be even at this day some less indispensable one is discovered fallen into some crevice or pool—first bestowed by divine hand. The potatoe seems to have been one of those gifts which fell into a crevice when first bestowed.

It was even a lucky thought perchance of some early wight—the taking shelter in caves from sun and rain—a first doubtful step—uncertain whether of instinct or reason— It was a great deal better than the old way, which yet was not without its conveniences. After long experience of pelting storms on the bare skin, and the alternation of sunshine and shade, some inspired wit did discover how to use nature as a shield against herself, and doubtfully at first—yet impelled by the idea, crept into a cavity in the rock. And then some remote descendant of inventive genius pitying the hard fate of men, who were obliged to forego as yet, the fair plains and fertile vallies visible afar, and restrict their wandering to the porous hill country— Some genius (I say) nicely discriminating what was essential in the cave and what adventitious —invented the roof—the cave above ground—the portable cave invented to stand under a palm tree—to extend palm

leaves over head—impermeable to sun and rain—an
effectual protection—the record of which remains yet in
all languages; In the Latin tectum in English shelter or
roof— And in course of ages the slow conviction was
forced upon all men—that the roof was good, and should
prevail—nor would the gods be displeased thereby. And
lo! the plains and valleys too were populated, and the
dingy cramped and misinformed families of men were
dispersed into nimble and spreading nations.

And this invention has been patented in sun and rain
to this day—roofs of palm leaves with flickering sun beams
instreaming, and dates dates dropping upon table—of
bark or boughs—of grass and stubble—of linen woven and
stretched—of stone and tiles—of boards and shingles.—

And hence it may be this fair-complexioned Caucasian
race—so many ages in advance of its sun burnt brothers.

> On fields oer which the reaper's hand has passd
> Lit by the harvest moon and autumn sun,
> My thoughts like stubble floating in the wind
> And of such fineness as October airs,
> There after harvest could I glean my life
> A richer harvest reaping without toil,
> And weaving gorgeous fancies at my will
> In subtler webs than finest summer haze.

The writer should be as vigorous as a sugar maple
(which can well bear to be tapped) with sap enough to
maintain his own verdure beside what runs into the
troughs. But alas for the most part his top being already
withered—he can only shed a few tears for the public
weal. Or he is like a vine pruned late in the spring which
bleeds to death in the endeavor to heal its wounds.

I like the round emphatic manner in which the old
naturalists speak of the operations of nature. They love
to have their books filled with fine striking truths, and

even when modern science has disproved their
assertions–they are still almost as good as true. "The
Greeks," says Gesner, "had a common proverb (Λαγος
καθευδον), 'a sleeping hare,' for a dissembler or counterfeit,
because the hare sees when she sleeps; for this is an
admirable and rare work of nature, that all the residue of
her bodily parts take their rest, but the eye standeth
continually sentinel."

Hist Anim. by Toplis

In October the air is really the fine element the poets
describe The fields emit a dry and temperate odor– There
is some thing in the refined and elastic air which reminds
us of a work of art. It is like a verse of Anacreon or a
tragedy of Eschylus.

All parts of nature belong to one head as the curls of
a maiden's hair. How beautifully flow the seasons as one
year, and all streams as one ocean– In all her various
products she only developes her own germs– The hawk
perchance, which now takes its flight over the tops of the
trees, was at first only a leaf which fluttered at their feet.
From rustling leaves came in the course of centuries the
lofty flight and clear carol of the bird. Look up at the tree
tops and see how finely she finishes off her work there
as if she would never have done. See how the pines spire
without end higher and higher, and give a graceful fringe
to the earth. And who shall count the finer cobwebs that
soar and float away from their utmost tops–and the
myriad insects that dodge between them!

The poet is he that hath fat enough–like bears and
marmots to suck his claws all winter. He hybernates in
this world and feeds on his own marrow– I love to think
as I walk over the snowy fields of those happy dreamers
that lie under the sod–of dormice and all that tribe of

dormant creatures, which have such a superfluity of
life–enveloped in thick fold of fur–impervious to winter.
The poet is a sort of dormouse that early in the autumn
goes into winter quarters of deep and serene thoughts
– But most men lead a starved existence like
hawks that would fain keep on the wing and trust to pick
up a sparrow now and then.

I hate museums–there is nothing so weighs upon my
spirits. They are the catacombs of nature– One green
bud of Spring–one willow catkin–one faint trill from a
migrating sparrow–would set the world on its legs again.
The life that is in a single green weed is of more worth
than all this death. They are dead nature collected by
dead men. I know not whether I muse most–at the bodies
stuffed with cotton and saw-dust–or those stuffed with
bowels and fleshy fibre outside the cases. V p. 78

It is one great and rare merit in the old English
tragedy–that it says something. The words slide away very
fast but toward some conclusion. It has to do with things
and the reader feels as if he were advancing– It does not
make much odds what message the author has to deliver
at this distance of time–since no message can startle us,
but how he delivers it–that it be done in a downright and
manly way. They come to the point–and do not waste
the time.

They say that Carew was a laborious writer–but his
poems do not show it– They are finished, but do not show
the marks of the chisel. Drummond was indeed a
quiddler–with little fire or fibre–and rather a taste *for*
poetry than a taste *of* it.

After all we draw on very gradually in English literature
to Shakspeare–through Peele and Marlowe–to say

nothing of Raleigh & Spenser–and Sidney. We hear the
same great tone already sounding to which Shakspeare
added a serener wisdom and clearer expression. Its chief
characteristics of reality and unaffected manliness are
there– And they constitute a more important distinction
than the more or less of wisdom.

The more we read of the literature of those times–the
more does acquaintance divest the genius of Shakspeare,
of the in some measure false mystery which has thickened
around it–and leave it shrouded in the grander mystery
of day light. His critics have for the most part made their
contemporaries less that they might make Shakspeare
more.

The distinguished men of those times had a great flow
of spirits–a cheerful wit far removed from the solemn
wisdom of these days. What another thing was fame and
a name then than now. This is seen in the familiar
manner in which they were spoken of by each other and
the nation at large–*Kit* Marlowe–and *George* (Peele)
and *Will* Shakspeare and *Ben* Jonson. Great *fellows–chaps*

To the indifferent and casual observer the laws of
nature are science– To the enlightened and spiritual they
are morality–or modes of divine life.

Where is the proper Herbarium–the true cabinet of
shells–and Museum of skeletons–but in the meadow
where the flower bloomed–by the sea side where the tide
cast up the fish–and on the hills and in the vallies where
the beast laid down its life–and the skeleton of the
traveller reposes on the grass. What right have mortals
to parade these things on their legs again–with their
wires–and when heaven has decreed that they shall
return to dust again–to return them to sawdust?

Would you have a dried specimen of a world–or a
pickled one?

Embalming is a sin against heaven and earth. Against heaven who has recalled the soul—and set free the servile elements—and against the earth which is thus robbed of her dust.

I have had my right-perceiving senses so disturbed in these haunts as to mistake a veritable living man for a stuffed specimen—and surveyed him with dumb wonder as the strangest of the whole collection.

For the strangest is that which being in many particulars most like is in some essential particular most unlike

We pass through all degrees of life from the least organic to the most complex. Sometimes we are mere pudding stone and scoriae

How suddenly and silently do the eras we call history awake and glimmer in us—and there is room for Alexander and Hannibal to march and conquer.

V. n.p.

The present—is the instant work and near process of living—and will be found in the last analysis to be nothing more nor less than digestion—sometimes, it is true, it is indigestion.

It was a fine imagination which first taught that the stars are worlds, and conferred a great favor on man

Waves of serene life pass over us from time to time—like flakes of sunlight over the fields in cloudy weather. In some happier moment when more sap flows in the withered stalk of our life—Syria and India stretch away from our present as they do in history.

Daniel deserves praise for his moderation—and sometimes has risen into poetry before you know it. Strong sense appears in his epistles—but you have to

remember too often in what age he wrote and yet that
Shakspeare was his contemporary. His style is without
the tricks of the trade–and really in advance of his age.
We can well believe that he was a retired scholar who
would keep himself shut up in his house two whole
months together.

We continued up along the banks on foot–until from
Merrimack it became the Pemmigewasset that leaped by
our side–and after we had passed its fountain head–the
wild ammonusuck became our guide to its source amid
the mountains.

I have seen where the mildew on a jar had taken the
form of perfect leaves–thick–downy–and luxuriant. What
an impulse was given some time or other to vegetation
that now nothing can stay it. Some one has said he could
write an epic to be called the leaf–and this would seem
to have been the theme of the creator himself. The leaf
either plain or variegated–fresh or decayed–fluid or
crystalline–is natures constant cypher.

The low of cattle in the street sounds like a low
symphony or running base to the hurry scurry of the
leaves.

The wind goes hurrying down the country, gleaning
every loose straw that is left in the fields–while every
farmers lad too seems to scud before it–having donned
his best pea-jacket and pepper and salt waistcoat–his (as
yet) unbent trowsers–outstanding rigging of duck or
kersymere, or corduroy–and his furry hat withal–to
county fairs and Cattle-shows–to this Rome amid the
villages where the treasures of the year are gathered.– All
the land over they go leaping the fences with their tough
idle palms which have not yet learned to hang by their
sides, amid the low of calves and the bleating of
sheep.– Amos–abner–Elnathan Elbridge
    "From steep pine-bearing mountains to the plain."

I love these sons of earth–every mothers' son of
them–with their great hearty hearts rushing tumultuously
in herds–from spectacle to spectacle, as if fearful that
there should not be time between sun and sun to see them
all.– And the sun does not wait more than in haying time.

> "wise Nature's darlings, they live in the world
> Perplexing not themselves how it is hurl'd."

They may bring their fattest cattle and their fairest
fruits–but they are all eclipsed by the show of men.

These are stirring autumn days When men sweep by
in crowds amid the rustle of leaves, like migrating
finches– This is the true harvest of the year when the
air is but the breath of men–and the rustling of leaves
is as the trampling of the crowd.

We read nowadays of the ancient festivals games and
processions of the Greeks and Etruscans with a little
incredulity–or at least want of sympathy–but how
childlike–how natural and irrepressible must be in all
people some hearty palpable greeting of nature. The
Corybantes the Bachannals–the rude primitive tragedians
with their procession and goat song and the whole
paraphernalia of the Panathenaea–which seems so
antiquated and peculiar are easily parralleled now. The
husbandman is always a better Greek than the scholar
is prepared to understand–and the old custom still
survives while antiquarians & sholars grow grey in
commemmorating it

The farmers crowd to the fair today–in obedience to
the same ancient law of the race–which Solon or
Lycurgus did not enact–as naturally as bees swarm and
follow their queen.– I love to see the herd of men feeding
heartily on coarse succulent pleasures–as cattle feed on
the husk and stalks of vegetables Many of them it is true
are crooked and crabbed specimens of humanity, run all
to thorn and rind and crowded out of shape by adverse
circumstances like the third chestnut in the bur–yet fear
not that the race will fail or waver in them–like the crabs

which grow in hedges they furnish the stocks of sweet
and thrifty fruits still– Thus is nature recruited from
age to age while the fair and palatable varieties are
dying out and have their period.

This is that mankind.

How cheap must be the material of which so many
men are made– And where is that quarry in the earth
from which these thousands were dug up?

> Epitaph
> Here lies an honest man,
> Rear Admiral Van.
> Faith, then ye have
> Two in one grave,
> For in his favor
> Here too lies the engraver.

> Epitaph on an Engraver.
> By Death's favor
> Here lies the engraver,
> And now I think o't,
> Where lies he not?
> If the archangel look but where he lies,
> He ne'er will get translated to the skies.

> On a goodman
> Here lies–the world,
> There rises one.

Here rose the spirit of Capt. Jonathan Foster–the 19th
day of May, and the 50th year of our independence.
Such was his character on earth that even his nearest
friends were reconciled to his departure. Having reached
the term of his unnatural life he has gone in the fulness
of hope to meet his reward in that land beyond the
grave, where he is anxiously expected by a disconsolate
wife and nine small children.

And now that his soul has returned to him who
gave it

May the worms be merciful to his body.

Donne was not a poet–but a man of strong sense–a sturdy English thinker–full of conceits and whimsicalities, hammering away at his subject–be it eulogy or epitaph –sonnet or satire with the patience of a day laborer, without taste, but with an occasional fine distinction or poetic phrase. He was rather *Doctor* Donne, than the *poet* Donne. His letters are perhaps best.

Lovelace is what his name expresses–of slight material to make a poet's fame. His goings and comings are of no great account. His taste is not so much love of excellence as fear of failure, though in one instance he has written fearlessly and memorably.

Running hither and thither with appetite for the coarse pastimes of the day–now with boisterous speed at the heels of the inspired negro–from whose larynx the melodies of all Congo and Guinea Coast had broke loose into our streets.– Now to see the procession of a hundred yoke of oxen all as august and grave as osiris–or the droves of neat cattle and milch cows as unspotted as Isis or Io. Such as had no love for nature before
          "Went lovers home from this great festival."

Though we wanderers are thus far down the stream–still a subtler tide rises in us both to an equal height– And like the stars our thoughts rise up in his horizon still. Hearts put in 'circulation' a finer blood than Lavoisier has detected. The lover is the only man of science.– who knows the value of magnanimity and truth.

As in the bones of man are found the various earths which entered into their composition, so no doubt some finer soils are found in which the most delicate flowers grow, and the oxide and other coloring matter which impart to them their hues. This answers to the instinct which we call love of flowers, by which they answer a certain etherial utility to our higher nature.

All nations make flowers express the sentiments and finer qualities of the character.

The human eye is the first of flowers and one of fairest hue. Its perennial and unfading colors attest its superiority– The hard avaricious man is not more conscious of this fair azure or hazel blossom which he bears than of those which spot the fields. It is in young and old alike an unwrinkled feature like the soul which abides behind it. So is every flower in the field an eye–with a seer as near behind it–and at some period its elements have coursed in our veins

Toward the end of the summer when the reign of sunshine is drawing to a close and the earth has absorbed enough of golden rays, the flowers of the sun begin to bloom. On every hill side and in every valley stand countless asters, coriopses tansies, golden rods, and the whole race of yellow flowers, like Brahminical devotees–turning steadily with their luminary from morning till night. It is the floral solstice a little after mid-summer. As if the particles of golden light–the sun-dust, had fallen like seeds upon the earth, and produced these blossoms.

{*One-fourth page blank*}

The characteristics and pursuits of various ages and races of men are always existing in epitome in every neighborhood. The pleasures and pursuits of my earliest youth have become the inheritance of other men–and not a mile from where I write are even now enjoyed. Peter and George are still fishers though I have wandered

on—about other pursuits. They perchance are not
confounded by many knowledges, and have not sought
out many inventions. How to take many fish before the
sunset, with their slight willow twigs and hempen lines,
that is invention enough for them. To them nature is
still natural, They are still natural to nature.

It is good to be a fisherman in summer and in winter.
Some men are judges, and serve the state, sitting on
benches, even till the court rises. They sit judging in
their ermine between the seasons and between meals
leading a civil-politic life— Arbitrating in the Case of
Spaulding versus Cummings—from the first phospher
light till the red vesper sinks into the west.

The fisherman meanwhile stands in three feet of water
at high noon, arbitrating in other cases between
muck-worm and shiner, amid the scent of water
lillies—mint—and pontederia. Leading his life—still many
rods from the dry land—within a pole's length of where
the larger fishes swim. Human life is to him very much
like a river,
                    Aye flowing downward to the sea
He was the first to observe this. His honor made a great
discovery in bailments.

How wholsesome are the natural laws to contemplate
—as gravity heat—light—moisture—dryness.
Only let us not interfere. Let the soul withdraw into the
chambers of the heart—let the mind reside steadily in the
labyrinth of the brain, and not interfere with hands or
feet more than with other parts of nature,

Thompson was a true lover of of nature—and seems to
have needed only a deeper human experience, to have
taken a more vigorous and lofty flight. He is deservedly
popular and has found a place on many shelves and in

many cottages. There are great merits in the Seasons,–and
the Almanack

In Autumn

"attemper'd suns arise"

*   *   *

–; while broad, and brown, below,
"extensive harvests hang the heavy head.
Rich, silent, deep, they stand;–"

—

The moon in Autumn

, her spotted disk,
Where mountains rise, umbrageous vales descend,

—

, gives us his blaze again,
void of its flame, and sheds a softer day.
Now through the passing cloud she seems to stoop,
Now up the pure cerulean rides sublime.

—

The whole air whitens with a boundless tide
Of silver radiance, trembling round the world.

The friend is a fair isle of palms, floating perchance,
cheering the mariner in the Pacific sea, near whose coast
he in vain stands off and on–sounding for some safe
entrance within its coral reef.

My friend thou art not of some other race or family of
men–thou art flesh of my flesh, bone of my bone. Has
not nature associated us in many ways. Water from the
same fountain–lime from the same quarry–grain from
the same field, compose our bodies. And per chance our
elements but reassert their ancient kindredship. Is it of
no significance that I have so long partaken of the same

loaf with thee, have breathed the same air summer and winter–have felt the same heat and cold–the same fruits of summer have been pleased to refresh us both– And thou hast never had a thought of different fibre from my own.

Our kindred–of one blood with us. With the favor and not the displeasure of the gods, we have partaken the same bread.

It is hard to know rocks, they are crude and inaccessible to our nature– We have not enough of the stoney element in us.

Who does not walk upon the plain as amid the columns of Tadmore of the desert.

It is hard to know men by rumor only– But to stand near somewhat living and conscious– Who would not sail through mutiny and storm farther than Columbus–to reach the fabulous retreating shores of some continent man?

There is on the earth no institution which friendship has established. It has no temple nor even a solitary column. It governs no where. It has no shrine. It is as a thing unheard of–and if you inquire for it–you will not hear. It is not taught by any religion– The wisest books of the ancient world do not contain its law–nor do the scriptures inculcate it

There goes a rumor that the earth is inhabited, but we have seen only a foot-print on its shores. The hunter has found fragments of pottery and the mounds of former inhabitants.

My friend can only be in any measure my foe, because he is fundamentally my friend; for everything is after all more nearly what it should rightfully be, than that which it is simply by failing to be the other.

All that has been said of friendship is like botany to flowers. It can never be recognised by the understanding.

It cannot be the subject of reconciliation or the theme of conversation even between friends. The true friend must in some sense disregard all professions of friendship and forget them.

Friendship is not so kind as is imagined–it has not much human blood in it. It has a certain disregard for men and their erections, while it purifies the atmosphere like electricity. It is as far from pity as from contempt. I should hesitate even to call it the highest sympathy since the word is of suspicious origin, and suggests suffering rather than joy. It was established before religion, for men are not friends in religion, but over and through it–and it records no apostacy or repentance, but there is a certain divine and innocent and perennial health about it. A certain disregard the Christian duties and humanities is consistent with its perfect integrity. For it is rather a society than sympathy as it were a fragmentary and godlike intercourse of ancient date, still kept up at intervals–which remembering itself–does not hesitate to neglect the humbler rights and charities of humanity. Its charity is generosity–its virtue nobleness– (Its religion trust.) We come nearer to friendship with flowers and inanimate objects–than with merely affectionate and loving men. It is not for the friend to be just even–at least he is not to be lost in this attribute–but to be only a large and free existence representative of humanity–its general court– Admirable to us as the heavenly bodies, but like them affording rather a summer heat and day-light–the light and fire of sunshine & stars–rather than the intense heats and splendors which our weakness and appetite require. All its deeds are gratuitous. It is free and irresponsible. How slight & evanescent it has been in every man's experience–like the fluttering of a leaf over his head–remembered like heat lightning in past summers.

Yesterday I skated after a fox over the ice. Occasionally he sat on his haunches and barked at me like a young wolf. It made me think of the bear and her cubs mentioned by Capt. Parry–I think–.

All brutes seem to have a genius for mystery–an oriental aptitude for symbols and the language of signs. & this is the origin of Pilpay & Aesop. The fox manifested an almost human suspicion of mystery in my actions. While I skated directly after him, he cantered at the top of his speed, but when I stood still, though his fear was not abated some strange but inflexible law of his nature caused him to stop also, and sit again on his haunches. While I still stood motionless, he would go slowly a rod to one side, then sit and bark, then a rod to the other side, and sit and bark again, but did not retreat, as if spell-bound. When however I commenced the pursuit again he found himself released from his durance.

Plainly the fox belongs to a different order of things from that which reigns in the village. Our courts, though they offer a bounty for his hide, and our pulpits, though they draw many a moral from his cunning, are in few senses contemporary with his free forest life.

To the poet considered as an artist his words must be as the relation of his oldest and finest memory–and wisdom derived from the remotest experience.

How cheering is the spring to all creatures, and the steady revolutions of nature. It cannot but affect our philosophy favorably to know of the schools of migratory fishes–of Salmon shad alewives and herring which penetrate up the innumerable rivers of our coast–some even to the interior lakes.– and again of the young fry which in still greater numbers wend their way downward to the sea.

Occasionally I hear a remote sound with so
unprejudiced a sense, far sweet and significant–that I
seem for the first time to have heard at all. It has a larger
meaning and a wider undulation than I knew.

{One-fifth page blank}

I have thought when walking in the woods–through a
certain retired dell, bordered with shrub oaks and pines,
far from the village and affording a glimpse only through
an opening of the mountains in the horizon–how my life
might pass there, simple and true and natural, and how
many things would be impossible to be done there. How
many books I might not read–how, under such
circumstances, I should select my reading. Might I not
read only henceforth serene truth! Never statistics, nor
news, nor reports–nor periodicals, only great poems, and
when they failed, read them *again*, or write more.

Scholars are wont to sell their birth-right for a mess of
learning. Is it necessary to know of Greek art and
philosophy–of Hindoo wisdom, or German criticism?
Does the sun shine to light us to these things?

All that are printed and bound are not books–they
belong not of course to letters–but are to be ranked with
other luxuries and conveniences of civilized life– In one
sense every Commercial and Railroad and stage company
has its books–and there are new and patented inventions
in this shape for the elevation of the race–which many a
pure scholar and genius who has learned to read is
deceived by, and finds himself reading a horse rake or
spinning jenny–or steam power press, or kitchen range,
who was seeking serene truths, as in Zoraster.
Alas! paper is cheap and authors do not have to erase
one book, before they write another.

Why avoid my friends and live among strangers–why not reside in my native country!

Books are written with intentions and as part of a system– Books which contain the elements of knowledge–and the science of things–that is men's ignorance of things. elements which lead to human solutions–methods to a method–but never to a ray of absolute or divine knowledge. The scholar is taught the method of arriving at that dilemma in which men of science and philosophers–professors, now stand–and studies elements and the best classification with a view to this end soley.

Many a book is written which does not necessarily suggest or imply the phenomenon or object to explain which it professes to have been written. But we may begin anywhere with nature. Strictly speaking there is no such thing as elementary knowledge There is always a chasm between knowledge and ignorance which the steps of science can never pass.

One might say that the great mass of books were a part of the common school system. I have just seen advertised a "Popular Guide to the Observation of Nature"– They do not teach the divine view of nature but the popular.

Every child should be encouraged to study not man's system of nature but Nature's.

pine Drying out?–

Giles Fletcher knew how to write & has left English verses behind. He is the most valuable imitator of the Spenserian stanza, and adds a moral tone of his own.

{One-fifth page blank}

To a marsh hawk
In Spring–
There is health in thy grey wing
Health of nature's furnishing.
Say thou modern-winged antique,
Was thy mistress ever sick?
In each heaving of thy wing
Thou dost health and leisure bring,
Thou dost waive disease & pain
And resume new life again.

Man walks in nature still alone,
    And knows no one,
Discerns no lineament nor feature
    Of any creature.

Though all the firmament
    Is o'er me bent,
Yet still I miss the grace
    Of an intelligent and kindred face

I still must seek the friend
Who does with nature blend
Who is the person in her mask,
He is the friend I ask.

Who is the expression of her meaning,
Who is the uprightness of her leaning,
Who is the grown-child of her weaning.

We twain would walk together
    Through every weather,
And see this aged nature
    Go with a bending stature.

The centre of this world
The face of nature
The site of human life,
Some sure foundation
And nucleus of a nation,
At least, a private station.

It is the saddest thought of all, that what we are to others that we are much more to ourselves–avaricious, mean, irascible, affected–we are the sufferers– If our pride offends our humble neighbor much more does it offend ourselves–though our lives are never so private and solitary.

The offer
I make ye an offer,
Ye gods hear the scoffer,
The scheme will not hurt you,
If ye will find goodness I will find virtue.
Though I am your creature,
And child of your nature,
I have pride still unbended,
And blood undescended,
Some free independence,
And my own descendents.
If ye will deal plainly,
I will strive mainly,
If ye will discover
Great plans to your lover,
And give him a sphere
Somewhat larger than here.

Morning
Heathen without reproach,
Who dost upon the civil day encroach,
Who ever since thy birth
Hast trod the outskirts of the earth
–The cowards hope the brave man's way,
And distant promise of a day–
While the late risen world goes west
I'll daily bend my steps to east.

The Friend.
The great friend
Dwells at the land's end,
There lives he
Next to the sea.
Fleets come and go,

Carrying commerce to and fro,
But still sits he on the sand
And maketh firm that headland.
Mariners steer them by his light
Safely in the darkest night,
He holds no visible communion
For his friendship is a union.
Many men dwell far inland,
But he alone sits on the strand,
Whether he ponders men or books
Ever still he seaward looks,
Feels the sea-breeze on his cheek,
At each word the landsmen speak;
From some distant port he hears
Of the ventures of past years
In the the sullen ocean's roar
Of wrecks upon a distant shore;
In every companions eye
A sailing vessel doth descry;
Marine news he ever reads
And the slightest glances heeds.

Near is India to him
Though his native shore is dim,
But the bark which long was due,
Never–never–heaves in view,
Which shall put an end to commerce
And bring back what it took from us,
(Which shall make Siberia free
Of the climes beyond the sea)
Fetch the Indies in its hold,
All their spices and their gold,
And men sail the sea no more
The sea itself become a shore,
To a broader deeper sea,
A profounder mystery.

As in the treaties of states there are secret articles
inserted of vital importance to the parties–so in our
treaties with heaven the most indistinct and secret articles
are the most vital.

{*One-third page blank*}

What a fine and beautiful communication from age to
age of the fairest and noblest thoughts, even such as have
never been communicated by speech, is music. The
aspirations of ancient men preserved in these simple
notes. It is the flower of language. thought painted
–colored and curved–tinged and wreathed. The
crystal fountain tinged with the suns rays. It is the
only fluent and flexible thought. Notes of music are like
the ripples of a purling stream–reflecting the green grass
and the red clouds.

It teaches us again & again to trust the remotest and
finest as the divinest instinct. It makes a dream our only
real experience. All that we have imagined of heroism it
reminds and reassures us of.

In the forward part stands a brawny New Hampshire
man, bare headed and in simple shirt and trowsers–a
rude apollo of a man coming down from that "vast
uplandish country"–to the main–of nameless age–with
flaxen hair and vigorous weather bleached and suntried
countenance, in whose wrinkles the sun still lodged– As
fresh as a mountain maple. An undressed–unkempt
–uncivil man.

There is reason in the distinction of civil and uncivil.
The manners are sometimes so rough a rind that we
doubt whether they conceal any core or sap wood. We
sometimes meet uncivil men–children of Amazons, who
dwell by mountain paths, and are said to be inhospitable
to strangers. Their salutation is as rude as the grasp of
their brawny hands, and they naturally deal with men as
unceremoniously as they are accustomed to deal with the
elements. They have only to extend their clearings and
let in more of sun light, to seek out the southern slopes
of the hills from which they may look out upon the civil
plain or ocean, and temper their diet duly with the cereal

fruits, consuming less wild meat and acorns, to become
like the inhabitants of cities.

I was once travelling through a distant and
mountainous part of the country, along the banks of a
stream whose course I had followed for several days,
through a succession of shady vallies, sunken deep
among the hills–where dwelt a few mild and hospitable
inhabitants–while on either hand–high up on the level
tops of the mountains dwelt a different & less cultivated
race who had but little intercourse with themselves–so
near indeed though inaccessible that I occasionally heard
the bleating of their flocks–

As the day was not yet spent and I was anxious to
improve the light though my path was gradually rising
to these higher levels I took leave of my kind hosts–who
directed me to the dwelling of the nearest of the race
–whom we will call Satyrus, who they said was a rude
and inhospitable man.

At length as the sun was setting behind the mountains
in a still darker and more solitary vale, where the shaggy
woods almost joined their tops over the torrent I reached
the dwelling of my host.

I observed as I drew near to his abode that he was
less savage than I had feared, for he kept herds and dogs
to watch them, and I saw where he made maple sugar
on the sides of the mountains, and detected the voices of
children mingling with the murmur of the torrent
before the door.

As I passed his stable I met one whom I took to be a
hired man attending to his cattle, and inquired if they
entertained travellers at that house. "Some times we
do"–he answered gruffly, and immediately went to the
farthest stall from me– And I perceived that it was Rice
himself whom I had addressed. But pardoning this
incivility to the wildness of the surrounding scenery–I
bent my steps to the house– There was no sign post

Before it nor invitation to the traveller though I saw by the road that many went and came there–but the owner's name only was fastened to the outside–a sort of implied and sullen invitation, as I thought.

I passed from room to room without meeting any one, at first, till I came to what seemed the guests apartment, which was neat and even had an air of refinement, and I was glad to find a chart on the wall which would direct me upon my journey on the morrow.

At lenght I heard a step in a distant apartment which was the first I had entered, and went to see if the master of the house had come in, but it proved to be only a child, one of those whose voices I had heard, probably his son, and between him and me stood in the door way a large watch dog, which growled upon me and looked as if he would presently spring, but the boy did not speak to him nor seem to observe the danger. And when I asked him for a glass of water he briefly said "It runs in the corner." So I took a mug and went outdoors again and searched round the corners of the house, but could find no well nor spring, nor any water, but the stream I have mentioned –which ran all along the front I came back therefore and set down the empty mug–thinking to ask if the stream was good to drink–saying I could not find it–whereupon the child seized the mug and going to the corner of the room where a cool spring trickled through a pipe into the apartment, filled it and drank, and gave it to me empty again–then calling to the dog rushed out of the room, and left me alone.

This spring was cool and pure and seemed to issue from the mountain behind the house, and was conducted through it in pipes, and thence flowed into the stream in front.

At length some of the men came in and drank and washed and combed their hair. And some of them sat down, as if weary; and fell asleep, without having spoken.

All the while I saw no females, but sometimes heard a bustle in that part of the house, from which the spring came and whither the child had gone.

At length Rice himself came in with an ox whip in his hand, breathing hard, and going to a corner drank some kind of liquor.

He sat down not far from me and when I asked if he could give me a bed, he said there was one ready, but in such a tone as if I ought to have known it, and the less said about that the better.

I observed that it was a wild and rugged country which he inhabited and worth coming many miles to visit–"not so very rough neither," said he, and appealed to his men to bear witness to the breadth and level of his fields, and the size of his crops, "And if we have some hills", said he, "there's no better pasturage any where."

I then asked if this place was not the one I heard of, calling it by the name I had seen on the map–or if it was a certain other, and he answered gruffly–that it was neither the one nor the other–that he had settled it–and cultivated it–and made it what it was–and I could know nothing about it–that it was a place between certain other places–and the books and maps were all wrong–for he had lived there longer than anybody.

To tell the truth I was very much pleased with my host's residence, and inclined even to exaggerate the grandeur of the scenery–and sought in many ways to make known my contentment.

Observing some guns and other implements of hunting on the wall, and his hounds now sleeping on the floor, I took occasion to change the discourse, and inquired if there was much game in that country–and he answered this question more graciously for he was evidently fond of the chace–but when I asked if there were many bears, he answered impatiently that he did not loose more sheep than his neighbors—he had tamed and civilized that region.

After a pause, thinking of my journey on the morrow, and of the few hours of day-light in that hollow and mountainous country, which would require me to be on my way betimes, I remarked that the daylight must be shorter by an hour there than in the neighboring plains, at which he gruffly asked what I knew about it. And affirmed that he had as much light as his neighbors—he ventured to say the days were longer there than where I lived as I should find if I stayed—that some how or rather as I could'nt be expected to understand the sun came over the mountains a half an hour earlier and lingered a half an hour later, than elsewhere.

Without regarding his rudeness I said with a little less familiarity that he was a fortunate man, and I trusted he was grateful for so much light—and rising said I would take a light, and I would pay him then for my lodging, for I expected to commence my journey on the morrow, even as early as the sun rose in his country, but he answered somewhat more civilly as I thought that I should not fail to find some of his household stirring however early, for they were no sluggards, and I could take my breakfast with them before I started if I chose, and as he lighted the lamp I could see a gleam of true hospitality and ancient civility—a beam of pure and even gentle humanity, from his bleared and moist eyes, for the effect of the liquor had in some measure worked off— And he led the way to my apartment stepping over the limbs of his men who were sound asleep on the floor, and showed me a clean and comfortable bed. But I arose by star light the next morning as usual, before my host or his men or even his dogs were awake, and having left a ninepence on the counter, was already half way over the mountain with the sun, before they had broken their fast.

But before I had quite left the country of my host, while the first rays of the sun slanted over the mountains, as I had stopped by the wayside to gather some wild berries, a very aged man came along with a milking pail in his hand, and turning aside also began to pluck the berries with me, but when I inquired the way he answered in a low rough voice without looking up, or seeming to take any notice of me–which I imputed to his years–and presently mutturing to himself he proceed to collect his cows in a neighboring pasture, and when he had again returned to the wayside, he suddenly stopped while his cows went on before, and uncovering his head prayed aloud to God for his daily bread, and also that he who letteth his rain fall on the just and on the unjust, and without whom not a sparrow falleth to the ground–would not neglect the stranger–meaning me–

And when he had done praying I made bold to ask him–if he had any cheese in his hut which he would sell me, but he answered without looking up and as gruffly as before–that they did'nt make any–and went to milking.

"The stranger who turneth away from a house with disappointed hopes, leaveth there his own offences, and departeth, taking with him all the good actions of the owner."

Everyone finds by his own experience that the era in which men cultivate the apple and the amenities of the garden, must be different from that of the forest and hunter's life– Gardening is civil and sociable but it wants the vigor and freedom of the forest and the outlaw. Talk of civilizing the Indian! By his wary independence and aloofness he is admitted to a refinement in his untrimmed mistress, which is like the distant but permanent light of the stars, compared with tapers. There are the innocent pleasures of country life,–but the heroic paths are rugged and retired in another sense, and he who treads them

studies his plots and parterres in the stars, he gathers
nuts and berries by the way and orchard fruits with such
heedlessness as berries.

There is something less noble in gardening even than
in savage life. It conciliates–soothes–tames Nature. It
breaks the horse and the ox, but the Indian rides the
horse wild and chases the Buffalo, and not the less
worships them both as his gods.

The gardiner takes plants out of the forest and sets
them in his garden, but the true child of nature finds
them in his garden already wherever they grow, and does
not have to transplant them. If the Indian is somewhat of
a stranger in nature the gardener is too much a familiar.
There is something vulgar and foul in the latter's closeness
to his mistress, something noble and cleanly in the
formers distance.

Yet the hunter seems to have a property in the moon
which even the farmer has not.

Ah!–the poet knows uses of plants which are not easily
reported, though he cultivates no parterre; see how the
sun smiles on him while he walks in the gardener's
aisles, rather than on the gardner.

Not only has the foreground of a picture its glass of
transparent crystal spread over it, but the picture itself is
a glass or transparent medium to a remoter background.
We demand only of all pictures–that they be perspicuous
–that the laws of perspective have been truly
observed– It is not the fringed foreground of the
desert–nor the intermediate oases that detain the eye and
the imagination–but the infinite, level, and roomy horizon,
where the sky meets the sand, and heavens and earth–the
ideal and actual, are coincident.– The back ground into
which leads the path of the pilgrim.

There is a persevering and serene reserve in friendship,
which implies such qualities as the warrior prizes. The
simple but determined friendship which Wawatam

testified for Henry the fur trader, so almost bare and
leafless—yet not blossomless nor fruitless, the reader
remembers with satisfaction and security.

The stern imperturbable man, comes to my lodge, and
affirms that I am the white brother whom he saw in his
dream, and adopts me henceforth. And we practise not
hostility but friendship thereafter as children of one
father—having always a welcome ready for one
another Wawatam has buried the hatchet as it regards
his friend; and they hunt and feast together—not coveting
each other's scalps. The friend will be a *necessarius*
and he shall meet ever on the homely ground of
necessity—not on cushions but on the ground and on rocks
we shall sit.

{*One-third page blank*}

All things are in revolution it is the one law of nature
by which order is preserved, and time itself lapses and
is measured.

Yet some things men will do from age to age and some
things they will not do.– I find among the papers of an
old Justice of the Peace—and Deacon of this town, this
memorandum—
"Men that Travil^d with teams on the Sabbath
December 18th 1803 ware
    Jeremiah Richardson &
    Jonas Parker both of Shirley
    They had teams with riging such as used to
carry Berrells and they ware travilling to the
westward Richardson was Questioned by Hon Eph^m Wood
Esq–& he said that Jonas Parker was his fellow traveller
& he farther said that a Mr. Longley was his Employer
who promis^d to bare him out."

We were the men that were gliding northward on the
Sabbath this Sept. 1st 1839—with still team and rigging

such as are not used to carry barrells, unquestioned by
any squire or church Deacon, and who were ready if need
be to bear ourselves out. Men have relaxed a little from
their strictness one would say—but I presume if the
ligature is found to be loosened in one part, it is only
drawn the tighter in another.

The Concord or Musketaquid or Grass-ground-river,
(the original name, it is conjectured, being "formed of
the Indian words, *moskeht*, signifying 'grass', and ohkeit,
signifying 'ground'; and unitedly 'grass-ground,'"
describing accurately enough the country through which
it flows, and hence justly applied to the stream
itself)—though as old as the Euphrates and Nile, did not
begin to have a place in history until the fame of its
broad meadows and open uplands—and abundance of
fish, attracted settlers out of England in 1635— And the
other kindred name of Concord it derived from the quiet
and peaceable lives of these settlers upon its banks both
with one another and with the Indians
    According to our faithful town history—"One branch of
it rises in the south part of Hopkinton; and another from
a pond and a large cedar-swamp in Westborough, and
running into Hopkinton, forms the boundary line between
that town and Southborough. Thence in a northerly
direction it passes through Framingham, and forms the
boundary line between Sudbury and East sudbury (where
it is sometimes called Sudbury River), and enters Concord
at the south part of the town. After passing through it in
a diagonal direction, it receives the North River, and,
going out at the north east part between Bedford and
Carlisle and through Billerica, empties into the Merrimack
at Lowell. It is remarkable for the gentleness of its
current, which is scarcely perceptible by the eye. At low
water mark? it is from 4 to 15 feet deep, and from 100 to
300 feet wide. Where it enters Concord it is 200 feet, and

where it leaves it 330. At the former place it is 114 feet
above low-water mark in Boston. In times when the river
is highest, it overflows its banks, and is in many places
more than a mile wide."— The North or Assabeth River
which has its source a little farther to the north and
west—and is neither so wide nor so long, unites with it near
the middle of the town.

Its general course is from south west to North east, and
its length about 50? miles.

Salmon—Shad—& Alewives—were formerly abundant in
this river and taken in weirs by the Indians, and afterward
by the settlers who used them as food and as manure—until
the dam and afterward the canal at Billerica, and the
factories at Lowell put an end to their migrations
hitherward.—

Perchance after a few thousands of years if the fishes
will be patient and pass their summers elsewhere in the
meanwhile, nature will have levelled the Billerica dam
and the Lowell factories—and the "grass-ground" river
will run clear again, inviting the fins of migratory
schools to explore its sands again—their scales be seen
sparkling in the sun again in many a deserted pond and
a new primeval age begin.— Knocking for entrance at
some other river's gates—

Even within recent years there have been men who
paid their £5 per year for the exclusive right to fish
here—a race now extinct though never numerous. Whose
seins lie now rotting in the garrets of their children One
would like to read a little more distinctly the history of
those days when there were those who openly professed
the trade of fishermen, and even fed their townsmen to
their credit—not needing to skulk through the meadows on
the rainy afternoons only to this sport. But unfortunately
no record of their lives has been preserved, unless it be
one page of brief but unquestionable and hard history

which occurs in day book no 4 of an old trader long since
dead, which shows plainly enough what constituted a
fisherman's stock in trade in those days. It is worth
preserving entire for many reasons.

"Fisherman's Acc^t for 1805 Began March 25

	cts.
D^d Mr. Saml Potter 2 q^{ts} W.I. 3/ 1 lb sugar 10^d	\$0 64
One Cod line 5/ – – – – – – – – – – – – – –	84
April 8 Q^t WI 1/6 & 1 lb Sugar 10^d & Brown	
Mug – – – – – – – – – – – – – – – – – – –	48
9 Q^t NE rum 1/ 10th D^o a^e D^o 1/ – – – –	33
13 Q^t NE rum & 1 lb Sugar 15th 2 Q^{ts} NE	
rum 2/ – – – – – – – – – – – – – – – –	62
17 Q^t WI 1/6 D^o NE 1/ lb Sugar 9^d & Q^t	
NE rum – – – – – – – – – – – – – – – –	71
22 Q^t NE rum 1/ lb sugar 9^d & Q^t NE rum	
1/	44½
23 Q^t NE rum 1/ D^o a^e D^o & sugar 5^d – –	39
24 Q^t NE rum 1/ lb sugar 9^d	28½
29 Q^t NE rum 1/ & lb sugar 9^d 30th Rum 1/	44½
May First Q^t rum 1/2 lb Sugar 1/5^d – – – – –	22
Q^t NE rum 1/ & 1/2 lb Loaf Sugar 9^d	29
4 Q^t rum 1/ Sugar 5^d	22
6 Q^t NE rum 1/ & lb good Sugar 11^d – –	31
7 Q^t NE rum 1/ 8th Q^{ts} NE rum 1/	
& 1/2 lb Sugar 5^d	40
11 Q^t NE rum /11^d lb sugar 10^d – – – – –	29
15 Q^t rum & lb Sugar 1/9 & Q^t NE rum –	44
16 To a Line for the Sceene 3/	0.50
20 To Q^t NE rum/11^d lb sugar 10^d – – –	0.29
21 To Q^t NE rum 11^d & lb sugar 10^d – – –	0.29
27 To Q^t WI 1/6 & lb sugar 10^d – – – – –	0.39
June 5th 1805 Settled this Acc^t by Recev.g Cash	
in Full	\$8:82½

—

This was probably during the fishing season. With salmon–shad–and alewife fresh and pickled–he was there after independent on the groceries Rather a preponderance of the fluid elements we would say, however, yet such is the fisherman's nature

As the poet says

> Standing upon the margent of the main,
>> Whilst the high boiling tide came tumbling in, &c

*   *

> Soon could my sad imagination find
> A parallel to this half world of flood,
> An ocean by my walls of earth confined,
> And rivers in the channels of my blood;
>> Discovering man, unhappy man, to be
>> Of this great frame Heaven's epitome.–

In the Merrimack shad and alewives are still abundant. But salmon are at present rare, though formerly more numerous than shad. Bass also are taken at the same time with the former.

The shad make their appearance at the same time with the blossoms of the Pyrus which are so conspicuous among the early flowers–and which is for this reason known by the name of the Shad blossom. An insect called the shad fly appears at the same season–covering the houses and fences– They continue to go up the river during the whole of the month–

But they are said to ascend in greatest numbers 'when the apple trees are in full blossom'–and return in August & September

Shad are still taken in the basin of Concord river at Lowell, where they are said to be distinguished by the fisherman from the Merrimack shad. Still patiently almost pathetically with instinct not to be discouraged not to be taught revisiting their old haunts–as if their

stern Fate would relent. And still met by the Corporation
with its dam. Poor dumb fish not to be instructed!

—

   Poor shad When nature gave thee instinct–gave she
the heart to bear thy fate–where is thy redress? Still
wandering the sea in thy scaly armor to inquire humbly
at the mouths of rivers, if man has perchance left them
free to thee Ye countless schools loitering uncertain
meanwhile–merely stemming the tide–in danger from
sea foes in spite of thy bright armor–so tender–awaiting
new instructions–until the sands until the water itself
tells thee if it be so or not– Thy ancient race–thus, by
whole migrating races full of instinct which is thy
faith–thus in this late spring to be turned adrift–and
perchance knowest not where men do *not* dwell–where
there are *not* factories in these days– Armed with no
sword no electric shock–but mere shad armed only with
innocence–and a just cause– I for one am with
thee.– And–who knows–what may avail a crow bar
against that Billerica dam! With tender dumb mouth only
forward–and scales easy to be detached. Not despairing
utterly–when whole myriads have gone to feed those
sea-monsters–during thy suspense–but still brave,
indifferent–as a shad reserved for higher destinies–willing
to be decimated for man's behoof–after the spawning
season only demanding protective laws–even game
laws–silently–of man and the God of nature.
   Away with the superficial selfish charities of men–who
knows what admirable virtue of fishes may be below low
water mark–not admired by that fellow creature who
alone can appreciate it. Only for nature to admire
& reward.

But dumb instinctive living nature is mighty–with right on its side. The time is approaching and is not far off–when thou shalt have thy way up the rivers–up all rivers if I am not mistaken and thy nature and everlasting justice prevail. Yea even thy dull watery dream shall be more than realized– If it were not so but thou were to be over looked at first *and* at last, then would not *I take* their heaven. Yes, *I* say so, who think I know better than thou canst. Keep a stiff fin and stem all the tides thou mayst meet

How many young finny contemporaries of various character and destiny, form and habits, we have even in this water– And it will not be forgotten by some memory that we *were* contemporaries. It is of *some* import– We shall be some time friends I trust and know each other better. Distrust is too prevalent now. We are so much alike? have so many faculties in common!– I have not yet met with the philosopher who could in a quite conclusive undoubtful way–show me *the* and if not *the* then how *any*–difference, between man and a fish. We are so much alike– How much could a really tolerant patient humane and truly great and natural man make of them, if he should try? For they are to be understood, surely, by no other method than that of sympathy. It is easy to say what they are not–to us–i.e. what we are not to them–but what we might and ought to be is another afair.

The common perch–(perca-flavescens, describing well the bright golden reflections of its scales as it is drawn out of the water) is very numerous. It rather prefers the clear water and sandy bottoms, though it has not much choice. It is the firmest and toughest of our fishes and by those who are not epicures most preferred for food. It is the handsomest and most regularly formed of our fishes, and reminds of the fish in the picture which asked to be restored to its element, until it had grown larger– And indeed most that are caught are not half grown. It has from 7 to 10 'transverse dark bands' When fully grown it weighs from 1/2 a pound to a pound. and is about a foot long

In the ponds they swim in schools of a thousand at once–in company with the shiner (Leuciscus Crysoleucas) and on account of their size–being commonly from six to eight inches long only–and from the fact that the larger ones are comparatively rare–are thought to be a different species. But perhaps the fact that the smaller are preyed upon by the larger of their own and other species may account for the disproportion.

They bite readily at the common baits without nibbling.

It is a true fish–such as the angler loves to put into his basket or hang at the top of his willow string, in sunny afternoons along the banks of the stream. So many unquestionable fishes he counts–and so many shiners which he counts, and then throws away.

The chivin is a rare fish–of about the same size but more slender than the perch–a silvery soft scaled fish–but of a trim and neat form. It loves a swift current and a sandy bottom– It is caught but rarely and accidentally. The young are used as bait for pickerel in the winter.

The Bream–or Ruff (Pomotis vulgaris) is the most common of all our fishes A most simple and inoffensive fish. Of very various colors. Its nests are seen all along the shore–hollowed in the sand–where like a water clock it is steadily poised through the summer hours on waving fin.

A perfect jewel of the river–a concentration of rays–green–red coppery and golden reflections–such rays as struggle through the floating pads and flowers to the bottom of the river are reflected from its mottled

sides. behind its watery shield how far from many
accidents–many events inevitable to human life!

It enhances the grand serenity & security of nature to
watch the still undisturbed content and confidence of the
fishes of this century–their happiness the birth of their
summer. The Fresh water sun Fish–as it were without
ancestry without posterity–still represents the Fresh water
sun Fish in nature. Seen on every urchin's string.

The shiner (Leuciscus Crysoleucas) a slight tender
fish–timid and sprightly–found in all places deep and
shallow–clear and turbid picking up an uncertain
subsistence– The prey of its stronger neighbors. Generally
the first nibbler at the bait– And with its small mouth
and propensity to nibble not easily taken. I have seen the
young fry–when frightened by any thing thrown in to the
water–leap out in schools and loose themselves on a
floating plank.

It is a tolerably firm fish in the spring but too soft to
be edible in mid summer.

In the tributaries the Brook-minnow & the trout. Even
in the rills emptying into the river–over which you stride
at a step you may see small trout not so large as your
finger glide past–or hide under the bank.

The pickerel (Esox Reticulatus) is very common along
the shallow weedy sides of the river. It is a solemn stately
and shy fish–but exceedingly ravenous–darting at anything
which suddenly falls into the water and swallowing it at
once–a sort of fresh water shark. I have caught one which
had swallowed a brother pickerel half as large as himself
–the tail still visible in his mouth while the head
was already digested in his stomach. They are frequently
caught by being entangled in the line the instant it is cast.
They are the swiftest of fishes. When the urchin thinks to

annihilate his victim at a thrust holding his pole within a
foot–suddenly he discovers him poised in calm water far
from the commotion–chewing the cud– A ruminant fish.

Darting at other fish & frogs from time to time–slowly
taking up his station–choosing his ground. 7 3/4 to 8 is
the largest I have heard of being taken in this
river–farther north they are said to grow to an indefinite
size.

{*One-fourth page blank*}

The Horned Pout (Pimelodus Nebulosus) A dull
blundering fish–like the eel vespertinal in its habits–fond
of the mud. And biting slowly and deliberately, as much
prized by some epicures as its undervalued by others.
They are taken at night–with a light to attract them–and
a mass of worms strung on thread and coiled up–which
catches in their teeth–and sometimes 3 or more are drawn
out at once–with the eel. They are extremely tenacious of
life–opening and shutting their mouths for hours after
their heads are cut off. These are very abundant in our
slow and muddy streams. I have seen the young not an
inch long–darkening the shore, with their myriads.

The character of this as indeed of all fishes–depends
directly upon that of the water it inhabits. Those taken in
clear and sandy water being of brighter hue and cleaner
and of firmer & sweeter flesh. It makes a curious
squeaking noise when drawn out which has given it the
name of the Minister or preacher.

The Suckers in schools of a hundred or more are seen
stemming the current in the sun, at which time they
sometimes as it were one accidentally swallow the hook
and is taken. With their migrations I am not acquainted.
At one time in the spring (and in the fall) they are very
plenty, but the mere angler may never catch them. Some

with horns and some without. They are a good fish early
in the season.

To our village eyes these schools have a most foreign
aspect–and set us a dreaming of the fertility of the seas
They are perhaps on an average the largest of our
fishes. A rather dull fat fish soft–getting its living
sucking–with mouth wide opening–without a careful
selection.

The Common Eel–a slimy–squirming creature–leading
an obscure life in the mud. Still squirming–whether from
acute feelings or inveterate habits–in the frying pan. A
choice morsel to some. Speared and hooked up from
various recesses. A perpetual screw– It is a worm that
goes on its belly (Muraena Bostoniensis)

It is doubtful whether the Lamprey (Petromyzon
Americanus) still frequents this part of the river on
account of the dams.

{*One-fifth page blank*}

As the truest society approaches always nearer to
solitude–so the most excellent speech finally falls into
Silence. We go about to find Solitude and Silence, as
though they dwelt only in distant glens and the depth of
the wood, venturing out from these fortresses at
midnight–and do not dream that she is then imported into
them when we wend thither– As the butcher busied
himself with looking after his knife when he had it in his
mouth. For where man is there is silence, And it takes a
man to make any place silent.
Silence is the communing of a conscious soul with
itself– When we attend for a moment to our own
infinity–then and there is silence–audible to all men–at

all times—in all places— It is when we hear inwardly
—sound when we hear outwardly.

Silence is ever less strange and startling than noise
and is any where intense and profound just in proportion
as we find ourselves there. Creation has not displaced her
but is her visible frame work and foil— She is always at
hand with her wisdom, by road sides and street corners
—lurking in belfries, the cannon's mouth, and the
wake of the earthquake, gathering up and fondling their
puny din in her ample bosom.

All sounds are her servants and purveyers, proclaiming
not only that their mistress is, but is a rare mistress, and
earnestly to be sought after. The thunder is only the
signal of her coming.

All sound is nearly akin to silence—it is a bubble on her
surface which straightway bursts, an evidence of the
strength and prolificness of the under current. It is a
faint utterance of silence—and then only agreeable to our
auditory nerves when it contrasts itself with and relieves
the former. In proportion as it does this, and is a
heightener and intensifier of the Silence—it is harmony
and purest melody.

Accordingly every melodious sound is an ally of
silence—a help and not a hindrance to abstraction.

Silence is the universal refuge. The sequel to all dry
discourses, and all foolish acts—as balm to our every
chagrin—as welcome after satiety as disappointment.
That background which the painter may not daub, be he
master or bungler, and which, however awkward a figure
we may have made in the foreground, remains ever our
inviolable asylum.

Where no indignity can assail no personality—disturb
us.

The orator puts off his individuality and is then most eloquent, when most silent. He listens while he speaks and is a hearer along with his audience.

Who has not hearkened to her infinite din? She is Truth's speaking trumpet– She is the sole oracle, the true Delphi and Dodona, which kings and courtiers would do well to consult, nor will they be balked by an ambiguous answer. Through her all revelations have been made – Just in proportion as men have consulted her oracle they have obtained a clear insight, and their age been marked as an enlightened one. But as often as they have gone gadding abroad to a strange Delphi and her mad priestess, their age has been Dark or Leaden. These have been garralous and noisy eras which no longer yield any sound, but the Grecian or silent & melodious era, is ever sounding and resounding in the ears of men.

A good book is the plectrum with which our silent lyres are struck. We not unfrequently refer the interest which belongs to our own unwritten sequel to the written and comparatively lifeless body of the work. Of all books this sequel is the most indispensable part. It should be the authors aim to say once and emphatically "he said" 'ἐφη' ε This is the most the book maker can attain to If he make his volume a foil whereon the waves of silence may break it is well.

It were vain for me to interpret the silence–she cannot be done into English. For six thousand years have men translated her with what fidelity belonged to each, and still is she little better than a sealed book. A man may run on confidently for a time–thinking he has her under his thumb, and shall one day exhaust her–but he too must at last be silent, and men remark only how brave a beginning he made. For when he at length dives into her–so vast is the disproportion of the told to the untold, that the former will seem but the bubble on the surface where he disappeared.

Never the less will we go on, like those Chinese Cliff swallows, feathering our nests with the froth, which may one day be bread of life to such as dwell by the sea shore.

{One-fourth page blank}

We read Marlowe as so much poetical pabulum— It is food for poets, water from the Castalian spring—some of the atmosphere of Parnassus—raw and crude indeed, and at times breezy, but pure and bracing. Few have so rich a phrase. He had drunk deep of the Pierian spring—though not deep enough, and had that fine madness, as Drayton says,

"Which justly should possess a poet's brain."

We read his Dr Faustus—Dido Queen of Carthage—and Hero & Leander, especially the last, without being wearied. He had many of the qualities of a great poet, and was in some degree worthy to precede Shakspeare. But he seems to have run to waste for want of seclusion and solitude—as if mere pause and deliberation would have added a new element of greatness to his poetry. In his unquestionably fine heroic tone it would seem as if he had the rarest part of genius, and education could have added the rest. The Hero and Leander tells better far his character than the anecdotes which survive.

I have sometimes passed down the river in my boat before sunrise on a summer morning between fields of lilies still closed in sleep—and when the flakes of sun light fell successively on the water, fields of white blossom were opened before me, almost at a flash,—like the sudden unfolding of a banner. So sensible is this flower to the influence of the sun-light.

And now our boat was already grating against the bullrushes of its native port—and its keel again recognized the Concord mud where the flattened weeds still preserved some semblance of its own outline having scarce yet recovered themselves since its departure. And we leaped gladly on shore—drawing it up and fastening it to the little apple tree whose stem still bore the mark which its chain had worn—in the chafing of the spring freshets.

—

I fain would stretch me by the highway side,
　To thaw and trickle with the melting snow,
That mingled soul & body with the tide
　I too might through the pores of Nature flow.

—

Might help to forward the new spring along,
　If it were mine to choose my toil or day,
Scouring the roads with yonder sluice-way throng,
　And so work out my tax on *Her* highway.

—

A stir is on the Wooster hills,
And Nobscot too the valley fills,
Where scarce you'd dip an acorn cup
In summer when the sun is up,
No more you'll find a cup at all,
But in its place a waterfall.

Yet let us thank the purblind race,
　Who still have thought it good
With lasting stone to mark the place
　Where braver men have stood.

In concord, town of quiet name
　And quiet fame as well,

Ive seen ye, sisters, on the mountain-side
When your green mantles fluttered in the wind
Ive seen your foot-prints on the lakes still shore
Lesser than man's, a more etherial trace,

I have heard of ye as some far famed race–
Daughters of gods whom I should one day meet–
I reverence your natures so like mine
Yet strangely different, like but unlike
Thou only stranger that hast crossed my path
Accept my hospitality–let me hear
The message which thou bring'st
   Made different from me
   Perchance thou'rt made to be
   The creature of a different destiny.
I know not who ye are that meekly stand
Thus side by side with man in every land.
Reveal but that which ye can now tell
Wherein ye are not I, wherein ye dwell
Where I can never come.
What boots it that I do regard ye so
Does it make suns to shine or crops to grow?
What boots that I never should forget
That I have sisters sitting for me yet
And what are sisters
The robust man who can so stoutly strive
In this bleak world is hardly kept alive.
And who is it protects *ye* smoothes *your* way
Ye children of the moon in placid nights
Vaulted upon the hills and sought this earth.
When did ye form alliance with our race

We can afford to lend a willing ear occasionally to
those earnest reprovers of the age– Let us treat them
hospitably– Shall we be charitable only to the poor. What
though they are fanatics–their errors are likely to be
generous errors–and these may be they who will indeed
put to rest the american Church and the American
Government, and awaken better ones in their stead.

Let us not meanly seek to maintain our delicate lives
in chambers or in Senate halls by a timid watchfulness of
the rude mobs that threaten our baby-houses. Let us not
think to raise a revenue which shall maintain our our
domestic quiet by an impost on the liberty of speech.

Let us not think to live by the principle of self defence–have we survived our accidents hitherto think you by virtue of our great swords–that 3 foot lathe that dangles by your side–or those brazen mouthed pieces under the burrying hill which the trainers keep to hurrah with in the April & July mornings Do our protectors burrow under the burying ground hills–on the edge of the bean-field which you all know gorging themselves once a year with powder & smoke–and kept bright & in condition by a chafing of oiled rags and rotten stone

Have we resigned the protection of our hearths and civil liberties to that feathered race of wading birds & marching men who drill but once a month–& I mean no reproach to our Concord train bands–who make a handsome appearance–and dance well– Do we enjoy the sweets of domestic life undisturbed because the naughty boys are all shut up in that white-washed "stone-yard" as it is called–and see the concord meadows only through a grating.

No–let us live amid the free play of the elements– Let the dogs bark–let the cocks crow–& the sun shine–and the winds blow

{*One-third page blank*}

> Ye do command me to all virtue ever
> And simple truth the law by which we live
> Methink that I can trust your clearer sense
> And your immediate knowledge of the truth.
> I would obey your influence–one with fate

There is a true march to the sentence as if a man or a body of men were actually making progress there step by step–and they are not the mere disjecta membra–the dispersed and mutilated members even though it were of heroes–which can not walk any longer– They are not merely carrions–nor even liberated specimens for the galleries, but stand on the natural and broader pedestal of the living rock–and have a principle of growth in them still–have that human nature from which they spring.

Yet perhaps enough has been said in these days of the charm of fluent writing.

We hear it complained of some modern books of genius that they are irregular and have no flow, but perhaps we should consider that the flow of thought, is more like a tidal wave than a prone river, and is the effect of celestial influence, and not of any declivity in its channel. The river flows because it runs down hill, and descends the faster as it flows more rapidly. The one obeys an earthly attraction, the other a heavenly attraction. The one runs smoothly because it gravitates toward the earth alone, the other irregularly because it gravitates toward the heavens as well.

The reader who expects to float down stream for the whole voyage may well complain of nauseating groundswells, and choppings of the sea, when his frail shore craft gets amidst the breakers of the ocean stream, which flows as much to sun and moon, as lesser streams to it– But if he would appreciate the true flow that is in these books he must expect to feel it rising from the page like an exhalation and wash away his critical brains like burr millstones, flowing to higher levels, above and behind himself.

There are many books which ripple on like a freshet –and flow as glibly as a mill-stream sucking under a race way– And when their authors are in the full tide of their discourse Plato and Jamblichus and Pythagoras and Bacon, halt beside them. Their long stringly slimy sentences do naturally flow and run together. They read as if written for military men–men of business–there is such despatch in them–a double quick time–a Saratoga march, with beat of drum. Compared with them–the grave

thinkers and philosophers seem not to have got their
swaddling clothes off They are slower than a Roman
army in its march, the rear encamping tonight where the
van camped last night. The wise Jamblichus eddies and
gleams like a watery slough.

The writer seizes the pen–the reviewer offttimes it
is–and shouts Forward! Alamo & Fanning! and after rolls
the tide of war.

The very walls and fences seem to travel– And when
the author discovers himself launched and if the slope
be easy–and there be grease enough–who shall say how
fast and far he will go. But the most rapid trot is no flow
after all– And thither you & I at least will not go.

We have now for the third winter had our spirits
refreshed and our faith in the desstiny of the common
wealth strengthened by the presence and the eloquence
of Wendell Philips, and we wish to tender to him our
thanks and our sympathy. The admission of this
gentleman into the Lyceum has been strenuously opposed
by a large & respectable portion of our fellow citizens, who
themselves we trust, or whose descendants we trust, will
be as faithful conservatories of the new order of things,
when at length it shall be the order of the day–and in
each instance the people have voted that they *would hear
him*, by carrying all their ears and all their cousins to the
lecture room–and being very silent that they might hear.
One young woman as we hear, walked 5 miles through
the snow from a neighboring town to be present on the
occasion. We saw some men and women who had long
ago *come out*, *going in* once more through this free and
hospitable portal–and our neighbors confessed that they
had had a sound season this once–

It was the lecturers aim to show what the state &
especially the church had to do, and now alas had
done–with Texas and slavery–and how much the

individual should have to do with the state & the Church. These were fair themes and not misstimed–addressed to a fit audience–and not a few.

We give Mr Philips the credit of being a clean, an erect, and what was once called, a consistent man– He at least is not responsible for Slavery–nor our American Independence–for the hypocrisy and superstition of the Church–or the timidity and selfishness of the state–or for the indifference and willing ignorance of individuals. He stands so distinctly, so firmly, & so effectively, alone, and one honest man's voice is so much more than a host–that we cannot but feel that he does himself injustice when he reminds us of "the American society which he represents."

It is rare that we have the pleasure of listening to so clear and sound a speaker. to one who has obviously so few cracks and flaws in his moral nature–who having words at his command to a remarkable degree, has much more than words if these should fail in his unquestionable sincerity and integrity–secures the genuine respect of his audience, aside from their admiration of his rhetoric.

He unconsciously tells his biography as he proceeds –and *we* seem to see him early and earnestly deliberating on this subject–and wisely and bravely–without counsel of man–occupying a ground at once–from which the varying tides of public opinion cannot drive him.

No one could mistake–the genuine modesty & truth with which he affirmed–when speaking of the framers of the Constitution "I am wiser than they"–who with him improved these seventy year's additional experience of its working. Or the consistently and unhesitating prayer which does not conclude like the Thanksgiving proclamations with "God save the Commonwealth of Mass"–but "God dash it into a thousand pieces;" And make us a new one of course.

v n p b 1

We consider Mr P as one of the most conspicuous and
earnest champions of a true church & state at present in
the field, and perhaps no one is laboring more efficiently
toward an immediate & practical end. The degredation
& suffering of the black man–will not have been in vain
if they contribute thus indirectly to give a loftier tone to
the religion and politics of this country–

We would fain express our appreciation of the wisdom
and steadiness, so rare in the reformer–with which he
declared that he was not born to abolish slavery, or
reform the church–but simply to do the right. His
positions have the advantage of being not only morally
& politically sound and expedient, but philosophically
true, and a rare clearness and singleness of perception
is coupled with a still rarer felicity of expressive
utterance We have heard a few, a very few, good
political speakers–Webster & Everett–who afforded us the
pleasure of larger intellectual conceptions–strength and
acuteness–of soldier like steadiness and resolution–and
of a graceful and natural oratory– But in this man there
was a sort of moral worth and integrity–which was more
graceful than his rhetorick and more discriminating than
his intellect which was more stable than their firmness.
A something which was not eloquence which was not
oratory–or wit or scholarship which was working not for
temporary–but for worthy & untrivial ends.

It is so sweet rare and encouraging to listen to the
orator who is content with another alliance, than with
the popular party–or the sympathy of the martyrs– Who
can afford sometimes to be his own auditor when the
mob stay away–and hears him self without reproof. That
we feel ourselves in danger of slandering all mankind by
affirming that there is one man who is at once an eloquent
speaker and a righteous man.

While there remains a fragment on which a man can
stand–and dare not tell his name"–referring to the case

of Frederick _____, to our disgrace we know not what to
call him, unless Scotland will lend us one of her hero
Douglasses out of history or fiction for a season–till we
be trustworthy and hospitable enough to hear his proper
name.– A fugitive slave, in one more sense than we–who
has proved himself the possessor of a *White* intellect, and
has won a colorless reputation among us–who we trust
will prove himself as superior to temptation from the
sympathies of freedom, as he has done to the degradation
of slavery. When he communicated his purpose said
Mr. Philips the other day to a New Bedford audience of
writing his life and telling his name and the name of his
master and the place he ran from– This murmur ran
round the room, and was timidly whispered by the sons
of the Pilgrims "he had better not"–and it was echoed
under the shadow of Concord monument–"he had better
not." But he is going to England where this revelation
will be safe.

v 1 p b 1

Perhaps on the whole the most most interesting fact
elicited by these addresses is the readiness of the people
at large, of whatever sect or party, and the more liberal
and least timid of the conservatives to entertain with
good will and hospitality the most heretical opinions thus
frankly and plainly expressed–proving that all men are
easily convertible to the right if you will only show it
to them
    Such clear and candid declarations of opinion whetted
and clarified the intellect of all parties like an electuary
and furnished each with additional arguments to support
what he deemed that right. "Well," says one; "He put it on
to us poor Democrats pretty hard". "That's a severe dose"
says another, "Well", responds the minister it's all true,
every word of it." One of our most impartial and
discriminating neighbors affirmed that he had perfectly
demonstrated to his mind the truth of principles which

he knew to be false. One elderly & sensible lady told us
that she was much pleased–but as we inquired did you
like it wholly every part of it–and she answered she must
confess as she had heard but one antislavery lecture
before she was not used to hearing the church so spoken
of, but yet she liked it–and she was one of those who sit
with honor under the very nave of the church.

We have no desire to be overly critical and in the
present complexion of affairs we would only say to him
and such as are like him–God speed you.

As the spanish Chronicler said that from Cape Alfaetio
the easternmost part of terra firma on which columbus
landed–travellers might walk due west till they came
quite round again to cape saint Vincent in Spain– "And
God grant them a pleasant journey–"–but we suspect that
there may be a Pacifica ocean to be crossed, which is to
this atlantic as 10 to 3–before they come to the Cape St
Vincent we have heard of–and will not remember ever to
have seen it before. However westward lies the way. and
Fare well.

No wonder, said one who is a judger of these matters,
no wonder the people wanted to hear   "we cant do better
than get him again."

But it becomes the many who yield their so easy assent
to his positions, and suffer not the sometimes honest
prejudice of their neighbors to hinder his free speech to
hear him with seriousness & with a spirit at least as
prepared and as resolved as his own for the issue.

He does not bewilder and mystify his audience with
sophistry–as the mere partisan always does–but furnishes
a light which all may use to their profit.

It is a marvel how the birds contrive to survive in this
world– These tender sparrows that flit from bush to bush
this evening–though it is so late do not seem improvident,
to have found a roost for the night. They must succeed

by weakness and reliance, for they are not bold and
enterprising as their mode of life would seem to require,
but very weak and tender creatures. I have seen a little
chipping sparrow come too early in the spring shivering
on an apple twig, drawing in its head and striving to
warm it in its muffled feathers, and it had no voice to
interceed with nature but peeped as helpless as an infant
and was ready to yield up its spirit and die without any
effort— And yet this was no new spring in the revolution
of the seasons.

Some have thought that the gales do not at present waft
to the voyageur the natural and original fragrance of the
land, but that we breathe a tainted atmosphere—that the
loss of many odoriferous native plants by the grazing of
cattle and the rooting of swine—many sweet-scented
grasses and medicinal herbs, since the settlement of the
country, which formerly sweetened the atmosphere and
rendered it salubrious is the source of many diseases
which now prevail.

It may be that from these portions of the globe which
have long been subjected to extremely artificial and
unclean methods of cultivation—where the fields are
turned into pens or hot beds as men increase by art the
decay of nature—husbandry being devoted to the fattening
of swine and cattle—and the pampering of depraved tastes
and appetites—the surface of the earth is deprived of these
sweet and wholesome fragrances which would naturally
come up from it.

Our offence is rank, it smells to heaven. In the midst of
our village as in most villages there is a slaughter
house—and—through out the summer months—day and
night—the air filled with such scents as we instinctively
avoid in a country walk—and doubtless if our senses were
once purified and educated by a simpler and truer life,
we should not consent to live in such a neighborhood.

Whether we live by the sea side–or by the lakes and rivers, or in the prairie it concerns to attend to the nature of fishes, since they are not phenomena

{*Two leaves missing*}

> By a lonely isle a far azore
> Where it is, where it is, the treasure I seek
> On the barren sand of a desolate creek

Between Sudbury and Wayland the Meadows acquire their greatest breadth, and when covered with water in the spring–they form a chain of handsome lakes– The greatest expanses just above Shermans bridge and Talls Island, where there is a single reach of two miles–by a half a mile–looks like some lake Huron skirted in the distance with smoky maples and dense groves of alder– The farm houses along the Sudbury shore, which rises gently to a great height command fine water prospects These waters are resorted to by gulls and ducks.

The farmers tell me that thousands of acres are flooded land wherein they remember to have seen the honeysuckle or clover growing once and they could go dry with shoes in summer–now there is nothing but a coarse sedge grass, piper-grass–and blue-joint. standing in water all the year round. When the wind blows strong over these vernal lakes in a raw march day, heaving up the surface into dark and sober billows, or regular swells, it is very pleasant and exciting to row and sail here.

and the farmer looks sadly to his upland and woodlot as his last resource

Geo Melvin–our Concord Trapper, told me that on going to the spring near his house where he kept his minnows for bait, he found that they were all gone, and immediately suspected that a mink had got them, so he removed the snow all around and so laid open the trail of

a mink underneath–which he traced to his hole and then
he set his trap and baited it with fresh minnows. Going
again soon to the spot, he "found the minks fore-legs in
the trap gnawed off near the body," and having set it again
he caught the mink with his three legs, the fourth having
only a short bare bone sticking out.

When I expressed some surprise at this and said that
I heard of such things but did'nt know whether to believe
them–and was now glad to have the story confirmed– Said
he– Oh the muskrats are the greatest fellows to gnaw
their legs off. Why I caught one once that had just
gnawed his third leg off, this being the 3d time he had
been trapped, and he lay dead by the trap, for he could'nt
run on one leg. Such tragedies are enacted even in this
sphere and along our peaceful streams, and dignify at
least the hunters trade. Only courage does any where
prolong life–whether of man or beast

When they are caught by the leg and cannot get into
the water to drown themselves they very frequently gnaw
the limb off. They are commonly caught under water in
close to the edge and dive immediately with the trap and
go to gnawing and are quackled and drowned in a
moment though under other circumstances they will live
several minutes under water. They prefer to gnaw off a
fore leg to a hind leg–and do not gnaw off their tails. He
says the wharf rats are very common on the river and
will swim and cross it like a muskrat and will gnaw their
legs and even their tails off in the trap.

These would be times that tried mens souls–if men
had souls to be tried. Even the the water rats lead sleepless
nights.– and live Achillean lives– There was "the strong
will & the endeavor" Man even the hunter naturally has
sympathy with every brave effort even in his game to
maintain that life it enjoys. The hunter regards with awe
his game and it becomes at last his medicine.

Of Cadew or Case worms there are the Ruff-coats or
Cockspurs—whose cases are rough and made of various
materials & the Piper Cadis or Straw-worm—made of reed
or rush & straight & smooth.

Stones which began to revolve perchance before
thoughts revolved in the brains of men. What are the
periods of Hindoo and Chinese history running back to
the times when gods walked on the earth—to the periods
which these have inscribed. What ears listened to the
music of their revolution?

{*Three-fourths page blank*}

Carlyle's works are not to be studied—they are not to be
re-read—the first impression is the truest and the deepest
– If you look again you will be disappointed and
find nothing adequate to the mood they have excited. All
things are but once and never repeated– They are true
natural products too in this respect. The first faint blushes
of the morning gilding the mountain tops—with the pale
phosphorus & saffron colored clouds—they do verily
transport me to the morning of creation—but what avails
it to travel Eastward or look again an hour hence–
We should be as far in the day as the sun ourselves
—mounting toward our meridian– There is no
double entendre in fact—this work was designed for such
complete success that it answers but a simple use, a single
occasion. It is the luxury of wealth & art when for every
deed its own instrument is manufactured.
The knife which sliced the bread of Jove ceased to be a
knife when that service was rendered

—

There is very little of what is called criticism here. It is
love & reverence which deal with qualities not relatively

but absolutely great. Whatever is admirable in a man is something infinite–to which we cannot set bounds. It allows the mortals to die–the immortal the divine to survive– Among contemporaries almost he alone preserves the antique view Jove & the Fates & the Furies all survive The earthy man–after death–becomes a hero or a demi god–and has a place in heaven His men are heroes or they are mannikins. It is what every child demands– Give us the meagerest history and it shall still have its Agamemnons and Achilles–and we constantly and necessarily pay this compliment to our companions of exaggerating them to something more than actual and mortal– We do not know them till we allow them the largest frame and broadest margin.– He revives the old fact of apotheosis which the moderns do not recognise.

—

There the sun lighted me to hoe beans pacing slowly backward and forward over that yellow gravelly upland between the long green rows–15 rods–the one end terminating in a shrub oak copse–where you could rest in the shade–the other in a blackberry field–where your repast awaited you– Over this the wind blew on this the rain fell and the sunbeams and the nocturnal dews and shades. removing the weeds–and putting fresh soil about the bean stems. I got twelve bushels but I have not got all my crop yet? Encouraging this weed I had sown. Making the yellow soil express its summer thought in bean leaves and blossoms rather than in wormwood & piper & millett grass– Making the earth say beans instead of grass

A very agricola laboriosus to the travellers bound westward through Wayland

One field not in Mr Coleman's report   who estimates what crop nature yields in the fields unimproved by man.

The crop of English hay is carefully weighed the moisture calculated the silicates the potash

But in all dells & pond holes in the wood and in remote pastures and swamps grows a rich & various crop –ungathered by man–only waiting to be improved.

Before yet any woodchuck or squirrel has run across the road–or the sun has got round the corner of the wood (world) While all the dew was on. My hoe began to tinkle against the stones of my bean-field– I heard from time to time of oratorio's concerts operas in distant temples but attended none of them–but this was my oratorio when my steel hoe plate struck against a pebble–and vibrated some chord of nature–ah it has dignified the bean grower's life this divine accompaniment yielding an instant crop– As I hoed and gathered still fresher soil about my rows–I disturbed the ashes of unrecorded nations–whose primeval lives were passed under these same heavens, and their small implements of war and hunting and perhaps more ancient hoes–were brought to the light of this modern day.

The night-hawk circled over my head in the sunny afternoons–like a mote in my eye–or in heaven's eye–falling from time to time with a swoop and a sound as if the heaven's were rent–torn at last to very rags–and yet a seamless cope at last. Small imps that fill the air–and lay their eggs on the ground or on bare rocks on the top of the hills. Graceful and slender like waves and ripples of the pond caught up like leaves by the wind–to float in the heavens. such kindred is in nature–the hawk is aerial brother of the ocean wave–which he sails over and surveyes– Those his perfect air-inflated wings answering to the elemental unfledged pinions of the sea.– When you pause to lean upon your hoe these sights you behold–any where in the row–such inexhaustible entertainment does the country offer.

At hand upon the topmost spray of a birch sings the brown thrasher–the red mavis–glad of your society–who would find out another farmer's field if you were not there–while you are planting corn–drop it &c You may wonder what his rigmarole his amateur paganini performance on one string or on none at all–may have to do with planting corn or beans, and yet prefer it to ashes or plaster.

The passage of wild pigeons from this wood to that–with their slight tantivy–and carrier haste– Now from under some rotten stump your hoe turns up a spotted salamander–your own contemporary– A small trace of Egypt & the nile in New-England– Where is the priest of Isis.

Digging to find worm bait in my dry pasture where earth worms did not inhabit–I found the ground nut on its pearly string– A sort of fabulous hesperides fruit of my childhood found there by the mill brook long ago–or was it dream and illusion of childhood–and now here the dream is confirmed. A possible far future unexpanded fruit for man–between his grosser diet & ambrosia– A faint promise of nature to feed him worthily–as large as his trust is–to be infinitely expanded.

Its crimpled red velvety blossom–hanging from a foreign stem–is a small ambrosial discourse on the repasts of the gods–pleasant to read by such light as we have.

A place of eagles once–

—

In C. is the completeness and success of talent not the obscurity & depth of Genius.

Verily another soldier than Buoneparte rejoicing in the "triumph" of a psalm "exceeding high and great"

– Appealing to psalms as his authority his Herald's
book (the 68th or 110th psalm

"And the close of it,–that closeth with my heart, and I
do not doubt with yours, 'The Lord shakes the hills &
mountains, & they reel."

At the ceremony of installation "Does the reader see
him?" His victories are "crowning mercies" "intercalated"
"annotations" by "the latest of the Commentators"

"Say Major-General Harrison and a number of men,
founding on Bible Prophecies, Now shall be a Fifth
Monarchy, [to succeed the Assyrian–Persian–Greek–&
Roman ones] by far &c v p 94 v 2d by far the blessedest
and the only real one,–the Monarchy of Jesus Christ,
his Saints reigning for him here on Earth,–if not he
himself, which is probable or possible,–for a thousand
years, &c., &c– – O Heavens, these are tears for human
destiny; and immortal Hope itself is beautiful because it
is steeped in Sorrow, and foolish Desire lies vanquished
under its feet! They who merely laugh at Harrison take
but a small portion of his meaning with them. Thou, with
some tear for the valiant Harrison, if with any thought of
him at all, tend thou also valiantly, in thy day &
generation, whither he was tending; and know that, in far
wider and diviner figure than that of Harrison, the
Prophecy is very sure,–that it *shall* be sure while one
brave man survives among the dim bewildered
populations of this world. Good shall reign on this Earth:
has *not* the Most High said it?"

He too has his dreams.

I have endeavored to acquire strict methodical business
habits–they are indispensable– My trade is mainly with
the celestial Empire that on which I count–sometimes of
course you will touch at the Cape–and other intermediate
ports for refreshment–or to refit–

I may say that I am wholly devoted to business–and love
to oversee all the details myself–personally–some small

counting house on the–coast at any convenient port–is
ware house enough

My vessels arrive at long and uncertain intervals

Exchange or good houses there I have always to sell.

I export such as the country affords–purely *native*
products–much ice–and pine timber and a little granite
–which have proved good ventures–

To superintend the discharge of imports–night & day to
be upon many parts of the coast at once–often the richest
freight will be discharged upon an open beach where is
no anchorage–to be your own telegraph unweariedly
sweeping the horizon–speak all passing vessels–mostly
coastbound–some times in danger from custom house
officers–

–A steady despatch of commodities and supply of such
distant and most exorbitant markets–in all weathers and
in all seasons no omissions being allowed for–always in
native bottoms.

It is a labor to task the intellect–such problems in profit
& loss–interest–tare & tret–& guageing–of all kinds it
demands a universal knowledge–account of stock to be
taken from time to time–to know where you are. It is a
good port–Walden pond–a safe–anchorage– No Neva
marshes to be filled– – Though I suppose you must every
where build on piles–good spruce or pine timber of your
own driving–

–I have thought it would be a good place for
business.– not to be undermined and swept away in
freshets–with easterly winds. It is said that a flood
tide–with a westerly wind and ice in the Neva–would after
all sweep st Petersburg from the face of the earth.

not solely on account of the railroad and the ice trade
either–

It offers advantages–which it may not be good policy to
divulge.

To keep informed of the state of the markets–prospects of war & peace–and anticipate the tendencies of extended trade & civilization–taking advantage of the results of all exploring expeditions–at the earliest date.

–Improving new passages–all improvements in navigation–charts to be studied–the position of reefs and of new buoys & lights ascertained–and ever and ever the logarithmic tables are to be corrected.– Universal science to be kept pace with–which bears upon all things.

You will seek to be familiar with the lives of all great discoverers–& navigators great adventurers & merchants from Hanno & the Phonicians down to our day.

To know how little can be done by a clerk–factor–agent –that these are well nigh useless–you must be both pilot & captain & owner and underwriter–buy & sell & keep the accounts.–

Plant the common white bush bean in the first week of June–in straight rows, three feet by eighteen inches apart.– fresh–round & unmixed seed. And first look out for worms, and supply vacancies by planting afresh.– then look out for wood chucks–which will nibble off the earliest tender leaves almost clean as they go– And again when the young tendrils make their appearance they have notice of it–and will clip off their stems with both buds & young pods–sitting erect like a squirrel– Harvest as early as possible if you would have fair and saleable beans.– You may save 2/3 of your labor by the last means.

The space between the bricks in my fire place was filled with stones from the shore of the pond– And the white sand for my mortar & plastering was brought over the pond in a boat.

A few tall arrowy pines still in their youth–were felled for King and Queen posts–& sills–

James Collins shanty was considered an extra fine one–when I called he was not at home– I walked about to

reconoitre–the dirt raised 5 feet all around–concealing
much– Mrs C. came to the passage and asked me to view
it from the inside–the hens were driven in by my
approach–. She lighted a lamp to show me that the board
floor extended under the bed–good boards over head–good
boards all around–only smoky–good window of two
squares–only the cat went through one lately.– be careful
not step into the cellar–of small compas highest cottage
roof–dirt floor–mostly–hard–dank–dull–opaque
–smotherish–agueish–here a board and there a board
–which might not bear removal not a fossil board– Stove
–bed–& place to sit–& infant in the house where it was
born– Silk parasol–gilt-framed looking-glass–&
patent-coffee mill nailed to to a white oak sapling– All
told.

It was a bargain– James returns–tis 425– I vacate at
six tomorrow morn you pay tonight– I sell in the
meantime to nobody else– Prudent men anticipate the
so-calld last owner–you understand–6 is your hour. At
six I pass James on the road–one large Bundle holds
all–Bed–coffee mill–looking glass hens–only the cat
omitted–she took to the woods.– became wild cat–trod
in a trap for wood chucks–became rabid cat–became dead
cat–and buried at last.

Lintel none but perennial passage for hens I threw
down this dwelling next day–drawing the nails–and
removed it to the pond side in small cart-loads– Penurious
neighbor Irishman–as I was informed transferring in
the intervals the still tolerable–straight driveable
nails–staple spikes to his pocket–and then stood to look
on unconcerned and pass the time of day. There by the
pondside they bleached–warped back again in the sun
upon the grass

Gazing freshly up at the devastation–seeing there is a
dearth of work– –he to represent spectatordom.

For every inferior earthly pleasure we forego a superior celestial one is substituted.

To purify our lives requires simply to weed out what is foul & noxious– And the sound and innocent is supplied–as nature purifies the blood–if we will but reject impurities.

Nature and human life are as various to our several experiences as our constitutions are various– Who shall say what prospect life offers to another? Could a greater miracle take place than if we should look through each other's eyes for an instant. What I have read of Rhapsodists–of the primitive poets–Argonautic expeditions–the life of demigods & heroes–Eleusinian mysteries–&c–suggests nothing so ineffably grand and informing as this would be.

We know not what it is to live in the open air–our lives are domestic in more senses than we had thought. From the hearth to the field is a great distance. A man should always speak as if there were no obstruction not even a mote or a shadow between him & the celestial bodies. The voices of men sound hoarse and cavernous–tinkling as from out of the recesses of caves–enough to frighten bats & toads–not like bells–not like the music of birds, not a natural melody.

Of all the Inhabitants of Concord I know not one that dwells in nature.– If one were to inhabit her forever he would never meet a man. This country is not settled nor discovered yet

Circumstances & employment have but little effect on the finer qualities of our nature. I observe among the rail-road men–such inextinguishable ineradicable refinement & delicacy of nature–older and of more worth than the sun & moon. A genuine magnanimity–more than Greek or Roman–equal to the least occasion–of unexplored of uncontaminated descent. Greater traits I observe in them–in the shortest intercourse–than are recorded of

Epaminondas Socrates–or Cato– The most famous
philosophers & poets seem infantile–in comparison with
these easy profligate giants. with faces homely–hard and
scarred like the rocks–but human & wise–embracing–copt
& musselman–all races & nations. One is a famous
pacha–or sultan in disguise

A fineness which is commonly thought to adorn the
drawing rooms only There is no more real rudeness in
laborers–and washerwomen than in Gentlemen &
ladies Under some ancient wrinkled–almost forlorn
visage–as of a Indian chieftain slumber the world famous
humanities of man. There is the race–& you need look
no farther. You can tell a nobleman's head among a
million–though he may be shovelling gravel six rods off in
the midst of a gang–with a cotton handkerchief tied about
it– Such as are to succeed the worthies of history– It
seems no disadvantage, their humble occupation and that
they take no airs upon themselves Civilization seems to
make bright the superficial film of the eye

Most men are wrecked upon their consciousness
–morally–intellectually–and humanly.

—

A place of pines–of forest scenes and events visited by
successive nations of men all of whom have successively
fathomed it– And still its water is green & pellucid not
an intermittent spring–somewhat perennial in it– While
the nations pass away. A true well–a gem of the first
water–which concord wears in her coronet.

looking blue as amethyst or solidified azure far off as
it is drawn through the streets. Green in the deeps–blue
in the shallows– Perhaps the grass is a denser deeper
heaven

—

The works of Landor–Coleridge–Wordsworth–contain
quotable sentences–gems–in the midst of much that is
dull and comparatively of little value– In Carlyle there
is as little to quote as in the conversation of a vivacious and
eloquent speaker– What you would quote is his vivacity.

But some deliberate–tedious–stuttering old gentleman
will say some thing more memorable.

—

Some whiter & cleaner sand I brought over from the
opposite shore of the pond in a boat sunk to its edge by
the load–scarcely rippling the surface–convey me and my
spade and wheel barrow and several cart loads at once
– There is no more beautiful conveyance–than this
of water carriage.– without jar–or scar. a high-way that
never need be mended.

In winter nights the booming of the ice in the pond
restless in its bed, that would fain turn over– And the
cracking of the ground with frost. At evening regularly at
half past seven the whip or–I will–emphasizing the last
word–sat on a stump by my door or on the ridge pole–and
sung its vespers–as regularly as a clock–. Sometimes it
circled round and round me at a few feet distance in the
woods.

Often a red or grey squirrel awaked me in the dawn
–coursing over my roof–and up and down the sides
of my house–by fits & starts. sent out of the woods by
nature to awaken me–with sleepless frisking–

A little flock of tit mice came daily in the winter–to peck
a dinner out of my wood pile–or the crumbs at my
door.– with fast flitting lisping song–with sprightly
day-day-day–and airy–summery–phe-be–from the woods
side

The pewee? came in to my house to find a place for its nest–flying through the windows.

Sometimes I hear the bells–the Lincoln bell at night–the Acton bell–the Bed-ford bell and the Concord bells–a faint & sweet almost natural melody there. Now up they go ding &c

It was a bright thought that of mans to have bells–no doubt the birds hear them with pleasure.

The faint rattle or tinkle which marked the passage of a carriage or team along the distant highway.– The shrill whistle of the steam engine too penetrated the woods–sounding like the scream of a hawk sailing over some farm yard. informing me that many restless city merchants are arriving within the circle of the town – – or adventurous country traders from the other side–. as they come under one horizon they shout in warning get off our track heard to the other–aye and some times through the circle of two towns even.– Here come thy groceries thou country–thy rations countrymen–and is there any independent man on his farm can say them nay– And heres your pay for them shrieks the countryman's whistles–timber like long catapults going 30 miles an hour against the city walls.– The country sends down most bulk the city sends out most tempting wares–& chairs enough to seat all the weary & heavy laden

Here comes your cotton–but lo in the down train comes your cloth–to shirt ye citizens.

Here comes the silk–down goes the cotton & woolen–up whirls the books and the news down goes the the wit to write them down goes the wood to warm–and the ice to cool ye.

But my object is not to live cheaply nor to live dearly –but to transact a little private business there with the fewest obstacles.– Some business more or less private or public engages us all and to be prevented from accomplishing it for want of a little calculation & fore thought–seems not so sad as foolish.

My house is 10 feet wide by 15 long–with a garret & closet–2 windows one door at the end–and a fire place A cellar six feet square and seven deep with shelving sides not stoned–but having never come to the sun the sand still keeps its place.

I laid up a half bushel of chestnuts which were an important item in the winter's store–which cost me only a pleasant ramble in the October woods.

Flints pond lies east a mile or more–a walk to which through the woods by such paths as the Indians used is a pleasant diversion summer or winter– Our greatest lake– Worth the while if only to feel the wind blow–and see the waves run–and remember those that go down upon the sea– I went a nutting there in the fall–one windy day–when the nuts were dropping into the water & were washed ashore.– and as I crawled along its long sedgey shore the fresh spray flung in my face–I came upon what seemed a large pad amid the reeds–which proved the mouldering wreck of a boat still distinctly preserving its well modelled outline–as when it was first cast up upon that beach–but ready to furnish the substance of new pads and reeds.

———

To compete with the squirrel's in the chestnut harvest–picking ofttimes the nuts that bear the mark of their teeth.

———

And again in winter to cross this pond on the ice–is our Davis' straits or Baffin's Bay–as a pleasant adventure.– to see the Lincoln hills rise up around it as a center–Mount

Tabor–& Bare Hill & the rest– It is a somewhat novel scenery, and not often seen in summer. Also the men seen far over the ice–at an indefinite distance–fishing for pickerel and moving slowly to and fro– You are uncertain whether giants or pigmies–like sealers with their wolvish dogs– They loom up like something fabulous & incredible. Norse-like.

Where 190 acres of the ocean stream have flown under the ground to make their appearance here. And west fair Haven lake not quite so far– This is our lake country.

Flints–going to which you cross Goose pond–where a whole colony of muskrats inhabits & have raised their cabins high above the ice–but not one is seen abroad.

—

I expect of any lecturer that he will read me a more or less simple & sincere account of his life–of what he has done & thought. Not so much what he has read or heard of other mens lives–and actions– But some such account as he would put into a letter to his kindred if in a distant land–describing his outward circumstance and any little adventures that he might have–and also his thoughts and feelings about them there.

He who gives us only the results of other men's living though with brilliant temporary success–we may in some measure justly accuse of having defrauded us of our time– We want a man to give us that which was most precious to him–not his lifes blood but even that for which his life's blood circulated what he has got by living–

If any thing ever yielded him pure pleasure or instruction–let him communicate it. The Miser must tell us how much he loves wealth and what means he takes to accumulate it– He must describe those facts which he knows & loves better than any body else.

He must not lecture on Missions & the Temperance The mechanic will naturally lecture about his trade the farmer about his farm and every man about that which he compared with other men–knows best.

Yet incredible mistakes are made– I have heard an Owl lecture with a perverse show of learning upon the solar microscope–and chanticlere upon nebulous stars When both ought to have been sound asleep in a hollow tree–or upon a hen roost. When I lectured here before this winter I heard that some of my towns men had expected of me some account of my life at the pond–this I will endeavor to give tonight.

I find that no way of doing or thinking however ancient is to be trusted. What every body echoes or in silence passes by may turn out to be sheer falsehood at last– As it were the mere smoke of opinion falling back in cinders which some thought–a cloud that would sprinkle fertile rain upon their fields.

One says you cant live so and so–it is madness–on vegetable food solely–or mainly–for it furnishes nothing to make bones with–walking behind his oxen–and so religiously devotes a part of his day to supplying his system with the raw material of bones.

Certain things are absolute necessaries of life in some circles–the most helpless and diseased–in others certain other or fewer things–and in others fewer still–and still what the absolutely indispensable are has never been determined I know a robust and hearty mother who thinks that her son who died abroad–came to his end by living too low, as she had since learned that he drank only water– Men are not inclined to leave off hanging men–today–though they will be to-morrow. I heard of a family in Concord this winter which would have starved, if it had not been for potatoes–& tea & coffee.

—

It has not been my design to live cheaply but only to
live as I could not devoting much time to getting a
living– I made the most of what means were already got.

—

To determine the character of our life and how
adequate it is to the occasion–just try it by any test–as for
instance that this same sun is seen in Europe & in
America at the same time–that these same stars are
visible in 24 hours to 2/3 the inhabitants of the globe–and
who shall say to how many inhabitants of the universe–
What farmer in his field lives according even to this
somewhat trivial material fact.

I just looked up at a fine twinkling star–and thought
that a voyager whom I know now many days sail from this
coast–might possibly be looking up at that same star with
me– The stars are the apexes of important triangles.

There is always the possibility–the possibility I say of
being *all*–or remaining a particle in the universe

Perhaps we may distribute the necessaries of life under
the several heads of food–clothing–shelter–& fuel And
this suggests how nearly the expression "animal heat"–is
to being synonymous with animal life.

Clothing–shelter–& fuel *warm* us outwardly– I have
read that the New Hollander goes naked in a pretty cold
winter–and warms his body by putting his feet close to
a hot fire–though the rest of the body may be in frost– On
the other hand food according to Liebig is the fuel which
keeps up the internal combustion which is going on in
the lungs. In cold weather weather we want more of this
fuel–in summer less

It is necessary then to keep warm to keep the vital
heat in us–to banish cold from the trunk and the
extremities.

The summer is a sort of elysian life time to
man— fuel—except to cook his food—is is then unnecessary
and the sun is his fire—and the fruits are many of them
cooked by its rays. Clothing and shelter are more than
half dispensed with even in our climate— And food is
more various & more easily obtained—

To many creatures there is only one necessary of
life—food— to the Bison—it is the palatable grass of the
prairie. And none of the brute creation require more than
food & shelter.

To the elevation & ennoblement of mankind what are
called the luxuries & even many of the comforts of life
are not only not indispensable but hinderances

With respect to luxuries & comforts the wise have ever
lived a more simple & meagre life than the poor Some
not wise will go to the other side of the globe—to barbarous
& unhealthy regions—and devote themselves to trade for
ten years—in order that they may live in New England
at last.

The ancient philosophers were a class of men than
whom none were poorer in respect to outward riches—none
so rich in respect to inward. None can be an impartial and
wise observer of human life—but from the vantage ground
of the barest the most simple & independent life.

when a man is warmed by the several modes I have
described—what next does he want—not surely more
warmth of the same kind—as more and nicer food—larger
and more splendid houses—& the like—but to adventure into
life—a little—his vacation having commenced— As
science which is poetry *professed* by the civilized
state—measuring the unfathomed with its telescope—&
microscope—but feebly & partially—we want something
more comprehensive & assertive which may be called
con-science perhaps—and signify a practical growth—

—

Critics have been very lavish of the word philosopher of late– Every century has had several. But we have forgotten what the name implies. These men were perhaps professors of philosophy–readers of it–sometimes even speakers of it partially–but never livers of it– It is admirable to read–to profess to speak–simply because it was admirable to live–

To be a philosopher is not even to have subtle thoughts and found a school–but rarer still to live a life of simplicity–of independence–of magnanimity & trust–such as all men should live. The weak–the unwise–the dependent cannot live so

Some modern men have skill & ambition enough to lead partially graceful & pleasing lives under the circumstances–but there was no bending of circumstances under their hands. Man stands very near to the helm of his life– It is a courtier like success–not kingly–not manly. With the actual life of man for the problem to see how you can solve it. But where are the progenitors of a nobler race of men? We are pigmies & dwarfs– –The founders of nations

———

In these days in in this country a few implements –light–& stationary and access to a few books–will rank next to the necessaries–but can all be obtained at a very trifling cost Under the head of clothing is to be ranked bedding or night-clothes.

We are very anxious to keep the animal heat in us–what pains we take with our beds–robbing the nests of birds & their breasts–this shelter within a shelter–as the mole has a bed of leaves and grass at the end of its burrow.

———

In the summer I caught fish occasionally in the pond—but since sept. have not missed them.

—

Of a life of luxury—the fruit is luxury in literature or in art.

—

In a man or his work over all special excellence or failure, prevails the general authority or value

Almost any man knows how to earn money—but not one in a million knows how to spend it. If he had known how to spend it he would never have earned it.

—

The philosopher is in advance of his age not merely in his discourse but in his life—in the form & outward mode of it. He is not fed—clothed—warmed—sheltered like other men—

How can a man be a philosopher and not maintain his vital heat by better methods than other men.

The body is so perfectly subjugated by the mind that it prophecies the sovereignty of the latter over the whole of nature. The instincts are to a certain extent a sort of independent nobility—of equal date with the crown. They are perhaps the mind of our ancestors subsided in us. The experience of the race—

I have thought sometimes when going home through the woods at night—star-gazing all the way—till I was aroused from my reflections by finding my door before me—that perhaps my body would find its way home if its master should have forsaken it— As the hand finds its way to the mouth without assistance.

All matter indeed is capable of entertaining thought.

—

Why do men degenerate.– what makes families
run-out? What is the nature of that luxury that
ennervates nations and is there none of it in our lives?
Are we the founders of a race.

Men frequently say to me I should think you would
feel lonely down there– I should think you would want
to be nearer to folks rainy days & nights especially. How
far apart dwell the most distant inhabitants of those
stars the breadth of whose disks cannot be appreciated
by our instruments.

But what after all do we want to dwell near to?– not
mainly to the depot or to many men–not to the post office
or the bar room–or the meeting house or school house–or
Beacon hill or the Five points where men are more
numerous than any where– –but rather I should say to
the source of our life–whence in all our experience we
have found that to issue. As the willow stands near the
water and sends out its roots in that direction.

But most men are not so wise as a tree or rather are like
those trees which being badly located make only wood &
leaves and bear no fruit.

This will vary with different natures of course–but this
is the place where a wise man will dig his cellar.

What is the great attraction in cities? It is universally
admitted that human beings invariably degenerate
there–and do not propagate their kind.– Yet the
prevailing tendency is to the city life–whether we move
to Boston or stay in Concord.

We are restless to pack up our furniture and move into
a more bustling neighborhood but we are proportionally
slow to rent a new mode of living–or rather to rend the
old.

—

I one evening overtook one of my towns men on the Walden road–driving a pair of cattle to market–who enquired of me how I could bring my mind to give up so many of the comforts of life– I answered that I was very sure I liked it passably well.– I was not joking. And so I went home to my bed–& left him to pick his way through the darkness and the mud to Brighton which place he would reach some time in the morning.

At another time I over took another towns-man in the same woods going to Boston by night with a single horse-load of wood–he was plainly a hard working and rather straitened man–getting on to his wheel when he ascended a hill to assist his horse– He told me how much it cost him to live–he must have so much pork–and tea & coffee and molasses–and beside lay up something against a sick day–for he had already come near dying several times.

In fact I never saw a rich man who knew how to spend his money–commonly they wear no better clothes–they build no better houses–than their neighbors– For while they have been accumulating property, they have not been cultivating taste nor wisdom.

Even with money you might do something grander–& more imposing–

What they give is not a gift but rather so much abandoned to mankind–though it be the tenth part of their income annually relinquished

A small sum would really do much good if the donor spent himself with it and did not relinquish it to some distant society whose managers & secretary & treasurers do the good or the evil with it– How much might be done for this town–with a hundred dollars! I could provide a select course of Lectures for the summer or winter–which would be an incalculable benefit to every inhabitant of the town–with a thousand-dollars I could purchase for this town a more complete & select library than exists in the

state out of Cambridge & Boston–perhaps a more
available one than any.

–Men sit palsied and helpless–their money–buried.

After all those who do most good with money do it with
the least–because they can do better than to acquire it.

—

March 13th 1846 The Songsparrow & Black bird heard
today–the snow going off–the ice in the pond 1 foot thick.

—

Men speak–or at least think much of cooperation
nowadays–of working together to some worthy end– But
what little there is, is as if it were not–being a simple result
of which the means are hidden–a harmony inaudible to
men– If a man has faith–he will cooperate with equal
faith every where– If he has not faith he will continue
to live like the rest of the world. To cooperate in the
lowest & in the highest sense–thoroughly–is simply to get
your living together. I heard it proposed lately that two
young men should travel together over the world–the one
making his way as he went, seeking his fortune,–before
the mast–behind the plow–walking and sleeping on the
ground–living from hand to mouth–and so come in
immediate contact with all lands and nations–the other
carrying a bill of exchange in his pocket as a resource in
case of extremity– It was easy to see that they could not
be companions to one another–or cooperate. They would
part company at the first interesting crisis the most
interesting point in their adventures

I live about a mile from any neighbor no house is visible
within a quarter of a mile or more–

The pond furnishes my water which 8 or 9 months in the year I think is the best in the town– In the summer I set it in my cellar and found that it became sufficiently cool.–

It seemed to me that it would become colder–than well water under the same circumstances–but I never tried the experiment

{*One-fifth page blank*}
{*One leaf missing*}

I know a man whom I do not know–who carries as much mystery about him as can consist with any acquaintanceship– He is cast outwardly in the rudest and coarsest mould–a woodchopper by profession– He is about 29 somewhat sluggish but stout of body–eats much meat–and sometimes drinks till he is drunk. In him there is the animal man developed, but the intellectual and divine is infantine slumbering like an infant. Of the world he knows nothing– If other men think he does not know it. I do not know whether he is as wise as Shakspeare, or as simple as a child–whether to suspect him of consciousness and deception or something more miraculous

We sometimes tell our friends of a man whom we value whome we have met with–and we tell him also of our friends whom we wish him to know–and when they meet our hero knows that he has a part to perform and performs it.

But this man is so genuine–& unsophisticated that no introduction will serve–more than if you introduced a woodchuck to your neighbor–he has got to find him out as you did. He will not play any part. Like all children he lives alone not in society–nor where rumor & fame reach– Men help to feed him & clothe him and pay him wages for work–but he never exchanged opinions with them. He never heard the sound of praise.

If I tell him that a wise man is coming to see him he
does not know nor think how he shall behave more than
If I told him an archangel had come—but does as if he
thought that anything so grand would expect nothing
of himsef but take all the responsibility on himself—and
let him be forgotten still.

In due time in the spring I heard the martins twittering
over my clearing though it had not appeared that the
town contained so many that it could afford any to
me They were rather of the ancient stock that dwelt in
hollow trees before the white man came than the modern
village race that live in boxes.

Let a man live in any part of the globe and he will hear
the same simple spring sounds to cheer him. Along the
Nile and the Orinoco and the Mississippi birds of the same
genus—migrate. Everywhere the frog and the turtle greet
the season The temperate and Frigid salute the Torrid
zone again—and birds fly & plants and winds blow to
correct this oscillation of the poles and preserve the
equilibrium of nature. This slight oscillation how it is
painted by the seasons and heralded by the songs and the
glancing plumage of migrating birds—

The Pewee (Phoebe?) came and look in at my door or
window to see if my house were cave like enough for
her—sustaining herself on humming wings—with clenched
talons as if she held by the air—while she surveyed the
premises.

Girls and boys generally seemed glad to be in the woods
& young women they looked in the pond and at the
flowers and improved their time.

But men of business only thought of Solitude and
employment. though they said they loved a ramble in the
woods occasionally it was obvious that they did not.

Restless committed men whose time is all taken up in getting a living–Ministers Doctors–lawyers generally suggested in one way or another the importance of doing good.

Conscientious preachers–(the way of their profession) –uneasy house keepers–young men who had ceased to be young and had concluded that it was safest to follow the beaten track of the professions generally said it was not possible to do so much good in my position.

The old and infirm thought of sickness & sudden death–to them life seemed full of danger–any where–and a prudent man would carefully select the safest position

{*One page blank*}
{*One leaf missing*}
{*Seven leaves and endpapers blank*}

[Walden 1]

JULY 5, 1845–MARCH 27, 1846

Walden Sat. July 5th–45

Yesterday I came here to live. My house makes me think of some mountain houses I have seen, which seemed to have a fresher auroral atmosphere about them as I fancy of the halls of Olympus. I lodged at the house of a saw-miller last summer, on the Caatskills mountains, high up as Pine orchard in the blue-berry & raspberry region, where the quiet and cleanliness & coolness seemed to be all one, which had this ambrosial character. He was the miller of the Kaaterskill Falls, They were a clean & wholesome family inside and out–like their house. The latter was not plastered–only lathed and the inner doors were not hung. The house seemed high placed, airy, and perfumed, fit to entertain a travelling God. It was so high indeed that all the music, the broken strains, the waifs & accompaniments of tunes, that swept over the ridge of the Caatskills, passed through its aisles. Could not man be man in such an abode? And would he ever find out this grovelling life?

It was the very light & atmosphere in which the works of Grecian art were composed, and in which they rest. They have appropriated to themselves a loftier hall than mortals ever occupy, at least on a level with the mountain brows of the world.

There was wanting a little of the glare of the lower vales and in its place a pure twilight as became the precincts of heaven Yet so equable and calm was the season there that you could not tell whether it was morning or noon or evening. Always there was the sound of the morning cricket

July 6th

I wish to meet the facts of life–the vital facts, which where the phenomena or actuality the Gods meant to show us,–face to face, And so I came down here. Life! who knows what it is–what it does? If I am not quite right here I am less wrong than before–and now let us see what they will have. The preacher, instead of vexing the ears of drowsy farmers on their day of rest, at the end of the week, (for sunday always seemed to me like a fit conclusion of an ill spent week and not the fresh and brave beginning of a new one) with this one other draggletail and postponed affair of a sermon, from thirdly to 15thly, should teach them with a thundering voice –pause & simplicity.

stop– Avast– Why so fast? In all studies we go not forward but rather backward with redoubled pauses, we always study *antiques*–with silence and *re*flection. Even time has a depth, and below its surface the waves do not lapse and roar. I wonder men can be so frivolous almost as to attend to the gross form of negro slavery–there are so many keen and subtle masters, who subject us both. Self-emancipation in the West Indies of a man's thinking and imagining provinces, which should be more than his island territory One emancipated heart & intellect– It would knock off the fetters from a million slaves.

July 7th

I am glad to remember tonight as I sit by my door that I too am at least a remote descendent of that heroic race of men of whom there is tradition. I too sit here on the shore of my Ithaca, a fellow wanderer and survivor of Ulysses. How Symbolical, significant of I know not what the pitch pine stands here before my door unlike any glyph I have seen sculptured or painted yet– One of nature's later designs. Yet perfect as her Grecian art. There it is, a done tree. Who can mend it? And now

where is the generation of heroes whose lives are to pass
amid these our northern pines? Whose exploits shall
appear to posterity pictured amid these strong and
shaggy forms?

Shall there be only arrows and bows to go with these
pines on some pipe stone quarry at length.

If we can forget we have done somewhat, if we can
remember we have done somewhat. Let us remember this

The Great spirit of course makes indifferent all times &
places. The place where he is seen is always the same,
and indescribably pleasant to all our senses. We had
allowed only near-lying and transient circumstances to
make our occasions– But nearest to all things is that
which fashions its being. Next to us the grandest laws are
being enacted and administered.

Bread may not always nourish us, but it always does
us good   it even takes stiffness out of our joints and
makes us supple and boyant when we knew not what ailed
us–to share any heroic joy–to recognise any largeness in
man or nature, to see and to know– This is all cure and
prevention.

Verily a good house is a temple– A clean house–pure
and undefiled, as the saying is. I have seen such made of
white pine. Seasoned and seasoning still to eternity.
Where a Goddess might trail her garment. The less dust
we bring in to nature, the less we shall have to pick up.
It was a place where one would go in, expecting to find
something agreeable; as to a shade–or to a shelter–a more
natural place.

I hear the far off lowing of a cow and it seems to heave
the firmament. I at first thought it was the voice of a
minstrel whom I know, who might be straying over hill

and dale this eve–but soon I was not disappointed when
it was prolonged into the sweet and natural and withal
cheap tone of the cow. This youths brave music is indeed
of kin with the music of the cow. They are but one
articulation of nature.

Sound was made not so much for convenience, that we
might hear when called, as to regale the sense–and fill
one of the avenues of life. A healthy organization will
never need what are commonly called the sensual
gratifications, but will enjoy the daintiest feasts at those
tables where there is nothing to tempt the appetite of the
sensual.

There are strange affinities in this universe–strange
ties stranger harmonies and relationships, what kin am
I to some wildest pond among the mountains–high up
ones shaggy side–in the gray morning twilight draped
with mist–suspended in low wreathes from the dead
willows and bare firs that stand here and there in the
water, as if here were the evidence of those old contests
between the land and water which we read of. But why
should I find anything to welcome me in such a nook as
this– This faint reflection this dim watery eye–where in
some angle of the hills the woods meet the waters edge
and a grey tarn lies sleeping

My beans–whose continuous length of row is 7 miles,
already planted and now so impatient to be howed–not
easily to be put off. What is the meaning of this service
this small Hercules labor–of this small warfare–I know
not. I come to love my rows–they attatch me to the
earth–and so I get new strength and health like Antaeus

–My beans, so many more than I want. This has been
my curious labor– Why only heaven knows–to make this
surface of the earth, which yielded only blackberries &
Johnswort–& cinqfoil–sweet wild fruits & pleasant flowers
produce instead this pulse What shall I learn of beans or

beans of me– I cherish them– I hoe them early & late I
have an eye to them.– And this is my days work. It is a
fine broad leaf to look upon.

My auxiliaries are the dews and rains–to water this dry
soil–and genial fatness in the soil itself, which for the
most part is lean and effoete. My enemies are worms cool
days–and most of all woodchucks. They have nibbled for
me an eigth of an acre clean. I plant in faith–and they
reap–this is the tax I pay–for ousting Jonswort & the
rest But soon the surviving beans will be too tough for
woodchucks and then–they will go forward to meet new
foes.

July 14th 1845

What sweet and tender, the most innocent and divinely
encouraging society there is in every natural object, and
so in universal nature even for the poor misanthrope and
most melancholy man. There can be no really *black*
melan-choly to him who lives in the midst of nature,
and has still his senses. There never was yet such a storm
but it was Aeolian music to the innocent ear. Nothing can
compel to a vulgar sadness a simple & brave man. While
I enjoy the sweet friendship of the seasons I trust that
nothing can make life a burden to me. This rain which is
now watering my beans, and keeping me in the house
waters me too. I needed it as much. And what if most are
not hoed–those who send the rain whom I chiefly respect
will pardon me.

Sometimes when I compare myself with other men
methinks I am favored by the Gods. They seem to whisper
joy to me beyond my deserts and that I do have a solid
warrant and surety at their hands, which my fellows do
not. I do not flatter myself but if it were possible *they*
flatter me. I am especially guided and guarded.

And now I think of it–let me remember–

What was seen true once–and sanctioned by the flash
of Jove–will always be true, and nothing can hinder it. I

have the warrant that no fair dream I have had need fail of its fulfilment.

Here I know I am in good company–here is the world its centre and metropolis, and all the palms of Asia–and the laurels of Greece–and the firs of the Arctic Zones incline thither.

Here I can read Homer if I would have books, as well as in Ionia, and not wish myself in Boston or New-york or London or Rome or Greece– In such place as this he wrote or sang. Who should come to my lodge Just now–but a true Homeric boor–one of those Paphlagonian men? Alek Therien–he called himself– A Canadian now, a woodchopper–a post maker–makes fifty posts–holes them i.e. in a day, and who made his last supper on a woodchuck which his dog caught– And he too has heard of Homer and *if it were not for books would not know what to do*–rainy days. Some priest once who could read glibly from the Greek itself–taught him reading in a measure his verse at least in his turn–at Nicolet away by the Trois Riviers once.

And now I must read to him while he holds the book –Achilles' reproof of Patrocles on his sad countenance
> "Why are you in tears,–Patrocles? Like a
> young child (girl) &c. &c
>
> Or have you only heard some news from Phthia?
> They say that Menoetius lives yet, son of Actor
> And Peleus lives, son of AEacus, among the Myrmidons,
> Both of whom having died, we should greatly grieve."

He has a neat bundle of white-oak bark under his arm for a sick man–gathered this Sunday morning– "I suppose there's no harm in going after such a thing today."? ? The simple man. May the Gods send him many wood chucks.

And earlier today came 5 Lestrigones–Railroad men who take care of the road, some of them at least. They

still represent the bodies of men–transmitting arms and
legs–and bowels downward from those remote days to
more remote. They have some got a rude wisdom
withal–thanks to their dear experience. And one with
them a handsome younger man–a sailor like Greek like
man–says "Sir I like your notions– I think I shall live so
my self Only I should like a wilder country–where there
is more game. I have been among the Indians near
Apallachecola I have lived with them, I like your kind of
life– Good-day I wish you success and happiness."

Therien said this morning (July 16th Wednesday) If
those beans were mine I should'nt like to hoe them till
the dew was off–" He was going to his wood chopping.
Ah said I that is one of the notions the farmers have
got–but I dont believe it.
"How thick the pigeons are" said he, "if working every
day were not my trade I could get all the meat I should
want by hunting. Pigeons woodchucks–Rabbits
–Partridges–by George I could get all I should want for a
week in one day."

I imagine it to be some advantage to live a primitive
and frontier life–though in the midst of an outward
civilization. Of course all the improvements of the ages
do not carry a man backward nor forward in relation to
the great facts of his existence.
Our furniture should be as simple as the Arab's or the
Indians'– At first the thoughtful wondering man plucked
in haste the fruits which the boughs extended to him–and
found in the sticks and stones around him his implements
ready. And he still remembered that he was a sojourner
in nature. When he was refreshed with food and sleep he
contemplated his journey again. He dwelt in a tent in this
world. He was either threading the vallies or crossing the
plains or climbing the mountain tops

Now the best works of art serve comparatively but to dissipate the mind–for they are themselves transitionary and paroxismal and not free and absolute thoughts.

Men have become the tools of their tools–the man who independently plucked the fruits when he was hungry–is become a *farmer*

There are scores of pitch pine in my field–from one to three inches in diameter, girdled by the mice last winter– A Norwegian winter it was for them–for the snow lay long and deep–and they had to mix much pine meal with their usual diet– Yet these trees have not many of them died even in midsummer–and laid bare for a foot–but have grown a foot. They seem to do all their gnawing beneath the snow. There is not much danger of the mouse tribe becoming extinct in hard winters for their granary is a cheap and extensive one.

Here is one has had her nest under my house, and came when I took my luncheon to pick the crumbs at my feet. It had never seen the race of man before, and so the sooner became familiar– It ran over my shoes and up my pantaloons inside clinging to my flesh with its sharp claws. It would run up the side of the room by short impulses like a squirrel–which resembles–coming between the house mouse and the former– Its belly is a little reddish and its ears a little longer. At length as I leaned my elbow on the bench it ran over my arm and round the paper which contained my dinner. And when I held it a piece of cheese it came and nibled between my fingers and then cleaned its face and paws like a fly.

{*One-third page blank*}

There is a memorable intervale between the written and the spoken language–the language read and the

language heard. The one is transient—a sound—a tongue—a
dialect—and all men learn it of their mothers—

It is loquacious, fragmentary—raw material— The other
is a reserved select matured expression—a deliberate word
addressed to the ear of nations & generations. The one is
natural & convenient—the other divine & instructive— The
clouds flit here below—genial refreshing with their
showers—and gratifying with their tints—alternate sun &
shade— A grosser heaven adapted to our trivial wants—but
above them—repose the blue firmament and the stars. The
stars are written words & sterotyped on the blue parchment
of the skies—the fickle clouds that hide them from
our view—which we on this side need though heaven
does not These are our daily colloquies our vaporous
garrulous breath.

Books must be read as deliberately and reservedly as
they were written. The herd of men the generations who
speak the Greek and Latin, are not entitled by the accident
of birth to read the works of Genius whose mother tongue
speaks every where, and is learned by every child who
hears.

The army of the Greeks and Latins are not coaeternary
though contemporary with Homer & Plato Virgil & Cicero.
In the transition ages nations who loudest spoke the
Greek and Latin tongues—whose mothers milk they were,
learned not their nobler dialects, but a base and vulgar
speech

The men of the middle ages who spoke so glibly the
language of the Roman & in the eastern empire of the
Athenian mob prized only a cheap contemporary
learning— The classics of both languages were virtually
lost and forgotten. When after the several nations of
Europe had acquired in some degree rude and original
languages of their own—sufficient for the arts of life &
conversation—then the few scholars beheld with advantage
from this more distant stand-point the treasures of

antiquity–and a new Latin age commenced the era of
reading– Those works of genius were then first classical.
All those millions who had spoken Latin and Greek–had
not read Latin & Greek– The time had at length arrived
for the written word–the *scripture*–to be heard. What the
multitude could not *hear*, after the lapse of centuries a
few scholars read. This is the matured thought which was
not spoken in the market place unless it be in a market
place where the free genius of mankind resorts today.

There is something very choice & select in a written
word. No wonder Alexander carried his Homer? in a
precious casket on his expeditions. A word which may be
translated into every dialect and suggests a truth to every
mind, is the most perfect work of human art, and as it
may be breathed and taken on our lips and as it were
become the product of our physical organs as its sense is
of our intellectual–it is the nearest to life itself. It is the
simplest and purest channel by which a revelation may be
transmitted from age to age. How it subsists itself whole
and undiminished till the intelligent reader is born to
decypher it. These are the tracks of Zoroaster–of
Confucius and moses–indelible in the sands of the
remotest times.

There are no monuments of antiquity comparable to the
Classics for interest and importance. It does not need that
the scholar should be an antiquarian for these works of
art have such an immortality as the works of nature and
are modern at the same time that they are ancient–like
the sun and stars–and occupy by right no small share of
the present.

This palpable beauty is the treasured wealth of the
world and the proper inheritance of each generation.
Books, the oldest and the best, stand rightfully on the
shelves of every cottage. They have not to plead their
cause–but they enlighten their readers and it is gained.

When the illiterate and scornful rustic earns his imagined leisure and wealth, he turns inevitably at last, he or his children, to these still higher and yet inaccessible circles, And even when his descendant has attained to move in the highest rank of the wise men of his own age and country he will still be sensible only of the imperfection of his culture and the vanity and inefficiency of his intellectual wealth, if his Genius will not permit him to listen with somewhat of the equanimity of an equal to the fames of godlike men–which yet as it were form an invisible upper class in every society.

I have carried an apple in my pocket tonight–a Sopsinwine they call it till now that I take my hand kerchief out it has got so fine a fragrance that it really seems like a friendly of trick of some pleasant daemon to entertain me with. It is redolent of sweet scented orchards of innocent teeming harvests I realize the existence of a goddess Pomona–and that the gods have really intended that men should feed divinely, like themselves, on their own nectar & ambrosia They have so painted this fruit and freighted it with such a fragrance that it satisfies much more than an animal appetite. Grapes peaches berries nuts &c are likewise provided for those who will sit at their sideboard. I have felt when partaking of this inspiring diet that my appetite was an indifferent consideration–that eating became a sacrament–a method of communion–an extatic exercise a mingling of bloods–and sitting at the communion table of the world. And so have not only quenched my thirst at the spring but the health of the universe
The indecent haste and grossness with which our food is swallowed, have cast a disgrace on the very act of eating itself. But I do believe that if this process were rightly conducted, its aspect and effects would be wholly changed, and we should receive our daily life and

health–Antaeus like–with an extatic delight–and with upright frank–innocent and graceful behavior–take our strength from day to day. This fragrance of the apple in my pocket has I confess deterred me from eating of it– I am more effectually fed by it another way.

It is indeed that common notion that this fragrance is the only food of the gods. and inasmuch as we are partially divine we are compelled to respect it.

> Tell me ye wise ones if ye can
> Whither and whence the race of man.
> For I have seen his slender clan
> Clinging to hoar hills with their feet
> Threading the forest for their meat
> Moss and lichens bark & grain
> They rake together with might & main
> And they digest them with anxiety & pain.
> I meet them in their rags and unwashed hair
> Instructed to eke out their scanty fare
> Brave race–with a yet humbler prayer
> Beggars they are aye on the largest scale
> They beg their daily bread at heavens door
>   And if their this years crop alone should fail
> They neither bread nor begging would know more.
>   They are the Titmans of their race
>   And hug the vales with mincing pace
>   like Troglodites, and fight with cranes,
>   We walk mid great relations feet
>   What they let fall alone we eat
>   We are only able
>   to catch the fragments from their table
>   These elder brothers of our race
>   By us unseen with larger pace
>   Walk oer our heads, and live our lives
>   embody our desires and dreams
>   Anticipate our hoped for gleams
>   We grub the earth for our food
>   We know not what is good.
>   Where does the fragrance of our orchards go
>   Our vineyards while we toil below–
>   A finer race and finer fed
>   Feast and revel above our head.

The tints and fragrance of the flowers & fruits
Are but the crumbs from off their table
While we consume the pulp and roots
Some times we do assert our kin
And stand a moment where once they have been
We hear their sounds and see their sights
And we experience their delights—
But for the moment that we stand
Astonished on the Olympian land.
We do discern no traveller's face
No elder brother of our race.
To lead us to the monarch's court
And represent our case.
But straightway we must journey back
retracing slow the arduous track
Without the privilege to tell
Even, the sight we know so well

In my father's house are many mansions.

Who ever explored the mansions of the air—who knows who his neighbors are. We seem to lead our human lives amid a concentric system of worlds of realm on realm, close bordering on each other—where dwell the unknown and the imagined races—as various in degree as our own thoughts are. A system of invisible partitions more infinite in number and more inconceivable in intricacy than the starry one which Science has penetrated.

When I play my flute tonight earnest as if to leap the bounds that narrow fold where human life is penned, and range the surrounding plain—I hear echo from a neighboring wood a stolen pleasure occasionally not rightfully heard—much more for other ears than ours for tis the reverse of sound. It is not our own melody that comes back to us—but an amended strain. And I would only hear myself as I would hear my echo—corrected and repronounced for me. It is as when my friend reads my verse.

The borders of our plot are set with flowers—whose seeds were blown from more Elysian fields adjacent—which our

laborious feet have never reached–and fairer fruits and
unaccustomed fragrance betray another realm's vicinity.
There too is Echo found with which we play at evening.

There is the abutment of the rainbow's arch

{One-fifth page blank}

Walden Aug 6–45

I have just been reading a book called "The Crescent &
the Cross" till now I am somewhat ashamed of myself.
Am I sick, or idle–that I can sacrifice my energy
–America–and to-day–to this mans ill remembered and
indolent story– Carnac and Luxor are but names, and
still more desert sand and at length a wave of the great
ocean itself are needed to wash away the filth that
attaches to their grandeur. Carnac–Carnac–this is carnac
for me and I behold the columns of a larger and a purer
temple.

May our childish and fickle aspirations be divine, while
we descend to this mean intercourse. Our reading should
be heroic–in an unknown tongue–a dialect always but
imperfectly learned–through which we stammer line by
line, catching but a glimmering of the sense–and still
afterward admiring its unexhausted hieroglyphics–its
untranslated columns.

Here grow around me nameless trees and shrubs each
morning freshly sculptured–rising new stories day by
day–instead of hideous ruins– Their myriad-handed
worker–uncompelled as uncompelling

This is my carnac–that its unmeasured dome–the
measuring art man has invented flourishes and dies upon
this temples floor nor ever dreams to reach that ceilings
height. Carnac & Luxor crumble underneath–their
shadowy roofs let in the light once more reflected from the
ceiling of the sky

Behold these flowers–let us be up with Time not
dreaming of 3000 years ago. Erect ourselves and let

those columns lie–not stoop to raise a foil against the
sky– Where is the *spirit* of that time but in this present
day–this present line 3000 years ago are not agone–they
are still lingering here aye every one,

> And Memnon's mother sprightly greets us now
> Wears still her youthful blushes on her brow
> And Carnac's columns why stand they on the plain?
> T'enjoy our Opportunities they would fain remain

> This is my Carnac whose unmeasured dome
> Shelters the measuring art & measurer's home
> Whose propylaeum is the system nigh
> And sculptured facade the visible sky

Where there is memory which compelleth time the
muse's mother and the muses nine–there are all ages–past
and future time unwearied memory that does not forget
the actions of the past–that does not forego–to stamp
them freshly– That old mortality industrious to retouch
the monuments of time, in the world's cemetery through
out every clime
 The student may read Homer or Aeschylus in the
original Greek–for to do so implies to emulate their
heroes–the consecration of morning hours to their page–
 The heroic books though printed in the character of
our mother tongue–are always written in a foreign
language dead to idle & degenerate times, and we must
laboriously seek the meaning of each word and line,
conjecturing a larger sense than the text renders us at last
out of our own valor and generosity.

 A man must find his own occasions in himself. The
natural day is very calm, and will hardly reproove our
indolence. If there is no elevation in our spirits–the pond
will not seem elevated like a mountain tarn, but a low
pool a silent muddy water–a place for fishermen.
 I sit here at my window like a priest of Isis–and
observe the phenomena of 3000 years ago, yet

unimpaired. The tantivy of wild pigeons, an ancient race of birds–gives a voice to the air–flying by twos and threes athwart my view or perching restless on the white pine boughs occasionally–a fish-hawk dimples the glassy surface of the pond and brings up a fish And for the last half hour I have heard the rattle of rail-road cars conveying travellers from Boston to the country.

After the evening train has gone by and left the world to silence and to me The Whippoorwill chants her vespers for half an hour– And when all is still at night the owls take up the strain like mourning women their ancient ululu. Their most dismal scream is truly Ben-Jonsonian –wise midnight hags It is no honest and blunt Tu whit Tu who of the poets but without jesting a most solemn graveyard ditty–but the mutual consolation of suicide lovers remembering the pangs and the delights of supernal love–in the infernal groves.

And yet I love to hear their wailing their doleful responses trilled along the wood side reminding me sometimes of music and singing birds as if it were the dark and tearful side of music–the regrets and sighs that would fain be sung The spirits–the *low* spirits–and melancholy forebodings–of fallen spirits–who once in human shape night-walked the earth and did the deeds of darkness now expiating with their wailing hymns –threnodia their sins in the very scenery of their transgressions. They give me a new sense of the vastness and mystery of that nature which is the common dwelling of us both.

Oh-o-o-o-o–that I never had been bor-or-or-or-orn–sighs one on this side of the pond and circles in the restlessness of despair to some new perch in the grey oaks. "That I never had been bor-or-or-or orn" echoes one on the farther side with a tremulous sincerity–and "born or-or-or-orn" comes faintly from far in the Lincoln woods.

And then the frogs–bull Frogs– They are the more sturdy spirits of ancient wine bibbers and wassailers still unrepentant–trying to sing a catch in their stygian lakes. They would fain keep up the hilarious good fellowship and all the rules of their old round tables–but they have waxed hoarse and solemnly grave and serious their voices mocking at mirth–and their wine has lost its flavor and is only liquor to distend their paunches–and never comes sweet intoxication to drown the memory of the past but mere saturation and waterlogged dulness and distension– Still the most Aldermanic with his chin upon a pad, which answers for a napkin to his drooling chaps under the eastern shore quafs a deep draught of the once scorned water– And passes round the cup–with the ejaculation–tr-r-r-r r-oonk–tr-r-r-r-oonk–tr-r-r-oonk. And straightway comes over the water from some distant cove the self-same pass word where the next in seniority and girth has gulped down to his mark– And when the strain has made the circuit of the shores–then ejaculates the master of ceremonies with satisfaction Tr-r-r-oonk –and each in turn repeats the sound–down to the least distended, leakiest–flabbiest paunched–that their be no mistake–

And the bowl goes round again until the sun dispels the mornings mist and only the Patriarch is not under–the pond–but vainly bellowing–Troonk from time to time –pausing for a reply.

All nature is classic and akin to art– The sumack and pine and hickory which surround my house remind me of the most graceful sculpture. Some times the trees do not make merely a vague impression–but their tops or a single limb or leaf seems to have grown to a distinct expression and invites my life to a like distinctness and emphasis.

Poetry Painting Sculpture claim at once and associate with themselves those perfect pieces of art–leaves–vines acorns–

The critic must at last stand as mute though contented before a true poem–as before an acorn or a vine leaf. The perfect work of art is received again into the bosom of nature whence its material proceeded–and that criticism which can only detect its unnaturalness has no longer any office to fulfill.

The choicest maxims that have come down to us are more beautiful or integrally wise–than they are wise to our understandings– This wisdom which we are inclined to pluck from their stalk is the fruit only of a single association. Every natural form–palm leaves and acorns–oak-leaves and sumack and dodder–are untranslateable aphorisms

{One-fifth page blank}

I love to gaze at the opposite or south side of the pond which has a foreign shore–low hills skirted with oaks and pines which seem but the front rank of a forest beyond which stretches a level country, the earth I read of, as far as Tartary and the empire of the Grand Khan–where tribes of men dwell in tents.

The struggle of the hero Ajax are thus forcibly described in the 16th book of the Iliad. He endeavors to ward off fire from the ships while Patroclus is interceeding with Achilles for his armor and his Myrmidons.

> "Thus *they* spoke such things to oneanother.
> But Ajax no longer stood fast; for he was
>   forced by javelins;
> Both the will of Zeus overcame him & the
>   illustrious Trojans,
> Hurling (their darts); and his bright helmet
>   being struck
> Had a terrible clanging about his temples; and
>   he was struck incessantly
> Upon his well-made armor. He was disabled in
>   his left shoulder

Always holding firm his variegated shield;—nor
were they able
(Around him to make an impression), striving with
their weapons.
But all the while he was breathing hard, and
the sweat
And much sweat ran down from him on every
side from his limbs, nor ever had he
To breathe; and on every side misfortune
succeeded surely to misfortune.

or better

Thus they were speaking such words to oneanother.
i.e (Patroclus & Achilles)

But Ajax no longer stood his ground; for he was
compelled by weapons;
The will of Zeus subdued him, and the illustrious
Trojans,
Hurling (their javelins); and his bright helmet
being struck
Had a terrible clang about his temples, & he was
struck incessantly
Upon his well-made armor; he was wounded in his
left shoulder
Always holding firm his variegated shield; nor
were they able
Around to stagger him, striving with their weapons.
But constantly he breathed with difficulty; and
much sweat
Ran down on every side from his limbs, nor ever
had he
(A chance) to breathe; And on every side
misfortune was riveted to misfortune

Twenty three years since when I was 5 years old, I was
brought from Boston to this pond, away in the country
which was then but another name for the extended world
for me—one of the most ancient scenes stamped on the
tablets of my memory—the oriental asiatic valley of my
world—whence so many races and inventions have gone
forth in recent times. That woodland vision for a long time

made the drapery of my dreams. That sweet solitude my
spirit seemed so early to require that I might have room to
entertain my thronging guests, and that speaking silence
that my ears might distinguish the significant sounds.
Some how or other it at once gave the preference to this
recess among the pines where almost sunshine & shadow
were the only inhabitants that varied the scene, over that
tumultuous and varied city–as if it had found its proper
nursery.

Well now to-night my flute awakes the echoes over this
very water, but one generation of pines has fallen and
with their stumps I have cooked my supper, And a lusty
growth of oaks and pines is rising all around its brim and
preparing its wilder aspect for new infant eyes.

Almost the same johnswort springs from the same
perennial root in this pasture.–

Even I have at length helped to clothe that fabulous
landscape of my imagination– –and one result of my
presence and influence is seen in the bean leaves and corn
blades and potatoe vines.

Seek to preserve the tenderness of your nature as you
would the bloom upon a peach.

Most men are so taken up with the cares and rude
practice of life–that its finer fruits can not be plucked by
them. Literally the laboring man has not leisure for a
strict and lofty integrity day by day   he cannot afford to
sustain the fairest and nobelest relations. His labor will
depreciate in the market.

How can he remember well his ignorance who has so
often to use his knowledge

August 15th

The sounds heard at this hour 8 1/2 are the distant
rumbling of wagons over bridges–a sound farthest heard
of any human at night–the baying of dogs–the lowing of
cattle in distant yards

What if we were to obey these fine dictates these divine suggestions which are addressed to the mind & not to the body–which are certainly true–not to eat meat–not to buy or sell or barter &c &c &c?

I will not plant beans another summer but sincerity –truth–simplicity–faith–trust–innocence–and see if they will not grow in this soil with such manure as I have, and sustain me. When a man meets a man–it should not be some uncertain appearance and falsehood–but the personification of great qualities. Here comes truth perchance personified along the road– Let me see how Truth behaves– I have not seen enough of her– He shall utter no foreign word–no doubtful sentence–and I shall not make haste to part with him.

I would not forget that I deal with infinite and divine qualities in my fellow. All men indeed are divine in their core of light but that is indistinct and distant to me, like the stars of the least magnitude–or the galaxy itself–but my kindred planets show their round disks and even their attendant moons to my eye.

Even the tired laborers I meet on the road, I really meet as travelling Gods, but it is as yet and must be for a long season, without speech.

Sat Aug 23d 1845

I set out this afternoon to go a fishing–for pickerel to eke out my scanty fare of vegetables– From Walden I went through the woods to Fair Haven–but by the way the rain came on again and my fates compelled me to stand a half hour under a pine–piling boughs over my head, and wearing my pocket handkerchief for an umbrella–and when at length I had made one cast over the pickerel weed, the thonder gan romblen in the Heven with that gristly steven, that Chaucer tells of–(the gods must be proud with such forked flashes and such artillery

to rout a poor unarmed fisherman) I made haste to the
nearest hut for a shelter. This stood a half a mile off the
road and so much the nearer to the pond– There dwelt a
shiftless Irishman John Field & his wife–and many
children from the broad faced boy that ran by his father's
side to escape the rain to the wrinkled & Sybil like
–crone-like infant, not knowing whether to take the part of
age or infancy that sat upon its father's knee as in the
palaces of nobles and looked out from its home in the
midst of wet and hunger inquisitively upon the stranger
with the privilege of infancy The young creature not
knowing but it might be the last of a line of kings instead
of John Fields poor starveling brat–or I should rather say
still knowing that it was the last of a noble line and the
hope and cynosure of the world. An Honest hard working
–but shiftless man plainly was John Field. And his wife
she too was brave to cook so many suceeding dinners in the
recesses of that lofty stove–with round greasy face and
bare breast–still thinking to improve her condition one
day–with the never absent mop in hand–and yet no effects
of it visible anywhere– The chickens like members of the
family stalked about the room–too much humanized to
roast well– They stood and looked in my eye or pecked at
my shoe– He told me his story–how hard he worked
bogging for a neighbor–at ten dollars an acre–and the use
of the land with manure for one year– And the little
broad faced son worked cheerfully at his fathers side the
while not knowing alas how poor a bargain he had made.
Living–John Field–alas–without arithmetic.– Failing to
live– Do you ever fish said I– Oh yes–I catch a mess
when I am lying by–good perch I catch– whats your
bait– I catch shiners with fish worms & bait the perch
with them.

You'd better go now John, said his wife with with
glistening hopeful face– But poor John Field disturbed
but a couple of fins while I was catching a fair string–&

he said it was his luck–and when he changed seats–luck
changed seats too.

Thinking to live by some derivative old country mode in
this primitive new country e.g. to catch perch–with
shiners.

I find an instinct in me conducting to a mystic spiritual
life–and also another–to a primitive savage life–

Toward evening–as the world waxes darker I am
permitted to see the woodchuck stealing across my path,
and tempted to seize and devour it. The wildest most
desolate scenes are strangely familiar to me

Why not live a hard and emphatic life? not to be
avoided–full of adventures and work! Learn much–in
it. travel much though it be only in these woods I
some-times walk across a field with unexpected expansion
and long-missed content–as if there were a field worthy
of me. The usual daily boundaries of life are dispersed
and I see in what field I stand.

When on my way this after noon shall I go down this
long hill in the rain to fish in the pond "I ask myself"–and
I say to my-self yes roam far–grasp life & conquer it–learn
much–& live– Your fetters are knocked off–you are really
free. Stay till late in the night–be unwise and daring– See
many men far and near–in their fields and cottages before
the sun sets–though as if many more were to be seen– And
yet each rencontre shall be so satisfactory and simple that
no other shall seem possible Do not repose every night as
villagers do– The noble life is continuous and
unintermitting At least, live with a longer radius– Men
come home at night only from the next field or
street–where their house hold echoes haunt–and their life
pines and is sickly because it breathes its own breath.
Their shadows morning & evening reach farther than
their daily steps. But come home from far–from ventures

& perils–from enterprise and discovery–& crusading–with faith and experience and character.

Do not rest much. Dismiss prudence–fear–conformity – Remember only–what is promised. Make the day light you and the night hold a candle–though you be falling from heaven to earth–"from morn to dewy eve a summer's day."

for Vulcan's fall occupied a day but our highest aspirations and performances fill but the interstices of time.

Are we not reminded in our better moments that we have been needlessly husbanding somewhat–perchance –our little God-derived capital–or title to capital guarding it by methods we know? but the most diffuse prodigality a better wisdom teaches–that we *hold* nothing–we are not what we were–

By usurers craft–by Jewish methods–we strive to retain and increase the divinity in us–when the greater part of divinity is out of us.

Most men have forgotten that it was ever morning– But a few serene memories–healthy & wakeful natures there are who assure us that the Sun rose clear, heralded by the singing of birds

This very day's sun which rose before memnon was ready to greet it.

In all the dissertations–on language–men forget the language that is–that is really universal–the inexpressible meaning that is in all things & every where with which the morning & evening teem. As if language were especially of the tongue. Of course with a more copious hearing or understanding–of what is published the present *languages* will be forgotten.

The rays which streamed through the crevices will be forgotten when the shadow is wholly removed.

Sunday Aug 24th 1845

Again I remember as I was leaving the Irish man's roof after the rain and bending my steps again to the shore of the lake–my haste to catch pickerel wading in retired meadows in sloughs & bog holes in forlorn and in savage places–seemed for an instant trivial to me who had been sent to school and college–but then in an instant–my genius said–from the western heaven–go fish & hunt far & wide day by day–and rest thee by many hearth-sides without misgiving– Rise free from care before the dawn, and seek adventures Let the noon find thee by other brooks–and the night over take thee every-where at home. Lead such a life as the children that chase butterflies in a meadow. There are no larger fields than these–no nobler games–no more extended earth. with thy life uninsured live free and forever as you were planted Grow wild and rank like these ferns and brakes–which study not morals nor philosophy. nor strive to become tame and cultivated grass for cattle to eat–these bull rushes–behind which yon the red evening sky over the lake–as if they were the masts of vessels in a crowded venice harbor. Let the thunder rumble in thy own tongue– What if it brings rain to farmer's crops that is not its errand to thee–take shelter under the cloud–while they fly to carts & sheds.

Enjoy thy dominion–and name anew the fowl and the quadruped and all creeping things Seek without toil thy daily food–thy sustenance–is it not in nature?

Through want of confidence in the gods men are where they are–buying and selling–*owning* land–following trades–and spending their lives ignobly.

{*Three-fourths page blank*}

Left house on account of Plastering wed. Nov. 12 at
night—returned sat. Dec 6th—

Man does not live long in this world without finding out
the comfort there is in a house the domestic comforts
—which originally belong to the house—more than
to the family. Man was not made so large limbed
and tough but that he must seek to narrow his world and
wall in a space such as fitted him. He found himself all
bare and out of doors (and out doors is there still, and has
remained all bare and unchanged, serene and wintry by
turns since Adam) and though this was pleasant enough
in serene and warm weather by day light—the rainy
seasons and the winters would perchance have nipped his
race in the bud—if he had not first of all clothed himself
with the shelter of a house of some kind. Adam and Eve
according to the fable wore the bower before other clothes.
Where is home—without a house?

Though the race is not so degenerated but A man
might possibly live in a cave today and keep himself
warm by furs Yet as caves and wild beasts are not plenty
enough to accommodate all at the present day—it were
certainly better to accept the advantages which the
invention and industry of mankind offer.

In thickly settled civilized communities boards &
shingles lime & brick are cheaper and more easily come at
than suitable caves.— or the whole logs or bark in
sufficient quantity—or even clay or flat stones.

A tolerable house for a rude and hardy race that lived
much out of doors was once made here without any of
these materials. According to the testimony of the first
settlers of Boston an Indian wigwam was as comfortable
in winter as an English house with all its wainscoting.
And they had advanced so far, as to regulate the effect of
the wind by a mat suspended over the hole in the roof,
which was moved by a string.

Such a lodge was in the first instance erected in a day
or two and every family had one–and taken down and put
up again in a few hours.

Thus (to try our civilization by a fair test) in the ruder
states of society every family owns a shelter as good as
the best–and sufficient for its ruder and simpler
wants–but in modern civilized society–though the birds
of the air have their nests and woodchucks and foxes
their holes–though each one is commonly the owner of
his coat and hat though never so poor–yet not more than
one man in a thousand owns a shelter–

but the 999 pay an annual tax for this outside garment
of all–indispensable summer and winter which would buy
a village of Indian wigwams and contributes to keep
them poor as long as they live.

But, answers one, by simply paying this annual tax the
poorest man secures an abode which is a palace compared
to the Indian's. An annual rent of from 20 to 60 or 70
dollars entitle him to the benefit of all the improvements
of centuries. Rumford fire place–Back plastering–Venitian
blinds–copper pump Spring lock–&c &c–

But while civilization has been improving our houses
she has not equally improved the men who should occupy
them. She has created palaces but it was not so easy to
create noblemen and kings– The mason who finishes the
cornice of the palace returns at night perchance to a hut
no better than a wigwam.

If She claims to have made a real advance in the
welfare of man–she must show how she has produced
better dwellings without making them more costly– And
the cost of a thing it will be remembered is the amount
of life it requires to be exchanged for it. An average house
costs perhaps 1500 dollars and to earn this sum will
require from 15 to 20 years of the day-laborer's life even
if he is not incumbered with a family–so that he must

spend more than half his life before a wigwam can be earned– And if we suppose he he pays a rent instead this is but a doubtful choice of evils

Would the savage have been wise to exchange his wigwam for a palace on these terms?

When I consider my neighbors–the farmers of Concord for instance, who are at least as well off as the other classes, what are they about? For the most part I find that they have been toiling 10 20 or thirty years to pay for their farms and we set down one half of that toil to the cost of their houses, and commonly they have not yet paid for them.

This is the reason they are poor and for similar reasons we are are all poor in respect to a thousand savage comforts though surrounded by luxuries.

But most men do not know what a house is–and the mass are actually poor all their days because they think they must have such an one as their neighbors– As if one were to wear any sort of coat the tailor might cut out for him–or gradually leaving off palm leaf hat and cap of woodchuck skin should complain of hard times because he cannot by him a crown.–

{*One-fourth page blank*}

It reflects no little dignity on Nature–the fact that the Romans once inhabited her.– That from this same unaltered hill, forsooth, the Roman once looked out upon the sea–as from a signal station.

–The vestiges of military roads–of houses and tessellated courts and baths– Nature need not be ashamed of these relics of her children.– The heroes' cairn– One doubts at length whether his relations or nature herself raised the hill. The whole earth is but a hero's cairn.

How often are the Romans flattered by the Historian
and Antiquary   their vessels penetrated into this frith
and up that

> The Earth
> Which seems so barren once gave birth
> To heroes—who oerran her plains,
> Who plowed her seas and reaped her grains

—

river of some remote isle—their military monuments still
remain on the hills and under the sod of the valleys— The
oft repeated Roman story is written in still legible
characters in every quarter of the old world, and but today
a new coin is dug up which repeats or confirms their
fame. Some "Judaea Capta"—with silent arrgument and
demonstration puts at rest whole pages of history

{*One-fourth page blank*}

Some make the Mythology of the Greeks to have been
borrowed from that of the Hebrews—which however is not
to be proved by analogies—the story of Jupiter dethroning
his father Saturn, for instance from the conduct of Cham
towards his father Noah, and the division of the world
among the three brothers—
But the Hebrew fable will not bear to be contrasted with
the (Grecian (?). The latter is infinitely more sublime
and divine. The one is a history of mortals—the other a
history of gods & heroes—therefore not so ancient. The one
God of the Hebrews is not so much of a gentleman not so
gracious & divine not so flexible and Catholic does not
exert so intimate an influence on nature than many a one
of the Greeks. He is not less human though more absolute
and unapproachable

The Grecian were youthful and living gods–but still of godly–or divine race and had the virtues of gods– The Hebrew, had not all of the divinity that is in man–no real love for man–an inflexible justice

The attribute of the one god–has been infinite power –not grace–not humanity–nor love–even–wholly Masculine–with no sister Juno–no Apollo no Venus in him

I might say that the one God was not yet Apotheosized –not yet become the current material of poetry–

The Wisdom of some of those Greek fables is remarkable The God Apollo (Wisdom–Wit Poetry) condemned to serve–keep the sheep of *King* Admetus– So is poetry allied to the State

To AEacus Minos, Radamanthus, Judges in hell, only naked men came to be judged– As Alex. Ross comments "In this world we must not look for Justice; when we are stript of all, then shall we have it. For here something will be found about us that shall corrupt the Judge."

– When the island of AEgina was depopulated by sickness at the instance of AEacus Jupiter turned the ants into men–ie.–made men of the inhabitants who lived meanly like ants.

The hidden significance of these fables which has been detected–the ethics running parallel to the poetry and history–is not so remarkable–as the readiness with which they may be made to express any Truth They are the skeletons of still older and more universal truths than any whose flesh and blood they are for the time made to wear– It is like striving to make the sun & the wind and the sea signify the propositions of our day.

Piety–that carries its father on its shoulders.

Music was of 3 kinds–mournful–martial & effeminate –Lydian–Doric & Phrygian– Its inventors Amphion –Thamiras–& Marsias– Amphion was bred by shepherds. He caused the stones to follow him & built the walls of Thebes by his music– All orderly and harmonious or beautiful structures may be said to be raised to a slow music.

Harmony was begotten of Mars & venus.

Antaeus was the son of Neptune & the Earth– All physical bulk & strength is of the earth & mortal   when it loses this point d'appui it is weakness; it cannot soar. And so vice versa you can intepret this fable to the credit of the earth.

They all provoked or challenged the Gods–Amphion –Apollo & Diana and was killed by them– Thamiras the Muses who conquered him in music, took away his eyesight & melodious voice–and broke his lyre. Marsyas took up the flute which Minerva threw away–challenged Apollo–was flayed alive by him & his death mourned by Fauns Satyrs & Dryads whose tears produced the river which bears his name.

The fable which is truly and naturally composed–so as to please the imagination of a child–harmonious though strange like a wild flower–is to the wise man an apothegm and admits his wisest interpretation.

When we read that Bacchus made the Tyrrhenian mariners mad, so that they leapt into the sea mistaking it for "a meadow full of flowers", "and so became dolphins–we are not concerned about the historical truth of this, but rather a higher poetical truth. We seem to hear the music of a thought and care not if our intellect be not gratified

The mythologies–those vestiges of noble poems the
world's inheritance–still reflecting some of their original
hues–like the fragments of clouds tinted by the departed
sun–the wreck of poems–a retrospect as the loftiest
fames. Some fragment will still float into the latest
summer day–and ally this hour to the morning of creation.

They are materials and hints for a history of the rise
and progress of the race. How from the condition of ants
we arrived at the condition of men, how the arts were
invented gradually– Let a thousand surmises shed some
light on this history. We will not be confined by
historical–even geological periods–which would allow us
to doubt of a progress in human events– If we rise above
this wisdom for the day–we shall expect this morning of
the race–in which they have been supplied with the
simplest necessaries–with corn and wine and honey–and
oil–and fire–and articulate speech and agricultural and
other arts–reared up by degrees from the condition of ants
will be succeeded by a day of equally progressive
splendor–that in the lapse of gods summers–other divine
agents and godlike man will assist to elevate the race of
men as much above its present condition

Aristeus "found out honey and oil", "He obtained of
Jupiter and Neptune, that the pestilential heat of the dog
days, wherein was great mortality, should be mitigated
with wind."

Friday Dec 12th 1845 the pond skimmed over on the
night of this day–excepting a strip from the bar to the
N.W. shore Flint's pond has been frozen for some time.

16th 17th 18th 19th 20th Pond *quite free* from ice–not
yet having been frozen quite over.

Tuesday Dec 23d
The pond froze over last night entirely for the first
time, yet so as not to be safe to walk upon.

{*One-third page blank*}
{*Three leaves missing*}

I wish to say something tonight not of and concerning the Chinese and Sandwich Islanders as *to* and concerning those who hear me–who are said to live in New England. Something about your condition–especially your outward condition or circumstances in this world–in this town. what it is–whether it is necessarily as bad as it is–whether it can't be improved as well as not.

It is generally admitted that some of you are poor find it hard to get a living–haven't always something in your pockets, haven't paid for all the dinners you've actually eaten–or all your coats and shoes–some of which are already worn out. All this is very well known to all of you by hearsay and by experience.

It is very evident what–a mean and sneaking life you live always in the hampers–always on the limits–trying to get into business–and trying to get out of debt–a very ancient slough called by the Latins aes alienum anothers brass–some of their coins being made of brass–and still so many living and dying and buried today by anothers brass–always promising to pay–promising to pay–with interest tomorrow perhaps and die–to day–insolvent.

Seeking to curry favor to get custom–lying–flattering voting–contracting yourselves into a nutshell of civility–or dilating into a world of thin and vaporous generosity–that you may persuade your neighbor–to let you make his

{*Nineteen leaves missing*}
{*One-fifth page missing*}

him to be–that these "Letters & Speeches" now for the first time we might say–brought to to light–edited–& published together with the elucidations, have restored unity and the wanting moral grandeur to his life. So that we can now answer for ourselves and others wherefore–, by what means, and in what sense he came to be protector in England.

We learn that his actions are to be judged of as those of a man who had a steady religious purpose unparalled in the line of kings Of a remarkable common sense and practicalness yet joined with such a divine madness, though

{*One-fifth page missing*}

There is a civilization going on among brutes as well as men– Foxes are *Indian* dogs. I hear one barking raggedly, wildly demoniacally in the darkness to night–seeking expression laboring with some anxiety–striving to be a dog–struggling for light. He is but a faint man–before pigmies–an imperfect–burrowing man.– Goules are also misformed, unfortunate men. He has come up near to my window attracted by the light, and barked a vulpine curse at me–then retreated.

{*Six leaves missing*}

Reading suggested by Hallam's Hist. of Literature.

1 Abelard & Heloise

2 Look at Luigi Pulci–his Morgante Maggiore (published in 1481 "was to the poetical romances of chivalry what Don Quixote was to their brethren in prose."

3 Lionardo da Vinci–the most remarkable of his writings still in manuscript–for his universality of Genius–"the first name of the 15th century."

4 Read Boiardo's Orlando Innamorato–published between 1491–& 1500–for its influence on Ariosto–and its intrinsic merits– Its sounding names repeated by Milton in Paradise Regained

{*One-fourth page blank*}

Landor's works are
1st A small volume of poems 1793 out of print
next Poems of "Gebir" "Chrysaor", the "Phocaeans" &c
 The "Gebir" eulogized by Southey & Coleridge
 Wrote verses in Italian & Latin.
 The dramas "Andrea of Hungary" "Giovanna of Naples"
  and "Fra Rupert."
 "Pericles & Aspasia"
 "Poems from the Arabic & Persian" 1800 pretending to
  be translations.
 "A Satire upon Satirists, and Admonition to Detractors"
  printed 1836 not published
 Letters called "High & Low Life in Italy"
 "Imaginary Conversations"
 "Pentameron & Pentalogia"
 "Examination of William Shakspeare before Sir
  Thomas Lucy, Knt., touching Deer-stealing."

{*One-fourth page blank*}

Vide again Richard's sail in "Rich. 1st & the Abbot"
 Phocion's remarks in conclusion of "Eschines &
  Phocion"
 "Demosthenes & Eubulides"
In Milton & Marvel speaking of the Greek poets–he says
 "There is a sort of refreshing odor flying off it
perpetually; not enough to oppress or to satiate; nothing
is beaten or bruised; nothing smells of the stalk; the flower
itself is half-concealed by the Genius of it hovering
round."
 Pericles & Sophocles
 Marcus Tullius Cicero & his Brother Quinctus in this
a sentence on Sleep and Death.
 Johnson & Tooke for a criticism on words.

{*Three-fifths page blank*}

It is worth the while to have lived a primitive wilderness
life at some time–to know what are after all the
necessaries of life–and what methods society has taken to
supply them– I have looked over the old day Books of the
merchants with the same view to see what it was that
men bought– They are the grossest groceries–salt is
perhaps the most important article of all.– most
commonly bought at the stores. Of articles commonly
thought to be necessaries–salt–sugar–molasses–cloth &c
by the Farmer.– You will see why stores or shops
exist / not to furnish tea and coffee–but salt &c   here's
the rub then.

{*One-fifth page blank*}

Have you seen my hound sir– I want to know What
–Lawyer's office–law Books if you've seen anything of a
hound about here– why, what do you do here? I live
here. no I have'nt   haven't you heard one In the woods
anyplace O yes I heard one this morning– What do you
do here– but he was someway off– Which side did he
seem to be– Well I should think here this other side of
the pond.– This is a large dog makes a large track–he's
been out hunting from Lexington for a week. How long
have you lived here– Oh about a year Some body said
there was a man up here had a camp in the woods
somewhere and he'd got him Well I dont know of any
body– There's Brittons camp over on the other road– It
may be there– Is'nt there anybody in these woods– Yes
they are chopping right up here behind me– how far is
it– only a few steps–hark a moment–there dont you hear
the sound of their axes.
    Therien the wood chopper was here yesterday–and
while I was cutting wood some chicadees hopped near
pecking the bark and chips and the potatoe skins I had
thrown out– What do you call them he asked– I told

him–what do *you* call them asked I– *Mezezence* I think
he said. When I eat my dinner in the woods said he sitting
very still having kindled a fire to warm my coffee–they
come and light on my arm and peck at the potatoe in my
fingers– I like to have the little fellers about me–

Just then one flew up from the snow and perched on the
wood I was holding in my arms and pecked it and looked
me familiarly in the face. Chica-a-dee–dee-dee-dee-dee,
–while others were whistling phebe–phe-bee–in the woods
behind the house.

{Three-fifths page blank}

"It is related that the ancient Loeri, a people of Greece,
were so charmed with the sound of the Cicada, that they
erected a statue to its honor."

Davis' notes to Morton's Memorial.

The Dutch of Surinam call it the Lyre-player.   Ibid.

{One-fourth page blank}

March 26th 1846

The change from foul weather to fair from danck
sluggish hours to serene elastic ones is a memorable
crisis which all things proclaim.

The change from foulness to serenity is instantaneous.
Suddenly an influx of light though it was late filled my
room– I looked out and saw that the pond was already
calm and full of hope as on a summer evening–though the
ice was dissolved but yesterday– There seemed to be some
intelligence in the pond which responded to the unseen
serenity in a distant horizon I heard a robin in the
distance the first I had heard this spring repeating the
assurance The green pitch suddenly looked brighter and
more erect as if now entirely washed & cleansed by the
rain.

I knew it would not rain any more. A serene summer
evening sky seemed darkly reflected in the pond–though
the clear sky was no where visible over head. It was no
longer the end of a season but the beginning– The pines
& shrub oaks which had before drooped and cowered the
winter through with myself–now recovered their several
characters and in the landscape revived the expression of
an immortal beauty– Trees seemed all at once to be fitly
grouped–to sustain new relations to men & to oneanother
– There was somewhat cosmical in the arrangement
of nature. O the evening robin–at the closse of a
New England day– If I could ever find the twig he sits upon.

Where does the minstrel really roost. We perceive it is
not the bird of the ornithologist that is heard–the *turdus
migratoria*? The signs of fair weather are seen in the
bosom of ponds before they are recognised in the
heavens It is easy to tell by looking at any twig of the
forest whether its winter is past–or not.

We forget how the sun looks on our fields as on the
forests & the prairies–as they reflect or absorb his ray. It
matters not whether we stand in Italy or on the prairies of
the west, in the eye of the sun the earth is all equally
cultivated like a garden–and yields to the wave of an
irresistible civilization.

My beans this brod field which I have looked on so long
looks not to me as the farmer– These beans have results
which are not harvested in the autumn of the year.

Our grain fields make part of a beautiful picture which
the sun beholds in his daily course– And it matters little
comparatively whether they fill the barns of the
husbandman The true husbandman will cease from
anxiety & labor with every day and relinquish all claim
to the produce of his fields.

The avaricious man would fain plant by himself–

A flock of geese have just got in late from the Canada
line, now in the dark flying low over the pond They came

on, indulging at last like weary travellers in complaint &
consolations, or like some creaking Evening mail late
lumbering in with regular anserine clangor I stood at my
door and could hear their wings when they suddenly
spied my light & ceasing their noise wheeled to the East
and apparently settled in the pond.

27th

This morning I saw the geese from my door through
the mist sailing about in the middle of the pond—but
when I went to the shore they rose and circled round like
ducks over my head so that I counted them 29 I after
saw 13 ducks.

[Walden 2]

SUMMER 1845–FEBRUARY 1846

distant capes. perhaps he thinks there may be neighbors still–since there used to be.

to the frequented curb where you see your long forgotten–unshaven faces–at the bottom–in juxtaposition with new made butter & the trout in the well. I repeat it that if men will believe it–there are no more quiet Tempes or more poetic & Arcadian life than may be lived in these New E. dwellings– It seemed as if their employment by day would be to tend the flowers & herds–and at night like the shepherds of old to cluster & gives names to the stars.

I could not imagine what they would be doing these summer nights–but giving names to the stars from the banks of the Merrimack. And in the middle of the sunny days they would converse with the flowers & the bees

> What doth he ask?
> Some worthy task.
> Never to run
> Till that be done,
> And that never done
> Under the sun.
> Here to begin
> All things to win
> By his endeavor
> Forever and ever–
> Happy and well
> On this ground to dwell
> This soil subdue
> Plant and renew.
> By might & main
> Health & strength gain
> So to give nerve
> To his slenderness

Some mighty pain
He would sustain.
So to preserve
His tenderness.
Not be deceived
Of suffring bereaved
Not lose his life
By living too well
Not escape strife
In his lonely cell
And so find out Heaven
By not knowing Hell.
Strength like the rock
To withstand any shock–
Yet some Aaron's rod
Some smiting by god
To open his veins
And increase his gains–
Occasion to gain
To shed a few tears
And sometimes to entertain
Still divine fears.
Not once for all, forever, blest,
Still to be cheered out of the east
Not from his heart to banish all sighs
Still be encouraged by the suns rise
Forever to love And to love and to love
Within him, around him–beneath him above
To love is to know, is to feel, is to be.
At once 'tis our birth & our destiny
Having sold all
Something would get–
Furnish his stall
With better yet–
For earthly pleasures
Celestial pains
Heavenly losses
For earthly gains.
Still to begin–unheard of sin
A fallen angel–a risen man
Never returns to where he began.
Some child like labor
Here to perform
Some baby house

To keep out the storm
Which will make the sun laugh
While he doth warm—
And the moon cry
To think of her youth—
Of the months gone by—
 And wintery truth.

How long to morning?
Can any tell?
How long since the warning
On our ears fell
We know very well.
Are we not ready
Our packet made
Our hearts steady
Last words said
Must we still eat
The bread we have spurned
Must we rekindle
The faggots we've burned—
 Must we go out
 By the poor man's gate
 Die by degrees
 Not by new fate.
Is there no road
This way my friend
Is there no road
Without any end—
Have you not seen
In ancient times
Pilgrims go by here
Toward other climes
With shining faces
Lusty and strong
Mounting this hill
With speech & song?
Oh my good sir
I know not the ways
Little my knowledge
Though many my days.
 When I have slumbered
 I have heard sounds
 As of travellers passing

Over my grounds–
Unless I have dreamed it
This was of yore–
Though I never told it
To mortal before–
I did not fear for my pulse or my grain
What the Lord gave man
He took again–
Twas a sweet music
Wafted them by
I could not tell
If far off or nigh.
Never remembered
But in my dreams
What to me waking
A miracle seems
If you will give of your pulse or your grain
We will rekindle those flames again
Here will we tarry still without doubt
Till a miracle putteth that fire out.

{Four leaves missing}

Frequent the church & schools–the courts & marts
And multiply supplies from near & far.

At midnight's hour I raised my head
The owls were seeking for their bread
The foxes barked impatient still
At their mean fate they bear so ill–
I thought me of eternities delayed
And of commands but half obeyed–
The night wind rustled through the glade
As if a force of men there staid
The word was whispered through the ranks
And every hero seized his lance
The word was whispered through the ranks
   Advance.

To live to a good old age such as the ancients
reached–serene and contented–dignifying the life of
man– Leading a simple epic country life–in these days of

confusion and turmoil– That is what Wordsworth has done– Retaining the tastes and the innocence of his youth– There is more wonderful talent–but nothing so cheering and world famous as this.

The life of man would seem to be going all to wrack & pieces And no instance of permanence–and the ancient natural health–notwithstanding Burns–& Coleridge–& Carlyle– It will not do for men to die young–the greatest Genius does not die young– Whome the gods love most–do indeed die young, but not till their life is matured–and their years are like those of the oak– For they are the products half of nature and half of god– What should nature do without old men–not children but men.

The life of men not to become a mockery and a jest–should last a respectable term of years– We cannot span the ages of those old Greek Philosophers.

They live long who do not live for a near end–who still forever look to the immeasurable future for their manhood.

All dramas have but one scene   there is but one stage–for the peasant–and for the actor and both on the farm and in the theatre the curtain rises to reveal the same majestic scenery. The globe of earth is poised in space for his stage under the foundations of the theatre– And the cope of heaven out of reach of the scene shifter over arches it. It is always to be remembered by the critic that all actions are to be regarded from a distance at last as performed upon some rood of earth–and amid the operations of nature.

Rabelais too inhabited the soil of France in sunshine & shade in those years.– And his life was no "farce" after all.

> I seek the present time
> No other clime,

Life in today–
Easy it is to sail another way–
To Paris or Rome
Or farther from home–
That man whoeer he is
Lives but a moral death
Whose spirit's not coeval
With his breath.
My feet forever stand
On Concord fields
And I must live the life
Which this soil yields
What are deeds done
    Away from home
What the best essay
    On the Ruins of Rome.
The love of the new
The unfathomed blue
The wind in the wood
And all future good
The sun lit tree
And the small chicadee
The dusty highways
What scripture says
This pleasant weather
And all else together
The river's meander
All things in short
Forbid me to wander
In act or in thought
In cold or in drouth
I would not seek the south
But of the sunny present hours
I would make the tour

For here if thou should'st fail
Where couldst thou prevail
If you love not
Your own land most
You'll find nothing lovely
On a distant coast.
If you love not
The latest sun set

What is there in pictures
Or old gems set
If no man should travel
Till he had the means
There'd be little travelling
For kings or for Queens
The means what are they
life got, and some to spare
Great works on hand
& freedom from care.
They are the wherewithal
   Great expenses to pay
   Plenty of time well spent
   To use
   Clothes well earned and no rent
   In your shoes
   Something to eat
   And something to burn
   And above all no need to return.
   For they who come back
   Say have they not failed
   However they've ridden
   & steamed it & sailed?

   All your grass hay'd
   All your debts paid
   All your wills made
   Then you might as well have stay'd
   For are you not dead
   Only not buried?
The way unto "today"
The rail road to "here"
They never'll grade that way
Nor shorten it, I fear.
There are plenty of depots
All the world oer
But not a single station
At a man's door—
If I would get near
To the secret of things
I shall not have to hear
When the engine bell rings

Exageration–was ever any virtue attributed to a man
without exaggeration–was ever any vice–without infinite
exagggeration? Do we not exaggerate ourselves to
ourselves–or Do we often recognise ourselves for the
actual men we are– The lightning is an exaggeration of
light. We live by exaggeration Exaggerated history is
poetry–and is truth referred to a new standard. To a
small man every greater one is an exaggeration. No truth
was ever expressed but with this sort of emphasis–so that
for the time there was no other truth. The value of what is
really valuable can never be exaggerated. You must speak
loud to those who are hard of hearing–so you acquire a
habit of speaking loud to those who are not. In order to
appreciate any even the humblest man–you must not only
understand but you must first love him– And there never
was such an exaggerator as love– Who are we   are we
not all of us great men And yet what actually– Nothing
certainly to speak of– By an immense exaggeration we
appreciate our Greek–Poetry–& Philosophy–Egyptian
Ruins–our shakspears & Miltons our liberty & christianity.
We give importance to this hour over all other hours– We
do not live by justice–but

{Two-thirds page missing}

{MS torn} different *{MS torn}*ses. Love never perjures
itself. Nor is it mistaken.

He is not the great writer–who is afraid to let the world
know that he ever committed an impropriety– Does it not
know that all men are mortal–? I dont

{Two-thirds page missing}

Carlyle told R.W.E. that he first discovered that he was
not a Jack ass on reading Tristram Shandy–& Rousseau's

Confessions especially the last— his first essay is an ariticle
in Fraser's Magazine on two boys' quarreling

{*Three leaves missing*}

Youth wants something to look up to–to look forward
to— As the little boy who enquired of me the other day
– How long do those Old-agers live? and expressed
the intention of compassing 200 summers at least The
old man who cobbles shoes without glasses at a hundred
and cuts a handsome swarth at a hundred and five–is
indispensible to give dignity & respectability to our life

{*Three-fifths page missing*}

is a receded Splendor–forever memorable–and shedding
still reflected light on all his scenes.
    Blacksmiths, though stout stalwart and tough–I should
not call the healthiest of men There is too much sweat
and puffing–too great extremes of heat & cold–and
incessant ten pound ten & thrashing of {*MS torn*} The

{*Three-fifths page missing*}
{*Fourteen leaves missing*}

of Genius are embalmed the souls of heroes
    But if Carlyle does not take two steps in philosophy–are
there any who take three? Philosophy having creeped
clinging to the path so far puts out its feelers many ways
in vain.

    From all points of the compass from the earth beneath
and the heavens above have come these inspirations and
been entered duly in such order as they came in the
Journal. Thereafter when the time arrived they were
winnowed into Lectures–and again in due time from
Lectures into Essays– And at last they stand like the

cubes of Pythagoras firmly on either basis–like statues on their pedestals–but the statues rarely take hold of hands– There is only such connexion and series as is attainable in the galleries. And this affects their immediate practical & popular influence.

Carlyle we should say more conspicuously than any other represents though with little enough expressed or even conscious sympathy–the Reformer class– In him the universal plaint is most settld most reasonable & serious Until the thousand named and nameless grievances are righted there will be no repose for him in the lap–of nature–or the seclusion of Science and literature.

And all the more for not being the visible leader of any class

There is no prolonged contemplation of the manifold life of man– There is no philosophy–properly speaking of Love or Friendship–or Religion or politics or Education–or nature

{*Four leaves missing*}
{*One-third page missing*}

{*MS torn*} started his {*MS torn*}

Consider the endless tide of speech–forever flowing in countless cellars garrets–*parlors*– that of the French says Carlyle "only ebbs towards the short hours of night." and what a drop in the bucket is the printed word.

Feeling–thought–speech–writing–how they gradually dwindle passing through successive colanders– But this writer reports more of the speech of man than any others–how they all dwindle at length

{*One-third page missing*}

All places, all positions–all things in short are a medium
happy or unhappy. Every Realm has its centre and the
nearer to that the better while you are in it– Even health
is only the happiest of all mediums   there may be excess
or there may be deficiency–in either case there is disease.
A man must only be *virtuous* enough.

I went over to neighbor Hugh Quoil's the waterloo
soldier–the Colonels house the other day. He lay lately
dead at the foot of the hill–the house locked up–and wife
at work in town but before key reaches padlock or news
wife–another door is unlocked for him and news is
carried farther than to wife in town–

In his old house–an "unlucky castle now" pervious to
wind & snow–lay his old clothes his outmost cuticle curled
up by habit as it were like himself upon his raised plank
bed. One black chicken still goes to roost lonely in the
next apartment–stepping silent over the floor–frightened
by the sound of its own wings–never–croaking–black as
night and silent too, awaiting reynard–its God actually
dead.

And in his garden never to be harvested where corn and
beans and potatoes had grown tardily unwillingly as if
foreknowing that the planter would die– –how how
luxurious the weeds–cockles and burs stick to your
clothes, and beans are hard to find–corn never got its
first hoeing

I never was much acquainted with Hugh Quoil–the
Ditcher dubbed Colonel sometime–killed a Colonel in
some war and rode off his horse? Soldier at Waterloo–son
of Erin. though sometimes I met him in the path, and
can vouch for it that he verily lived and was once an
inhabitant of this earth–fought toiled joyed sorrowed
drank–experienced life and at length Death–and do
believe that a solid shank bone or skull which no longer
aches lie somewhere and can still be produced which

once with garment of flesh and broad-cloth were called and
hired to do work as Hugh Quoil.

I say I have met him–got and given the nod–as when
man meets man and not ghost– At distance seemingly a
ruddy face as of cold biting January–but nearer–clear
bright carmine with signs of inward combustion It would
have made the ball of your finger burn to touch his cheek
–with sober reflecting eye that had seen other sights.
Straight-bodied snuff colored coat long familiar with him,
he with it, axe or turf knife in hand–no sword nor firelock
now–fought his battles through still but did not conquer
–on the Napoleon side at last–and exiled to this
st Helena Rock– A man of manners–gentleman like–who
had seen this world–more civil speech than you could
well attend to.

He and I at length came to be neighbors not speaking
nor ever visiting hardly seeing neighbors–but nearest
inhabitants mutually.

He was thirstier than I–drank more–probably–but not
out of the pond– It was never the lower for him–perhaps
I ate more than he. The last time I met him the only time
I spoke with him it was at the foot of the hill in the
highway where I was crossing to the spring one warm
afternoon in summer–the pond water being too warm for
me– I was crossing pail in hand–when Quoil came down
the hill still in snuff colored coat as last winter–shivering
as with cold rather with heat–delirium tremens they
name it– I greeted him and told him my errand to get
water at the spring close by only at the foot of the hill over
the fence– he answered with stuttering parched lips
–bloodshot eye–staggering gesture–he'd like to see
it– Follow me there then. But I had got my pail full and
back before he scaled the fence– And he drawing his coat
about him to warm him to cool him answered in delirium
tremens–hydrophobia dialect not easy to be written here
he'd heard of it but had never seen it–and so shivered his

way along toward the town–not to work there nor transact special business–but to get whack at a sweet remote hour to liquor & to oblivion.

Sundays–and even on days of the moon and consecrated to other gods sons of Erin and of New England crossed my bean field with jugs or with unstoppled mouths as capacious–toward Quoil's– But what for?– did they sell rum there? "Respectable people they" know no harm of them" "never heard that they drank too much" is the answer of all wayfarers

Travellers went sober stealthy silent–skulking–no harm to get elm bark sundays–return loquacious sociable, having long intended to call on you.

At length one afternoon Hugh Quoil feeling better, with snuff-colored coat–has paced solitary soldier look not forgetting waterloo along the woodland road to the foot of the hill by the spring–and there the fates meet him–and throw him down in his snuff-colored coat on the grass–and get ready to cut his thread–but not till travellers pass–who would raise him up–get him perpendicular–then settle – – lay me down says Hugh hoarsely– House locked–key –in pocket–wife in town–and the the fate cuts–and there he lies by the way side–5 feet 10–looking taller than in life–.

He had half contemplated a harvest much corn and many beans–but that strange trembling of the limbs delayed the hoeing.

–Skin of woodchuck just stretched never to be cured–no cap no mittens wanted. Pipe on hearth no more to be lighted–best buried with him

He tells us wisely whom & what to mark–saving much time.

Only the convalescent are conscious of the health of nature.

No thirst for glory, only for strong drink.

He has gone away–his house house here "all tore to pieces" he will not come back this way– But how it fares with him whether his thirst is quenched–whether there is still some semblance of that carmine cheek–struggles still with some liquid demonic spirit–perchance on more equal terms–till he drinks him up I cannot by any means learn.

–What his salutation is now what his January morning face what he thinks of waterloo what start he has gained or lost what work still for the ditcher & forester and soldier now– There is no evidence. He was here the likes of him for a season standing in his shoes like a faded gentleman–with gesture almost learned in drawing rooms– Wore clothes hat shoes–made ditches felled wood–did farm work for various people kindled fires–worked enough–ate enough–drank too much. He was one of those unnamed countless sects of philosophers–who founded no school.

—

Poor John Frost he has let go the anchor in the Fair Haven mud even now perchance and sits there with his shiner bait & his alder rod to see what his luck will be this time.

His horizon all his own none to intrude–and yet he a poor man–born to be poor.

I asked for water hoping to get a sight of the well bottom–but there alas are shallow quick sands–and rope broken bucket irrecoverable– Meanwhile the right culinary vessel is selected–water is distilled and passed out to the thirsty one–not yet suffered to cool not yet to settle–such gruel sustains life here   exclude these motes and those by a skilful undercurrent–and drink responsive to genuine hospitality a hearty brave draught. John Frost with his inherited Erse poverty or poor life his Adams grandmother–and boggy ways–not to rise in this world he or his posterity till their wading webbed feet get talaria light membranous wings.

In case of an embargo there will be found to be old clothes enough in every body's garrett to last till the millenium–

We are fond of news novelties new things– The bank bill that is torn in two will pass if you save the pieces, if you have only got the essential piecce with the signatures Lowell & Manchester and Fall river think you will let go its broad cloth currency when it is torn–but hold on have an eye to the signature clout the back of it–and endorse the mans name from whom you received it– And they will be the first to fail and find nothing at all in their garretts– Every day our garments become more assimilated to the man that wears them– More near and dear to us and not finally to be laid aside but with such delay and medical appliance & solemnity as our other mortal coil We know after all but few men a great many coats and breeches– dress a scare crow with your last shift you standing shiftless by–who would not soonest address the scarecrow and salute it?

King James loved his old shoes best– Who does not? Indeed these new clothes are won and worn only after a painful birth   at first moveable prisons oyster shells which the tide only raises opens and shuts–washing in what nutriment may be– Men walk on the limits–carrying their limits with them–in the stocks they stand, not without gaze of multitudes only without rotten eggs–in old torturing boots. the last wedge but one driven.

–Why should we be startled at death–life is constant putting off of the mortal coil– Coat–cuticle–flesh and bones all old clothes–

Not till the prisoner has got some rents in his prison walls possibility of egress without lock and key some

day–result of steel watch spring on iron grate–will he rest
contented in his prison

Clothes brought in sewing–a kind of work you may
call endless

A man who has at length found out something
important to do will not have to get a new suit to do it
in–for him the old will do lying dusty in the garrett–for
an indefinite period– Old shoes will serve a hero–longer
than they have served his valet–bare feet are the oldest
of shoes–and he can make them do– Only they who go
to legislatures and soirees they must have new coats–coats
to turn as often as the man turns in them. Whoever saw
his old shoes his old coat actually worn out–returned to
their original elements–so that it were not a deed of
charity to bestow them on some poorer boy.– and by him
to be bestowed on some poorer still–or shall we say on
some richer who can do with less

Over eastward of my bean field lived Cato Ingraham
slave–born slave perhaps of Duncan Ingraham Esqr
–gentleman of Concord village–who built him a house and
gave him permission to live in Walden woods– –and
then on the N E corner Zilpha–colored woman of
fame–and down the road on the right hand Bristow
–colored man–on Bristow's hill–where grow still those little
wild apples he tended now large trees but still wild–and
farther still you come to Breeds location and again on the
left by well and roadside Hilda lived Farther up the road
at the ponds end Wyeman the potter who furnished his
towns men earthen ware–the squatter–

Now only a dent in the earth marks the site of most of
those human dwellings–sometimes the well dent where a
spring oozed now dry and tearless grass–or covered deep
not to be discovered till late days by accident with a flat
stone under the sod.

These dents like deserted fox burrows old holes. Where once was the stir and bustle of human life over head and man's destiny—fate free will foreknowledge absolute were all by turns discussed— Cato and Bristow pulled wool— Universally a thirsty race. drank of the ton—only the strongest of waters—

Still grows the vivacious lilack for a generation after the last vestige else is gone—unfolding still its early sweet-scented blossoms in the spring to be plucked only by the musing traveller planted tended nursed watered by children's hands—in front yard plot— Now by wall side in retired pasture, or giving place to a new rising forest.

The last of that stirp sole survivor of that family little did the children think that this weak slip with its two eyes which they watered—would root itself so—and out live them—and house in the rear that shaded it—and grown man's garden & field.— and tell their story to the retired wanderer a half century after they were no more —blossoming as fair smelling as sweet—as in that first spring—

Its still cheerful—tender—civil lilack colors

The woodland road though once more dark and shut in by the forest—resounded with the laugh and gossip of inhabitants—and was notched and dotted here and there with their little dwellings Though now but a rapid passage to neighboring villages or the woodmans team it once delayed the traveller longer—and was a lesser village in itself—

You still hear from time to time the whinnering of the raccoon still living as of old in hollow trees washing its food before it eats it—the red fox barks at night The loon comes in the fall to sail and bathe in the pond—making the woods ring with its wild laughter in the early morning— At rumor of whose arrival all Concord sportsmen are on the alert in gigs on foot two by two

three with patent rifles–patches conical balls–spy glass
or pin hole on the barrel–they seem already to hear the
loon laugh–these on this side those on that for the poor
loon cannot be omnipresent   if he dive here must come
up somewhere– The october wind rises rustling the
leaves–ruffling the pond water–so that no loon can be
seen ruffling the surface– Our sportsmen sweep the pond
with spy glass in vain–for the loon went off in that
morning rain with one loud long hearty laugh–and our
sportsmen must beat a retreat to town & stable and daily
routine–

Or in the grey dawn the sleeper hears the long ducking
gun explode over toward goose pond and hastening to
the door sees the remnant of a flock black-duck–or teal–go
whistling by with out stretched neck with broken ranks
but in ranger order– –

And the silent hunter emerges into the carriage road
with ruffled feathers at his belt–from the dark pond side
where he has lain in his bower since the stars went out.

And for a week you hear the circling clamor clangor
of some solitary goose through the fog–seeking its mate
–peopling the woods with a larger life there than they
can hold.

For hours you shall watch the ducks cunningly tack
and veer and hold the middle of the pond far from the
sportsman on the shore–tricks they have learned and
practised in far Canada lakes or in Louisiana bayous.

The waves rise & dash taking sides with all waterfowl.

Then in dark winter mornings in short winter
afternoons the pack of hounds–threading all woods with
hounding cry & yelp unable to resist the instinct of the
chace–and note of hunting horn at intervals showing that
man too is in the rear– And the woods ring again and
yet no fox bursts forth onto the open level of the pond
and no following pack after their actaeon.

But this small village–germ of something more–why
did it fail while Concord grows apace– No natural
advantages–no water privilege–only the Walden pond
and Bristow's spring privileges alas all unimproved by
those men but to dilute their glass– Might not the basket
making–broom mat-making corn parching–potters
business have thrived here making the wilderness to
blossom as the rose? Now all too late for commerce–this
waste depopulated district has its rail road too. And
transmitted the names of Bristows Catoes Hildas Zilphas
to a remote and grateful posterity–

Again nature will try–with me for a first settler–and
my house to be the oldest in the settlement.

The sterile soil would have been proof against any
lowland degeneracy.

Farmers far and near call it the Paradise of beans

And here too on winter days while yet is cold January
and snow and ice lie thick comes the prudent foreseeing
land lord or housekeeper from the village to get ice–to
cool his summer-drink–a grateful beverage if he should
live, if time should endure so long– How few so wise so
industrious to lay up treasures which neither rust nor
melt–"to cool their summer drink" one day

And cart off the solid pond the element and air of
fishes held fast with chain & stake like corded wood–all
through winter air to wintery cellar.– to underlie the
summer there. And cut and saw the cream of the
pond–unroof the house of fishes.

And in early mornings come men with fishing reels and
slender lunch–men of real faith and let down their fine
lines & live minnows through the snowy field to hook the
pickerel & perch.

With buried well stones & strawberries raspberries
thimbleberries growing there–some pitchy pine or gnarled

oak in the chimney nook or the sweet scented black birch where the hearth was.

Breeds—history must not yet tell the tragedies enacted there—let time intervene to assuage—and lend an azure tint to them.

There is something pathetic in the sedentary life of men who have travelled. They must naturally die when they leave the road.

{*One-third page blank*}

From Gilfillan's Sketches of Eminent Literary Men" I learn that Carlyle "was born at Ecclefechan, Anandale of parents who were "good farmer people" father of "strong native sense"

Father dead mother still lives.

"Intimate with Ed. Irving" from previous to his college life till the former's death.

At college had to "support himself" partly by "private tuition, translations, for the booksellers" &c.—corresponded with Goethe till the latter's death.—

Destined for the church.—

"Taught an academy in Dysart, at the same time that Irving was teaching in Kirkaldy" after marriage "resided partly at Comely Bank Edinburg; and for a year or two at Craigenputtock, a wild and solitary farm house in the upper part of Dumfriesshire" among barren heather-clad hills. here visited by our Countryman Emerson who passed one day with him. His conversation "coming to its climaxes, ever and anon, in long, deep, chest-shaking bursts of laughter"

"An amicable centre for men of the most opposite opinions".

"Smoking his perpetual pipe"

"listened to as an oracle"

"come to see our Scholmaster, who had also been his"
     The poet Stirling his only intimate acquaintance latterly
in England.

{*One leaf missing*}

up the soil—or that there is a "Brest Shipping" that now at
length only after some years of this revolution there
should be some falling off in the importation of sugar— I
am strangely surprised— Perhaps I had thought they
sweetened their coffee? their water? with Revolution still.
     We want one or two chapters out of some English or
German Almanac at least—headed "work for the
month"— Including Revolution work of course— Altitude
of the sun"—"State of the Crops" "State of the markets"
"Meteorological observations" "Attractive Industry" "Day
labor" just to remind the reader that the French
peasantry—did something beside go without breeches
—burning chateaus, or getting ready knotted cords—embrace
& throttle one another ie we want not only a back ground
and a fore ground to the picture—but literally a ground
under the feet also.
     An omission common to most epics—a want of epic
integrity

     What seems so fair and poetic in antiquity—almost
fabulous—is realized too in Concord life— As poets and
historians brought their work to the Grecian games—and
genius wrestled there as well as strength of body—so have
we seen works of kindred genius read at our Concord
games—by their author in this our Concord Amphitheatre
It is virtually repeated by all ages and nations.

     Moles nesting in your cellar & nibbling every third
potatoe—a whole rabbit warren only separated from you

by the flooring– To be saluted when you stir in the dawn
by the hasty departure of Monsieur–thump thump thump
striking his head against the floor timbers

Squirrels & field mice that hold to a community of
property in your stock of chestnuts.

The blue jays suffered few chestnuts to reach the
ground–resorting to your single tree in flocks in the early
morning, and picking them out of the burs–at a great
advantage

The crop of blackberries small & vines not yet grown
–ground nuts not dug.

One wonders how so much after all was expressed in
the old way– –so much here depends upon the emphasis
–tone–prounciation–style & spirit of the reading–

No writer uses so profusely all the aids to intelligibility
which the printers art affords–

You wonder how others had contrived to write so many
pages without emphatic Italicised words–they are so
expressive so natural & indispensible here.

As if none had ever used the demonstrative pronoun
–demonstratively.

In anothers sentences the thought though immortal is
as it were embalmed and does not *strike* you–but here it is
so freshly living–not purified by the ordeal of death–that
it stirs in the very extremities–the smallest particles &
pronouns are all alive with it– You must not say it–but
it It is not simple it–your it–or mine, but *it*

His books are solid workmanlike–like all that England
does–they tell of endless labor–done–well done and all the
rubbish swept away–like this bright cutlery in the
windows while the coak & ashes–turnings–filings borings
dust–lie far away at Birmingham unheard of.

The words did not come at the command of grammar
but–of an inexorable meaning

not like the standing soldiers by vote of parliament

–but any able-bodied man pressed into the service It is
no China war–but a revolution

    This style is worth attending to as one of the most
important features of the man that we at this distance
know.

    What are the men of N. E. about? I have travelled some
in New England–especially in Concord–and I found that
no enterprise was on foot which it would not disgrace a
man to take part in. They seemed to be employed
everywhere in shops and offices & fields– They seemed
like the brahmins of the east to be doing penance in a
thousand curious unheard of ways–their endurance
surpassing anything I had ever seen or heard of–Simeon
Stylites–Brahmen looking in the face of the sun–standing
on one leg–dwelling at the roots of trees–nothing to it Any
of the twelve labors of Hercules to be matched– The
Nemaean Lion–Lernaean hydra–OEnoean stag
–Erymathian boar–Augean stables–Stymphalian birds
–Cretan bull–Diomedes' mares–Amazonian girdle–monster
Geryon–Hesperian apples–three headed Cerberus
– Nothing at all in comparison–being only twelve and
having an end– For I could never see that these men
ever slew or captured any of their monsters–or finished
any of their labors– They have no "friend Iolas to burn,
with a hot iron, the root" of the Hydra's head.– for as
soon as one head is beaten, two spring up.

    Men labor under a mistake–they are laying up
treasures which moth and rust will corrupt & thieves
break through & steal– Northern slavery–or the slavery
which includes the southern eastern western and all
others.

    It is hard to have a southern over-seer it is worse to
have a northern one but worst of all when you are
yourself the slave driver. Look at the lonely teamster on
the highway–wending to market by day–or night–is he a

son of the morning–with somewhat of divinity in
him–fearless because immortal–going to receive his
birth-right–greeting the sun as his fellow bounding with
youthful gigantic strength over his mother earth– See
how he cowers & sneaks–how vaguely indefinitely all the
day he fears–not being immortal not divine– The slave
and prisoner of his own opinion of himself–fame which
he has earned by his own deeds–

Public opinion is a weak tyrant compared with private
opinion– What I think of myself–that determines my fate.

I see young men my equals–who have inherited from
their spiritual father a soul–broad fertile uncultivated
–from their earthly father–a farm–with cattle and barns
and farming tools–the implements of the picklock–& the
counterfeiter– Better if they had been born in the open
pasture and suckled by a wolf–or perhaps cradled in a
manger–that they might have seen with clear eye what
was the field they were called to labor in. The young man
has got to live a man's life then in this world pushing all
these things before him and get on as well as he can– how
many a poor immortal soul I have met well nigh crushed
and smothered–creeping slowly down the road of life
–pushing before him a barn 75–by 40 feet and 100 acres of
land tillage–pasture woodlot– This dull opaque garment
of the flesh is load enough–for the strongest spirit–but
with such an earthly garment superadded–the spiritual
life is soon ploughed into the soil with compost.

Its a fool's life as they will all find when they get to the
end of it. The man that goes on acumulating property
when the bare necessaries of life are cared for is a
fool–and knows better.

There is a stronger desire to be respectable to one's
neighbors than to ones self–

However such distinctions as Poet Philosopher–Literary
man–&c do not much assist our final estimate– We do not

lay much stress on them–'a man's a man for a' that'– Any
man who interests us much is all and more than these–

It is not simple dictionary it–

Talent at making books–solid workman-like graceful
–which may be read.

Some Idyllic chapter or chapters are needed

In the French Revolution are (Mirabeau–king of
men)–(Danton–Titan of the Revolution)–(Camille
Desmoulins–poetic Editor)–(Roland–heroic woman)
–(Dumouriez–first efficient general)–on the other side
(Marat friend of the people) (Robespierre) (–Tinville
Infernal judge) St. Just. &c &c

Nutting & Le Gros–by the wall side– The Stratten
house & Barn where the orchard covered all the slope of
Brister's hill–now killed out by the pines–

Brister Freeman a handy negro–(slave once of Squire
Cummings? and Fenda his hospitable pleasant wife)
–large–round black–who told fortunes–

Zilpha's little house where "she was spinning
linen" Making the walden woods ring with her shrill
singing–a loud shrill remarkable voice–when once she
was away to town–set on fire by English soldiers on parole
in the last war–and cat and dog and hens all burned up.

And Cato the the Ginea negro–his house a little patch
among the walnuts–who let the trees grow up till he
should be old–& Richardson got them

Where Breeds house stood–tradition says a tavern once
stood, the well the same and all a swamp between the
woods & town & and road made on logs

{*Five leaves missing*}

It makes a dull man's dreams

Bread I made pretty well for awhile while I remembered the rules—for I studied this art methodically—going clear back to the primitive days and first invention of the unleavened kind—and coming gradually down through that lucky accidental souring of the dough which taught men the leavening process—and all the various fermentations thereafter—till you get to "good sweet wholesome bread" the staff of life. I went on very well mixing ry & flour & Indian meal & potatoe with success till one morning I had forgotten the rules—and thereafter scalded the yeast—killed it out—and so after the lapse of a month was glad after all to learn that such palatable staff of life could be made out of the dead and scalt creature and risings that lay flat.

I have hardly met with the housewife who has gone so far into this mystery— For all the farmers wives pause at yeast—give this and they can make bread—it is the axiom of their argument—what it is—where it came from—in what era bestowed on man—is wrapped in mystery— It is preserved religiously like the vestal fire—and its virtue is not yet run out—some precious bottle full first brought over in the May Flower—did the business for America—and its Influence is still rising—swelling—spreading like Atlantic billows over the land— The soul of bread—the spiritus —occupying its cellular tissue.

The way to compare men is to compare their respective ideals— The actual man is too complex to deal with.

Carlyle is an earnest honest heroic worker as Literary man—and sympathising brother of his race.

Idealize a man and your notion takes distinctness at once.

Carlyle's talent is perhaps quite equal to his genius—

Striving to live in reality—not a general critic —philosopher or poet—

Wordsworth with very feeble talent has not so great
and admirable as persevering genius
    heroism–heroism–is his word–his thing.
He would realize a brave & adequate human life. & die
hopefully at last.

—

Emerson again is a critic poet philosopher–with talent
not so conspicuous–not so adequate to his task– – Lives
a far more intense life–seeks to realize a divine life–his
affections and intellect equally developed.– has advanced
farther and a new heaven opens to him– Love &
Friendship–Religion–Poetry–The Holy are familiar to
him The life of an Artist–more variegated–more
observing–finer perception–not so robust–elastic–practical
enough in his own field–faithful–a judge of men
    There is no such general critic of men & things–no
such trustworthy & faithful man.– More of the divine
realized in him than in any.
    A poetic-critic–reserving the unqualified nouns for the
gods

—

Alcott is a geometer–a visionary– – The Laplace of
ethics– More intellect–less of the affections–sight beyond
talents–a substratum of practical skill and knowledge
unquestionable–but overlaid and concealed by a faith in
the unseen and impracticable
    Seeks to realize an entire life– A catholic observer
–habitually takes in the farthest star & nebula–into his
scheme.
    Will be the last man to be disappointed as the ages
revolve His attitude is one of greater faith & expectation

than that of any man I know–with little to show–with undue share for a philosopher of the weaknesses of humanity.

The most hospitable intellect–embracing high & low–for children how much that means–for the insane and vagabond–for the poet and scholar.

—

Emerson has special talents unequalled– The divine in man has had no more easy methodically distinct expression.

His personal influence upon young persons greater than any man's

In his world every man would be a poet– Love would reign– Beauty would take place– Man & nature would harmonize–

—

When Alcotts day comes Laws unsuspected by most will take effect–the system will crystallize according to them–all scales and falsehood will slough-off. Every thing will be in its place.

His responsive "yes" and "no" and and attentive alert "hah!"

Like a happy merchant in the crowd all on the alert and sympathetic nudging his friends–"hear that" listening to his favorite speaker–going for protection–impatiently attentive– "I say, at the same time we had a War with France. [Yes, your Highness said so,–and we admit it!]" all good–that which I didnt hear and that which I did–are means to it.

He not only makes him speak audibly but he makes all parties listen to him and gives us their comments–"groans"

or "blushes"–or or "assent"–for this side or that–not a
man speaking alone but with England sitting round.

The merchant listens restless with shake of his
head–dumb [hum-m-m!] and reiteration of his last words–

We have from time to time pleasant congratulations,
when the speech grows dim and involved of any "little
window in to his Highness" and intimations of a "Speech
getting ready in his interior."

with triumphant malicious appeals from time to time
when there is a palpable hit to [My honorable friends?]

–Supplying his looks and attitudes and sound of his
voice and even his unutterable and wrecked submerged
thought.

even the moderns are made to hear and respond as they
best can. "O Secretary of the Home Department, my right
honorable friend!" must bethink himself of his duties

–when the speech lags or stumbles reassuring &
encouraging his fellow auditors–hearing not for himself
only but for all–in more silent soliloquy exclaiming "Poor
Oliver, noble Oliver!"– "Look in that countenance of
his Highness!"

"Courage, my brave one!"

Cromwell begins speaking only within sight of the
beginning & stops short when the conclusion is visible.

And the sentence frequently "breaks down" in the
middle and never gets up again

Feb. 22d Jean Lapin sat at my door today 3 paces from
me at first trembling with fear–yet unwilling to move–a
poor wee thing lean & bony–with ragged ears–and sharp
nose–scant tail & slender paws– It looked as if nature no
longer contained the breed of nobler bloods–the earth
stood on its last legs– Is nature too unsound at last I took
two steps–and lo away he scud with elastic spring over
the snowy crust in to the bushes a free creature of the
forest–still wild & fleet–and such then was his nature–and
his motion asserted its vigor and dignity.– Its large eye

looked at first young–and diseased–almost dropsical unhealthy. But it bound free the venison straitening its body and its limbs–into graceful length.

and soon put the forest between me & itself.

—

Emerson does not consider things in respect to their essential utility but an important partial & relative one–as works of art perhaps

His probes pass one side of their centre of gravity. His exaggeration is of a part not of the whole {MS torn}

—

{Three-fifths page missing}

and other things, 'in a buzzing tone', which the impartial hearer could not make out. The single rider is a raw-boned male figure, 'with lank hair reaching below his cheeks;' hat drawn close over his brows; 'nose rising slightly in the middle;' of abstruse 'down look', and large dangerous jaws strictly closed: he sings not; sits there covered, and is sung to by the others bare. Amid pouring deluges, and mud knee-deep: 'so that the rain ran in at their necks, and they vented it at their hose & breeches'. a spectacle to

{Three-fifths page missing}
{Three leaves missing}

wood choppers going to their work To be sure I never pryed it up very high–but a very little crack is an unspeakable satisfaction– Though it should fall back again after all.–

How many an afternoon has been stolen from more profitable–if not more attractive industry–afternoons when a good run of custom might have been expected on the main street such as tempt the ladies out a shopping. Spent I say–by me in the well nigh hopeless attempt to set the river on fire or be set on fire by it–with such tinder as I had–with such flint as I was–

Trying at least to make it flow with milk & honey as I had heard of–or liquid gold–and drown myself without getting wet– A laudable enterprise I assure you–though I have not much to show for it.

So many Autumn days spent out side the town trying to hear what was in the wind–to hear it and carry it express– I well nigh sunk all my capital in it–and lost my own breath into the bargain.– depend upon it, if it had concerned either of the parties it would have appeared in the Yeoman's Gazette the Freeman–with the earliest intelligence.

For many years I was self appointed inspector of snow-storms & rainstorms and did my duty faithfully –though I never received one cent for it. Surveyor if not of higher ways then of forest paths and all across lot routs –keeping many open ravines bridged and passable at all seasons–where the public heel had testified to the importance of the same–all not only without charge but even at considerable risk & inconvenience. Many a mower would have foreborne to complain had he been aware of the invisible public good that was in jeopardy.

So I went on I may say without boasting I trust –faithfully minding my business without a partner–till it became more and more evident that my townsmen would not after all admit me into the list of town offices–nor make the place a sinecure–with moderate allowance

I have looked after the wild stock of the town–which pastures in common–and every one knows give you a good deal of trouble in the way of leaping fences. I have counted and registered all the eggs I could find at

least–and have had an eye to all nooks & corners of the
farm–though I did'nt always know whether Jonas or
solomon worked in this field today–that was none of my
business. I had to make my daily entries in the general
farm book–and my duties may sometimes have made me
a little stubborn and unyielding

Many a day spent on the hill tops waiting for the sky to
fall that I might catch something–though I never caught
much only a little manna-wise–that would dissolve again
in the sun.

My accounts indeed–which I can swear to have been
faithfully kept–I have never got audited still less
accepted. Still less paid & settled– However I haven't
set my heart upon *that*.

I have watered the red-huckleberry & the sand
cherry–and the hopwood-tree–& the cornel–& spoonhunt
–and yellow violet which might have withered else–in dry
seasons. The white grape

To find the bottom of walden Pond–and what inlet &
outlet it might have

I found at length that as they were not likely to offer
me any office in the court house–any curacy or living
any where else, I must shift for myself

Now watching from the observatory of The cliffs–or
Anursnack–to telegraph any new arrival–to see if
Watchusett Watatic or Monadnoc had got any nearer.
– Climbing trees for the same purpose–

The unlimited anxiety strain & care of some persons is
one very incurable form of disease– Simple arithmetic
might have corrected it– For the life of every man has
after all an epic integrity–and nature adapts herself to
our weaknesses and deficiencies as well as talents.

No doubt it is indispensable that we should do *our*
work between sun & sun–and only a wise man will know
what that is– And yet how much work will be left not
done put off to the next day and yet the system goes on.

We presume commonly to take care of our selves–and trust as little as possible–vigilant more or less all our days–though we say our prayers at night and commit ourselves to uncertainties.– As if in our very days and most vigilant moments the great part were not a necessary trust still. How serenity anxiety–confidence fear paint the heavens for us–

All the laws of nature will bend and adapt themselves to the least motion of man.

All change is a miracle to contemplate   when all is ready it takes place and only a miracle could stay it.

We compelled to live so thoroughly and sincerely –reflecting on our steps reverencing our life–that we never make allowance for the possible changes

We may waive just so much care of ourselves as we devote of care elsewhere–

{*Paste-down endpaper*}

[Berg Journal]

APRIL 17, 1846–DECEMBER 1846

Walden April 17 1846

Even nations are ennobled by affording protection to
the weaker races of animals When I read of some custom
by which an ancient people recognized the migrations of
birds and beasts, or any necessity of theirs, they seem
not more savage but more god like– The Greeks were not
above this humane intercourse with nature. They were as
happy as children on the arrival of the swallow in the
spring–and the passage of cranes from the sources of the
Nile. They took note of and delight in such trifling events
like Indians. Anacreon sings

> Behold how the crane travels
> Behold how the duck dives.

The partridge & the quail the swan and the stork were
also mentioned by the poets with distinction.

According to Hare "The children in Rhodes greeted the
latter (i.e. the swallow) as herald of the spring in a little
song. Troops of them, carrying about a swallow
(χελιδονίζοντες), sang this from door to door, and
collected provisions in return." I give my own translation
as most literal

> The swallow has come,
> The swallow has come,
> Bringing beautiful hours,
> Beautiful seasons,
> White on the belly,
> Black on the back.
> —Wilt thou bring forth figs
> From thy fat house,
> And a cup of wine,
> And a canister of cheese,
> And wheaten bread? The swallow

Does not reject even
The yolk of eggs. Shall we go away or shall
　　we receive something?
If indeed thou wilt give anything–but if not
　　we will not leave thee;
We will carry away either the door, or the
　　lintel,–
—Or the wife sitting within.
She is little, easily we shall bear her off.
But if thou wilt bring anything, then bring
　　something ample.
Open open the door to the swallow,
For we are not old men, but children.
　　　　　　　　　　　　Athenaeus viii. c 60

The Greeks were such worshippers of beauty that this
peculiarity is observable whenever the word καλος is
used–as in καλὰς ὥρας καλὼς ἐνιαυτὼς in the above– I take
an unwearied delight in their repetition of this word– It
does not degenerate into the French bel or fine Theirs is
a simple & temperate use of the word after all. It is hard
to be lovers of beauty without being sentimental.

In the beginning of the 3d book of the Iliad sings
Homer–

But when they were arrayed each under his leader,
The Trojans rushed with a clang & a shout like
　　birds;
As when there is a clangor of cranes in the heavens
Who avoid winter & unspeakable rain,
They fly with clangor toward the streams of Ocean
Bearing slaughter & Fate to Pygmaean men;
Passing through the air these bear along
　　disastrous strife.

the lexicon says Ἠέριαι in the morning here

Husbandry is universally a sacred art–pursued with too
much heedlessness and haste by us– To have large farms
and large crops is our object. Our thoughts on this subject
should be as slow and deliberate as the pace of the ox.

"According to the early laws of Greece, the ploughing
ox was held sacred, & was entitled, when past service, to

range the pastures in freedom & repose. It was forbidden,
by the decrees of Triptolemus, to put to death this faithful
ally of the labors of the husbandman, who shared the toils
of ploughing & threshing. Whenever, therefore, an ox was
slaughtered, he must first be consecrated or devoted as a
sacrifice (ἱερειον), by the sprinkling of the sacrificial
barley; this was a precaution against the barbarous
practice of eating raw flesh (βουφαγια). A peculiar
sacrifice (Διπόλια) at Athens, at which the slayer of the
ox fled, and the guilty axe was thrown into the sea, on
the sentence of the Prytanes, yearly placed before the
people a visible type of the first beginnings of their social
institutions."

                                          Ap 18th The morning
must remind every one of his ideal life– Then if ever we
can realize the life of the Greeks We see then Aurora.
The morning brings back the heroic ages.

    I get up early and bathe in the pond–that is one of the
best things I do–so far the day is well spent.
    In some unrecorded hours of solitude whether of
morning or evening whose stillness was audible–when the
atmosphere contained an auroral perfume the hum of a
mosquito was a trumpet that recalled what I had read of
most ancient history and heroic ages. There was somewhat
that I fancy the Greeks meant by ambrosial about it–more
than Sybilline or Delphic– It expressed the infinite fertility
and fragrance and the everlastingness of the κοσμος It was
θειον Only Homer could name it. The faintest is the most
significant sound.

    I have never felt lonely or in the least oppressed by a
sense of solitude but once, and that was a few weeks after
I came here to live when for an hour I doubted if the near
neighborhood of man was not essential to a healthy

life– To be alone was something. But I was at the same time conscious of a slight insanity–and seemed to foresee my recovery–in the midst of a gentle rain while these thoughts prevailed– There suddenly seemd such sweet and beneficent society in nature–and the very pattering of the drops–& in evry sound & sight around my house–as made the fancied advantages of human neighborhood insignificant. I was so distinctly made aware of the presence of my *kindred*, even in scenes which we are accustomed to call wild, that the nearest of blood to me & humanest was not a person nor a villager–that no place could be strange to me.

Cheerful society is worthy employment.

The morning which is the most memorable season of the day–is the awaking hour–then there is least somnolence in us–and for an hour at least some part of us seems to awake which slumbers all the rest of the day and night– After a partial cessation of our sensual life–the soul of man, or its organs–seem to be reinvigorated each day. And the Genius tries again what noble life it can make. I know of no more encouraging fact than the unquestionable ability of man to elevate his life–by a conscious endeavor. All memorable events in my experience transpire in morning time–and a morning atmosphere– Their atmosphere is auroral– Greek poetry & art are auroral to me– And the evening & the morning are one. The wood thrush sings at morning & at evening–and to him who has kept pace with the sun there is no difference

It is some thing to be able to paint a particular picture–or carve a statue–and so to make a few objects beautiful–but it is far sublimer to carve & paint the very atmosphere & medium through which we look–which morally we can do.

To affect the quality of the day that is the highest of arts.

It matters not what the clocks say or the attitudes & labors of men–morning is when I am awake & there is a dawn in me.

Moral reform & improvement is the effort to throw off sleep & somnolency– How is it that men can give so poor an account of their day if they have not been slumbering – They are not such poor calculators If they had not been over come with drowsiness they would have performed some-what. The millions are awake enough for physical labor & activity–but only one in the million is awake enough for mental exertion–only one in a hundred million–spiritually–(more than intellectually) awake. To be awake is to be alive.

My thoughts which are either the memory or the expectation of my actions–are the causes which determine life & death.

Every man is tasked to make his life even in its details worthy the contemplation of his most elevated and critical hour

{*Two leaves missing*}

man could have consciously devised.

Commerce is brave & serene–alert–adventurous –unwearied–

It is very natural–much more than many fantastic enterprises–sentimental experiments and hence its success–

I am refreshed and expanded when the freight-train rattles past me on the rail road–and I smell the stores which have been dispensing their odors from long-wharf last–which remind me of foreign parts of coral reefs & Indian oceans and tropical climes–& the extent of the

globe– I feel more a citizen of the world at the sight of
the palm leaf which will cover so many new England
flaxen heads the next summer–the manilla cordage–&
the cocoanut husks– The old Junk & scrap iron, and worn
out sails–are full of history more legible & significant
now these old sails than if they could be wrought into
writing paper.

Here goes lumber from the Maine woods which did not
go out to sea in the last freshet–risen 4 dollars on the
thousand by reason of what *did* go out or was split
up–pine spruce cedar–1st 2nd–3d & 4th quality so lately
all of one quality, to wave over the bear & moose &
caribou.

–next rolls of Thomaston lime a prime lot which will
get far among the hills before it gets slacked– These rags
in bales of all hues & qualities the last and lowest
condition of dress–of patterns which are now no longer
cried up those splendid articles–poplin & muslin de
laines–& pongees–from all quarters both of fashion & of
poverty–going to become paper of one color–or a few
shades

This closed car smells of salt fish the strong scent–the
commercial scent–reminding me of the grand banks & the
fisheries & fish flakes

A hogshead of molasses or rum–directed John Brown
–Cuttings-ville Vt.–some trader among the growers who
imports for the farmers near his clearing and now
perchance stands over his bulk head and thinks of the
last arrivals on the coast

Is telling his customers perhaps–has told 20 this
morning that he expects some by the next arrivalls– It is
advertised in the cuttingsville Times

I know a woman who possess a restless & intelligent
mind–interested in her own culture & that of the family
and earnest to enjoy the highest possible advantages. I

meet her with pleasure as a natural person who a little
provokes me–& I suppose is stimulated in turn by
myself– Yet our acquaintance plainly does not attain
that degree of confidence & sentiment–which women
–which all–covet–

I am glad to help her, as I am helped by her, I like very
well to know her with a sort of strangers privelege–and
hesitate to visit her often like her other friends– My
nature pauses here & I do not well know why. Perhaps she
does not make the highest demand on me–not a religious
demand. Some with whose prejudices or peculiar bias I
have no faith–yet inspire me with confidence–and I trust
they confide in me also as a religious heathen at least,–a
good Greek– I too have principles as well founded as
their own–

If this person would conceive that without wilfulness I
associate with her as far as our destinies are coincident–as
far as our good geniuses permit–and still value such
intercourse it would be a grateful assurance to me.

I feel as if I appeared careless & indifferent & without
principle–or requisition–to her–not expecting more & yet
not content with less– If she could know that I make an
infinite demand on myself, as well as all others–she
would see that this true though incomplete intercourse
was infinitely better than a more abandoned & unreserved
though falsely grounded one–without the principle of
growth in it.

For a companion I require one who will make an equal
demand on me with my own genius– Such a one will
always be rightly tolerant It is suicide–it corrupts good
manners to welcome any less than this. I value & trust
those who love & praise my aspiration and tendency–not
my performance–

If you would not stop to look at me,–but look whither
I am looking & further–then my education could not
dispense with thy company.

The struggle in me is between a love of contemplation
and a love of action–the life of a philosopher & of a hero.
The poetic & philosophic have my constant vote–the
practic hinders & unfits me for the former.

How many things that my neighbors do bunglingly
could I do skilfully & effectually–but I fain would not
have leisure– My tendency is, on the one hand to the
poetic life–on the other to the practic–and the result is the
indifference of both–or the philosophic.

In the practic the poetic loses its intensity–and fineness
but gains in health & assurance–

The practical life is the poetic making for itself a
basis–and in proportion to the breadth of the base will be
the quantity of material at the apex– The angle of slope
for various materials is determined by science. The fabric
of life is pyramidal.

The man of practice is laying the foundations of a
poetic life

The poet of great sensibility is rearing a superstructure
without foundation.

To make a perfect man–the Soul must be much like
the body not too unearthly & the body like the soul. The
one must not deny & oppress the other.

The line of greatest breadth intersects the line of
greatest length at the point of greatest depth or height

A law so universal–and to be read in all material–in
Ethics as well as mechanics–that it remains its own most
final statement.

–It is the heart in man– It is the sun in the system–it
is the result of forces– In the case of the pond it is the
law operating without friction. Draw lines through the
length & breadth of the aggregate of a man's particular
daily experiences and volumes of life into his coves and
inlets–and where they intersect will be the height or depth
of his character.

You only need to know how his shores trend & the character of the adjacent country to know his depth and concealed bottom.

There is a bar too across the entrance of his every cove—every cove is his harbor for a season—and in each successively is he detained—land locked.

There is no exclusively moral law—there is no exclusively physical law.

Carlyle is a brave and genuine man earnest & sincere

A most talented writer of English—an art of which he is master

If he is sometimes an extreme praiser he is never a fatal detractor

A Detector of shams

A practical bent.

He inspires us to greater earnestness & effort—and useful activity

I find I cannot fish without falling a little in my own respect. I have tried it again & again—and have skill at it—and a certain instinct for it which revives from time to time but always I feel that it would have been better if I had not fished I think I am not mistaken. It is perhaps a faint intimation— Yet so are the streaks of morning. It tempts me as one means of becomming acquainted with nature not only with fishes but with night & water and the scenery—which I should not see under the same aspects;—and occasionally though

{*Two leaves missing*}

boat

I seem to hear a faint music from all the horizon— When our senses are clear and purified we always may hear the notes of music in the air— This is the tradition under

various forms of all nations–the statue of Memnon– The
music of the spheres–of the sun flower in its circular
motion–with the sun &c. &c.

Carlyles place & importance in English Literature is
not yet recognised–

For the most part I know not how the hours go.
Certainly I am not living that heroic life I had dreamed
of– And yet all my veins are full of life–and nature
whispers no reproach– The day advances as if to light
some work of mine–and I defer in my thought as if there
were some where busier men– It was morning & lo! it
is now evening– And nothing memorable is
accomplished– Yet my nature is *almost* content with
this– It hears no reproach in nature.

What are these pines & these birds about? What is
this pond a-doing? I must know a little more–& be forever
ready. Instead of singing as the birds I silently smile at
my incessant good fortune but I dont know that I bear any
flowers or fruits– Methinks if they try me by their
standards I shall not be found wanting–but men try one
another not so. The elements are working their will
with me.

As the fields sparrow has its trill sitting on the hickory
before my door–so have I my chuckle as happy as
he–which he may hear out of my nest.

Man is like a plant and his satisfactions are like those
of a vegetable–his rarest life is least his own– One or two
persons come to my house–there being proposed it may
be to their vision the faint possibility of intercourse–&
joyous communion. They are as full as they are silent and
wait for your plectrum or your spirit to stir the strings of
their lyre. If they could ever come to the length of a
sentence or hear one–on that ground they are thinking
of!! They speak faintly–they do not obtrude themselves

They have heard some news which none, not even
they themselves can impart. What come they out for
to seek? If you will strike my chord?

They come with somethings in their minds no particular
fact or information–which yet is ready to take any form
of expression on the proper impulse It is a wealth they
bear about them which can be expended in various ways.
Laden with its honey the bee straightway flies to the hive
to make its treasure common stock– The poet is impelled
to communicate at every risk and at any sacrifice.

I think I have this advantage in my present mode of
life over those who are obliged to look abroad for
amusement–to theatres & society–that my life itself is my
amusement and never ceases to be novel–the
commencement of an experiment–or a drama which will
never end.

Sunday May 3d
I heard the whippoorwill last night for the first time.

Carlyle's books are not to be studied but read with a
swift satisfaction–rather– Their flavor & charm–their
gust is like the froth of wine which can only be tasted
once & that hastily. On a review I never can find the pages
I had read– The book has done its work when once I have
reached the conclusion, and will never inspire me again.

They are calculated to make one strong and lively
impression–and entertain us for the while more entirely
than any–but that is the last we shall know of them They
have not that stereotyped success & accomplishment
which we name classic–

It is an easy and inexpensive entertainment–and we
are not pained by the author's straining & impoverishing
himself to feed his readers.

It is plain that the reviewers and politicians do not
know how to dispose of him– They take it too easily &

must try again a loftier pitch– They speak of him within
the passing hour as if he too were one other ephemeral
man of letters about town who lives under Mr. Somebody's
administration. Who will not vex the world after burial–

But he does not depend on the favor of reviewers–nor
the honesty of booksellers–nor on popularity– He has
more to impart than to receive from his generation

He is a strong & finished journeyman in his craft–&
reminds us oftener of Samuel Johnsson than of any other.
So few writers are respectable–ever get out of their
apprenticeship– As the man said that as for composition
it killed him he did'nt know which thought to put down
first–that his hand writing was not a very good one–&
then there was spelling to be attended to– So if our able
stock writer can take care of his periods & spelling–and
keep within the limits of a few proprieties–he forgets that
there is still originality & wisdom to be attended to, and
these would kill him.

There is always a more impressive and simpler
statement possible than consists with any victorious
comparisons.

We prize the good faith & valor of soberness & gravity
when we are to have dealings with a man If this is his
playful mood we desire so much the more to be admitted
to his serious mood.

May 5th

Now I hear the whippoorwill every night–they are my
clock–now two are singing one a stanza behind the other.
Like Scotland's burning, now together in exact time now
one lags.

The subject of sex is a most remarkable one–since
though it occupies the thoughts of all so much, and our
lives & characters are so affected by the consequences
which spring from this source– Yet mankind as it were
tacitly agrees to be silent about it–at least the sexes

do one to another. Here is the most interesting of
all human facts or relations still veiled, more completely
than the Eleusinian mystery– Out of such secresy & awe
one would think that some religion would spring. I am
not sorry for the silence– It is a golden reserve which
speech has not yet desecrated– I believe it is unusual for
the most intimate friends to impart the pleasures–or the
anxieties connected with this fact– This is wonderfully
singular–& when from this soil our flowers grow and
music has its root here.

I love men with the same distinction that I love
woman–as if my friend were of some third sex–some other
or stranger and still my friend.

I do not think the shakers exaggerate this fact–but all
mankind exaggerate it much more by silence. In the true
and noblest relations of the sexes there is somewhat akin
to the secret of all beauty & art in the universe The
imagination of the Greeks filled the heavens full of love &
benignity in a thousand forms–flitting from this side to
that– From Apollo in the sun to Aurora in the
morning–still charming the world with this inexplicable
variety– What sort of Dualism or difference there is who
ever conceived? If there are Gods there are Goddesses
Apollo & Venus–Neptune & Ceres– And the Hebrew's God
is Love too.

What the difference is between man and woman–that
they should be so attracted to one another I never saw
adequately stated.

Man and man are more nearly of the same sex.

What an infinite and divine demand is made on us
forever to sustain this relation worthily

–It is easy to see that the education of mankind has not
commenced–there is so little interaction– The life of the
Greek would be forgotten in noble relations of the sexes
to one another–and to themselves– What can the
university do to develope the inert faculties of men–if they

go not hence to the more catholic university of friendship

–The end of love is not house keeping–but it consists as much or more with the letting go of the house.

Men can help one another indeed but not by money or by kindness & just & upright & neghborly behavior much–but by being gods to oneanother–objects of adoration– The wisest philosopher that ever lived is not such an instructor as the illiterate love of any human-being– – The world is full of suspicion when it might be full of love– There is contempt where there might as well be respect & adoration. Instead of imprisoning or executing the criminal we might so easily apotheosize him or translate him by love and admiration for what is god-like in him– And it is not done.

If men would steadily observe realities only and not allow themselves to be deluded–life would be like a fairy tale & the Arabian nights entertainments. When I am calm & wise and unhurried I perceive that only great and worthy things have any permanent & absolute existence– That petty fears and petty pleasures–are but the shadows of the reality. By closing the eyes and slumbering–and consenting to be deceived by shows–men establish their daily life of routine and habit everywhere–which however is built on imaginary foundations

If men could discriminate always and were never deluded by appearances life would never be mean–nor unworthy.

Children who play life discern its true law & relations more clearly than men who fail to live it worthily–but think they are wiser by experience.

{*One leaf missing*}

Carlyle was 50 years old on the 4th Dec. 1845.

—

Caught pouts from the boat–in 20 ft water off Cove
May 2nd–
   People had caught them from the shore four or five
nights previous.

—

   Early in May or by the last of April the oaks hickory
–maples & other trees–just putting out amidst the
pine woods–give them the appearance in cloudy days
especially of the sun just breaking through mists and
shining on them– Their green bursting buds or expanding
leaves scatter a slight sun-shine over the hillsides– It is
moist bright & spring-like
   The first week in May I hear the Whippoorwill–the
brown-thrasher–the veery–the wood pewee–the
chewink The wood thrush long before
   The 3d or 4th of may I saw a loon? in the pond

{*One-fourth page blank*}

May 15th

   Capt. Fremont describes the prairies as covered with
sun-flowers–and traversed occasionally by a clear &
shallow creek

   At the approach of evening I hear the note of the
tree toad–and the veery & wood thrush–and sometimes
late in the night some small bird in the forest the
pine warbler? or the tree sparrow? sings aloud a distinct
and pleasant strain as if awakened by its dreams. What
should impel it to such an expression of its happiness
   I think that an important difference between men of
genius or poets and men not of Genius–is in the inability

of the latter to grasp and confront the thought that
visits them. It is too faint for expression or even
conscious impression– What merely quickens or retards
the blood in their veins–and fills their afternoons with
pleasure they know not whence–conveys a distinct
assurance to the finer organization of the poet

How to make my life of finer quality–to transplant it
into futurity that is a question

Chapman seems to have come to his task the
translation of Homer with the right spirit–to supply
a want to England–

> "O! 'tis wondrous much
> (Though nothing prized) that the right virtuous
>   touch
> Of a well-written soul, to virtue moves,
> Nor have we souls to purpose, if their loves
> Of fitting objects be not so inflam'd:
> How much then were this kingdom's main soul
>   maimed
> To want this great inflamer of all powers
> That move in human souls? – –

> being so far from cause
> Of prince's light thoughts, that their gravest laws
> May find stuff to be fashioned by his lines;
> Through all the pomp of kingdoms still he shines
> And graceth all his gracers."

He says of those who had translated him into other
languages

> They fail'd to search his deep & treasurous heart,
>   The cause was, since they wanted the fit key
> Of Nature, in their downright strength of Art;
>   With poesy to open poesy.

When my friends reprove me for not devoting myself
to some trade or profession, and acquiring property I feel
not the reproach– I am guiltless & safe comparatively
on that score– But when they remind me of the

advantages of society of worthy and earnest helpful relations to people I am convicted–and yet not I only but they also.

But I am advised by thee Friend of friends to strive singly for the highest–without concern for the lower – The integrity of life is otherwise sacrificed to factitious virtues–and frittered away in morbid efforts & despair.

Disturb not the sailor with too many details–but let him be sure that he keep his guiding star in his eye. It is by a mathematical point that we are wise–but that is a sufficient guidance for all our lives– The blind are led by the slightest clue.

When I am reproved for being what I am I find the only resource is being still more entirely what I am.

Carry yourself as you should and your garments will trail as they should.

I am useless for keeping flocks & herds, for I am on the trail of a rarer game.

To the mariner the faint star is the chief light though he will avail himself of the light in the binnacle.

{*One-fifth page blank*}

In may the pollen of the pine (pitch) began to cover the pond with its yellow dust.

There was a frost on the night of June 12th which killed my beans tomatoes & squashes–and my corn & potatoes to the ground.

June 20th
    Caught a chivin in the river–
14 3/4 inches long
  2 1/2 wide
  1 1/2 thick behind the eyes
  1 1/4 between   ”
  3 1/4 from snout to edge of gill cover

A regular graceful fish with coppery red reflections—the back & belly curving very slightly and regularly from end to end. the width of the body being nearly the same for some distance.

Above dusky—olivaceous—head above dark blue—snout blue—(scales on the sides edged with black & a black membrane covering their base with golden and red copper reflections lighter above redder below) (below & on belly lustrous red copper—) P.V.A fins reddish but dusky at extremities D. slightly reddish at base—rest dusky — C dusky.

head bare—a dull buried golden spot behind the eyes —1/2 inch in diameter—forming a temple like prominence Sides of head remarkably red coppery & smooth & bright —eyes about 1/2 inch in diameter. pupils blue black—irises golden. Jaws toothless upper jaw retractile—projecting beyond the lower when the mouth is closed.

Under the edge of gill cover a silvery spot 1—by 1/2 inch—with a broad black border. belly flattish—scales crowded behind gills. Lat line distinct after it commences to be straight.

Single Dorsal fin 10 rays about as high as wide 1st ray 1/3 2°

> P.   17—rounded
> V.   8   "
> A.   10
> C   19 or 22 deeply forked

Answers very nearly to Leuciscus pulchellus

1st   But is not so deep in proportion to length by 1/2 inch

2nd   Gill covers not silvery

3d   Eye twice as large.

4th   no appearance of bands

5th   2 or 3 more scales below the lat. line

6th   D fin not high again as long– And as near the
         center of body.

7th   The spines of D fin not reddish.

   differs from common Sucker in not being white
beneath–opercula not golden– Anterior nostril not
larger–in position of ventral fin–& shape of anal. & in
the number of rays in each fin.

   In some parts of the river, the water willow when it is
of large size and entire–is the lightest & most graceful
of all our trees seeming to float upon the water masses of
finely cut foliage being piled upon one another
–occasionally the slight grey stems seen between. It has
more than any a foreign aspect– It reminds us of Persian
luxury and of the trim gardens and artificial lakes of
the east.

   No tree is so wedded to the water and harmonises so
well with a still stream And I think it more graceful than
the weeping willow or any pendulus trees which dip
their branches in the water and are not buoyed up by it.
It is rare that you see a perfect specimen–though the
decayed but vivacious trees which line the stream
everywhere are grotesque & pleasing objects enough.

   It certainly surpasses every other tree for lightness both
stem & shore being concealed.

   Now you paddle along the edge of a dense palisade of
bull rushes–as straightly bounding the water as if clipped
by art–reminding us of Indian forts. Alternate shore &
bank & precipitous bank– The bank is over hung with
graceful branches grasses–& various species of brake
–whose stems stand close & visible grouped as if in
a vase, while their heads spread many feet on either hand.

   A river or any water especially if placid is a place of
singular enchantment– Nature exhibits a fabulous

wealth there for not only are you struck by the weedy luxuriance of the bottom–but this is doubled by the flection of all the fertility upon the banks. The shallowest water is unfathomed–wherever a boat can float–there is more than Atlantic depth & no danger of fancy or imagination running aground.

He who has not hooked the red chivin is not yet a fisherman–all other fishes are amphibious at least this is one of the true anglers fishes– His cork goes dancing down the swift rushing stream amid the weeds & sands, when suddenly emerges this fabulous inhabitant of another element–as if it were the instant creation of an eddy–at last a true product of water & running streams. It is among the things heard of but not yet seen. And this bright cupreous dolphin had long inhabited your native fields and dwelt so low the bright creature beneath your feet.

It would seem as if a few elements made all nature–the metals are told upon your fingers–and their hues are but repeated in the plumage of birds–the morning & evening clouds and in the tints of fishes they are golden or silvery–or bright cupreous as this–still representing some mine where their armor was wrought. I have heard of mackerel visiting the copper banks– Many a fish must have been there

The east furnishes the religion of the wise and contemplative man–as the west of him that is mixed in affairs Christianity is more personal and moral The religion of the Brahmens' is more philosophical & constitutional.

The life of the Hindoo passes without violent emotions– No valuable gift of the gods–is lost or diminished by moderation or even by renunciation.

Renunciation takes up the safe & better part of a gift. To
eternize moods to still the chord that vibrates–to reduce
passions to states and conditions is the Brahmen's
philosophy. Only youth is in haste & concentrates its life
–(grown older in mod europe it postpones enjoyment
wholly to the future) the oriental mind preserves a just
medium.

Inferior gifts are easily avoided, only a look or a
gesture is sufficent–but the gifts of the gods are not
avoided by denial– He who conscientiously refuses them
receives more than they.

The gods do not require that we be moved by their
gifts In the Bhag vat-Geeta I read "The man whose
passions enter his heart as waters run into the unswelling
passive ocean, obtaineth happiness; not he who lusteth
in his lusts."

It is philosophically conservative, not selfishly or
timidly so.

—

The sincere ruggedness of Cromwell–not easily
prevailing by the truth and grandeur of his character but
honestly striving to bend all things to his will–is grateful
to consider in this, or any, age. "He was a strong man,"
as John Maidstone said, "in the dark perils of war; in the
high places of the field, hope shone in him like a pillar
of fire, when it had gone out in the others." His conduct
was not always what christianity teaches, or the best
philosophy–yet it was noble and will always be pardoned
at last to the consistent greatness of the man.

The wisest conservatism is that of the Hindoos
–"The man is praised, who, having subdued all his
passions, performeth with his active faculties all the

functions of life, unconcerned about the event. Perform
the settled functions: action is preferable to inaction. The
journey of thy mortal frame may not succeed from
inaction."

"Thou shouldst observe what is the practice of mankind
& act accordingly–" I myself Kreeshna "live in the
exercise of the moral duties" for the sake of example "As
the ignorant perform the duties of life from the hope of
reward, so the wise man, out of respect to the opinions &
prejudices of mankind, should perform the same without
motives of interest." He tells Arjoon the soldier to "be free
from hope."

Books are distinguished rather by the grandeur of their
topics than the manner in which they are handled– The
oriental philosophy treats of loftier themes than the
modern ever aspires to. It is greater to prattle on these
subjects than discuss learnedly on a lower platform.

The oriental unlike the western mind discerned action
in the inactive contemplative mind. And everywhere they
affirm that he who is actually & truly inactive is the best
employed– "He is a performer of all duty." – –

"Wise men call him a Pandeet, whose every undertaking
is free from the idea of desire, and whose actions are
consumed by the fire of wisdom". – – "Although he acteth,
he is not confined in the action. The work of him, who
hath lost all anxiety for the event, who is freed from the
bonds of action, and standeth with his mind subdued by
spiritual wisdom, and who performeth it for the sake of
worship, cometh altogether unto nothing. God is the gift
of charity; God is the offering; God is in the fire of the
altar, by God is the sacrifice performed; and God is to be
obtained by him who maketh God alone the object of
his works."

He who works from the highest motive and to the
highest end accomplishes nothing. Nothing is the net
result.

"In wisdom is to be found every work without exception."

– –"As the natural fire, O Arjoon, reduceth the wood to ashes, so may the fire of wisdom reduce all moral actions to ashes. There is not anything in this world to be compared with wisdom for purity. He who is perfected by practice, in due time findeth it in his own soul." – – "The human actions have no power to confine the spiritual mind, which, by study, hath forsaken works, and which, by wisdom, hath cut asunder the bonds of doubt."

Yet "Children only, & not the learned, speak of the speculative and practical doctrines as two. They are but one, for both obtain the selfsame end, and the place which is gained by the followers of the one, is gained by the followers of the other. That man seeth, who seeth that the speculative doctrines & the practical are but one."

They are impartial, they entertain no opinion exclusively–things are not opposed to one another–they reveal the agreement which exists.– they provoke no quarrel. They are too wise to side with any. *to continue* the last quotation.

"To be a Sannyasee, or recluse, without application, is to obtain pain & trouble; whilst the Moonee, who is employed in the practice of his duty, presently obtaineth Brahm, the Almighty. The man who, employed in the practice of works, is of a purified soul, a subdued spirit, and restrained passions, and whose soul is the universal soul, is not affected by so being. The attentive man, who is acquainted with the principles of things, in seeing, hearing, touching, smelling, eating, moving, sleeping, breathing, talking, quitting, taking, opening & closing his eyes, thinketh that he doeth nothing; but that the faculties are only employed in their several objects. The man who, performing the duties of life, and quitting all interest in them, placeth them upon Brahm, the Supreme, is not tainted by sin; but remaineth like the leaf of the lotus

unaffected by the waters. Practical men, who perform the
offices of life but with their bodies, their minds, their
understandings, and their senses, and forsake the
consequence for the purification of their souls; and,
although employed, forsake the fruit of action, obtain
infinite happiness; whilst the man who is unemployed,
being attached to the fruit by the agent desire, is in the
bonds of confinement. The man who hath his passions
in subjection, and with his mind forsaketh all works, his
soul sitteth at rest in the 9-gate city of its abode, neither
acting nor causing to act."

"The Almighty createth neither the powers nor the
needs of mankind, nor the application of the fruits of
action: nature prevaileth. The Almighty receiveth neither
the vices nor the virtues of any one." – – "He whose soul is
unaffected by the impressions made upon the outward
feelings, obtaineth what is pleasure in his own mind.
Such an one, whose soul is thus fixed upon the study of
Brahm, enjoyeth pleasure without decline. The enjoyments
which proceed from the feelings are as the wombs of
future pain. The wise man, who is acquainted with the
beginning & the end of things, delighteth not in these. He
who can bear up against the violence which is produced
from lust & anger in this mortal life, is properly employed
and a happy man." – –

– –

"He cannot be a Yogee, who, in his actions, hath not
abandoned all intentions. Works are said to be the means
by which a man who wisheth, may attain devotion; so
rest is called the means for him who hath attained
devotion. * * He [the Sannyasee] should raise himself by
himself: he should not suffer his soul to be depressed.
Self is the friend of self; and, in like manner, self is its
own enemy. Self is the friend of him by whom the spirit

is subdued with the spirit; so self, like a foe, delighteth
in the enmity of him who hath no soul." * *

"He [The Yogee] planteth his own seat firmly on a spot
that is undefiled, neither too high nor too low, and
sitteth upon the sacred grass which is called Koos,
covered with a skin & a cloth."

"The Yogee of a subdued mind, thus employed in the
exercise of his devotion, is compared to a lamp, standing
in a place without wind, which waveth not. He delighteth
in his own soul, where the mind, regulated by the service
of devotion, is pleased to dwell, and where, by the
assistance of the spirit, he beholdeth the soul. He
becometh acquainted with that boundless pleasure which
is far more worthy of the understanding than that which
ariseth from the senses; depending upon which, the mind
moveth not from its principles; which having obtained,
he respecteth no other acquisition so great as it; in which
depending, he is not moved by the severest pain." * * "The
man, O Arjoon, who from what passeth in his own breast,
whether it be pain or pleasure, beholdeth the same in
others, is esteemed a supreme Yogee."

No race of thinkers occupies so lofty a platform—such
a table land— They do not quite fail when they personify
Brahma and speak as from the mouth of Divinity "I plant
myself on my own nature, and create again & again, this
assemblage of beings, the whole, from the power of
nature, without power. Those works confine not me,
because I am like one who sitteth aloof uninterested in
those works"

* * "They also who serve other Gods with a firm belief,
in doing so, involuntarily worship even me. I am he who
partaketh of all worship, & I am their reward." *

"I am the same to all mankind: there is not one who is
worthy of my love or hatred. * *

"And learn, O Arjoon, that every being which is worthy
of distinction & pre-eminence, is the produce of the

portion of my glory. But what, O Arjoon, hast thou to do with this manifold wisdom? I planted this whole universe with a single portion & stood still."

They speak from solitude–men are not multiplied–it is the society of man and divinity–how far from ancient history. It is man–not men–and so is addressed to each one more directly & personally.

"This supreme spirit & incorruptible Being, even when it is in the body, neither acteth, nor is it affected, because its nature is without beginning & without quality."

— —

"A man's own calling, with all its faults, ought not to be forsaken. Every undertaking is involved in its faults, as the fire in its smoke."

The elevation of the thought & the power of abstraction & concentration possessed by the Hindoo philosophers is the subject of the following sensible remarks by Warren Hastings prefixed to the translation of the translation of the Bhagvat-Geeta–an episode to the Mahabharat, a voluminous ancient poem.

After describing an instance, which he witnessed, of the spiritual discipline which distinguishes the religion of the Brahmans from every other he says–

–"But if we are told that there have been men who were sucessively, for ages past, in the daily habit of abstracted contemplation, begun in the earliest period of youth, and continued in many to the maturity of age, each adding some portion of knowledge to the store accumulated by his predecessors; it is not assuming too much to conclude, that, as the mind ever gathers strength, like the body, by exercise, so in such an exercise it may in each have acquired the faculty to which they aspired, and that their collective studies may have lead them to the discovery of new tracks & combinations of sentiment,

totally different from the doctrines with which the learned
of other nations are acquainted: doctrines, which however
specullative & subtle, still, as they possess the advantage
of being derived from a source so free from every
adventitious mixture, may be equally founded in truth
with the most simple of our own."

The philosophy of the Hindoos is an immense a sublime
conservatism–at once ancient & modern–and world
wide–preserving the universe with asiatic anxiety in that
state–in which it appeared to their minds. They dwelt
upon the inevitability & immutability of the law–on the
power of temperament, and constitution–as the three
Goon, Truth–Passion–darkness. (or white red–black–on
the circumstances of birth and affinity–

The end and object is an immense consolation–to be
absorbed in Brahma.

Their speculations never adventure–they have such
periods in their dynasties– The boyant the free the
flexible–the various–the possible which also are qualities
of the unnamed–they deal not with The incalculable
promise of the morrow–they have weighed–

For them there is no bloom up on the blossom of
futurity.

The unaccountable & undeserved reward they earn, by
penance

Novelty is one with antiquity to them morning with
evening–future & past.

It would be a catholic enterprise for this age to print in a
series or collectively the Scripture or sacred writings of
the several nations the Chinese the Hindoos the Persians
the Hebrews or Selections from them–as the written and
the recorded truth– The New Testament is yet perhaps
too much on the lips & in the hearts of men–to be called
a scripture. But this is a work which time will surely &

faithfully edit. This would unquestionably be the Bible or book of books.

A precious volume which let the missionaries send to the uttermost parts of the earth–what God has revealed of himself to all nations. Will not at length the printing press itself by miracle address itself to so sacred & choice a labor.

A mere mechanical juxtaposition like this would serve to liberalize the faith of living men–

I do not know that any has attempted to compare the theological and mythological systems of antiquity as of the present day–but this too though a subtle subject is deserving our attention. I remember no comparison of the God of New Englanders with the god of the Greeks.

{*One-third page blank*}

It is the characteristic of great truths that they will yield of their sense in due proportion to the hasty and the deliberate reader– To the practical they are common sense and to the wise wisdom–as the traveller may either wet his lips or take a hearty draught at a full stream with equal satisfaction–and navies may as easily supply their wants.

As a copious stream quenches the thirst of the smallest animal.

The thought of the Bhag-vat-Geeta is less sententious & perhaps poetic but wonderfully sustained & developed.

It is more modern in its method.

Of the forsaking of works Kreeshna says "This never-failing discipline I formerly taught unto Veevaswat," –and it was handed down from one to another–"until at length, in the course of time, the mighty art was lost." – – "It is an ancient & supreme mystery."

– –

"Know, O Arjoon, that all the regions between this &
the abode of Brahm afford but a transient residence; but
he who findeth me, returneth not again to mortal birth."

Man is thus independent of his good or his evil
deeds– He having determined that an action shall be
performed appointeth a man to do it.

Some choice fruits has the harvest of thought already
yielded in this country which will endure–some small
books and newest testaments all which however we could
have conveniently stowed in the till of our chest– Poems
are already groping their way in the land from the
imperfect diaries of those whose ambition it has been, like
their busy country men, to "make something," and
perform their proper work.

Essays there are not all in vain–which, aiming high,
have hit not low. Sincere reports of some man's life.

But above all in our Bethel at home–in our native port
have we not been present at N England's peaceful
games–of the Lyceum–& from which new eras will be
dated as from the games of Greece–for though Herodotus
brought his history to Olympia to read–after the Cestus &
the race–yet we have heard there such histories far-fetched
and true as made Greece to be forgotten.

Philosophy too hath there her grove & portico Nor
has her school been wholly unfrequented in these days.

It reads like the argument to a great poem on the
primitive state of the country and its inhabitants–and the
reader imagines what in each case with the invocation of
some muse might be sung– He leaves off with suspended
interest as if the full account were to follow. The singular
moderation of his story leaves a history behind it. In what
school was this fur-trader educated? He travels the
immense snowy country with such purpose only as the

reader accompanies him–while it lies passive to be
observed by him.

In my short experience of human life I have found that
the outward obstacles which stood in my way were not
living men–but dead institutions It has been
unspeakably grateful & refreshing to make my way
through the crowd of this latest generation honest &
dishonest virtuous & vicious as through the dewy
grass–men are as innocent as the morning to the early
riser–and unsuspicious pilgrim and many an early
traveller which he met on his way v poetry–but the
institutions as church–state–the school property &c are
grim and ghostly phantoms like Moloch & Juggernaut
because of the blind reverence paid to them. When I have
indulged a poets dream of a terrestrial paradise I have
not foreseen that any cossack or Chipeway–would disturb
it–but some monster institution would swallow it– The
only highway man I ever met was the state itself– When
I have refused to pay the tax which it demanded for that
protection I did not want itself has robbed me– When I
have asserted the freedom it declared it has imprisoned me.
I love mankind I hate the institutions of their
forefathers–
What are the sermons of the church but the Dudleian
lectures–against long extinct perhaps always imaginary
evils, which the dead generations have *willed* and so the
bell still tolls to call us to the funeral services which a
generation can rightly demand but once.
It is singular that not the Devil himself–has been in
my way but these cobwebs–which tradition says were
originally spun to obstruct the fiend.
If I will not fight–if I will not pray–if I will not be
taxed–if I will not bury the unsettled prairie–my neighbor
will still tolerate me and sometimes even sustains me–but
not the state.

And should our piety derive its origin still from that exploit of pius Aenaeus who bore his father Anchises on his shoulders from the ruins of Troy

Not thieves & highwaymen but Constables & judges—not sinners but priests—not the ignorant but pedants & pedagogues—not foreign foes but standing armies—not pirates but men of war. Not free malevolence—but orgranized benevolence.

For instance the jailer or constable as a mere man and neighbor—with life in him intended for this particular 3 score years & ten—may be a right worthy man with a thought in the brain of him—but as the officer & tool of the state he has no more understanding or heart than his prison key or his staff— This is what is saddest that men should voluntarily assume the character & office of brute nature.— Certainly there are modes enough by which a man may put bread into his mouth which will not prejudice him as a companion & neighbor. There are stones enough in the path of the traveller with out a man's adding his own body to the number.

There probably never were worse crimes committed since time began than in the present Mexican war—to take a single instance— And yet I have not yet learned the name or residence and probably never should of the reckless vilain who should father them— all concerned —from the political contriver to the latest recruit possess an average share of virtue & of vice   the vilainy is in the readiness with which men, doing outrage to their proper natures—lend themselves to perform the office of inferior & brutal ones.

The stern command is—move or ye shall be moved—be the master of your own action—or you shall unawares become the tool of the meanest slave. Any can command him who doth not command himself. Let men be men & stones be stones and we shall see if majorities *do* rule.

Countless reforms are called for because society is not animated or instinct enough with life, but like snakes I have seen in early spring—with alternate portions torpid & flexible—so that they could wriggle neither way.

All men more or less are buried partially in the grave of custom, and of some we see only a few hairs upon the crown above ground.

Better are the physically dead for they more lively rot.

Those who have a stolen estate to be defended slaves to be kept in service—who would pause with the last inspiration & perpetuate it—require the aid of institutions—the stereotyped and petrified will of the past— But they who are something to defend—who are not to be enslaved themselves— —who are up with their time—ask no such hinderance

Carlyle's is not the most lasting word nor the loftiest wisdom—but for his genius it was reserved at last to furnish expression for the thoughts that were throbbing in a million breasts— It has plucked the ripest fruit in the public garden— But this fruit now least concerned the tree that bore it—which was rather perfecting the bud at the foot of the leaf stalk.

Carlyle is wonderfully true to the impressions on his own mind, but not to the simple facts themselves. He portrays the former so freshly and vividly—that his words reawaken and appeal to our whole Experience But when reinforced by this terrible critic we return to his page his words are found not to be coincident with the thing and inadequate and there is no host worthy to entertain the guest he has invited.

{One-half page blank}

On this remote shore we adventurously landed
unknown to any of the human inhabitants to this day
— But we still remember well the gnarled and
hospitable oaks, which were not strangers to us, the lone
horse in his pasture and the patient ruminating herd
whose path to the river so judiciously chosen to overcome
the difficulty of the ascent we followed and disturbed their
repose in the shade. And the cool free aspect of the wild
apple trees, generously proffering their fruit to the
wayfarers though still green and crude. The hard round
glossy fruit which if not ripe–still is not poison but New
English–brought hither its ancestor by our ancestors once.

And up the rocky channel of a brook we scrambled
which had long served nature for a sluice in these parts
leaping from rock–through tangled woods at the bottom
of a ravine, darker and darker it grew and more hoarse,
the murmur of the stream–until we reached the ruins of
a mill where now the ivy grew and the trout glanced
through the raceway and the flume.

And the dreams and speculations of some early settler
was our theme

> But now "no war nor battle's sound"
> Invades this peaceful battle ground
> But waves of Concord murmuring by
> With sweetly fluent harmony.
> But since we sailed, some things have failed
> And many a dream gone down the stream
> Here then a venerable shepherd dwellt
> Who to his flock his substance dealt
> And ruled them with a vigorous crook
> By precept of the sacred Book.
> But he the pierless bridge passed o'er
> And now the solitary shore
> Knoweth his trembling steps no more.
> Anon a youthful pastor came
> Whose crook was not unknown to fame

His lambs he viewed with gentle glance
Dispersed o'er a wide expanse,
And fed with "mosses from the Manse"
We view the rocky shore where late
With soothed and patient ear we sat
Under our Hawthorne in the dale
And listened to his Twice told Tale.

It comes on murmuring to itself by the base of stately
and retired mountains–through dark primitive woods
–whose juices it receives and where the bear still drinks
it– Where the cabins of settlers are still fresh and far
between, and there are few that cross its stream.
Enjoying still its cascades unknown to fame perhaps
unseen as yet by man–alone by itself–by the long ranges
of the mountains of Sandwich and of Squam with
sometimes the peak of Moose hillock the Haystack &
Kearsarge reflected in its waters. Where the maple and the
raspberry that lover of the mountains flourish amid
temperate dews. Flowing as long and mysterious and
untranslateable as its name Pemigewasset. By many a
pastured Pielion and Ossa where unnamed muses haunt,
and receiving the tribute of many an untasted
Helicon Not all these hills does it lave but I have
experienced that to see the sun set behind them avails as
much as to have travelled to them.
From where the old Man of the Mountain overlooks
one of its head waters–in the Franconia Notch, taking the
basin and the Flume in its way–washing the sites of future
villages–not impatient. For every mountain stream is
more than Helicon, tended by oreads dryads Naiads, and
such a pure and fresh inspiring draught gift of the gods
as it will take a newer than this New England to know
the flavor of.

Such water do the gods distill
And pour down hill
For their new England men.

A draught of this wild water bring
And I will never taste the spring
Of Helicon again.
But yesterday in dew it fell
This morn its streams began to swell
And with the sun it downward flowed
So fresh it hardly knew its road.

Falling all the way, not discouraged by the lowest
fall–for it intends to rise again.

There are earth air fire & water–very well, this is
water. down it comes that is the way with it.

It was already water of Squam and Newfound lake and
Winnipiseogee, and White mountain snow dissolved on
which we were floating–and Smith's and Bakers and
Mad rivers and Nashua and Souhegan and
Piscataquoag–and Suncook & Soucook & Contoocook
–mingled in incalculable proportions–still fluid yellowish
restless all with an inclination seaward but boyant.

Here then we will leave them to saw and grind and spin
for a season, and I fear there will be no vacation at low
water for they are said to have Squam and Newfound
lake and Winipiseogee for their mill ponds.

By the law of its birth never to become stagnant for it
has come out of the clouds, and down the sides of
precipices worn in the flood through beaver dams broke
loose not splitting but splicing and mending itself until
it found a breatheing plaace in this lowland– No danger
now that the sun will steal it back to heaven again before
it reach the sea for it has a warrant even to recover its
own dews into its bosom again with every eve

We wandered on by the side and over the brows of hoar
hills and mountains–& through notches which the stream
had made–looking down one sunday morning over
Bethlehem amid the bleating of sheep, and hearing as we

walked the loud spoken prayers of the inhabitants–like
crusaders strolled out from the camp in Palestine– And
looking in to learning's little tenement by the way–where
some literate swain earns his ten dollars by the
month–after the harvest–with rows of slates and well cut
benches round–as well cut as farther south–not noticing
the herd of swine which had poured in at the open door,
and made a congregation– So we went on over hill and
dale through the stumpy rocky–woody–bepastured
country–until we crossed a rude wooden bridge over the
Amonnoosuck and breathed the free air of the
Unappropriated Land.

Now we were in a country where inns begin– And we
too now began to have our ins and outs– Some sweet
retired house whose sign only availed to creak but bore
no Phoenix nor golden eagle but such as the sun and rain
had painted there– –a demi public demi private house
–where each apartment seems too private for your use–too
public for your hosts. One I remember where Landlord
and lady hung painted as if retired from active life–upon
the wall–remarkable one might almost say–if he knew
not the allowed degrees of consanguinity for a family
likeness–a singular deflexion of the nose turned each to
each–so that the total variation could not have been better
represented than in the picture.
    –But here at any rate the cream rose thick upon the
milk–and there was refreshment
    One "Tilton's Inn" tooo sheltered us which it were well
worth remembering, in Thornton it was where towns
begin to serve as gores only to hold the world together
–reached late in the evening and left before the sun rose.
But the remembrance of an entertainment still remains
and among publicans Tiltons name still stands
conspicuous in our diary.

But where we took our ease was no Canterbury street,
no Four corners nor Five points–no trivial place where 3
roads meet but hardly one road held together– A dank
forest path–more like an otter's or a marten's trail or
where a beaver had dragged his trap than where the
wheels of travel ever raised a dust. The pigeon sat
secure above our heads high on the dead limbs of the pine
reduced to robins size– The very yard of our hostelries
was inclined upon the skirts of mountains and as we
passed we looked up at angle at the stems of maples
waving in the clouds–and late at evening we heard the
drear bleating of innumerable flocks upon the mountains
sides seeming to hold unequal parley with the bears

Shuddered through that Franconia where the
thermometer is spliced for winter use, saw the blue earth
heaved into mountain waves from Agiocochook, and
where the Umbagog Ossipee and Squam gleamed like
dewy cobwebs in the sun– And like bright ribbons the
streamlets of Connecticut Saco & adroscoggin "take up
their mountain march–

Went on our way silent & humble through the Notch
–heard the lambs bleat in Bartlett on the mountains late at
night–looked back on Conway peak–threaded the woods
of Norway pine–and saw the Great Spirit smile in
Winnipiseogee

Varro advises to plant in the Quincunx order in order
not to "obstruct the beneficial effects of the sun and
moon and air," and adds "nuts, when they are whole,
which you might comprize in one modius, because nature
confines the kernels in their proper places, when they are
broken, can hardly be held in a measure of a modius and
a half." Vines thus planted produce more fruit "more
must and oil, and of greater value".

I read in Varro that "Caesar Vopiscus AEdilicius, when he pleaded before the Censors, said that the grounds of Rosea were the garden [(sedes)] of Italy, in which a pole being left would not be visible the day after, on account of the growth of the herbage." This soil was not remarkably fertile yet I was so well contented with myself it may be & with my entertainment–that I was really remind of this anecdote.

In speaking of "the dignity of the herd" Varro suggests that the object of the Argonautic expedition was a ram's fleece   the gold apples of the Hesperides were by the ambiguity of language [Μηλον] goats and sheep which Hercules imported–the stars and signs bear their names   the AEgean sea has its name from the goat and mountains and straits have hence their names–sic. The Bosphorus Piso makes Italy to be from Vitulis– The Romans were shepherds "Does not the fine [mulcta, a mulgendo] that was by ancient custom paid in kind refer to this?" The oldest coins bore the figures of cattle and the Roman names Porcius–Ovinus Caprilius & the surnames Equitius, Taurus, Capra Vitulus.

Vide Cato "Of purchasing an Estate–" "How an estate is to be planted–" &c in Lat & Eng.

{*One-third page blank*}

Aug 31st 1846 Concord to Boston–
    Rail road Station–tall man–sailors short of money–cars to Portland Passenger to Umbagog. Sea shore–Salem tunnel no water   hay cocks–Portsmouth North Berwick–Saco–Portland–Capt's office –White head light–sailor–owls head Thomaston –Camden–Belfast–Bangor–
Sept 1st
    Start in buggy 11 o clock–double barrelled guns–knapsack and carpet bag. North Bangor–Still

water lower and upper–lucus a non lucendo–Old
town–loggers with black man marking logs   batteaux
Ferry–pedlar–Indian island–Swing by a Canadian
–Milford Marks of freshet Ind Islands.–Olemon Green
bush–Sunkhaze? Houlton Military road–Passadumkeag
–politicians doctor and lawyer–&c–Enfield–temperance
house–treats–Orchard–

Sept 2nd

Cold stream lake–Apple trees Lincoln–Indians   dogs
–Salmon spear   rum–moose–No 4?, burnings–trees like
frnt yard–larch–ball spruce–cedar hemlock–fir–beach
birch Norway pine &c. shop   pencils–Mattawamkeag
–bridge   point–relics–Shallowness of river–60 miles
up–Houlton road to Aroostook do–Potatoes & turnips
Molunkus house–stage–Province man– –Pasture–oiled
map–Flash novels and statistical reports–companions

Thursday

Sept 3d

Woodland trail–Mattaseunk–mill & rail road 3 miles
–burnt land Salmon river & Crockers Pattagumpus
sp–7 miles from Pt. little Books Ma'rm Howards
books–via open land   patch Cucumbers & potatoes &
burrying ground–Fisk's at E branch–Nickatow–New
wife–10 miles from Pt–ferry–corn field–batteau
Opening and barn near rock Ebeeme–loggers camps
–cedar shingles–hovel–latches–fire place–benches–place
for waterpail & pork-barrel–& wash basin–chimney
rudiment of– –fresh sweet scent of the woods. Hairy
woodpecker–Yellow hammer blue jay–Ducks–loon
–chicadee–cedar bed–

Hale farm, now Waites' 13 miles from Pt Corn
field–fine view, too smoky–to see Mt. Table–mt
cranberries–books Eng. woman–to Mc Causlins Little
Schoodic–17 miles Gun–dogs–ferry–Jim–relics
–family Uncle Geo. Supper–farm Hut Milk   cheese
supper

Friday Sept 4th

    rain–books–Wand. Jew Crim. Calendar–Parishes
Geogr. Flash novels–table–holes in floor–butter to
grease boots No excursions into woods   logging roads
–no game   tea–molasses–no boards–clapboards
–chimney–wood colored a sort of buff color by smoke.
Dogs and hawks–no salt nor sugar   oats–grass
potatoes & rot   carrots turnips–little corn for hens
–White pine gone–Spruce white cedar–beach birch
maple–larch–fir left   harebell &c–bat in house.
    supply loggers in spring & winter–Beaver dam.
    Blue joint–& rush grass

Sat. Sept 5th

    Why this country not settled–9 shillings an acre
–Mc Causlin hired out by his wife–15 lbs hard bread
10 lbs pork–tea–kettle–frying pan–spirits–salt
matches–tent–blankets–burnt land   dogs–
    Little sturgeon gut   a run round 3 miles from
Mc. C's–Great sturgeon gut   shad pond–& Tho
Fowlers Millinocket river 8 miles from Millinocket
lake 4 from Mc C:–smaller than map is shad pond.
–Pam–& Thom   new house   window–spruce bark
–Beer–fife–Fish hawk–Eagles nest–Tom hired out
–haying–rush grass and meadow clover at mouth of
Millinocket, Cedar brooms   sucker or eel nests–musk
rats–determine rise of water–Summer duck–kingfisher
–robins fish hawks–brown ash–a still river   moose
meadows Old Fowlers 6 miles from Mc C. last
house Once lived on S side west branch where he built
his house 16 year ago– first house built above five
Islands–Kittens   mink-cat.– Intelligence of people–just
caught salmon here fresh in pickle–Salmon with
us. Wolves–traps   horses–carry–2 miles   sled–stones
building hog pen.– rocks   pipe–Dine–reach river above
Grand Falls at 2 to 4   thunder storm   under

batteau   making pins & singing songs–Geo & Tom
Fowler mild easy like, Geo. Melvin   & Jim who was
clearing   entrance to Quakish lake at 2 o'clock 8 miles
from Mc C. Grand Falls below Kettle Frying
pan   axe   getting ready to lie under a log. Camps on
route–poling up rapids–Ind. say river ran both ways
    rowing through Quakish of a thousand acres Joe
merry mt N of W–clear before sun set   ducks &
loon Cedar & spruce trees covered with moss like
ghosts. 1st view of Ktaadn in clouds 2 miles of double
lake then 1 of poling to dam–raise water 10 feet   take
out baggage   draw up sluice. John morrison & his
gang–fish poles   log sluices   toll pier Men of all
trades   camp   tea & white bread   tin cups–fire–no
milk   sweet cakes Em. Address & two converts
–Westminster Rev. for 1834 & Hist. of the Erection of
the Monument on the grave of Myron Holley. spring
–beds   benches   leaves of bible–Coffee pot–devour and
steal all–
    This camp 11 miles from Mc. C. 1 mile of river
thoroughfare & rapids N W–S of W N W–& W   then
4 miles in North Twin–by moon light S twin inlet
laughing loon   light house island–distant shores
Ghostly trees   mountain vailed– pausing to
hear wolves & see moose   hear hooting owls–alternate
rowing–rocks   camp at head of N Twin at 20 to
9 o clock–probably a dozen moose looking on. Great
fire   sandy shore   sand bed–sparks–boat   tent
shower in night–beautiful calm glassy lake by moon
light–little rill–rousing up fire–snoring–jokes   whispers
remarks. moving about fire–
Sept 6th
    Sunday morning 1/2 of river and thorough fare amid
rocks & poling to foot of Pamadumcook–across this 1
mile   lake makes N W 10 miles to hills &
mountains Joe Merry bears S W.   then thoroughfare

& across Deep cove 2   part of same lake   two miles
N E–men lost on lakes–could not find river–1 1/2
across Umbedegis lake   beautiful lake Joe Merry &
double top–to Rock & breakfast–rill–old camp and
Blacksmith's shop & brick–pond lilies   tea–black
–pork   hard bread   salmon–birch bark plates   forks
Booms & fencing stuff in water & laid up at entrance &
outlet of lake

 1/4 mile of thorough fare & rapids to carry of 90 rods
around Umbedegis falls   stream we were set over–Pork
barrel–carrying baggage & boat up hill through mossy
places   drag–& keep from rocking. bream. 500
weight–

 Then 1 1/2 miles of river & Passamagummuck
lake   a large cove or lake comes in on left through
meadow to falls   river like–Unbedegis stream coming
in on right–. poled up these falls–then 1/2 mile to
Thatcher's Rips–then 2 miles of Depskaneig lake
–Passamagummuck stream coming in on left–first more
northerly then more easterly–shallow & weedy & not
very large.– no trout   dinner   choak and break
tooth– –cliffy shore   tea kettle–carry of 90 rods–oak
hall–to Pockwockomus lake   river like 2 miles to
Consultation isle–rush & cut grass & moose track
–Depskaneig comes in from left 1/2 mile from
head.– Poke Logans 1 mile from Con. isle to carry
of 40 rods round Pockwockomus falls   small Concord
stream–willows   gravel–marks of pikes on stones
–barrel of pork–rocky–hard work warping up. then
poling & rowing through Aboljacarmegus lake 3/4
mile   river like   to carry around Aboljacarmegus
falls at flat rock   then poling 1/2 mile by jam of logs
like cannon to Sowdehunk dead water

 to Murch Brook & Aboljacknagesic 1 mile below
Gibson's clearing & sowdehunk and camp–13 3/4
from Head N. Twin.

trout & chivin   camp   moose bones   cedar bed
and tea Mt. visible   not 4 but 14 miles

Monday Sept 7th
        mount by moon light   trout by moonlight–large
white chivin–fish for breakfast   pack and start   how
leave things & batteau–carry fish & tent &c. bee line
from Abol–&c to base of high peak. burnt
land   poplars   blueberries   thick woods   moose
dung   bear dung   rabbits dung– moose
tracks   browsing–stripping off bark–cook fish on
sticks–Mount ash or round wood–cranberries–cornel
berries   birch–fir–spruce–solomon's seal   climb
tree   torrent–camping ground   leave party   go up
torrent   fir trees   lakes   rocks–clouds–sick and
weary   camp   green fish   fire at night–wind up
ravine

Tuesday 8th
        Hard bread–& pork getting short–go up–Mount
Cranberries and blue berries   clouds–wind–rain   rocks
lakes   return down stream   8 1/2   marks of
freshet–trout   all come from top   the inlet   trout
–slipping sliding–jumping–brook runs S & S W   wet
feet–climb tree   see meadow   hard bread & pork
–allowance–Moose tracks   muddy water– Burnt
lands–batteau 2 1/2   fish in sun

—

return 4 1/2   swiftly   dropped batteau over
Aboljacarmegus falls   carry around Pocwockomus
Falls– Camp at Oak hall carry leaving boat to bring
over in morning–old camp   high wind & smoke–goes
down before morn–

Wednesday Sep 9th

Around run down Passamagumuck falls   found
share   walking round–dropped down Unbedegis
falls   breakfasted at head of lake making haste lest
the wind should rise–rowing & steering
rapidly   Umbedegis a beautiful lake   deep
philosophy with Fowler on this lake–fine view of Mt.
NE   double top &c

from foot of Pammadumcook Joe Merry S W. 4
miles across N Twin. 12 1/2 minutes to mile   mt
visible from lakes commonly– Dam at 12 1/2
o clock   not visible here. 1/2 barrel pickerel   devour
all again   walk the millinocket 2–instead of 1 1/2
–partridges   young tree Indians   muskrat–moose
track–Mac causlins at sundown   dogs glad to see him.

Thursday Sept 10th

Walking 7 miles–batteauing–10 miles   school
house–ducks–1/2 past three   ride till 1/2 past one to
Bangor   fires by road–then sleep 3 hours and steam
it 17 hours to Boston 450 miles–

—

The Mt was first ascended by white men in 1804 V
Williamson's Hist Maine.
Prof. J. W. Bailey. West Point 1837.
Cedar–is Thuja occidentalis
Jackson in–38
Hale in 1845

{One-half page blank}

It was with pleasant sensations that we rowed over the
North Twin lake by moonlight–now fairly beyond the last

vestige of civilized, perhaps of human life–in the midst of
such environment and such civility there as nature
allows For still I could think of nothing but vaster cities
there concealed on the distant shore and ports and
navies–and the orient and occident–the levant and the
Pacific of trade–

Over that high table land so open to the sun and light
and yet uninhabited. Continuous forests bounded the view
on every side–the shore rising into gentle wooded
hills–and now and then a mountain reared itself above
the level woods–Joe Merry or Double-top–or Ktadn.

The loon laughed and dived as we held on our way–the
fir and spruce and cedar, occasionally hanging with
moss, stood like the ghosts of trees on the distant
shore– We sang, at least with enthusiasm, such boat
songs as we could remember–and listened to hear if any
wolf responded–aware that we had perchance disturbed
many a deer or moose quietly feeding on the shore–and
even then gazing at us–but we heard only the hooting of
owls

On entering the lake we steered for a little dot of an
island hardly visible in the dark–where we amused
ourselves with planning that the light house should
be–and how we should like to live and be the light-house
man. At length we drew up our batteau upon a smooth
white sandy shore at the head of the lake–gliding in
between some large dark rocks and proceeded to make our
camp–

It is difficult to conceive of an country uninhabited
by man   we naturally suppose them on the horizon
everywhere– And yet we have not seen nature unless we
have once seen her thus vast and grim and drear–whether
in the wilderness or in the midst of cities–for to be Vast is
how near to being waste.

Coming down the Mt perhaps I first most fully realized that that this was unhanselled and ancient Demonic Nature, natura, or whatever man has named it.

The nature primitive–powerful gigantic aweful and beautiful, Untamed forever. We were passing over burnt lands with occasional strips of timber crossing it, and low poplars springing up–open and pasture-like–with blue berries sloping away down toward the river–for our convenience I found myself traversing it familiarly like some pasture run to waste–or partially reclaimed by man–but when I reflected what a man–what brother or sister or kindred of our race farmed it–and made it firm ground and convenient for us to walk on– The earth seemed recent–and I expected the proprietor to dispute my passage– When then did my ancestors acquire the preemptive right? But only the moose browsed here, and the bear skulked–and the black partridge fed on the berries and the buds.

The main astonishment at last is that man has brought so little change– And yet man so overtops nature in his estimation.

The trout fishing at the mouth of the Aboljacknagesic–in that part of the river called the Sowdehunk still water, was as it were fabulous, to describe There those fishes made beautiful the lord only knows why, to swim there, leaped from the stream to our frying pan by some orphic process

It impressed me so like a vision that late at night or early in the morning I rose by moonlight to learn if I were indeed there and this dream were true. And there by the moonlight–in that wholly visionary dream land–the speckled trout again rose to the bait and the fable proved true again.– The outline of Ktadn was plainly visible a dozen miles off in the warm light–

I could understand the truth of mythology–and the fables of Proteus and all those beautiful sea monsters– How all history put to a terrestrial use is history, but put to a celestial is mythology ever.

There we lay where Indians once–and since adventurous loggers seeking the white pine had camped before us and caught trout like us. There were the moose on which some party had feasted, of which we brought away some teeth–and we used the birch poles that had been left by them.

One memorable evening and moon lighted dawn I first caught the trout in the Maine wilderness at the mouth of the Aboljacknagesic which comes into to the West Branch of the Penobscot from Mount Ktadn– And the fable of the trout was realized to me. I had long sought a larger specimen of its cousin the White Chivin or roach and here my first captive was the fish I sought–fishes larger than the red distinctly white or silvery–swam here and were forward to take the bait–at the mouth of Murch Brook–in dark water. I had come so far to catch my fish.

There are singular reminiscensces in the life of every man–of seasons when he was leading a wholly unsubstantial and as it were impossible life–in circumstances so strange–in company so unfit and almost this time the creature of Chance. As the hours spent in travelling by steam boat night or day– It is a transient and dream like experience–for which I have no other place in any memory but such as I assign to dreams. In a longer voyage no doubt the circumstances and scenery wold become familiar and we might realize how we too could be sailors–and so lead our lives But in these voyages of a night in which the power of a new genius or demon steam–surpassing the relations of eastern

fables are summoned to waft us to a distant spot–we pass
too rapidly from our associations to a new era– All men
but a few cooks and waiters and engineers and deck
hands seem as much in a dream as yourself– All are as
if they had taken something–wine or opium or beer– All
are familiar as in dreams and each represents a class Is
the best specimen of his class– See the man in a rich
fur cap and velvet cloak– Now trying to get sleep–now
pacing the deck and looking round upon us–with
assurance as if he were some prince and travelled there
rightfully and more entirely than we–we who are the
same old six pences any where just as homely and simple
the other side the Globe as where we belong–and the last
day as this hour–

He is a fabulous man–not fed and sustained as we
are– The Sea fareing man lighting his pipe at midnight
and pacing the deck once more–guessing we are now
about off white head whose light we see yonder–has often
sailed this shore knows all the lights– By the bye
Where's Jim   how many times has he been to bed and
got up again–not knowing but it was day light–hoping it
was– Now he'll borrow your pipe if you please– Has he
slept any–he says he slept well does'nt want any more–but
here he is up at mid night– He declares he sees the day
breaking–we shall be in the bay in an hour–thats' nigger
Island–that's Owl's head-light– It grows light apace– We
begin to trig up–slick hair–smooth pants snuff the
breeze a little and shake ourselves– By the by what time
is it? One says its 3 o clock   one says its one–one says
it's only eleven– And the cook passing answers half past
leven gentlemen– And that light was the moon rising
and the sailors who had sailed these shores–exeunt to
bed again and now determine to sleep this time– Some
not abaft the shaft choose again a soft recess among the
bales–some stagger down–seeming to the risen heads to

have come upon the business of the boat–or as if going
down town at leisure

{*One-fifth page blank*}

At about eleven oclock I started with one companion in
a buggy from Bangor–for "up river" expecting to be
overtaken at Matawamkeag Point the next day night. We
had each a knapsack or carpet bag–filled with such clothing
and conveniences as we could conveniently carry–and my
companion carried a double barrelled gun– We rattled out
of this depot of lumber–this worn Old Bangor–in to New
Bangor still in its swadling clothes–built of the lumber
saved from exportation–till some 6 or seven miles brought
us to Stillwater–lucus a non lucendo I suppose–for here
the river is particularly restless and uneasy and the falls
furnish the power which carries the mills night and day by
which the sorely driven logs are at last driven through
the narrowest gut of all and most finely slitted There
your inch stuff or your two or your three inch begin to
be And Mr Sawyer marks off those spaces which decide
the destiny of so many prostrate forests– Through this
jam over this fall they come out laths boards clapboards
shingles such as the wind can take–and very few logs
indeed get over whole
Through this steel riddle is the arrowy Main forest
from Chesuncook–& the head waters of the St John's &
from Ktadn relentlessly sifted
Here is a close jam a hard rub at all seasons and then
the Maine forest white as driven pine log–is lumber.
The log which has shot so many falls only with injury
to its sap wood–and bears the scars of its adventures–may
think here to lie quietly embraced by its boom with its
companion's as in a fold–but not so. for here comes the
closest rub of all–one inch–two 3 inches at a time–with

your sap pared off–and then you may go.– The best of
eastern stuff–to Boston or New Haven–or New York.

Then are they slit and slit again till you get a size that
will suit for the ship or house or lucifer match. Think
how stood the white pine tree with its branches soughing
with the four winds–think how it is trimmed now. loped
–scarified–soaked bleached–shaved–& slit–before yet the
mechanical gentry–with their cases of sharp cutting
instruments commence operations upon it.

Then Upper still water & its mills–leaving the railroad
still on our left away from–the river running through a
cedar swamp. Here we stopped in our waggon to observe
a party of watermen with spike poles in their hands
selecting logs from the mill– They were directed by a
mullatto celebrated for his skill and judgment–and in
their jumping from log to log got 3 or 4 duckings where
the water was 3 or 4 feet deep while we were looking on

At 12 miles we reached the village of Old Town, with
its mills–& its depot–quite a large and rambling country
town

While waiting for the Ferry man's scow to come over,
for the bridge had been carried off in the freshet and they
were now completing a new one 4 feet higher–we walked
into a batteau manufactory– There were some on the
stocks and new ones just painted outside to dry– They
were made of the clearest and widest stuff as slightly as
possible–secured to a few light maple knees with only two
boards to a side–from 20 to 25 feet long and only 4 or 5
wide–sharp at both ends–and sloping seven or 8 feet over
the water at the boughs–in order that they slip over
the rocks as gently as possible– The bottom is left
perfectly flat–not only from side to side by from end to
end–sometimes even they become hogging after long use,
and the boatmen then turn them over and straighten
them by a weight at each end.

The making of batteaux is quite a business here and at several other places—for the supply of the penobscot river— They told us that a batteau wore out in two years on the rocks—and they were sold for 14 to 16 dollars apiece. There was something refreshing to my ears in the very name of the white man's canoe, reminding me of Charlevoix and Canadian voyagers— The batteau the "paddle—the water"? is a sort of mongrel between the canoe and the boat—a fur traders boat—& I know not that this boat is used in other parts of the world.

They weigh from 5 to 800 pounds and commonly it takes 3 men to carry one over a portage one at each end and one in the middle underneath At a little distance when I first observed them on the water, they had the sparse straight stealthy look of a canoe.

Every log is marked by the chopper with the owners mark cut in the sap wood with the axe—and it requires considerable ingenuity to invent new marks where there are so many owners— They have quite an alphabet of their own—which only the practised can read— My companion read off from his memorandum book some marks of his own logs— Among which there were crows feet and girdles and various other devices—as Y-girdle-crowfoot

We at length drove into the scow which is used as a temporary ferry boat and had now returned and the two boatmen had already shoved off some rods when a tin pedlar appeared on the bank and hailed us—earnest to carry his wares still further into the woods.— we were fain to push back and take him in. With him we jested awhile for our amusement—and he proved of the right stuff especially when he watered his horse in one of his large pans dipping in the river—we declared it would leak—a pedlar trying his own wares—didnt he know better–it would certainly leak, and sure enough it did–but had'nt he a composition which he sold with them–sure to stop leaks–and so increased his trade. And as he held it to horse it ran a stream–

This ferry took us past the Indian Island–lying between that and the falls– Just as our boat left the shore we observed one short ill-looking washerwoman looking Indian land on the old town side–as if just from up river– And drawing up his canoe he took out a bundle of skins in one hand and an empty keg or half barrel in the other– Here was his history written

The island seemed nearly deserted this day– Yet I noticed some new houses among the weather stained as if the tribe had a design to live–but generally they have a very shabby and forlorn & cheerless look all backside and woodshed and not homestead even Indian homestead but in stead of home an abroad-stead–for their life is domi et militiae–or rather venatus–and most of the latter– The church is the only trim looking building–but that is not Abenakis That was Rome's doings.

Good Canadian it may be but poor Indian.

There was here a sort of swing somewhere called a fandango I believe erected by a Canadian for the amusement of strangers and his own profit–a contrivance by which you were carried round in the air as it were sitting in the circumference of a skeleton wheel–with a radius of 60 feet or so–not horizontally but vertically–and your seat kept upright by your weight I judged. It was altogether a frail and trembling structure and I should have preferred to see a heavier man "come full's circle" before I tried it.

We were at length landed in Milford and rode along on the east side of the Penobscot having a more or less constant view of the river and the islands in it–for they hold these as far up as Nickatow at the mouth of the East branch. It was the Houlton military road on which

we were travelling–the main almost the only road of much
importance in these parts It is straight and as well made
and kept in repair as you will find almost any where.
Everywhere we saw signs of the great freshet this house
standing awry–and that where it was not founded–and
that other with a water-logged look as it were still airing
and drying its basement–and logs with every body's
marks upon them–and sometimes the marks of their
having served as bridges–strewn along the road.

We crossed at the Sunk haze a summerish Indian
name–the Olemmon and other streams–which make a
greater show on the map than they now did from the road.

At Passadumkeag we found anything but what the
name implies–earnest politicians to wit on the alert to
know how the election is likely to go–men who talk one
can not help believing with factitious earnestness rapidly
in subdued voice at dusk one on each side your
chaise–endeavoring to say much in little for the time is
short   they see you hold the whip impatiently. Caucuses
they have had caucuses they are like to have–victory and
defeat and Some body–may be elected! somebody may
not– They grow warm–patently warm volatiely
warm   the man on the right frightens the horse with his
asseveration growing more solemnly positive as there is
less thought in him to be positive about– There are the
lights are they not being lit in yonder school house where
Cilley has the floor to night but you draw the rein
firmly– And they step resignedly aside–with a loook
which seems to say and must you go–and we have so
much to say? well we can endure it.

This is mister so and so who lives in that house
there–he does not know you or he does–he having just
been "made acquainted" with you, and now talks in a low
serious and long established voice with you– So did not
Passadumkeag look on the map.

We left the river road awhile for shortness and went by
a way of Enfield where we stopped for the night at
Treats temperance house in a retired country. An
orderly and domestic inn–where the traveller may really
be refreshed and make himself at home Here we found
quite an orchard of healthy and well grown bearing apple
trees–but all wild and comparatively worthless for want
of a grafter–and so is it generally here abouts though the
trees are generally much younger–than here This being
the oldest settlers house The apple is almost the only
fruit that can be raised–and yet a poor apple is put up
with.

And so it comonly happens the farmer in a new country
will go far to raise the trees but not to graft them. Here
abouts they told us deer were not uncommon in the
winter–& wolves some times still did them harm.

The next morning we drove along through a high
and hilly country–in view of Cold Stream Pond a very
beautiful lake 4 or 5 miles long–at least– It deserves to
make a greater show upon the maps– we observed that
every farmer hereabouts was raising an orchard though
there was no grafted fruit yet.

Lincoln which we passed through this forenoon is
quite a village for this country. I observed an
establishment for making pottery We stopped awhile to
learn if there were any Indians in the neighborhood as
we wished to engage them as guides–

We were told that there were several wigwams half a
mile from the road on one of their islands–

So we left our horse and waggon and walked through
the fields and woods to the river but it was not till after
considerable search that we discovered their
habitations–regular shanties–in a retired place out of
sight of settlers– Taking one of 2 canoes which we found
drawn up on the shore on the Lincoln side we paddled
across to what seemed their landing on the island

side There were some canoes and a curious fish spear
made of wood lying on the shore—such as they might have
used before white men came They afterward told us it
was a salmon spear. its point was an elastic piece of
wood somewhat like the contrivance for holding the
bucket on the end of a well pole. Near where we landed
sat an Indian girl on a rock in the water washing and
singing or huming a song meanwhile— This was an
aboriginal strain—her hair hung down like the long grass
at the bottom of the river— We walked up to the nearest
house—but were met by a sally of a dozen wolfish looking
dogs which might have been lineal descendants from the
ancient Indian dogs which the first voyageurs describe
as "their wolves."

The occupant soon appeared with a long pole in his
hand with which he beat off the dogs—while he parleyed
with us. He seemed half mullattoe He told us in his
sluggish way that there *were* Indians going "up river" he
and one other— And when were they going–? to-day
—before noon— And who was the other— Louis Neptune
who live in the next wigwam— Well let us go see Louis
– The same doggish reception–the same development
And Louis Neptune makes his appearance–a small
wirey man with a puckered and wrinkled face— The
same as I remembered who had guided Jackson to the Mt
in 37– The same questions were put to him–and the same
information obtained–while the other Ind. stood by. He
going by noon with two canoes up to Chesuncook
hunting–to be gone month— Well Louis suppose you get
to the Point tonight–we walk on on up the west branch
tomorrow four of us— You overtake us tomorrow–and
take us into your canoes– You stop for us we stop for
you— Yea May be you carry some provision for us and
so pay.– He said "me sure get some Moose–" and when
I asked if he thought Pomolar the genius of the Mt
–would let us go up he answered–we must plant one

bottle of rum on the top—he had planted a good many—and when ever he looked again the rum was all gone— No wonder—

He had been up 2 or 3 times— he had planted letter Eng—German—French. &c &c.— So we parted   he would reach Mattawamkeag point tonight to camp—and over take us up the west branch the next day or the next— When we reached the landing Mrs Neptune was just coming up the bank having been shopping in Lincoln and smilingly affirmed that we had stolen her canoe— We asked her too if Louis were going upriver and she answered "right away".

So we left the Indians thinking ourselves lucky to have secured such guides and companions.

These Ind. were bare headed and lightly dressed like laborers They did not ask us in to their houses but met us outside.

There were occasional burnings on this road—where some settler was enlarging his farm or some new comer making a clearing.— very few houses were built of logs— —but we passed some log houses which had been deserted The evergreen such as are rare with us stood by the road side like a long front yard—beautiful specimens of the larch & cedar or arbor vitae—ball spruce—fir balsam—& norway pine— Also beech & birch—growing luxuriantly in the soil of the road side.

We stopped a few moments at a place called the "cottage inn" to water the horse and walking into the bar room with the ostler following—and as if we showed him the way— Our heads as empty just at that moment of any serious purpose as the room was empty of men or the bar of decanters—as travellers use— Perhaps we stamped —shook our coats and looked out the window to see which way we had come in. one thing we did—that at at least would be reasonable   we looked full in the face of the

clock that hung on the wall, but alas it responded not to
our gaze or remotely like harvard college as from behind
the age–some life that had convened within it seemed to
have adjourned sine die–perchance it chronicled the
advent of the last travellers–like an empty Caucus
chamber–but we put our finger upon the springs here a
little and there a little and soon left the speaker running
over his minutes to a full house while the ostler grinned
his satisfaction behind– And said he "we have got another
in the dining room that has'nt been a going for some
time–should like to have you look at that–and that we
looked at over the bare tables ready set–but all desolate
and unsavory– –and so we let *him* water the horse.

We walked into a shop over against the inn–the *puny*
beginning of commerce which would grow at last in to a
"firm" in the future town or city   in deed it was already
"Somebody & Co. The woman came from the penetralia
of of the attached house–for Mr–was in the "burning"
perchance–and *she* sold percussion caps canalés or
smooth and knew their prices & qualities and which the
hunters preferred– Here was a little of everything–to
satisfy the wants and the ambition of the woods a stock
selected with what pains & care–but there seemed to me as
usual a preponderance of children's toys dogs to bark and
cats to mew and trumpets to blow where *natives* there
hardly are yet– As if a child born into the Maine woods
among the pine cones and the cedar berries couldnt do
without such a sugar man and skipping jack as the young
Rothschild has. It seems to me I was indebted to none of
these things but my one pewter soldier which *has* left an
impression.

I observed here pencils which are made in a bungling
way by grooving a round piece of cedar then putting in
the lead and filling up the cavity with a strip of wood.

About noon we reached the Matawamkeag–and dined
at a frequented house still on the Houlton Military

road–where the stage stops and dines–& sleeps–and here was a substantial *covered* bridge over the Matawamkeag built, I think they said some 17 years ago– After dinner–where by the way and even at breakfast as well as supper–at the public houses on this road the front rank is composed of various kinds of "sweet cakes" in a continuous line from one end of the table to the other I think I may safely say that there was a row of 10 or dozen plates of this kind before us two here– To account for this they say that when the lumberers come out of the woods they have a craving for cakes and pies and such sweet things which there are scarcer– And this is the supply to satisfy that demand. The supply is always equal to the demand–and these hungry men think a good deal of getting their money's worth

Well over this front rank I say you coming from the "sweet cake side" with a certain cheap philosophic indifference have to fight what there is behind which I dont by any means mean to insinuate is deficient to supply that other demand of men not from the woods but from the towns for venison and strong country fare.

After dinner we strolled down to the "point–or the junction of the two rivers–said to be the scene of an ancient battle between the Eastern Ind. & the Mohawks and a place still much used by Ind bound up or down the river for camping. We grubbed in a small potatoe patch and found some points of arrowheads and on the shore some colored beads and one small leaden bullet–but nothing more remarkable.

On our way back to the tavern we passed a singular mound regularly formed–and after deciding that it was a work of art speculated upon its design–and what we might do with a spade and leisure, when one of us stooping and looking narrowly at a clod–exclaimed I have it–the mystery is solved and held up a piece of charcoal.

The Matawamkeag was a mere rivers' bed exceeding
rocky & shallow—so that you could almost cross it dry
shod in boots and I could hardly believe my companion
when he told me that he had been 60 miles up it in a
batteau— A batteau could hardly find a harbor now at
its mouth.

Before our companions arrived we road on up the
Houlton road 7 miles to where the Aroostook road comes
into it—to Molunkus where there is a spacious mansion in
the woods called the Molunkus House kept by one
Libbey—which looked as if it had its hall for dancing and
for military drilling. Just as we stopped the Houlton stage
drove up and a Province Man addressed me as the
landlord—regretting the dryness the bars on this road
nothing since he left Houlton so— I asked him if it was
low water now that the bars were dry—and if he should
take in a little water whether he couldnt go over. I looked
off the piazza round the corner of the house up the
aroostook road which is a track well-worn by the shoes of
immigrants but showed no clearings in sight— And there
was a man just adventuring upon it this evening in a
rude original—what we will call Aroostook wagon—a *seat*
as it were with a wagon swung under it—a few bags and
a dog *asleep to watch* them. He offered to carry any
message to any body in that country—cheerfully— Here
too was a small trader who kept store but no great store
certainly in a small box over the way behind the
Molunkus sign post But his house—we could only
conjecture where that was. He may have rented a corner
of the Molunkus house. I saw him standing in his shop
door his shop so small that if a customer should make
demonstrations of coming in—he would have to go out—the
back way— And then perchance confer with him through
the window about his goods in the cellar— —or rather that
may be expected by the next arrivals— I was so green as

not to go in though I might have invented an errand
because I didn't see at first where he would go to

I think there was not more than one house on the road
to Molunkus– I remember one clearing where we got out
to examine the crop The mode of clearing & planting is
this to fell the trees and burn once what will burn–then
perhaps cut them up into lengths that may be rolled into
heaps and burn again–then with a hoe plant potatoes
where you can come at the ground between the
stumps–and charred logs   in the fall cut roll and burn
again–the ashes sufficing for manure and no hoeing
being necessary the first year–and soon it is ready for
grain or to be lain down. We got over the fence in to a
field here where the logs were still burning–and pulled
up the vines found good sized potatoes nearly ripe growing
like weeds and turnips mixed with them between the hills.

Let those talk of poverty and hard times who will in the
towns and cities   cannot the immigrant who can pay his
fare to N Y. or Boston pay 5 dollars more to get here and
be as rich as anybody–where land virtually cost
nothing–and houses only the labor of making And if he
will still remember the distinctions of poor and rich let
him bespeak him a narrower house forthwith.

When we returned to the Matawamkeag the stage had
already put up there and the Province man was betraying
his greenness to the Yankees.– Why Province money
wont pass here when states money is good at Fredricton
and st John. From what I saw then and after it appeared
that the Province man was *now* the only real Jonathan
and raw country bumpkin–left so far behind by his
enterprising neighbors–that he did'nt know enough to
put a question to them.

Here as every where in taverns there were men
educated to make the bar room their parlor Chamber &
withdrawing room who can sleep on a shelf or in a chest

or a sink with a lid to it–without stopping up the hole–with two eyes peering out at you–but silent and motionless till stage hours waiting for night to be gone.

On the parlor table we found a peculiar literaturre which I fancy never stops short of the frontiers and then only because there is no more illiterate place to go to– Flash novels manufactured in N Y and Boston expressly for these markets and never heard of there–by Prof. Ingraham and others–all printed as it were in colored ink red and yellow & blue with engravings interspersed–"the Belle of the Penobscots" and other thrilling stories– And also statistical reports for which we are indebted perchance to "our rep. at Congress

The last edition of Greenleaf's map of Maine hung on the wall and as this was the last opportunity of the kind and we had no pocket map we determined to trace a map of the lake country. But the paper our pocketbooks and the house afforded was too thick–so we even dipped a wad of tow into the lamp and oiled a sheet upon the oil-cloth –and in good faith traced a labyrinth of errors carefully following the outline of imaginary lakes.– And it was while engaged in this operation that our companions arrived.

Just at dusk there drove up 2 young ladies in a light wagon with a smart horse and leaped out upon the piazza with a bounce–displaying their full dresses in the height of the fashon–& delivering their horse to the bar keeper–and scud familiarly up stairs to take their places over the rear departments The driver proved to be the Landlords daughter who had been a shopping or visiting some 30 miles out and had probably thrown their dust in the eyes of the few travellers on the road.

Deer and caribou are some times taken here in the winter within sight of the house.

The next morning early we had mounted our packs and prepared for a tramp up the West Branch My companion

having turned his horse out to pasture for a week thinking
that a bite of fresh grass and experience of New
Country influence would do him as much good as his
master.– We observed a fresh deer skin stretched upon
an out house as we left the premise and leaping over a
fence began to follow a rather obscure trail up the
Penobscot There was now no road further and but few
log huts to be met with for 30 miles. The evergreen
woods had decidedly a sweet fragrance which was racy
and invigorating like root beer–the air was a sort of diet
drink and we walked on boyantly and full of expectation
getting our legs stretched

At the end of 3 miles we came to a mill, and a rude
wooden rail road running down to the Penobscot– This
was certainly the last rail road we were to see– The old
town road was not to be expected. At intervals there was
an opening on our left on the bank made for log rolling
by the lumberman where we got a sight of the river–a
rocky and rippling stream. this was my first sight
perhaps of a bran new country where the only roads
were of nature's providing and the few houses were
camps. Here then one could no longer accuse
institutions–and society but must front the true source of
the evil. We hearrd the sound of a whistler duck from
time to time on the river–and the omnipresent blue jay
& chicadee around and the yellow hammer in the
openings.

We crossed one tract of more than a hundred acres
which had just been burnt over and was still smoking.
Our trail lay through the midst of it and was well nigh
blotted out The trees lay at full length four or 5 feet deep
and crossing each other in all directions all black as
charcoal–but perfectly sound within, still good for fuel
or for timber– Soon the axe would reduce their size and
the fire be applied again. Here were thousands of cords
of wood which would keep amply warm the poor of Boston

and NY for a winter which only cumbered the ground and
were in the settlers way. At an early hour we reached
Crockers at the mouth of Salmon river 7 miles from the
point–and made our selves at home in his cabin–a house
made of logs & splints with a stone chimney and split
boards for the floor– Here one of my companions
commenced distributing a small store of little books
among the children to learn them to read as well as old
newspapers among the parents. There was a book for
Helen and a book for John–grinning flaxen headed
children–who were true enough not to say thank you sir
because they were told to–and so the diminished package
was tucked away again against a new demand– A few
miles further we came to Ma'rm Howards passing over
an extensive opening where were 2 or three log huts in
sight and a small ground surrounded by a wooden
paling–one day perchance to be the old burrying ground
of a village with its mossgrown grave stones. Here was
another distribution of books– We noticed turnips &
cucumbers growing by our path.

The next house was Fisks at the Mouth of the East
branch–at Nickatow. There was quite a field of corn here
now nearly ripe Our course here crossed the Penobscot
and followed the southern bank– One of the party who
entered the house in search of the ferryman–reported a
very neat dwelling–with plenty of books and a new wife
just imported from Boston–wholly new to the woods– We
proceeded up the E. branch a little way to the batteau and
were poled down and across the main stream by this man
and another.– I was astonished to find the East branch
so deep which was apparently so shallow–10 or 15 feet–

we passed some rapids in the river called rock
Ebeeme–and a rude barn filled with hay–to be sold to the
loggers in the winter–and not long after in the thickest
of the woods some loggers camps still new which were
occupied the previous winter. There were the camps and

the hovel for the cattle hardly distinguishable except that
the latter had no chimney. These camps were perhaps 15
by 20 feet built of logs–hemlock cedar or spruce–2 or 3
large ones first one above the other & notched together
at the ends to the height of 3 or four feet then of smaller
logs resting upon transverse logs at the ends successively
shorter–so that the roof sloped to the chimney or oblong
square hole 3 or 4 feet in diameter. The interstices filled
with moss and the roof shingled with long splints of
cedar or spruce rifted with a sledge & cleaver.

The fire place the most important place of all is in
shape and size like the chimney–defined by a fence or
fender of logs on the ground and a heap of ashes a foot
or two deep–with solid benches of split logs running
round it– Here the fire melts snow & dries rain before it
can descend to quench it. The beds of white cedar leaves
or Arbor Vitae extend under the roofs on either hand.
There was the place for the water pail and pork barrel and
wash basin–and generally a pack of cards left on a log.
Usually a good deal of whitling was expended on the latch
which was made of wood in the form of an iron one.
These are made comfortable houses by the hugeness of the
fires that can be afforded.

Usually the scenery is drear and savage and as
completely in the woods as a fungus at the foot of a pine
in a swamp–no outlook but to the sky. This is for
warmth & convenience The primitive wood is always and
every where damp and mossy so that I travelled
constantly with the impression that I was in a swamp And
when it was remarked that this or that tract would make
a profitable clearing I was reminded that if the sun were
let in it would make a dry field at once.

The woods abounded in beech and yellow birch of
which there were some very large specimens and spruce
cedar and fir & hemlock–but we saw only the stumps of
the white pine–some of great size–these having been

closely culled out–and being the only tree much sought after even in this neighborhood– It was the white pine that had tempted white travellers to preceed us on this route. There are now indeed 3 classes of inhabitants in this country first the loggers who for a part of the year are much the most numerous– 2nd the settlers we have named who raise supplies for the loggers the only permanent inhabitants–and there were but 3 log huts above where we now were– And 3dly the hunters mostly Indians–the most ancient of all.

At what is commonly called the Hale farm–now Waite's an extensive and elevated clearing–we got a fine view of the river rippling & gleaming far beneath us.

Here you commonly get a good view of Ktadn and other mts but today it was so smoky that we could see none. But we could over look an immense country of forest stretching away up the sebois toward the Allagash–& Canada–and toward the Aroostook vally in the N. E. Here was quite a large cornfield for this latitude–whose penetrating dry scent we perceived a 3d of a mile off before we discovered it. We here met with a very hospitable reception from Mrs Waite who would not be paid for the luncheon she provided but seemed contented with the sight of strangers– We nibbled a morsel from the corner of her table which was yet standing and some of the party were refreshed by a cup of tea– Mountain cranberries stewed and sweetened made the dessert. The table when cleared and set away turned out an arm armchair which we ocupied The arms of the chair formed the frame on which the table rested and when the round top was turned up against the wall it formed the back of the chair and was no more in the way than the wall itself.

This we noticed was the prevailing fashion in these log houses–probably to economise in room. Here was only

one little boy to receive a picture book–which he fell to
reading forthwith.

18 miles brought us in sight of Mc-Causlin's or Uncle
George's as he was called by my companions where we
intended break Our fast and spend the night. His house
was in the midst of an extensive clearing on the opposite
or north side of the river.– So we collected upon the
shore and fired our gun as a signal–which brought first
his dogs forthwith and thereafter their master–at once
recognized as uncle George–stalking in waterman's boots
still further down the stream to where his boat
lay. accompanied by his dogs & a younger man–. One
after the other other he recognised the strangers as he
poled his batteau nearer the shore–and then declared that
the whole family was there. He was notified of an addition
to his family– And with his pole soon set us all over this
swift but shallow stream–in which we finally grounded
at some distance from the shore.

Geo. Mc Causlin has a clearing of several hundred
acres of level intervale at the mouth of the little Schoodic
river a dark and swampy looking beaver-stream This
soil bore the evidence of having been occupied by the
Ind Mc C. having picked up many relics and we looked
for more this afternoon though with slight success

Here we concluded to spend the night as there was no
convenient stopping place above.

He had seen no Indians pass and this did not happen
except in the night without his knowledge His house
stands on the bank of the river and commands a wide
prospect up and down the river.

He keeps a couple of horses cows and oxen and quite
a flock of sheep– I think he said he was the first to bring
a plough and a cow so far

As the Afternoon was so far spent we made our dinner
& supper all in one–

Mc Causlin is Kennebec man of Scotch descent who has
been a waterman 22 years and drove on the lakes and
head waters of the Penobscot 5 or six springs in
succession– But is now settled here on the bank and
raises supplies for the lumberers and himself   he
entertained us with the true Scotch hospitality while we
stayed and would accept no recompense–for it. He was
well known to my companions and was familiarly
addressed as uncle Geo. by the whole party. A man of dry
wit and shrewdness and a general intelligence which I
had not looked for in the back woods.

Supper was got before our eyes in the ample kitchen by a
fire which would have roasted an oxe and was soon smoking
on the table–piping hot wheaten Cakes–the flour ground
below & brought up river in batteaux–ham and eggs the
produce of the farm–tea sweetened with molasses–and
sweet cakes in contradistinction to hot-cakes to wind up
with.

Butter was here in such plenty that it was commonly
used before it was salted to grease boots with. I observed
that here as elsewhere afterward–where the meats are
salted–no salt in the unadulterated state is used or set
upon the table.

The Indians do not use it any more as their ancestors
did not. We sat round the round table at which Mrs
Mc Causlin presided and did ample justice to the
ample fare.

Many whole logs, 4 feet long were consumed to boil our
tea-kettle. The same summer & winter.

The way to our bedrooms led through the dairy which
was teeming with new milk & cheeses in press– In the
night we were entertained by the sound of rain drops
and awaked with a drop or two in our eyes– It seemed
to have set in for a storm and we made up our minds not
to for sake such quarters as these with these prospects

but wait for Indians & fair weather. It rained and
drizzled–and gleamed by turns the live long day.– What
we did that day how we killed the time we could never
well tell. How many times we buttered our boots–how
often one was seen to sidle off to take a nap. When it held
up I strolled up and down the banks of the river–and
gathered the hare bell which grew there and the white
cedar berries– The White pine is gone–but in thick forests
of spruce white cedar–beach–birch–maple–larch & fir it
is not missed– The neighbor whom we had first seen
with Mc Causlin walked over to visit the nearest neighbor
Fowler four miles and had stayed.–

It appeared that the few inhabitants made no
excursions at least in summer from the river into the
forest–but only hauled logs in the winter by a few logging
paths. Only the hunter–and the explorer for lumber
–penetrates these forests in the summer. There
was comparatively no game to be counted on–and but
little life where there was yet no orchard to invite and
harbor singing birds.– Else we walked over his farm–and
visited his well filled barns with Mc C. The potatoe rot
had found out him out too the previous year–and the
seed was of his own raising– Oats grass & potatoes were
his staples–a few carrots & turnips.– and a little corn for
the hens The possibility of ripening a little Indian Corn
is a favorite theme with the remote settlers–but the
largest field we had seen for a day or two looked like an
experiment.

These few settlers on this stream were tempted by the
cheapness of the land– When we asked why more settlers
did not come in he told us that they could not by the
land– It belonged to individuals or companies who were
afraid of being taxed for it if a township should be
formed. But to settling on the state's lands there was no
such hindrance–

For his own part Mc Causlin wanted no neighbors
did n't wish to see any road by his house. Neighbors
might live across the river but on the same side there
would be trouble on the score of fences and cattle.

We were amused by the behavior of the dogs
here– After wondering how the chickens here were
saved from hawks we observed that the dogs allowed no
winged creature to alight within sight– As Mc C said
The old one took it up first–and she taught the pup–and
now they had taken it into their heads that it wouldn't
do to have any thing of the bird kind on the premises–a
hawk hovering over was not allowed to alight but barked
off by the dogs circling underneath–a pigeon or a yellow
hammer was instantly expelled.

Still no canoes hove in sight though we could command
a mile or two of the river– Some times our host thought
his dogs gave notice of the approach of Indians half an
hour before they arrived.

There was a beaver dam on the Little Schoodic half a
mile from the house which however we failed to see.

When it rained hardest we returned to the house again
and took down a tract from the shelf– There was the
Wandering Jew cheap Edition and fine print The Criminal
Calendar–& Parishes Geog–& Flash novels 2 or 3 Under
the pressure of circumstances we read a little– The press
is not so feeble an engine after all

This house as usual was built of huge logs which
peeped out every where–and were chinked with clay and
moss– There were no boards or shingles or clapboards,
and scarcely any tool but the axe used in its construction.
The partitions were made of long clapboard like splints of
spruce or Cedar turned to a sort of Salmon color by the
smoke–the roof was covered with the same

The chimney was of vast size and made of stone– I
noticed that the floor was full of small holes as if made

by a gimlet–which were made in the winter when
lumberers frequent the house–with spikes in their boots
to prevent slipping– we were surely on their trail.

Just above Mc C's there is a rocky rapid where logs
jam in the spring and many loggers are employed who
frequent his house for milk and butter and cheese &
hay &c.

Or else we tried by turns his long-handled axe upon
the logs before the door– The axe helves here are made
to chop standing on the log nearly a foot longer than
with us.

A bat flew round our heads for a few moments in the
house–after the lamp was lighted.–

{*One-fifth page blank*}

In the morning the weather proved fair enough for our
purposes and we prepared to start– As the Indians had
failed us we at length persuaded Uncle George to
accompany us in the capacity of guide & boatman, and
the more easily though not without some delay on account
of a lingering desire to revisit the Scene of his driving
–and to see the Mt. Mrs Mc C how could she be
left alone to drive up the cows & milk them–for
neighbor Jim had not yet returned–but at last she gave
her consent or rather as Mc C. phrased it he was hired
out by his wife and had nothing to say– A cotton
tent–and a blanket–15 lbs of hard bred and 10 lbs of
pork made up Uncle George's pack– Our tea kettle and
frying pan lent to neighbor Fowler, would complete our
outfit

We were soon out of Mc Causlin's clearing and in the
grim Evergreen woods again marked by one faint settlers
trail. We soon reach a narrow strip called the burnt land
over run with weeds–stretching northward to Millinocket
lake–9 or ten miles–where a fire had raged formerly.

At 3 miles we reached a run round in the river called Little Sturgeon gut and a short distance further another called Great Sturgeon Gut— hereabouts one of the party had seen a wolf when last here—his hind parts just disappearing between the trees.

Shad pond is laid down too large in proportion to the other lakes I should say—and the Millinocket river comes in too far from its outlet.

Thomas Fowlers house was in full sight 4 miles from Mc Causlins at the mouth of the Millinocket river—8 miles from the lake of the same name (over the latter stream)—which is 10 miles square—and full of islands This lake affords perhaps a more direct course to Ktadn but we followed the Penobscot—& Pamidumcook Young Fowler who has a farm here 2 miles this side of his father—was just completing a new log hut—and sawing out a window through the logs nearly 2 feet thick when we arrived— He had begun to paper his house with Spruce bark—inside out—which has a good effect and in keeping. Instead of water we got here a draught of beer—which it was allowed would be better— Such ale as Moor of Moore hall may have drunk—calculated "to make him strong and mighty"—even without the aqua vitae.— It was root beer it was spruce beer—cedar beer hemlock—the top most most fantastic and raciest sprays of this primitive wood steeped in it   what ever invigorating and stringent gum or essence these woods afford was dissolved in it. Clear and thin—but strong and stringent as the cedar sap.

It was as if one sucked awhile at the very teats of nature in these parts—the sap of all of Millinockets botany commingled—a lumberers-drink—a water proof cement which would acclimate and naturalize a man at once— A drink which would make him see green, and if he slept dream that that he heard the wind sough among the pines–and if he were one who'd "disafforested his mind"–all undo the work.

Here was a fife praying to be played on–brought hither to tame wild beasts.

As we stood upon the pile of chips by the door fish hawks were sailing over head–not to be reached by the harmless charge that was sent after them– And here over shad pond no doubt was daily enacted the tyranny of the bald-eagles over this bird. Tom Pointed away over the lake to an eagle's-nest which was plainly visible on a pine high above the surrounding forest, and was frequented from year to year & held sacred by him– They were the only houses in sight–his low hut–and the eagle's airy bed of fagots

Thomas Fowler too was soon "hired out by his wife"–for two men were necessary to manage the batteau–for that was soon to be our carriage–and those men needed to be cool & skilful for the navigation of the Penobscot– Toms pack was soon made for he had not far to look for his waterman's boots and a red flannel shirt– This is the favorite color with the new country men–and red flannel is reputed to possess some mysterious virtues–affording a more generous entertainment to the pespiration– On every gang of choppers & of water men there will be a sprinkling of red birds. It is reputed to have something wholesome in it.

We took here a poor and leaky boat and poled up the Millinocket 2 miles to the Elder Fowler's–where we were to exchange there our batteau for a better– Fowler was cutting his grass and making hay–on the meadows and on the small low islands of the millinocket– Of native grass land there is proportionally little in this vicinity–excepting the burnt lands and these few scanty meadows by the sides of still streams there is no open land at all.

This is a shallow & sandy stream quite free from
rapids for a considerable distance– There were frequent
traces of musquash in the banks and Their cabins
standing in the meadows– Uncle Geo. affirmed that
their height determined the rise of the water– The
summer duck sailed into the coves before us–the
kingfisher and the robin flitted past–and frequent fish
hawks sailed over head I observed a strange–irregular
and dead looking tree growing in swamps–which they
called the brown ash. on the small meadows & islands
were places in the grass as if a horse or an oxen had
lain down where our boatmen said a moose had lain
down the night before–"there were thousands in these
meadows"

Old Fowlers, 6 miles from Mc C. or 24 from the Point
is the last house– He is the oldest inhabitant of these
woods–and formerly lived on the south side of the west
Branch where he built his house 16 years ago.– The first
house built above the 5 islands.

Here our batteau would have to be carried over the
first portage on a horse sled made of saplings to jump
the rocks in the way– We had to wait here a couple of
hours for them to catch the horses which were pastured
at a distance and had wandered still further off– One
man was covering the hog pen with cedar or spruce
splints for shingles splitting with a sledge and cleaver.
This house was warmed by large and complicated
stoves–which struck me as rather singular– –portions of
it were lined with bark– There stood the cedar broom &
the pole hung high over the hearth to dry stockings &c
on. Kittens were exhibited which were web-footed–and
the mother was said to be part mink. The last of the
salmon had just been caught here and were still fresh
in pickle– From which however enough were extracted
to fill our empty kettle. They had lost 9 sheep out of their
first flock a week before this by the wolves– The sheep

came round the house and seemed frightened–which
induced them to go and look for them when they found
7 dead and two still alive which they took in and as
Mrs Fowler said they were merely scratched in the
throat– She sheared off the wool and washed them
and put on some salve and turned them out but
in a few moments they were missing and have not
been found since. They were all poisoned and swelled
up at once so that they used neither skin nor wool– There
were steel traps by the door of various sizes–for wolves
and for bear and otter–with large claws instead of
teeth.– The wolves are frequently poisoned. This realized
the old fables of the wolves and the sheep–. Here was an
instance of that old hostility revived– Verily the
shepherd boy needed not to sound a false alarm this time.

The pipe here was a part of the household furniture
which the traveller knew where to find– We dined here
before the horses arrived–on hot-wheaten bread fish
–salmon–& sweet cakes as usual– And tea sweetened with
molasses– Hot cakes–& sweet cakes had led the board
the main difference being that the former are white and
the latter yellow.

At length the horses arrived and we hauled our batteau
out of the water & lashed it to its wicker carriage &
throwing in our packs walked on before. The rout was
the roughest travelled by horses over rocky hills where
the sled bounced and slid along–while one was more
necessary at the stern to prevent the boat from being
wrecked than in the roughest sea.

At 2 we who had had walked on before reached the
river above the falls just at the outlet of Qakish lake and
waited for the batteau to come up.

This portage was a well worn Cart path through the
woods which had long been the rout of the hunter and
no doubt followed the course of an Indian trail round
these falls– batteaux weighing from 5 to 800 are

frequently carried over on the shoulders– On either side
the path from time to time were the traces of camps–the
two or more upright and single horizontal pole forming
the shed–and the heap of ashes–where lumberers and
Indians had camped.

We had been here but a short time bathing our feet
from off the rocks– When a heavy thunder shower was
seen coming up from the west and soon the heavy drops
began to rattle round us I had just looked the trunk of
a huge pine 5 or 6 feet in diameter and was crawling
under it for shelter. When luckily the boat arrived–and
the manner in which it was unlashed and whirled over
while the first water spout was bursting would have
amused a sheltered man to witness. Each one had
assumed the attitude of crawling under it before it was
fairly turned and down– How was the first man
amused to see the rest come riggling under like
eels– When all were in we proped up the lee side and
found our selves comfortably housed under a boat 20 feet
long and 4 or 5 wide.

Here under we busied ourselves whittling thole pins for
rowing–when we should reach the lakes and made the
woods ring with such boatsongs as we could remember
between the claps of thunder The horses stood sleek and
shining with the rain all drooping and crest fallen while
deluge after deluge washed over us before a streak of
fair weather appeared in the west. Anticipating fresh
adventures still deeper in the wilderness.

At length the clear sky appeared in the west or north
west whither our course now lay–promising a serene
evening for our voyage– And the driver returned with
his horses–leaving his long-handled axes with us– And
we made haste to launch our boat and commence our
voyage in good earnest.

With our packs heaped up near the bows with the
frying pan kettle and axe–and ourselves disposed as

baggage to trim the boat—and not to move in any case—if
we struck a rock more than a barrel of pork might—we
pushed out into the first rapid a slight specimen of the
stream we had to navigate. With Uncle Geo. in the stern
and Tom in the bows each using a spruce pole pointed
with iron—and poling on the same side, we shot up the
rapids like a salmon—the water rushing and roaring
around—so that only an experienced eye could discover
a path—grazing the rocks on either hand and literally
escaping by an ace as did the Argo—

I who had had some experience in boating had never
experienced any half so exhilarating before. We were
soon in the Quakish Lake—and smooth water where the
river was sunken and lost and we that were but freight
only could row

It is a small but handsome irregular lake with no sign
of man but perhaps some low boom in a distant cove
reserved for spring use.— The interminable uninhabited
forest shutting it in all around— The spruce and cedar
—hanging with grey, looked like the ghosts of trees—

We were lucky to have exchanged our Indians for these
men who were at once guides and companions The canoe
is more easily upset and worn out, and the Ind. is not so
skilful in the management of a batteau. The utmost
familiarity with still streams or the open sea would not
prepare a man for this peculiar navigation and the most
skillful boatman anywhere else—would here be obliged to
take out his boat and carry round still with great risk and
delay—where the practised batteau-man would pole up
with comparative ease and safety. Falls which a sailor
would not think of attempting he poles up successfully
—glancing between the rocks without striking or swamping
as by a miracle

All stores in the summer—the grindstone & plough of
the pioneer—Flour pork & hard bread for the lumberer
—must be conveyed in this way. And many a cargo & many

a boatman is lost in these waters. . . – In the winter
which is very equable and long–the ice is the great
highway and the logging team penetrates to Chesuncook
lake and still higher up.

The Ind. say that the river once ran both ways–one
half up & the other down–but since the white man came
it all runs down.– And he must laboriously pole his
canoe up and carry it over the portages.

Joe Merry Mt appeared in the NW–as if it were looking
down on this lake especially.– ducks and loon were
sailing here and there on the surface–and we had our
first but a partial view of Ktadn the summit veiled in
clouds–something betwixt earth & heaven in that quarter

We had two miles of smooth rowing across this
lake–when we found ourselves in the river again which
was a continuous rapid of one mile,–demanding all the
strength and skill of our boatmen to pole up it. Here we
hauled them through one of the log sluices by a rope and
walked up to the camp–whose smoke we saw curling up
through the trees on a hill side One of the party was
interested in this dam which is a very important and
expensive work–raising the whole river 10 feet–and
flooding I think they said some 60000 acres by means of
the innumerable lakes with which the river
connects– Here every log pays toll as it passes through
the sluices. It is a lofty & solid structure–with piers of logs
filled with stones to break the ice some distance up the
river above it.

Here we found a gang of men employed in repairing
damages occasioned by the great freshet in the spring
Though commonly there is nothing to call them to the
woods at this season

One after another we filed into the rude lumberers'
camp at this place built of logs like those I have described.
Here was only the cook to receive us A phlegmatic well

fed personage who set about preparing a cup of tea and
hot cakes for his visitors. His fire had been entirely put
out and his fire fire place filled several inches deep by
the rain but now it was kindled again—and we sat down
on the log benches around it to dry us. The chinks were
not filled against the winter—and light & air came in on
every side

Here was an odd leaf of the bible—some genealogical
chapter to prove their Christianity— And the next things
that turned up was Emerson Address on W I
Emancipation—which had made two converts to the
liberty party here, an odd number of the Westminster
Rev. for 1834–& a pamphlet entitled Hist. of the Erection
of the Monument on the grave of Myron Holley–& these
were well thumbed and soiled

The men employed in such works as this are Jacks at
all trade, who are handy at various things and accustomed
to make shifts—skilful with the axe and ruder implements
of good judgement and well skilled in wood and
water-craft. I observed by their poles that they sometimes
indulged in fishing.

Their hands not restricted to the processes of one trade
only—but free and as it were intelligent to practise many.

tea was served out to us in tin cups from a huge coffe
pot with molasses but no milk of course and hot cakes for
solid food

We did ample justice to this fare and when we had
done filled our pockets with the never failing sweet cakes
which remained—foreseeing that we were not soon to
meet such fare again. And so informing John Morrison
that we had pocketed all his sweet cakes and exchanging
our batteau for a better we made haste to improve the
little daylight that remained. The dam had smoothed
over many a rapid for us where formerly there was a
rough current to be resisted—

Beyond there was no trail–and the river and lakes was the only practicable rout. We were from 25 to 30 miles from the summit of the Mt–(though not more than 20 perhaps–in a straight line

We decided to row 5 miles by moon light–it being the full of the moon across the north Twin lake–lest the wind should blow on the morrow For a moderately stiff breeze makes quite a sea upon these lakes in which a batteau will not live a moment. One of our boatmen had been detained once a week by this cause. For though the lakes for the most part are not very wide–the journey round the shores would be long and difficult indeed

After one mile of river or what the boatmen call "thorough fare" the lakes prevail so–and of rapids which are in a great measure smoothed by the dam, we entered the North Twin Lake–by moon light and steered across for the river thorough-fare 4 miles– This is a noble sheet of water–where one may get the impression which a new country is fitted to create We could distinguish the inlet to the S twin which is said to be the larger– This lake is completely surrounded by the forest as savage and impassable now as to the first adventurers

There was the smoke of no log-hut nor camp of any kind to bid us welcome– No lover of nature or musing traveller was watching our batteau from the distant hills– Not even the Indian hunter was there, for he rarely climbs them, but hugs the rivers like ourselves

It was the first time I had realized my conception of a secluded Lake of the Woods.– The impression was, and I presume it agreed with the fact, as if we were upon a high table land between the states and Canada–where there was no bold mountainous shore but only isolated hills rising here and there from the plateau– The level of the innumerable lakes varies but a few feet and at high water they almost all connect with one another.

These lakes lay open to the light with a civilized aspect–or rather as if expecting trade & commerce and towns and villas– The shores rose gently to ranges of low hills still covered with the hardy evergreen-trees

No face welcomed us but the fine sprays of free and happy evergreens towering stately above their fellows.

the rugged and healthy pines–the spiring fir–with dark and regular cones like a chinese pagoda–the graceful cedar the sober beech

The country is an archipelago of lakes and the boatmen by short portages or by none at all pass easily from one into the other. They say that at very high water the Penobscot and the Kennebeck flow into each other or at any rate you can lie with your face in the one and your toes in Moose Head lake.

None of our party but the watermen had been above the dam before, and the younger of them only a few miles. so we trusted to Uncle Geo. to pilot us. And we could not but confess the importance of a pilot on these waters– While it is river you will not easily forget which way is up-stream but when you enter a lake the river is completely lost–there is no stream, and you scan the distant shores in vain to find where it comes in.– A stranger is for the time at least lost and must set about a voyage of discovery to find the river– To follow the windings of the shore when the lake is ten miles or more in breadth–and of an irregularity which will not soon be mapped–is a wearisome voyage and will spend his time & his provision– A gang of experienced woodmen were once sent they told us to certain location on this stream–and were thus lost in the wilderness of lakes– They cut their way through thickets and then carried their boat over from lakes to lake. Some times several miles– They carried into the millinocket which is on another stream and is 10 miles square and full of islands– They explored this thoroughly and then carried into another lake and it was a week—of no common toil & anxiety before they found the P. river.

While Uncle George steered for a small island near the head of the lake we rowed by turns swiftly over its surface—singing such boat songs as we could remember. The shores seemed at an indefinite distance by moonlight & whether nearer or more remote we could not say— At first the red clouds had hung over its western shore as gorgeously as if they illumined a city there

Occasionally we paused in our singing and rested on our oars to hear if any wolves howled which is the common serenade but we heard none only some uncivilized big throated owl hooted loud and stark and inhumanly in that drear wilderness—not nervous about his solitary life nor afraid to hear the echoes of his voice there. We remembered that possibly moose were silently watching us from the distant coves—and that some bear or timid red or rein deer had been startled by our singing.

It was with new emphasis that we sang there the Canadian boat song—which described precisely our own case and was inspired by the history of exactly this kind of life

For the rapids were near and the day light long since past except that there was no evening chime to be heard here—and no Ste Annes in this direction. The woods on shore had grown dim—and many a utawa's tide here emptied into the P. stream. It was indeed the realization of the fur traders experience and the Canadian boatman's life.

At last we glided past the little island which had been our landmark, and fancied how contentedly we might live there to tend the light house which should guide the future voyageur.

At length about 9 o clock we reached the mouth of the river and ran our boat into a natural haven between some rocks—and drew her up on the sand. This camping

ground Uncle Geo. had been familiar with in his
lumbering operations formerly.

The first business was to make a fire an operation
which was a little delayed at first by the wetness of the
fuel and the ground owing to the heavy rain of this
afternoon. The fire is a main comfort in a camp whether
in summer or winter and is about as ample at one season
as another– It is as well for cheerfulness as for warmth
and dryness. It forms one side of the camp–a bright side
at any rate–a wall of flame and crackling embers. Some
were dispersed to fetch in dead trees and boughs while
Uncle Geo. felled the birches and beeches which stood
convenient and soon we had a fire some ten feet long
by 3 or 4 feet high which rapidly dried the sand before it.
This was calculated to burn all night. Close by our boat a
little rill of pure water emptied into the lake and furnished
us with drink.

We next proceeded to pitch our tent which operation
is performed by sticking our spike poles into the ground
in a slanting direction about ten feet apart for rafters and
then drawing our cotton over them and tying it down–but
this evening the wind carried the sparks on to the tent
and burned it so we drew up the batteau and spreading
the tent on the ground to lie on–we lay with our heads &
bodies under the boat and our feet and legs on the sand
toward the fire– It was a bright moon light.

We lay at first side by side in a wakeful mood talking
of our course–and being in so convenient an attitude for
studying the heavens with the moon and stars shining in
our faces our conversation naturally turned upon
astronomy and by turns we recounted the anecdotes of
that science

At length one of the party having imposed a fine on
snoring, which penalty he was the first to incur–we
composed ourselves to sleep It was interesting when
awakened at midnight to watch the grotesque & fiendish

form and motions of one who had risen silently to arouse
the fire and add fresh fuel for employment–now
stealthily lugging a dead tree from the dark and heaving
it on–now stirring up the embers with his fork and
tiptoing about to observe the stars watched by half the
party in silent wakefulness while each supposes his
neighbor sound asleep.

Thus aroused I too brought fresh fuel to the fire–and
then walked along the sandy shore in the moon light
hoping to meet a moose come down to drink or a
wolfe– The little rill tinkled the louder and peopled all
the wilderness and the glassy smoothness of the lake
which might be the atlantic of 3 centuries ago and we the
discoverers on its western shore–the dark & fantastic
rocks rising here and there from its surface made a scene
not easily described. It had such a smack of wildness
about it as I had never tasted before.

Not far from midnight we were, one after another
awakened by rain–falling upon our extremities–and
gradually as each became aware of the fact by cold or wet
he drew a longer sigh & drew up his legs from the wet
side until gradually we had all sidled around from lying
at right angles with the boat till our bodies formed an
acute angle and were wholly protected. When next we
awoke the heavens were serene again and not a cloud to
be seen–and the signs of dawn in the east.

And we soon had launched and loaded our boat and
were off again before breakfast.

Our appearance excited no bustle amid the surrounding
hills as I read that when a ships boat approaches the bay
o Typee one of the Marquesan isles the news is shouted
from man to man–from the tops of cocoanut trees up the
valley 8 or 9 miles, and soon its whole population is on
the stir–stripping off the husks from Cocoa nuts–throwing
down bread fruit–and preparing leafen baskets in which to
carry them to the beach to sell. The young warrior may

be seen polishing his spear and the maiden adorning her
person for the occasion.

I cannot help being affected by the very fine–the slight
but positive relation of the inhabitants of some remote
isle of the Pacific to the mysterious white mariner It is a
barely recognised fact to the natives–that he exists and
has his home far away somewhere and is glad to by their
fresh fruits with his superfluous commodities.

Their customs are mutually unknown and yet this
commerce exists– The savage is still a dusky and
unexplored nature–the white man a mysterious demigod

No sooner is the mariner's boat seen to put off from
his vessel for the shore than the inhabitants of the
remotest recesses of these isles which stand like watch
towers in the Pacific make haste to repair to the
beach–with its fruits.

Such is commerce which shakes the cocoa nut and the
breadfruit tree in the remotest isle–and sometimes dawns
upon the duskiest and most ignorant savage

The savage & the civilized states offer no more striking
contrast than when referred respectively to the element
of fire– Fire is the white man's servant and is near to
him, and comes at his call. He subdues nature by
fire–steam powder the forge–the furnace–the oven–he
draws down lightning–and with heat comes enlightenment
and all amelioration & maturation– It is genial and
cordial–it imparts flavor–& comfort– With the friction
of a match the master calls his servant.

But how far from Fire stands the savage–cold–and
dark–how ineffectual his authority. With what pain &
sweat he rubs his two sticks together, before the fire
will come.

His fire as distant as the sun. There is no forge nor
furnace for him.

I am struck by the force of habit in considering the history of Salt We are accustomed to regard it as a necessary of life–and by some thing more than a figure of speech even go so far as to say sometimes that they have not salt enough to save their souls. The doctors say you cannot live without salt. Then to hear of a race who know not its use. We are at a loss to know what saves them–

All the good what are they but the salt of the earth–that which saves it– To do without salt why it is to live on air and as it were to find out some other principle of life.

What is the secret of the charm of invention and discovery? To find out the relation of something in nature to man. On which side to place it that the light may fall upon it aright– To put things in their place– To play a tune and put an end to discord. The savage splits the fibre of the breadfruit leaf and inserts his head in it–and is naturally delighted with his "superb head-dress"–for he has discovered a slight use of nature or relation to himself in her works.

The author of Typee describes the very simple and childlike behavior of the savages–who would sometimes when the freak took them as old Marheyo–hastily polish his spear–and don his finery–and go forthe to display himself to day light–not for display but but to give vent to his simple emotions and aspirations–his perchance magnanimity–training an hour of his life–and then doff his gear–and calmly resume his employments.

Not promenade Broadway or washington street–but the paths of his remote isle

It seems to me that in warm latitudes and among primitive races where clothing is dispensed with–tattooing is not necessarily the hideous and barbarous custom it is described to be. It is the same taste that prints the calico which he puts off and on—and the skin itself—which is always worn.

The consistent objection is to the style of the print—not to the practice itself. Where is the barbarity

{*One leaf missing*}

The first half mile was of river—a "Thorough fare—amid rocks and rapids which were poled up— Some of these like the smaller in our own stream were split quite in two in the middle in the direction of the stream— Then we rowed a mile across the foot of Pamadumcook Lake—which makes north west 10 miles to hills & mountains in the distance Joe Merry Mt now bore S W— by another thoroughfare—we past into deep cove—a part of the same lake which makes up two miles toward the north east beyond us— we rowed 2 miles across this and by another thorough fare entered Umbedegis lake—one of the most beautiful of all The lakes might all be regarded as one since they are so closely connected were it not that the river shows itself so distinctly between them with its narrow channel and rocky rapids.— and again it is Penobscot water you are poling in.

Generally at the entrance to these lakes we observed what is technically called the "fencing stuff"—or huge logs of which booms are made—either lashed together in the water or laid up on the rocks and lashed to trees against the spring and driving season. It startled me invariably to discover so plain a trail of the white man—here. I remember that I was strangely affected by the sight of a ring bolt well drilled into a rock and fastened with lead at the head of this beautiful but solitary lake of Umbedegis where there was no sound nor any other trace of civilized man to-day & I could hardly believe that he ever came— When the logs have gone down the rapids each on its own bark with more or less bruising and barking, they are collected together at the heads of the lake where they would otherwise be dispersed by the wind–and surrounded by a boom fence–of floating logs secured together at the ends–and thus towed together like a flock of sheep across the lake by a windlass or boom head which we frequently saw standing upon some island or headland. Sometimes the logs are dispersed in a lake by winds and freshet and it takes many days of hardships and exposure to collect them again–being landed on distant shores– The driver picks up one or two at a time and returns with them to the thorough fare. Driving hogs, which are said to drive best the contrary way to what you wish them to go is not to be named with driving logs which must be suffered to run–the gauntlets of the innumerable falls & rapids by themselves, and some times leap all fences and are dispersed over many miles of lake surface in a few moments.

And before the driver gets his flock all through Umbedegis or Pamadumcook he makes many a wet camp on the shore

{*One leaf blank*}

Umbedegis struck me this quiet Sunday morning as the most beautiful lake I had seen. It has the reputation of being the deepest– we rowed a mile & a half to near the head of the lake within the boom fence which there appeared like buoys embracing a large yard of water–and went ashore to cook our breakfast by the side of a large rock–where Uncle Geo. remembred a spring and the ground of former encampments.

The ketle was soon boiling on the shore and while the pork and fresh salmon were afrying–we proceeded to whittle us some forks of elder–or other twigs that

offered– The first mess of tea which was of an inky
blackness was condemned to the lake as the washing of
our unscoured kettle–but to my eyes the kettle never got
scoured to the end of the journey. Our plates were fresh
strips of birch bark and two tin dippers our tea cups

With Uncle Geo. & Tom I vistited the site of an old
camp on the hill side behind us overlooking the pond– He
lead the way confidently where the path once ran by the
spring at which we drank–to the ruins which were over
grown with weeds & underbrush. There were the remains
even of the Blacksmiths forge for even this worthy had
been in requisition here.

On our way up to this camp which was some distance
from the water we noticed a whole brick upon a rock
–which had been brought thus far to tamper with in
blasting–and was remembered with the ring bolts in the
rocks & the forge on the hill side– Uncle Geo afterward
regretted that we had not carried this brick on with us to
the Mt–for our mark. This would certainly be a simple
evidence of civilized man though rather cumbersome
in climbing mountains.

I could imagine what tales the loggers told here in hard
winters to keep their blood circulating–looking over to
Joe merry for exhiliration.

In the midst of a dense growth in the middle of the
little stream upon a rock–where there were no other
traces of man in sight–lay this brick–clean and red as in
the brick-yard.

–Thus had this lake shore its antiquity and ruins
allready.

Mc C said that large wooden crosses made of oak still
sound were sometimes found in this wilderness–which
were set up by the first Catholic missionaries who came
through to the Kennebeck. Go where you will somebody
has been there before you.

It is worth the while to feel the stark & grim wildness
of nature sometimes as to drink some stringent diet
drink of evergreens and roots and bark.

Having reached the head of the lake we made our way
along the shore leaping from rock to rock and creeping
under the bushes–while the boatmen poled up the rapids
stopping to take us in where a stream emptied in to the
river. A few rods above this we reached a portage of
90 rods round what is called Umbedegis Falls–where
it was necessary to carry over. Here was the roughest
path imaginable cut through the woods now up hill
at angle of nearly 45 degrees over rocks and logs
without end. By the shore stood a pork barrel with a hole
8 or 9 inches square cut in one side which was set against
the upright side of a large rock–but without turning or
upsetting the barrel the bears had gnawed a large hole in
the opposite sides big enough to put their heads in– It
looked precisely like an enormous rat hole–and at the
bottom of the barrel were still left a few mangled slices
of pork.

We first carried over our baggage and deposited it
upon the green bank at the other end While we were
resting here and quenching our thirst with the river
water–I noticed breams in the water–the first fishes I
had seen.

Returning to the batteau we fixed a couple of straight
sticks as yokes to the painter by which 2 couple stood
ready to pull abreast– While the boatmen stood at the
ends of the boat to steer & save it from rocks. Then at
the word from our driver at the stern we dragged it up
the first hill and so on with frequent pauses over half
the portage

Commonly 3 men walk over with the batteau on their
heads and shoulders–one standing under the middle of
the boat turned over–and one at each end– More cannot

well take hold at once. But this requires some use as well as strength and is in any case the hardest work that is done on these waters–

Our men at length took the batteau upon their shoulders and while two of us steadied the boat one upon each side to prevent it from rocking and wearing into their shoulders walked bravely over–with 2 or three pauses.

These carries where there are few strong and practised hands are the severest toil the boatman has to endure

With this weight they must climb and stumble along over slippery rocks of all sizes–while the men who walked by the side the widest part are continually brushed off by trees and rocks on account of the narrowness of the path.

We were an invalid party on the whole and could render our boatmen but little assistance.

Then we had a mile & a half of Passamagummuck lake which is narrow and river like to the falls of the same name. over a small meadow on our left we could see into a large cove or lake in that direction which connects with this. Umbedegis stream comes in some where on our right

Remembering the difficulty of the last portage our men determined to warp up the Passamagummuck Falls– So while the rest walked round carrying the baggage one of us remained in the batteau to assist in warping up. We were soon in the midst of the rapids which were more rapid and tumultuous than any we had poled up–and turning to the side of the stream to prepare for warping when–the boatmen who had observed me taking a few notes–feeling some pride in their skill and ambitious to do something more than usual took one more view of the rapids or rather falls–and in answer to ones question whether we could get up there the other answered that he guessed he'ed try it–so we pushed into the midst of the

fall–and then came the tug of war While I sat in the
mid of the boat to trim it moving slightly to the right
or left as it grazed a rock–with an uncertain and
wavering motion we wound and bolted our way up until
the bow was actually raised some feet above the stern in
the steepest pitch–and then when everything depended
upon his exertions the bowman's pole snapped in two but
before he had time to take the spare one I handed to
him–he had saved him self by the fragment, upon a
rock–and we got up by a hair's breadth– And Uncle
Geo. exclaimed that that was never done before–he had
not tried it if he had not known whom he had got in the
bow–nor he in the bow if he had not known him in the
stern. At This place there was a regular portage cut
through the woods & our boatman never had known a
batteau to ascend the falls.

I could not sufficiently admire the admirable skill &
coolness with which they performed this feat–never
speaking to each other–and the bowman not looking
behind–but knowing exactly what the other is
about–works as if he worked alone now springing to this
side now to that–and setting his pole afresh–now feeling
in vain in 15 feet of water for a bottom while the
sternman holds the bottom–and now barely holding his
ground for an instant with his feet braced against the
bows of the boat. The pole is set close to the boat–and the
bow is made to overshoot and just turn the corners of the
rocks in the very teeth of the rapids   nothing but the
length and lightness and the slight draught of the boat
enables them to make any headway– The bow man must
quickly choose his course–there is no time to
deliberate–frequently the boat is shoved between rocks
where both sides touch–and the waters on either hand
are a perfect maelstrom.

Taking in our companions we had proceeded a half a
mile to a slight rapid–where the boatman proposed that

two of us should try our hands at poling up We had got
over bravely and were just surmounting the last difficulty
when an unlucky rock confounded our calculations and
while the batteau was whirling round like a weather
cock–amid the eddies we were obliged to resign the poles
to more skilful hands.– These rips were christened with
the name of one of the party.

Think what a mean and wretched place this world
is–that half the time we have to light a lamp that we
may see to live in't.

Then we are begotten and our life has its source from
what a trivial and sensual pleasure.
That a trivial tittillation of the vulgar sense should be
the exciting cause that calls man into life
I thought as I waked from a transient sleep between
twilight and dark–hanging upon my chair aroused to
darkness deeper than daylight– I fell asleep one evening
in my chair Betwixt day-light and dark– Whither my
spirit went meanwhile I know not only it came back more
proud–and with some half expressed unquestionable
arguments sneered at its fate–when some trivial sound
which had authority called me back to life It was
thick darkness– I had to light a lamp that I might see.
And this is half our life? Who'd undertake the enterprize
if it were all? And pray what more has day to offer– A
lamp that burns more clear–a purer oil–and winter
strained–that so we may pursue our idleness with less
obstruction. Bribed with a little sunlight and a few
prismatic tints–we bless the maker–and deprecate his
wrath with hymns.
It is only your lean men that have a word to say about
life & the philosophies– The full orbed belly well encased
in fat in no place worn down to the bone rolls through
the world without a creak or sound

They are your dry and fleshless bones that rattle
eloquence–your empty gullets that sing hymns– Until
some care wears a man to the quick he's silent as the
grave–whether about good or ill or joy or pain.

Your epic poets must all be blinded first ere they can
see the Elysium of nature and the divinity in man.

To be so born and so continued in life–requiring the
veriest gentleman of us all daily every morning the
stay & support of some ridiculous potatoe saved from
the rot–by the hired cunning of men of science.

We next rowed 2 miles through Depskaneig lake–first
more northerly–then more easterly–Passamagummuck
stream coming in on the left– For this is generally the
order of names–as you ascend first the lake or dead
water, then the falls,–then the stream of the same name
emptying into the lake or river above.

This lake is not large–and very shallow and weedy,
and looked as if it might abound in pickerel– Pickerel
are caught in all these lakes along with trout–though
the former are said to have been put in originally by
the white man. They are now quite plenty–even up to
the sources of the river.

At Depskaneig Falls which are considerable and quite
picturesque we stopped to dine– While some of the party
were building a fire and getting dinner ready the rest
went to fishing for trout in the falls. This is a famous
place for trout well known to our skipper–who had seen
them caught here by the barrel full– But in this bright
sun light we could not get so much as a nibble. Leaping
from one slippery rock to another we soon learned to
walk as securely as our boatmen or as upon the flagstones
in the streets until we had reached the very middle of
the stream   we cast our lines into the very falls

them-selves–where the water was white with foam but no trout rose to our bait.

Some were fain to dine off the remnant of our salmon placed on chips with hard bread and pork and a dipper of black tea to wash it down.– One of the party who had lost a tooth in the encounter with a piece of hard bread which last had lodged fast in the esophagus–while taking a draught of river water in order to expel the obstruction–detected a larger–a larger and perhaps less rusty kettle than our own reposing on the bottom of the river–condemned and left by some party of lumberers

This portage was about the same length with that around Umbedegis falls, and mid way over in the woods we could see where frequent parties had encamped the slight rafters and cedar beds still remaining As before we first carried our packs over and then returned for the batteau–which after several stages–by the way–at one I remember Uncle George thrusting a dipper down into a hole in the ground the length of the arm for a drink of cool spring water– –we launched it in Pockwockomus lake– At the the further side we discovered another rusty and bruised tin dipper which we added to our tea set.

Half way over this carry thus far in the Main wilderness on its way to the Provinces we noticed a large flaming oak hall advertisement about 2 feet long wrapped round the trunk of a pine from which the bark had been stript to which it was fast glued by the pitch. This should be recorded among the advantages of this mode of advertising by handbills–that even bears and wolves–may learn where they can fit themselves according to the fashion–or at least recover some of their lost garments.

Through Pockwockomus lake which is but a slight expansion of the river we rowed for a couple of miles to a small grassy island–on which we landed to consult concerning our future progress whether we should leave

the river there and commence our tramp through the
woods to the Mt or go up the river 2 or 3 miles further
before we left it. we decided upon the last course–

This isle was covered with a kind of rush or cut
grass and near where we landed was the recent track of
a moose, a large roundish hole in the soft wet
ground–evincing great weight in the animal that made
it.– They visit all these island meadows swimming as
easily as they make their way through the thickets on
land. There were occasional small meadows of a few
acres waving with uncut grass up here which attracted
the regard of our boatmen–who regretted that they were
not a little nearer to their own clearings–and calculated
how much hay they might cut for the loggers the ensuing
winter.

It was 1 mile from this to the next portage– The
Depskaneig stream comes in on the left–and now and
then we passed what is called a poke logan–or what the
Drivers might have reason to call a "poke logs in"–which
is an inlet that leads no where–if you get in you've got to
get out again the same way– These and the frequent
run-rounds–which come into the river again–would
embarrass the inexperienced voyageur not a little.

We had soon reached the carry of 40 rods round
Pockwockomus Falls–passing through a small and
shallow channel divided from the main stream by an
island.

This little stream had a quite novel and peculiar
scenery–being overhung with alders and willows which
last we had not noticed lately, and so shallow that we
had to get out to lighten the boat–while the boatmen
walked in the stream shoving the boat along.

It reminded me of the scenery on Concord river. This
carry though short was exceeding rough & rocky– The
batteau having to be lifted directly from the water up

4 or 5 feet on to a rock–and launched again down a
similar bank. Here also was an empty pork barrel left by
a lumbering party.

The rocks in this portage were covered with the dents
made by the spikes in the lumberers' boots while
staggering over under the weight of their batteaux– We
also afterwards noticed that the rocks projecting above
water in the worst rapids were marked by the pike poles
of numerous voyageurs–who had braced themselves
against them.

You could see the surface of some larger rock whereon
they had rested their batteaux worn quite smooth
with use.

I am astonished at the singular pertinacity and
endurance of our lives The miracle is that what is–*is*
–precisely that–that our particular life succeeds so far.
That every man can get a living and so few can do any
more So much I can accomplish ere strength and health
are gone and yet this much suffices. I am never rich in
money and I am never meanly poor–if debts are incurred
why debts are in the course of events cancelled–as it
were by the same law by which they were incurred.

{*One leaf missing*}

the rapids as far as possible keeping close to the
shore– One seized the painter and leaped out upon a
rock but slightly exposed–but the spikes in his shoes
did not avail him and he was amid the rapids–but soon
recovering himself he passed me the painter–and took
his place in the bow– Leaping from rock to rock in the
shoal water close to the shore I held the boat while one
reset his pole–getting a bite each time round some large
rock–and so we progressed upwards through the worst
of it.

The man on shore bracing himself against a rock
holds the boat while those in the boat reset their
poles–and then all three work upward against any rapid.

When some of us walked round we generally took the
precaution to take out the most valuable part of the
baggage–for fear of swamping.

We next rowed and poled ourselves for 3/4 of a mile
through the Aboljacarmegus lake a slight expansion of
the river to the carry of an eighth of a mile around
Aboljacarmegus falls– This was a comparatively smooth
portage with a fine broad and flat rock at the end from
which to launch our boat. Just at the head of the falls.
Here were still the vestiges of a jam of logs which had
taken place in the famous freshet in the spring. As we
poled up a swift rapid about half a mile–the logs lay like
huge cannon piled up high and dry upon the rocks on
either hand–and pointing in every direction some
partially hollow to make the resemblance stronger– some
of our party read their own marks upon them. This last
half mile carried us to the Sowdehunk dead water
–occasioned by the Sowdehunk river which comes
in a mile above– Here at the mouth of Murch brook and
the Aboljacknagesac broad off from the Mt. and as our
experienced waterman said about 4 miles distant–but
eyes more accustomed to scanning mountains said to be
nearer 14.– Here we had been told by Uncle Geo. that
we should find trout enough– So while some prepared
the camp the rest fell to fishing–seizing the birch poles
which some party of Indians or lumberers had left on the
shore and baiting our hooks with pork–we cast our lines
into the shallow mouth of the brook standing in the
batteau which was moored. Instantly a shoal of white or
silvery roaches Cousin trout (Leucisci Pulchelli) or what
not large and small fell upon our bait and one after
another were landed on the shore amid the bushes. Anon
their cousins the true trout, took their turn–but they were

not heavy enough to content us So pushing up the stream about 40 rods to the mouth of the Aboljacknagesack a very different stream with a swift pure water and sandy bottom–and running our boat into the bushes–we recommenced the sport in good earnest– Alternately the trout and their cousins the roaches swallowed the bait as fast as we could throw in– And the finest specimens of both that I have ever seen–were heaved upon the shore in vain to wriggle down into the water again.

But soon we learned to remedy this accident for one who had lost his hook stood there to catch–and there they fell in a perfect shower about him–the heaviest near the shore the lighter farther off. While yet alive and before their tints had faded they glistened like the fairest flowers, and he stood over them as if in a trance unable to trust his senses–that these jewels should have swum away in that Aboljacknagesac water for so long! so many dark ages these bright flowers seen of Indians only!– It passed all the fables of Proteus Few things have seemed so incredible and strange to me– But there is the rough voice of Uncle Geo. who commands at the frying pan–to send over what you've got and then you may stay till morning– The pork sizzles and cries for fish– Luckily for that generation of trouts the night shut down at last–not a little deepened by the dark sides of Ktadn which like a permanent shadow reared itself from the eastern bank.

So we accompanied Tom into the woods to cut cedar twigs for our bed– While he went ahead with the axe and lopped off the smallest twigs of the flat-leafed ceadar–we gathered them up and returned with them to the boat, until it was loaded.

This was an old camping ground and there was the skeleton of a moose whose bones some Indian hunters had picked on this very spot.

Our bed was made with as much care and skill as a
roof is shingled beginning at the foot and laying the twig
end of the cedar upward we advanced to the head thus
successively covering the stub ends and producing a soft
and level bed– For us six it was about ten feet long by
six in breadth After supper which was eaten off a large
log while my companions were stretched upon their
couch–I sat up studying a large white roach which I had
reserved from the pan counting its fin rays and the
scales upon the lateral line to identify it by the light of
the fire sitting upon a log

This night we made an experiment and diversion–in
obedience to the satire and levity of one of the party who
thought that we might concoct some more savory drink
than the tea and more in harmony with our circumstances
out of the leaves and plants about– We made a dipper of
cedar tea But one who ventured the length of a few
swallows may be trusted when he declares that it
resembled nothing so much–at least in his experience as
a dose of rhubarb.

I waked before morning to dream of trout fishing– It
seemed an incredible fable that this painted fish swam
there and rose to our hooks last evening I doubted if I
had not dreamed it and rose by moon light to test its
truth while my companions were sleeping There stood
Ktadn at last with distinct and cloudless outline in the
moon-light–and the rippling of the rapids was the only
sound to break the stillness
     Standing on the shore I once more cast my line into the
mouth of Murch Brook–and found the dream to be real
and the fable truth. The speckled trout & silvery roach
like flying fish sped swiftly through the silvery moon
light air describing an arc upon the dark side of

Ktadn–until the moonlight now fading into daylight
brought satiety to my mind and the mind of my
companions who had joined me As Homer would say of
fishing ἐξ ἔρον ἔντο that is they had got enough of it– And
then we seated ourselves around the log where Uncle
Geo. presided–

οὐδέ τι θυμὸς ἐδεύετο δαιτος ἐΐσης

nor did any one fail of his fair share of the fish.

The largest trout would weigh 3 or 4 pounds and the
roach a pound and a half.

The trout fishing v 278

by 6 o'clock having mounted our packs and our tent
and a good blanket full of trout–and having swung up
such of their contents and such provision as we wished
to leave behind upon the tops of saplings to be out of the
way of bears–and fastened our batteau to a tree a few
rods up the Aboljacknagesac–we started for the Mt
–travelling up the north side of this stream through
burnt lands–now partially over grown with aspens and
shrubs Soon recrossing this stream upon logs and
rocks–we struck for the highest peak over a mile or more
of open land still.

Here it fell to the lot of the oldest mt climber to take
the lead–so scanning the woody sides of the mt–we
determined to steer for a slight spur which extended
south from the mt–keeping parallel to a dark seam in
the forest which marked the bed of a torrent and having
attained this lower but bare eminence, which afforded a
look out to steer directly up the peak which would be
close at hand.– So setting the compass for a north
eastern course we were soon buried in the wood.

Fresh blue berries still hung upon the bushes–and
bunch berries the fruit of the cornus Canadensis were
abundant We soon began to meet with bears and moose

dung and the tracks of the latter more or less recent
covered every square rod of the mt. Sometimes we
found our selves travelling in faint paths which they had
made—and every where the twigs had been browsed by
them—clipt as smoothly as by a scythe. The bark of the
trees was stript up by them to the height of 8 or 9 feet in
long narrow strips an inch wide—still showing the marks
of their teeth— We expected nothing less than to meet a
herd of them every moment—and our nimrod held his
shooting iron in readiness. At this season the bull moose
is dangerous to encounter, and frequently will not turn
out for the traveller but furiously rushes upon him. The
largest weigh 1200 weight—and are said to step over a
5 foot gate in their natural walk. They are an exceedingly
awkward looking animal with their extremely long legs
& short bodies making a ludicrous figure when in full
run—but making great headway nevertheless

It seemed a mystery to us how they could thread these
woods—which required all our suppleness to accomplish
climbing stooping winding alternately— They are said
to drop their long and branching horns upon their backs
and then make their way easily by the weight of their
bodies— Our boatmen said but I know not with how much
truth that their horns were gnawed away by vermin.

Rabbits dung was freqent along our rout. After
travelling about 4 or 5 miles in damp and thick woods for
the most part we reached the banks of a considerable
stream—whose channel was filled with rocks— This we
conjectured from its direction was Murch brook wich
entered the river exactly at camp.

Here was such a dash and flow of mountain water that
it seemed this was the old poets "river god" that sung

> I must make my waters fly,
> Lest they leave their channels dry,
> And beasts that come unto the spring
> Miss their morning's watering."

This fellow did make his waters fly with a witness as
if he were not afraid that his fontal springs would fail
in any case.

It is interesting to observe with what singular
unanimity the most sundered nations & generations of
men consent to give completeness and roundness to an
ancient fable. of which they appreciate the beauty and
the truth– By a faint and dream like effort–though it
were by the vote of a scientific body the dullest
posterity–slowly add some trait to the mythus– As when
astronomers call the lately discovered asteroid Astraea–for
this slightest recognition of poetic worth is significant,
and so the virgin that was driven from earth at the end
of the Golden ages–has her local habitation in the
heavens– In the same spirit Atlas is proposed as the
name of a newly discovered planet.

Here is some approach to a universal language– Even
Leibnitz with all his ingenuity advanced not so far.

This fond reiteration of the oldest truth by the latest
posterity using the very figures and metaphors of
antiquity, and content with slightly & religiously
retouching & modifying the old material is one of the
most impressive evidences of a universal and common
humanity.

By such slow aggregation has the mythology grown
from the first.

Under the cunning disguise of mythology and fable
truth has a firm hold upon the faith of men The
parables of the first children are lovingly &
magnanimously accepted and eked out by the last and
every age and nation adds some trait to the fable.

We had proceeded on thus till about noon with
frequent pauses to refresh the weary all the time in
woods–without having seen the summits–and very

gradually rising– When our watermen despairing a
little and fearing that we had gone astray and were
leaving the Mt on one side of us, Uncle Geo. climbed a fir
tree from the top of which he could see the peak–and it
appeared that we had not swerved from a right line.

The compass down below still pointed to the summit
with his arm.

Having reached a cool spring or mountain rill amid the
woods we determined to lighten our packs here by
cooking some of our fish. We had brought them in order
to save our hard bread & pork in respect to which we were
put upon allowance–

We had soon a fire blazing and each stood round with
a sharpened stick 3 or 4 feet in length upon which he
spitted his trout or roach which he had previously
salted– So we squatted round the fire our sticks
radiating like the spokes of a wheel from one centre–and
each crowding his particular fish into the most desirable
exposure not with the truest regard always to his
neighbors rights.

Thus we regaled our selves drinking meanwhile at the
spring till one mans pack was considerably lightened,
when we again took up our line of march.

The wood was chiefly birch spruce fir mountain ash
or round wood as Uncle Geo. called it which he prized
for its medicinal properties–& moose wood– The cornel
or bunch berries were very abundant as well as solomon's
seal and moose berries.

Blueberries were distributed along our whole rout and
in one place the bushes were drooping with the weight of
blue berries still as fresh as ever– Such patches afforded
a grateful repast–and served to bait the weary party
forward   when the hindmost lagged the cry of blue
berries was the most effectual to bring him up.

We again struck the torrent I have mentioned but our course as soon diverged again.

We crossed a moose yard 4 or 5 rods square–an opening caused by a large flat rock on which no trees grow–and such as the moose take advantage of as yards–where in the winter they tread down the snow.

At length we reached an elevation which was sufficiently bare to afford us a view of the summit still distant and blue–as if retreating from us. A torrent was seen tumbling down in front, literally from out of the clouds–not a ribbon like rill but a considerable stream white with foam–and apparently of undiminished breadth to the very clouds. But this glimpse at our whereabouts was soon lost again and we were buried in woods.

At length fearing that if we held the direct course to the summit we should not find any water near our camping ground we gradually swerved to the left till we struck the torrent we had seen at 4 o'clock Here the weary party decided to camp that night.

It was a drear and grim scenery–we looked long for a level and open space to pitch our camp.– at first there seemed only one of the thousand table rocks in the midst of the falls   while my companions were seeking a resting place for the night I endeavored to improve the short remnant of day-light in climbing the mt alone– Following the course of the torrent–and I would lay an emphasis on the word *up* pulling myself up perpendicular falls of 20 or 40 feet by the roots of firs and birches–and walking for a level rod or two in the thin stream– Thus ascending by huge steps–as if it were a giants stair way down which a river flowed–pausing on the successive shelves where the water was collected in pools or spread out in a thin sheet–to look back over the country beneath me– The stream was from 15 to 30 feet in width without a tributary and seemingly not diminishing in breadth as I advanced. Still it came

rushing and roaring with a copious tide where there was
nothing but barren rock interspersed with the meagerest
vegetation.

Leaving the stream at length when I had fairly cleared
the trees I began to work my way–more arduous than
satans in Pandemonium up the nearest peak. At first
scrambling on all fours over the tops of Ancient fir trees
old as the flood–from 2 to 10 and 15 feet in height– Their
tops were flat and spreading their foliage blue and nipt
with cold–as if for centuries they had ceased growing
upward against the bleak sky–the solid cold. Such was
the country with large rocks interspersed and a cold
wind that levelled all I walked some good rods erect upon
the tops of trees–where were overrun with moss and
cranberries. Once slipping through I look down 10 feet
into a dark and cavernous region and saw the stem of a
fir on which I stood fully 8 inches in diameter at the
ground.

–As if first rocks from the size of a table to a small
house had been dropped here and there upon the
mountain side–and then in the course of time these
venerable fir-trees had filled up the intervals and
levelled off the scene.

This was the sort of garden I made my way over not
seeing any path through it. Certainly the most treacherous
and porous country I ever travelled–but nothing could
exceed the toughness of the twigs not one snapped under
my weight They were slowly grown.

Having slumped scrambled rolled bounced & walked
over this firry country–I arrived upon a side hill–where
rocks grey silent rocks of every shape & size were the
flocks and herds that pastured–chewing a rocky cud at
sunset. They looked hardly at me without a bleat or low.
This brought me to the skirt of a cloud and bounded my
walk this night.

But I had seen maine waving flowing rippling–and now darkling down below.

A water it was less stained with earthyness than Helicon–truly a strong water–

When I returned my companions had selected a camping ground on the torrent's edge–and were resting on the ground–one was on the sick list & rolled in a blanket on a shelf of rock. We could camp no higher for want of fuel– And trees here seemed so forever green and moist and sappy–that we doubted if they would acknoledge the influence of fire.

It was a grand and desolate place for a nights lodging–the more so for the neighborhood of the trees and stream– We went supperless to bed tonight for our remaining fish had contracted a green hue from the green blanket in which they had been rolled and so were condemned and other food was scarce.

Some more aerial and finer spirited winds roared through the ravine all night–from time to time arousing our fire– It was as if we lay in the very nest of a young whirlwind. At midnight I remember my bed fellow startled in his dreams by one of these sudden upblazings of a fallen fir whose green boughs were suddenly lighted by the wind sprang up with a cry from his spruce leaf couch–thinking the world afire and drew the whole camp after him.

Here was was no cedar so we made our bed of coarser feathered spruce but they were plucked alive.

But fire prevailed and blazed here too like a good citizen of the world. In the morning after whetting our appetites on some pork and a hard wafer of bread–and a dipper of condensed cloud or waterspout, we all began to make our way up the falls I have described– this time we chose the right hand or highest peak–and soon my companions were lost to my sight behind the ever retreating mountain ridge   over huge rocks loosely

poised I climbed a mile or more–still edging toward the
clouds– The mtn was a vast conglomerate or aggregation
of loose rocks–as if sometime it had rained rocks–and
they lay as they fell upon the mt. sides Nowhere fairly
at rest but leaning on each other with cavities
between   rarely any soil or smoother shelf. At length I
entered within the skirts of the cloud which seemed
forever drifting over the summit–and yet would never
be gone–but was generated out of that pure air–fast as it
flowed away. Having reached the ridge summit and ridge
were alike enveloped in clouds. Now the wind would blow
me out a yard of clear sun light wherein I stood–then a
grey dawning light was all it could accomplish– The
cloud line ever rising and falling with the winds intensity.
At one moment it seemed as if the summit would be
cleared in a few moments and smile in sunshine but what
was gained on one side was lost on another– It was like
sitting on a Bakers chimney and waitting for the smoke
to blow away– – This was a cloud factory and the wind
turned them off from bare rocks. Occasionally when the
windy columnes broke in to me–I caught sight of a dark
damp crag to the right or left the mist driving
ceaselessly between it & me

It reminded of the creations of the old epic and
dramatic poets, of Atlas, Vulcan, the Cyclops, and
Prometheus– Such was Caucasus and the rock where he
was bound. AEschylus had no doubt visited such scenery
as this. It was vast titanic & such as man never inhabits.
Some part of the beholder, even some vital part seems to
escape through the loose grating of his ribs as he
ascends– He is more lone than one–there is less of
substance less of fair calculation & intellectual fullness
than in the plains where men inhabit Vast Titanic
inhuman nature has got him at disadvantage caught him
alone–& pilfers him She does not smile on him as in
the plains– She seems to say sternly why came Ye here

before your time– This ground is not prepared for. Is it not enough that I smile in the vallies I have never made this soil for thy feet, this air for thy breathing–these rocks for thy neighbors. I cannot pity thee then nor fondle thee here–but relentlessly drive thee where I am kind. Why seek me where I have not called you and then complain that I am not your genial mother.

These are among the unfinished parts of the globe–whither it is some slight insult to the Gods to climb and pry into their secrets and try their effect on our humanity. Simple races–as savages do not climb mountains Their tops are are sacred and mysterious tracts unvisited by them.

Pomola whom the Penobscot consider as the evil genius of the mt–or God in his angry mood is ever angry with him who climbs here.

For what canst thou pray here–but to be delivered from here.– And shouldst thou freeze or starve–or shudder thy life away–here is no shrine nor altar–nor access to my ear.

Knowing that my companions would be anxious to return and reach the river that night, and that the clouds might stand upon the mt for days I was at length compelled to descend. Occasionally the wind would blow me a vista open from which I could see the country eastward as the opposite–boundless forest and lake and streams gleaming in the sun– And a similar torrent which ran down that side–and probably emptied into the Seboois or E Branch. There were also new mts in sight. Now and then some small bird of the sparrow kind would flit away before–like a fragment of the grey rock unable to command its course.

I found my companions on the Mt side gathering the Mt cranberries which filled every crevice between the rocks–and also blue berries which we noticed had a

more sharp and racy flavor the higher up they grew. Not
the less agreeable to our palates.

From this elevation we could overlook the country west
and south Immeasurable forest–that eastern stuff we
had heard of Countless lakes–Moose-head close at hand
40 miles by 10 Chesuncook 18 by 3 without an island
–Millinocket on the south with its hundred islands
and a hundred others.– the P. river & our course–and
beneath us the very trees near which our boat was
moored. We had to console ourselves with the reflection
that this view was as good as from the peak as far as
it went–and what were a mt. without its clouds & mist.
We preferred in its every day dress

Returning still at an early hour in the day–we followed
the course of the torrent as long as it would not lead us
too far out of our course– Though after all its winds we
supposed it would prove to be the murch Brook which
emptied into the Main Stream exactly at our former
camping ground We thus travelled about 4 miles in the
very torrent itself continually crossing and crossing
leaping from rock to rock and jumping with the stream
itself down falls 7 or 8 feet–some times sliding down in
a thin sheet of water–sliping & rolling in it The cool air
of the torrent and the continual bathing of our
members–in mt. water–alternate foot and sitz and even
body baths–made this walk exceedingly refreshing. This
torrent had been the scene of a great freshet in the spring
apparently accompanied by a slide from the mt. For a rod
or two on either side its present channel the trees were
barked and splintered often to their tops–the birches
stood wrenched and twisted and deprived of their bark
like furies' hair– trees a foot in diameter were snapped
off–and whole clumps bent over with the weight of rocks
piled on them   in one place we noticed a large rock
lodged nearly twenty feet high in the limbs of a

tree– This ravine must have been filled with a stream
of stones and water at least 20 feet above its present level.

For the whole four miles we saw but one rill emptying
in–and the volume did not seem increased from the first.
With more leisure it would have been worth the while
to trace this torrent to its source.

In this way we travelled very rapidly with a downward
impetus which made it easier to run than to walk. It was
a pleasant picture when the foremost turned about and
look up the ravine   at intervals of a rod or two was seen
a red shirted highlander or a green jacket against the
white torrent walled in by forests and leaping down the
channel with his pack upon his back–or pausing upon a
convenient rock to unstrap his dipper and take a draught.

After diverging from the torrent we were in some doubt
about our course, and so Tom threw down his pack and
climbed the loftiest fir tree at hand to ascertain our
whereabouts– Up the bare trunk he went some 20 feet
and then through the green tower lost to our sight until
he held the topmost spray in his hand. Uncle Geo. had in
his younger days marched through the wilderness with
a body of troops under general somebody and with one
other man did all the scouting and spying service The
gens' word was "throw down the top of that tree"–and
there was no tree in the maine woods that it would not
lose its honors.

To Tom now we cried where away does the summit
bear–where the burnt lands– The last he could not
plainly see but conjecture– He reported however a little
meadow & pond lying apparently in our course which
we concluded to steer for.

Upon reaching this secluded meadow we found the
fresh tracks of moose upon the shore of the pond–and
the water was still muddy and unsettled as if they had
fled before us.

And after in dense under brush threaded by a stream
which emptied into the meadow we seemed to be still
upon their trail. It was a small meadow of a few acres
on the mt side–concealed by woods–where they might
browse and bathe and rest in peace.

Ere long we recovered our old land marks and reached
the open lands again wich went sloping down some
miles toward the river–and by two oclock we reached our
boat once more

Here we had expected to dine on trout but at this hour
in the broad sunlight we found them slow to take the
bait, and so took our allowance of hard bread and pork.
Here we deliberated whether we should not go up as far
as Gibson's clearing about a mile to get a half inch augur
to mend our spike poles with– There were young spruce
trees enough and we had reserved a spike but had nothing
to make a hole with– But as it was quite uncertain
whether we should find any one there at this time or any
tools left in camp–we patched up the broken pole as well
as we could for the downward voyage in which there
would be but little need of it.

At 4 1/2 we commenced our return voyage–which
would require comparatively little poling– The boatmen
substituted broad paddles instead of poles merely guiding
the batteau down the rapids– Though we glided so
swiftly and smoothly down where–it had cost an effort
to get up our present voyage was attended with far more
danger–for if we once fairly struck one of the thousand
rocks between which we were gliding the boat would be
swamped at once. When a boat is swamped under these
circumstances–the boatmen commonly find no difficulty
in keeping afloat at first whether they can swim or
not–for the current keeps them afloat along with their
freight and carries them far down the stream– If they

can swim they have only to sidle off gradually for the
shore But the greatest danger is of their being caught in
an eddy behind some large rock–where the water rushes
up faster than elsewhere it does down–and being carried
round under the surface till they are drownd– Some
times the body is not thrown out for several hours. One of
our company had performed such a circuit once only his
legs being visible to his companions–but he was fortunately
thrown out in season to recover his breath.

The boatman has this problem to solve– To choose
a circuitous and safe course amid a thousand sunken
rocks scattered over a quarter of a mile–at the same time
that he is moving steadily at the rate of 20 miles an hour.
Stop he cannot the only question is where will he go. The
bowman chooses the rout with all his eyes about him
striking broad off with his paddle and drawing the boat by
main force in to her course– The Stern man faithfully
follows the bow

We were soon at the Aboljacaremegus falls– Anxious
to avoid the delay as well as the labor of the portage
here our boatmen went forward to reconnoitre–and
concluded to let the batteau down the falls while we
carried the baggage round.

Jumping from rock to rock until nearly in the mid of
the stream we were ready to receive the boat and let her
drop over the first fall some 5 or 6 feet perpendicular
– The boatmen stand upon the edge of a shelf of
rock–where the fall is ten or twelve feet perpendicular
in from one to two feet of water one on each side of the
boat and let it slide gently over–then while one holds by
the painter the other leaps in–and his companion follows
and they are whirled down the rapids to a new falls or
to smooth water.

So in a very few minutes they had accomplished a
passage in saftey which would be as fool hardy to the
unskilful as the descent of Niagara itself.

It seemed as if it needed only a little more familiarity
and confidence to navigate down such rapids as Niagara
in perfect safety and save the expense of your Welland
canals.– One might have thought these were falls and
that falls were not to be waded through with impunity
like a mud puddle. There was really danger of their
losing their sublimity in losing their power to harm
us.– Familiarity breeds contempt

The boatman pauses perchance upon some shelf
beneath a table rock standing in some two feet of
water–and you hear his gruff voice come up through the
spray coolly giving directions how to launch the boat this
time. Having carried around Pockockomus falls we soon
carried in to the Depskaneigh or Oak hall carry where we
decided to camp half way over–leaving our batteau to
be carried over in the morning on rested shoulders One
shoulder of each of these men showed a red spot as
large as your hand worn by the batteau. And this
shoulder, since it does all the work, was lower than its
fellow–from long service– This toil soon wears out the
boatman.

The Drivers habitually work in the cold water in the
spring–rarely ever dry–and if one falls into the river he
never changes his clothes till night– Such a one is called
by a particular nick name–if he does–or is turned
off– None can lead this life who are not amphibious Uncle
geo. said he had seen where six men were wholly under
water at once with their shoulders to handspikes If the
log did'nt start–then they had to poke up their heads to
breathe.

The driver works as long as he can see from Dark to
dark–and at night has no time fairly to dry his clothes
and eat his supper before he is asleep upon his cedar bed.

We lay this night upon the very bed spread by such a
party–spreading our tent over the poles which were still

standing–but reshingling the damp & faded bed with
fresh twigs.

We concluded not to lose any time by going up to
Gibson's lest the wind should rise before we reached the
larger lakes and detain us.– for a moderate wind on
these waters produces waves which will swamp a
batteau–and on one occasion Uncle Geo. had been delayed
a week at the Head of the North Twin.

We were short on't for provisions–and ill prepared in
this respect for a journey round by the shore should our
boat be swamped–

In the night the wind rose and roared through the
woods presaging a windy morrow–but before day-light
it went down and offered a fair day for our return.

In the morn. we carried our boat over and launched
it–making haste lest the winds should rise– The boat
men ran down Passamagummuck & Umbedegis falls
while we walked round and carried a part of the baggage.
At the last falls we found a share with the owners name
on it left on the portage. We breakfasted at the Head of
Umbedegis lake on the remains of our pork–and were
soon rowing across its smooth surface again–under a
pleasant sky. The Mt now clear of clouds–rose near at
hand in N E and double top with two sharp cones to the
North of it Tom and I lolling in the bow discoursed
philosophy across this fair lake–while the rest set us
ahead like galley slaves. Tom was a young and ingenuous
waterman with that indolent but mild and mellow
expression of those who had had much intercourse with
rude nature– The noble franknes of a forest child– The
lake How deep is it!– 4 hundred feet perhaps and
more– See that ring bolt–where that large rock lies on
the sand– Thats a stiff boom-head down there But as the
Geologists say that stone is not in its place–it doesn't
belong there–perhaps it came from Ktadn.

I should like to see the bottom of this lake– Who do
you think made it?– who made it?– who? why think
what's in a name This isnt Umbedegis– Thats an Indian
word– just think– What is it then?– Why its a long
pull–this morning. Our arms know that   what do we
know of Umbedegis– I knew as much of Umbedegis from
the map before I ever saw this water– Do you believe
there's any heareafter?– Why where's Pamadumcook
isn't that hereafter? Pull away Boys we shall soon
see– But any other would say after death– Why after
Pammadumcook–we expect–The North Twin–and after
the North Twin Mattawamkeag and stranger places
which we never saw– The world never failed of morrows
and of news– So during this life we expect another.

Why here is but a "thoroughfare" and ever the stream
runs fastest just here–with rapids & falls.

Did you ever find when you went over the falls that
there were no rapids or smooth water below?–

You have curious notions.

Taking turns at the oars we thus shot rapidly across
Deep Cove & Foot of Pamadumcook and then 4 miles
across the North Twin–at the rate of a mile in 12 1/2
minutes–the wind not high enough to disturb us– We
reached the dam at 12 1/2–firing a gun by way of signal
when a mile off. Here again the cook got dinner for us
and we devoured all before us– They had a fine lot of
pickerel in pickle here which they had caught.

Uncle Geo & Tom went through a log sluice here in the
boat where the falls was 4 or 5 feet and took us in
below–

Here was the longest rapid in our route– And perhaps
the paddling down this was as dangerous & arduous a
task as any Shootting at the rate of 25 miles an hour
if–we struck a rock–we were split from end to end–in an
instant– It was tempting the waters We and our boat

now like a bait bobbing for pickerel or some other river
monster–now shootting this way now that–now gliding
swift and smooth near its destruction now our boatmen
paddling to right or left with all their might to avoid a
rock– We soon ran through and floated in the Quakish
lake– Rowing rapidly over this we left our batteau to be
hauled over at leisure and walked over the portage 2
miles to Old Fowlers on the Millinocket– here the batteau
we had expected to find was gone–and we walked round
2 miles instead to Tom Fowlers House. When we reached
the Millinocket opposite to Toms House–waiting for his
folks to set us over–we discoverd two canoes just
turning into the river from shad pond   one took the op.
side of small island before us while the othre took the
near–examining the banks carefully for muskrat.

The nearest proved to be Nep–& his companion–now
at last on their way up to Chesuncook after Moose– – But
they were so disguised that we hardly knew them– At a
a little distance they might have been taken for
Quakers–seeking a settlement in Pensylvannia–with
broad brimmed hats & cast off coats They looked like
London dandies the morning after a spree–

Neptune at first was only anxious to know "what we
kill"–seeing some partridges in our hands–but we had
assumed too much anger to permit of a reply– We
thought Ind. had some honor before– But me been
sick– O me unwell now– You make bargain then me go.

–He was still plainly under the influence of the disease
that had attacked him, his bottle– They had some young
muskrat in their canoe–which they had dug out of the
banks–for food not for their skins– They are their
principal food on these expeditions–

So they went on up the Millinocket–and we kept down
the banks of the Penobscot. Leaving Tom at home. At
the little sturgeon gut was the fresh track of a moose
calf made since we came up– After having passed the

night & buttered our boots at Uncle Geo. we kept on down
the river the next day about 8 miles and then took a
batteau with a man to pole it, to Mattawamkeag 10 more.

Near the mouth of the East branch we passed the
school house–whither it may be 10 or a dozen children
are poled to school in batteaux over the rapids–the
contribution of the woods. At first I thought it was all a
jest but–it was even true.– At middle of that very night
we dropped over the half finished bridge at Old town and
heard the clink of a hundred saws which never rest–and
at 6 o clock the next morn one of the party was steaming
his way to Massachusetts.

V launch in Quakish

There were six of us. Uncle Geo. Thatcher–Lowel
–Raish–Tom–& Henry–

> Nor speak I this, that any here exprest
> Should think themselves less worthy than the rest
> Whose names have their full syllables and sound;
> Or that Frank, Kit, or Jack, are the least wound
> Unto their fame and merit. I for my part
> (Think others what they please) accept that heart,
> Which courts my love in most familiar phrase;
> And that it takes not from my pains or praise,
> If any one to me so bluntly come:
> I hold he loves me best that calls me Tom."
>
> Thomas Heywood.

{Three-fourths page blank}

It was M. de Bonald who used the expression "The
Turks have encamped in Europe" and the traveller
confirms the justice of the conception. The customs of the
Turk are still those of the Tartar in his Tent–on a foray
into the plains

Chateaubriand thinks that love of country increases as
a man advances in years– "There are two things, which

grow stronger in the heart of man, in proportion as he
advances in years; the love of country and religion. Let
them be ever so much forgotten in youth, they sooner or
later present themselves to us arrayed in all their charms,
and excite in the recesses of our hearts, an attachment
justly due to their beauty." This may be so— But even
this infirmity of noble minds suggests the gradual decay
of youthful hope and faith— It is the sweet infidelity of
age. It is comparatively a faint & reflected beauty that is
admired. Not their essential and intrinsic charms. It is
because the old are weak—feel their mortality—and think
they have measured the strength of man. They will not
boast— They will be frank and humble Well let them
have the few poor comforts they can keep They look back
on life and so see not into the future—the prospect of the
young is forward and unbounded.

In the declining day the thoughts make haste to rest in
darkness—and hardly look forward to the ensuing
morning— All things prepare for night and rest— – The
same hopes and prospects are not for him who stands
upon the rosy mountain tops of the morning—and him
who expects the setting of his earthly day.

Humility is still a human virtue.

The traveller still sees the storks forming their ranks
and directing their flight to Africa from the hills of
Athens— Thus as Chateaubriand suggests they have
remained independent—preserving their customs
still—while other races have taken the place of those that
formerly sung them.

As we are told by the traveller that "The serene sky and
the brilliant sun of Greece merely communicate to the
marble of Paros & Pentelicus, a golden tint resembling
that of ripe corn, as the autumnal foliage."

So time lends to the monuments of their literature only
a golden–and a maturer tint *still*.

The poetry of the Greeks wears even now after the
lapse of 2000 summers–only a cereal and autumnal hue.

It is their atmosphere that preserves–as it were
enveloped in the inspiration which first breathed
them They carry with them their own serene and
heavenly atmosphere into all lands to protect them
against the corrosion of time.

If you doubt if Grecian valor and heroism is not wholly
a fiction of the poets– Go to athens and see still upon
the walls of the temple of Minerva the circular marks
made by the shields taken from the enemy in the Persian
war–which were suspended there.

When we begin to doubt the signs of the Past come
out on every hand with such freshness and with such
proximity–that we are silent lest she should arise entire
and reinstate herself upon the ruins of the Present
– – The very dust takes shape and confirms some
story we had read Times sundered (orderly) in the
grave record of history–seem rushing to confound their
spheres in one wide Present.

If history is a lifeless record and dust acumulates in
libraries as well as on the ruins of cities–and *books*
may easily deceive or be mistaken– The traveller has
not far to seek for more unquestionable and living
testimony– As Fuller said commenting on the zeal of
Camden–"A broken urn is a whole evidence; or an old
gate still surviving, out of which the city is run out."

Ruins of a nobler period do not grow old–but grow
young by age They are some trophies which nature
loves to preserve adorning them with moss and ivy to
the end of time. Does not our country furnish antiquities

as durable as any? Rocks as well grown with moss and
ivy– A soil which if it is virgin–is at the same time
mould–the very dust of man and nature. What if we
cannot read Rome or Greece

{*One leaf missing*}

Our fields are as old as God and the rocks we have to
show stamped with his hand.

And snow that old mortality whose youngest child
was Phidias comes evry year and fills our fields with
masterpices done in a whiter than Parian marble– Which
time by the effect of the sun has wasted

There is tradition of such a school which filled our
woods with every design which Greece has lately copied.

Whose ruins are now mingled with our meat and
drink–and sepulchres we are.

The century sun and unwearied rain has wasted
them–an incredible antiquity since no fragment from
that quarry now exists. The stone was brought from
heaven direct and no mortal ever saw its living rock–

As the springs and rivers–if they are not dry channels
what became of it and the clouds

{*One-fifth page blank*}

Chateaubriand says–"What particularly distinguishes
the Arabs from the tribes of the New World, is, that
amidst the rudeness of the former, you still perceive a
certain degree of delicacy in their manners; you perceive
that they are natives of that east, which is the cradle of
all the arts, all the sciences, and all religions. Buried at
the extremity of the west, in a by-corner of the universe,
the Canadian inhabits valleys shaded by eternal forests,
and watered by immense rivers: the Arab, cast as it were,

upon the high road of the world, between Africa and Asia, roves in the brilliant regions of Aurora, over a soil without trees and without water." The arab is still subject to a rude remnant of laws–the American is proudly independent– in his own words–"He is not connected by his origin with the great civilized nations; the names of his ancestors are not to be found in the annals of empires; the contemporaries of his ancestors are ancient oaks that are still standing. Monuments of nature and not of history, the tombs of his fathers rise unheeded among unknown forests. In a word, with the American, everything proclaims the savage, who has not yet arrived at a state of civilization; in the Arab, everything indicates the civilized man who has returned to the savage state."

{*Nine-tenths page missing*}

The naked the embalmed unburied death of Jerusalem–! In Tasso's poem I trust some things are sweetly buried.

{*Nine-tenths page missing*}

–Some unaffected tears shed by a pilgrim on Mt Calvary within the week.–

To the old mythology one memorable addition is due to this era–the Christian fable– With what pains and tears and blood these centuries have woven the christian fable–and added that to the mythology of mankind! The New Prometheus.

With what miraculous consent and patience is this mythus stamped on the memory of the race?

Nations and centuries combine to dress old truth in a new garb–to adorn it and set it forth.

As if by the watery links of rivers and of lakes we were about to float over unmeasured zones of earth–bound on unimaginable adventures–

And our voyage should be an episode in the life of man.

> Saint of this green isle hear our prayers,
> Grant us cool days and favoring airs.

Sir Thomas Browne says nobly for a Christian that "they only had the advantage of a bold and noble faith, who lived before his coming; and upon obscure prophecies and mystical types, could raise a belief."

All material things are in some sense man's kindred, and subject to the same laws with him.

Even a taper is his relative–and burns not eternally, as some say of lamps found burning in ancient sepulchres–but only a certain number of his hours.

These things belong to the same dynasty or system of things. He witnesses their wasting and decay as well as his own What mans experience does not embrace is to him stationary and eternal Whether he wakes or sleeps the lamp still burns on and burns out–completing its life within his own.

He sees such objects at a very near angle. They have a very large parallax to him–but not so those tapers the fixed stars which are not both lit and burnt out in the life of a man–yet they too are his distant relations.

Usually we read history but as a fable–and connect it not livingly by the links of centuries to our own times Some chasm of a Dark age at least

{*Three-fourths page missing*}

that tedium or ennui which presumes to have exhausted the variety and joys of life is as old as Adam.

Dec 2nd 23 geese in the pond this morn. flew over my
house about 10 'oclock in morn within gun shot. The
ground has been covered with snow since Nov. 25th

{*Three-fourths page missing*}
{*One leaf missing*}

add lest one ray more than usual come into our eyes–a
little information from the western heavens–and where
are we?– ubique gentium sumus!– where are we as it is?
Who shall say what *is*? He can only say *how* he *sees*.
One man sees 100 stars in the heavens–another sees
1000– There is no doubt of it–but why should they turn
their backs on one another, & join different sects– As
for the reality no man sees it–but some see more and some
less– what ground then is there to quarrel on? No man
lives in that world which I inhabit–or ever came
rambling into it– Nor did I ever journey in any other
man's– Our differences have frequently such foundation
as if venus should roll quite near to the orbit of the
earth one day–and two inhabitants of the respective
planets should take the opportunity to lecture one another
I have noticed that if a man thinks he needs 1000
dollars & cant be convinced that he does not–he will be
found to have it. If he lives & thinks a thousand dollars
will be forthcoming–though it be to by shoe-strings–they
have got to come. 1000 mills will be just as hard to come
to one who finds it equally hard to convince himself that
he needs them.

———

Of Emerson's Essays I should say that they were not
poetry–that they were not written exactly at the right
crisis though inconceivably near to it. Poetry is simply a
miracle & we only recognize it receding from us not
coming toward us– It yields only tints & hues of thought

like the clouds which reflect the sun–& not distinct propositions–

In poetry the sentence is as one word–whose syllables are words– They do not convey thoughts but some of the health which he had inspired– It does not deal in thoughts–they are indifferent to it–

A poem is one undivided unimpeded expression–fallen ripe into literature The poet has opened his heart and still lives– And it is undividedly and unimpededly received by those for whom it was matured–but mortal eye can never dissect it– while it sees it is blinded.

The wisest *man*–though he should get all the academies in the world to help him cannot add to or subtract one syllable from a line of poetry.

If you can speak what you

{Three leaves missing}

and crownings. As the youth studied minutely the order and the degrees in the imperial procession and suffered none of its effect to be lost on him–so the man at last secured a rank in society which satisfied his notion of fitness & respectability

He was defrauded of so much which the savage boy enjoys.

Indeed he himself has occasion to say in this very autobiography, when at last he escapes into the woods without the gates–"Thus much is certain, that only the undefinable, wide-expanding feelings of youth and of uncultivated nations are adapted to the sublime, which, whenever it may be excited in us through external objects, since it is either formless, or else moulded into forms which are incomprehensible, must surround us with a grandeur which we find above our reach."

He was even too well-bred to be thoroughly bred. He says that he had had no intercourse with the lowest class

of his townsmen– The child should have the full
advantage of ignorance as well as of knowledge–& is
fortunate if he gets his share of neglect and exposure.

"The laws of nature break the rules of art"

He further says of himself "I had lived among painters
from my childhood, and had accustomed myself to look at
objects, as they did, with reference to art." This was his
peculiarity in after years. His writings are not the
inspiration of nature into his soul–but his own
observations rather."

When I am stimulated by reading the biographies of
literary men to adopt some method of educating myself
and directing my studies–I can only resolve to keep
unimpaired the freedom & wakefulness of my genius. I
will not seek to accomplish much in breadth and bulk
and loose my self in industry but keep my celestial
relations fresh.

No method or discipline can supersede the necessity of
being forever on the alert– What is a course of History–no
matter how well selected–or the most admirable routine
of life–and fairest relation to society–when one is
reminded that he may be a *Seer* that to keep his eye
constantly on the true and real is a discipline that will
absorb every other.

How can he appear or be seen to be well employed to
the mass of men whose profession it is to climb resolutely
the heights of life–and never lose a step he has taken

Let the youth seize upon the finest and most memorable
experience in his life–that which most reconciled him to
his unknown destiny–and seek to discover in it his future
path. Let him be sure that that way is his only true and
worthy career.

Every mortal sent into this world has a star in the
heavens appointed to guide him– Its ray he cannot
mistake– It has sent its beam to him either through

clouds and mists faintly or through a serene heaven– He
knows better than to seek advice of any.

This world is no place for the exercise of what is called
common sense. This world would be denied.

Of how much improvement a man is susceptible–and
what are the methods?

When I meet the engine with its train of cars moving
off with planetary motion or say rather like a comet–for
the beholder knows not if with that velocity and that
direction it will ever revisit this system–its steam-cloud
like a banner streaming behind like such a fleecy cloud
as I have seen in a summer's day–high in the heavens
unfolding its wreathed masses to the light–as if this
travelling and aspiring man would ere long take the
sunset sky for his train in livery when he travelled
– When I have heard the iron horse make the
hills echo with his snort like thunder, shaking the
earth–with his feet and breathing fire and smoke– It
seems to me that the earth has got a race now that
deserves to inhabit it. If all were as it seems, and men
made the elements their servants for noble ends. If the
cloud that hangs over the engine were the perspiration of
heroes or as innocent and beneficent an omen as that
which hovers over the parched fields of the farmer.

If the elements did not have to lament their time
wasted in accompanying men on their errands.

If this enterprise were as noble as it seems. The stabler
was up early this winter morning by the light of the stars
to fodder and harness his steed–fire was awakened too to
get him off– If the enterprise were as innocent as it is
early– For all the day he flies over the country stopping
only that his master may rest– If the enterprise were as
disinterested as it is unwearied.– And I am awakened by
its tramp and defiant snort at midnight while in some far

glen it fronts the elements encased in ice and snow and
will only reach its stall to start once more
 If the enterprise were as important as it is protracted.

 No doubt there is to follow a moral advantage
proportionate to this physical one

 Astronomy is that department of physics which
answers to Prophesy the Seer's or Poets calling It is a
mild a patient deliberate and contemplative science. To
see more with the physical eye than man has yet seen to
see farther, and off the planet—into the system. Shall a
man stay on this globe without learning something
—without adding to his knowledge—merely sustaining
his body and with morbid anxiety saving his soul. This
world is not a place for him who does not discover its laws.
 Dull Despairing and brutish generations have left the
race where they found it or in deeper obscurity and
night—impatient and restless ones have wasted their lives
in seeking after the philosopher's stone and the elixir of
life— These are indeed within the reach of science—but
only of a universal and wise science to which an
enlightened generation may one day attain. The wise
will bring to the task patience humility (serenity)—joy
—resolute labor and undying faith.

 I had come over the hills on foot and alone in serene
summer days travelling early in the morning and resting
at noon in the shade by the side of some stream and
resuming my journey in the cool of the evening— With
a knapsack on my back which held a few books and a
change of clothing, and a stout staff in my hand. I had
looked down from Hoosack mountain where the road
crosses it upon the village of North Adams in the valley
3 miles away under my feet—showing how uneven the

earth sometimes is and making us wonder that it should ever be level and convenient for man, or any other creatures than birds.

As the mountain which now rose before me in the Southwest so blue and cloudy was my goal I did not stop long in this village but buying a little rice and sugar which I put into my knapsack and a pint tin dipper I began to ascend the mt whose summit was 7 or 8 miles distant by the path. My rout lay up a long and spacious valley sloping up to the very clouds, between the principle ridge and a lower elevation called the Bellows. There were a few farms scattered along at different elevations each commanding a noble prospect of the mountains to the north, and a stream ran down the middle of the valley, on which near the head there was a mill It seemed a very fit rout for the pilgrim to enter upon who is climbing to the gates of heaven– now I crossed a hay field, and now over the brook upon a slight bridge still gradually ascending all the while with a sort of awe and filled with indefinable expectations as to what kind of inhabitants and what kind of nature I should come to at last– And now it seemed some advantage that the earth was uneven, for you could not imagine a more noble position for a farm and farm house than this vale afforded farther or nearer from its head, from all the seclusion of the deepest glen overlooking the country from a great elevation–between these two mountain walls. It reminded me of the homesteads on Staten Island, on the coast of New Jersey– This island which is about 18 miles in length, and rises gradually to the height of 3 or 400 feet in the centre, commands fine views in every direction, whether on the side of the continent or the ocean–and southward it looks over the outer bay of New York to Sandy Hook and the Highlands of Neversink, and over long island quite to the open sea toward the shore of europe.

There are sloping valleys penetrating the island in
various directions gradually narrowing and rising to the
central table land and at the head of these the Hugenots
the first settlers placed their houses quite in the land in
healthy and sheltered places from which they looked out
serenely through a widening vista over a distant salt
prairie and then over miles of the Atlantic–to some faint
vessel in the horizon almost a days sail on her voyage to
Europe whence they had come. From these quiet nooks
they looked out with equal security on calm and storm
on fleets which were spell bound and loitering on the
coast for want of wind and on tempest & shipwreck. I
have been walking in the interior seven or eight miles
from the shore, in the midst of rural scenery where there
was as little to remind me of the ocean as amid these
N H hills when suddenly through a gap in the hills–a
cleft or "Clove road", as the Dutch settlers called it I
caught sight of a ship under full sail over a corn field
20 or thirty miles at sea. The effect was similar to seeing
the objects in a magic lantern, passed back and forth by
day-light since I had no means of measuring distance.

[I]

[WINTER 1846-1847–SPRING 1848]

{Four pages missing}

shorter and more adventurous way.

I had thoughts of returning to this house the next day–which was neatly kept & so nobly placed–for the husband was not at home though the mistress entertained me kindly–and perhaps remaining a week in the valley.

As I passed the last house a man called out to know what I had to sell, for seeing my knapsack he thought that I might be a peddlar who was taking this unusual rout for nearness over the ridge at the head of the valley to South Adams. He told me that–it was 4 or 5 miles to the summit by the path, which I had left but not more than 2 miles in a straight line–but nobody ever went this way–there was no path and I should

{Two-fifths page missing}

I was of that age when an unexplored country road furnishes objects of interest enough–when any deeper ravine–or higher hill–or novel bridge and unknown stream–detains us a long time–and once we go on with the interest and adventurous feeling of childhood not knowing what we shall see next. I was interested by such sights for instants as pigs and geese with yokes, which were new to me–bridges whose side rails only were covered with a projecting eve–virginia fences–and guide boards–which said right and left or Rt. Lt. or if it chanced to say so many miles to Esqr M'Gaws *{MS torn}* charmed and felt myself

{Two-fifths page missing}
{Thirty-two pages missing}

guage– And the vast majority of those who at one period
of their lives have been compelled to study Latin
& Greek–have remained as ignorant of the genius of their
authors as those inhabitants of the early centuries of our
era–who though they could speak the language of
Rome–erased the monuments of her noblest children to
make way for a Father–or a dull Romance.

I know it is advised by some to overlook at last and
forget what ancient and heroic men have done, what
wise and studious men have thought–what inspired poets
have sung– The most valuable monuments of human
labor and life– But it will be soon enough to forget when
we have the experience which will enable us well to
remember them– That age will be rich indeed when
those relics shall have still further accumulated–when
at some remote epoch the Vaticans shall be filled with
Homers & Shakespeares–where the ages shall have
successively deposited their trophies in a heap in the
forum. This way may we plausibly hope to scale the
heavens.

The works of the great poets have never yet been
read, for only great poets can read them. There was
never gathered an assembly of men who could appreciate
them–but they have ever been read partially and by
snatches in solitude as men view the stars. Only they
talk of forgetting the ancients who never knew them.

Ovid thus describes Chaos

> "And where there was Earth there also was
>   there sea & air;
> So was the earth not to be stood upon, the
>   waves not to be swum in,
> The air without light."

>   *   *

> And he secreted the liquid heavens from the
>   thick air

           *   *

And he confined the descending rivers within
    sloping banks;
Which in different places, are part absorbed
    by the earth,
Part reach the sea, and being received within
    the plain
Of its freer water, beat the shores for banks.

           *   *

The East Wind withdrew to Aurora & the Nabothaean
    kingdom
And the Persian, and the ridges placed under the
    morning rays

        *   *   *

Scarcely had he fenced off all these with
    certain {*MS torn*}
When the stars, which had long lain hid pressed
    down under
That mass, began to effervesce into every part
    of the heavens

The beautiful story of Phaeton and Apollo adds—
    The first part of the way is steep, and where
        scarcely the steeds
    Fresh in the morning strive; in the mid heaven
        it is highest;
    Whence to behold Sea and earth there is often fear
    To me myself, and my breast trembles with
        fearful dread
(He cannot translate a foreign language or even read
his own—who does not simply by his ear distinguish
some of the meaning of a word)
    The last part of the way is descending; and
        requires sure management
    Then even Tethys herself, is wont to fear, who
        receives
    Me with waves placed underneath, lest I be borne
        headlong.
    Add, that heaven is whirled with constant revolution;

And draws the lofty stars, and whirls them with
  swift revolution
I strive against it; nor does the impetus which
  conquers the rest,
Conquer me; and I am born contrary to the rapid
  sphere.
Suppose the charriot granted. What canst thou do?
  wilt thou be able
To go against the rotating poles, that the swift
  axis may not carry thee away,
Perhaps you conceive in your mind that there are
  groves there,
And cities of the gods and shrines rich with gifts.—
Through snares is the way, and the forms of wild
  beasts.
And although You should keep the way, and with no
  error be borne,
Nevertheless you will advance through the horns of
  Taurus, opposite.
And the Haemonian bows, and the features of the
  raging lion
And the Scorpion curving with long circuit its dread
Arms, and the Crab—bending its arms in another way
Nor is it possible for thee without preparation to
  manage the steeds
Excited with those flames which they have in their
  breasts
And breath forth from their mouths & nostrils.
  Scarcely do they endure me
When their sharp spirits have grown hot, and their
  necks spurn the reins.

Apollo tells his son he need not doubt of his descent
  Some proofs thou askest; I give sure proofs by fearing
  And prove myself father by my paternal fear—
His father cannot reveal his oath sworn by the
sacred marsh of Styx—but he may persuade—
            Nevertheless he resists his words
  And holds fast his purpose: and he burns with desire
  of the chariot.
  Therefore the father having delayed as far as it
  was lawful, conducts

The youth to the lofty chariot–the work of Vulcan
The axle was golden–the beam golden, golden the
    extreme
curvature of the wheel, of the spokes a silvery
    order–
About the yokes chrysolite and gems placed orderly
reflecting Phoebus gave back clear rays
And while high-minded Phaeton admires these things
    & surveys
The work; lo, wakeful Aurora from the glittering east
Opened the purple doors and the halls full of roses
The stars disperse; whose troops Lucifer
Drives away, and last of all withdraws from his station
    in the heavens,
But the father Titan when he saw the lands and
    world grow red
And the extremities of the moon's horns as it were
    to vanish
Commands the swift hours to yoke the horses.
The swift Goddesses perform his orders; and they
    lead the steeds
From the high stalls, breathing fire,
Filled with the juice of ambrosia; and they add the
    sounding bridles.
Then the father anointed the face of his son with
    the sacred
Tincture, and made it patient of the fervid flame.
And infixed the rays in his hair.

And of late the victor whom all our Pindars
praised–has won another palm. contending with

        "Olympian bards who sung
        Divine Ideas below,
        Which always find us young,
        And always keep us so."

Aspiring to guide that chariot which coursed olympia's
sky.– What will the Delphians say & Eleusinian
priests–where will the Immortals hide their secrets
now–which earth or Sea–mountain or stream–or Muses
spring or grove–is safe from his all searching eye–who
drives off apollo's beaten track–visits unwonted zones–&

makes the serpent writhe {*MS blotted*} a nile-like river
of our day flow back—and hide its head.

Spite of the eternal law, from his

> "lips of cunning fell
> The thrilling Delphic oracle."

I have seen some impudent connecticut or Down east
man in his crack coaster with tort sail, standing beside
his galley with his dog with folded arms while his cock
crowed aboard—scud through the surf by some fast
anchored Staten island farm—but just outside the line
where the astonished Dutchman digs his clams, or half
ploughs his cabbage garden with unbroken steeds &
ropy harness.— while his squat bantam whose faint voice
the lusty shore wind drownd responded feebly there for
all reply

I have awaked in the morning with the impression that
some question had beeen put to me which I had been
struggling to answer in my sleep—but there was dawning
nature, in whom all creatures live—looking in at the
window, with serene & satisfied face and no question
on *her* lips.

Men are not commonly greatly servicable to one
another—because they are not servicable to themselves
— Their lives are devoted to trivial ends, and
they invite only to an intercourse which degrades one
another. Some are too weakly sensitive by a defect of
their constitution, magnifying what

{*Twenty-eight pages missing*}

grown;—hoary tower—of azure tinted marble.— an acre
yielded about 1000 tons. They stacked up in a good day
about 1000 tons.

The parched inhabitants of Madras Bombay–Calcutta
–Havana–charleston & New Orleans drink at my well–

While I incredulous read the vast cosmogonal
philosophy of Ancient India–in modern New England
The Brahmen's Stoic descendant still sits in his native
temples and cools his parched lips with the ice of my
Walden well.

Though incredible ages ages have intervened–I am a
denizen of the same earth with their descendants–

The descendant of the religious devotee who dwelt at
the roots of trees with his crust of bread and water jug
cools his water today with ice from my well. If I am not
a modern hindoo we are near neighbors–and by the
miracle of commerce we quench our thirst and cool our
lips at the same well.

And concord fixed air is carried in that ice to mingle
with the sultry zephyrs of the Indus & the Ganges.

I bathe my intellect in the stupendous wisdom of the
Bhagvat Geeta–the Puranas–the Vedas–the laws of
menu–which last three make the Dharma Sastra of the
Hindoos– Since whose composition years of the gods have
lapsed–and in comparison with which this modern world
and its literature seem puny & trivial– And I wonder if
those are not to be referred to another state of existence
than this of ours.– So remote is that religion & sublimity
from our conceptions–

Where is that India where these sons of Brahma
dwelt– Alexander seems the most recent traveller to it.

Wondering at the remoteness of this my modern N E.
life from that fabluous life of theirs–and if by any link
I am related to them–I go to my well for a bucket of water
and there I meet the servant of the modern Brahmin
priest of veeshnóo & Indra & Brahma–come to draw a
bucket full for his master also.– And I refuse not to fill
his water-jug.

{Six pages missing}

for shoes. If the cormorant family would but begin with this little reading for I suppose it is elementary and introductry to better things–& read a little it would be a promising sign–

The result is dullness of sight–a stagnation of the vital circulations and a general deliquium of the intellectual facuties–

The "Skip of the tip-toe Hop" by the celebrated author of Tittle-tol-tan &c&c a romance–to appear in monthly parts–a great rush–dont all come together.

—

There was such a rush I hear at one of the offices to learn the foreign news by the last arrival as broke several large squares of plates glass– News which I seriously think a ready wit might right a twelve month–or 12 years before hand with sufficient accuracy– As for foreign news if one may judge who rarely looks into the newspapers I should say that nothing new ever does happen in foreign parts– As for spain for instance, if you know how to throw in Don carlos and the Infanta and don pedro & Seville & Gibraltar from time to time skilfully & serve up a bull fight when other entertainments fail–it will be true to the letter–

—

The best books are not read even by those who have learned their letters. What does our Concord culture amount to? There is in this town–with a very few exceptions, no taste for the best or the very good books even in English literature which all can read– Even college bred–& so called liberally educated men here &

elsewhere have no acquaintance with the English
Classics.– and as for the recorded wisdom of mankind
–which accesible to all who will know of it–there
are but the feeblest efforts made to study or to become
acquainted with it. One who has just come from reading
perhaps the best of English books will find how few to
converse with respecting it! It is for the most part foreign
& unheard of. One who comes from reading a Greek–or
Latin book–in the original–whose praisies are familiar
even to the illiterate will find nobody at all to speak to
and must keep silence about it.

Indeed there is hardly the professor in our colleges
who if he has mastered the difficulties of the language
has in any like proportion mastered the difficulty of the
wisdom & the poetry. And the zealous morning reader of
Homer or of the Greek Dramatic poets might find no
more valuable sympathy in the atmosphere of
Cambridge A man–any man will go considerably

{Thirty-four pages missing}

your gone–pull it up–pull it up But this–was Beans and
not corn & so it was safe from such enemies as he

–In summer days which some devoted to the fine
arts–away in Italy–and others to contemplation away in
India and some to trade in London & New York–I with
other farmers of N.E. devoted to field-labor

When my hoe tinkled on a stone it was no longer
beans that I hoed nor I that hoed beans.– By such sugar
plums they tempt us to live this life of man–however
mean and trivial

Or it was my amusement when I rested in the shrub
oaks to watch a pair of hen-hawks circling high in the
sky as silently as the humors on my eye–alternately
soaring and descending–approaching and leaving one

another–the imbodiment of some of my own thoughts
which some times soar as high & sail & circle as
majestically there.

—

I should not care if our village life were greatly
modified or totally changed It would be agreeable to me
if men dwelt more in the country–a more rural life a
life in the fields– I love to see a house standing in the
middle of a field away from any road–it is an evidence of
originality & independance in its inhabitants–& that they
do not in other respects copy their neighbors. The state &
the town should be a confederacy of independant families
living apart each with is own territory–or small families
may be united–like separate principalities A true
family is in my eyes more commannding of respect–& of
more authority and importance than the state– It is the
older and more venerable state– The nobility of every
country belong to families which are behind & prior to
and in some sense independent on the state & the state
can confer no honor equal to that of the family.

While the Robins are building their nest & rearing
their family in the apple tree in the orchard they attract
the favor and the interest of man–& represent all their
tribe–but when they are about to migrate in the fall and
have no further interest in the soil they band together in
flocks with a forlorn & alien look–commanding the
respect of none, and are at the mercy of every sportsman.
A flock {MS torn} hundred robins is not so interesting
{MS torn} me as a single family.

I could even dispense with the post office– I hardly
receive more than one letter in a year– And I think that
there are very few important communications made
through the post office– I am infinitely more interested in
the old books than in the new I had rather wait for the

new to become old before I read them than for the old to
become new– I never read any memorable news in a
newspaper in my life.– If we have read that one man
was robbed or murdered or killed by accident–or one
house was burned–or one mad dog killed or one vessel
wrecked–why need one ever read of another–one is
enough. I think that every man's private affairs his
bargains his adventures his accidents & his thoughts or
whims from morning till night are fully–as interesting
as uncle Sams– But every man unless he is naturally
stupid & a bore knows better than to trouble us with
these things.

Why should we live with such hurry & bustle–let us
spend one day as deliberately as nature– Let us rise
early & fast or break fast gently and without noise– What
if the milk-man does not come in season {*MS torn*}
white wash our coffee–let us murmur an inward prayer
that we may be sustained under this trial & forget
him Let company come & let company go determined to
make a day of it. Let the bells ring & the children
cry   why should we knock under–& go with the stream.
The sun has not got to the zenith yet. Let us not be upset
& overwhelmed in that terrible rapid & whirlpool called
a dinner–situated in the meridian shallows–weather this
danger and you are safe for the rest of the way is down
hill–   with unrelaxed nerves–with morning vigor sail
by it looking another way–tied to the mast– If the
engine wistles let it whistle for its pains–and we will
consider what kind of music it is like   Let us not be
starved before we are hungry.–   Men have the st Vitus'
dance. & cant possibly keep their heads still–   Why if
I should only give a few pulls at the bell-rope yonder
fiery like–i.e. without setting the bell why there is not a
man on his farm in the outskirts of the town
nothwithstanding that press of engagement

{*One-half page missing*}

sympathy with the devouring element. As for our work we
havent any–any thing can command– hardly a man
takes a half hour's nap after dinner but when he wakes
he holds up his head and inquires whats the news– some
give directions to be waked every half hour, doubtless
for no other purpose. & then in return they tell what they
have dreamed. Let us not be thrown off the track by
every nut-shell & mosquito's wing that comes in our way.

Men say that a stitch in time saves nine–and so they
take a thousand stitches today to save nine tomorrow
– They do nothing to stitch in time–when possibly
there may be

{*One-half page missing*}

In these woods ranged the {*MS torn*} fox the wood
chuck & the raccoon–the crow & the wood cock–in this
hollow willow & alder thicket the muskrats builded &
burrowed–along this meadow side the blackbirds
congregated– Under the grove of Elms & buttonwoods in
the horizon there was a village of busy men.– I I went
there frequently to observe their habits.– Mine was a
solitary fox or woodchuck hole

—

In the fall before my house was plastering but a fire
had become necessary in the cool evenings I passed

{*Twelve pages missing*}

but it was all gone out of the river–and he dropped down
without obstruction from Sudbury where he lived–to
Fair Haven pond–which he found unexpectedly was a

firm field of ice– It was a very warm spring day and he was astonished to see such a body of

{*Four-fifths page missing*}

Saw a woodchuck out 30 March snow fell 8 inches deep next day. heard a hyla Ap. 6th pond ice melted Ap 8th 1847

—

On the 15th March 142 years before this compelled her to rise from childbed–time to put on one shoe–dashed out the

{*Four-fifths page missing*}
{*Leaves missing*}

I

Robin Hood ballads, for instance, which I can recommend to travel by.

> Sweavens are swift, sayd lyttle John,
>   As the wind blows over the hill;
> For if it be never so loud this night,
>   To-morrow it may be still."

And so it went up hill & down till a stone interrupted the line, when a new verse was chosen.

> His shoote it was but loosely shot,
>   Yet flewe not the arrowe in vaine,
> For it met one of the sheriffe's men,
>   And William-a-Trent was slaine."

There is, however, this consolation to the most way worn traveller, upon the dustiest road, that the path his feet describe is so perfectly symbolical of human life–now climbing the hills, now descending into the vales. From the summits he beholds the heavens and the horizon, from the vales he looks up to the heights again. He is treading his old lessons still, & though he may be very weary & travel worn, it is yet sincere experience.

Thus we went on our way passing through Still river
village–at sundown–seen from whence the Wachusett
was already lost once more amid the blue fabulous mts
in the horizon.– Listening to the evening song of the
robin in the orchards–& contrasting the equanimity of
nature with the bustle & impatience of man– His words
& actions presume always a crisis near at hand, but she
is forever silent & unpretending.– Without stopping to
tell all of our adventures let it suffice to say that we
reached the banks of the Concord on the third morning
after our departure–before the sun had climbed many
degrees into the heavens

And now when we look again Westward from the hills
of concord Wachusett and Monadnock have retreated
once more among the blue & fabulous mts of the
horizon–though our eyes rest on the very rocks where
we boiled our hasty pudding amid the clouds.

What is hard not iron or stone–or adamant–but
necessity. Destiny. What is easy not not pleasure and
inclination indulgence but destiny–

What means this *tragical* change which has no
counterpart in nature–but is confined to the life of
man–from infancy to youth–from youth to
manhood–from manhood to age–while nature changes
not and is never more than one year old.

The individual that stands before you shall tell of
intervals as great as the Heavens & the earth are
asunder– Yet the most insignificant outward fact is
unchanged The winds blow as they were wont–grass
grows & water runs– And he enjoys one opportunity
with–all that is created & with the creator himself– We
are not born too late nor too early. We are never too old
nor too young & opportunity never fails.

{*Leaves missing*}

my sumachs & sweet briars tremble– Ah–Mr Poet is it
you– How dost thou like the world today–
Poet See the clouds yonder how they hang–thats
   great–the greatest thing I've seen–nothing like it in
   old books–nothing like it in strange lands– You know
   well I have my living to get–and as I have not eaten
   to day–I thought I would go a fishing–that is the true
   industry for us poets– I am truly a hungered. come?
   lets along.
Hermit. I cannot resist   my boiled chestnuts will soon
   be out– I will go with you nimbly soon– But I am
   just concluding a serious meditation–methinks I am
   near unto the end of it: Leave me alone then for
   awhile. But that we may not be delayed you shall be
   digging the bait mean while. Angle worms are indeed
   rare to be met with in these parts–where the soil was
   never fattened with manure–the race is nearly
   extinct The sport of digging the bait is well nigh equal
   to the fishing–when one's appetite is not too keen–and
   this thou mays't have all to thyself today– I would I
   would advice thee to set in the spade down yonder
   among the ground nuts–where you see the Johns wort
   waving– I think I may warrant you you one worm to
   every 3 sods you turn up if you look well in among the
   roots of the grass–as if you were weeding. Or if you
   choose to go further it may not be unwise for the
   increase of fair bait is very nearly as the squares of the
   distances.–
      If I should soon bring this meditation to an end is
   another so sweet occasion likely to offer. I was as near
   to being resolved into the essence of things as ever I
   was in my life. I am afraid that my thoughts will not
   come back to me– If it would do any good I would
   whistle for them– When they make us an offer is it
   good policy to say we will think of it.

My thoughts have left no track and I cannot find
the path again. What was it that I was thinking of– It
was a very hazy day.– I will just try these 3 sentences
of Con fut see–they are good pointers to fetch me into
the right course again. mem. They never give us but
one chance–though we may think there will be
another– There never is but one opportunity of a kind.
Poet
How now Hermit– I have got just 13 whole ones
beside several which are imperfect or not
matured. but they will do well for the smaller
fry.– They do not cover up the hook so much–
Hermit Well then lets be off– shall we to the Concord?
There's rare sport there– If the water be not too high–

—

Friendship has this peculiarity that it can never be
talked about. It is never established–as an understood
relation– Friends are never committed.

What it would say can never be expressed. All words
are gossip– what has speech to do with it.

When a man approaches his friend who is thus
transfigured to him, even his own hoarse salutation
sounds prosaic and ridiculous and makes him least
happy in *his* presence.

–It is an exercise of the purest imagination and the
rarest faith– I will be so related to thee– I will spend
truth on thee– the friend responds through his nature
and life and treats *his* friend with the same divine
civility– There is friendship–but without confession–in
silence as divine–

If the other is dull or engrossed by the things of the
world and does not respond to this lofty salute–or from
a lower platform–hears imperfectly– That friendship is
by necesity a profound secret which can never be

revealed– It is a tragedy that cannot be told. None ever knows what was meant.

There is no need that a man should confess his love of nature–and no more his love of man.– In any case what *sentence* is it indispensable should be framed and uttered Why a few sounds.

True love does not quarrel for slight reasons–such mistakes as mutual friends can explain away–but alas only for adequate & fatal & everlasting reasons, which can never be set aside.

That person is transfigured is God in the human form–henceforth– The lover asks no return but that the beloved will religiously accept & wear and not disgrace this apotheosis Whatever virtue or greatness we can conceive we ascribe to that one–of that at least his nature is capable–though he may

{*Leaves missing*}

Yet a fault may appear greater than it is in many ways.

I have never seen a person–who could bear criticism –who could not be flattered who would not bribe his judge.– Who would bear that truth should be loved always better than themselves

—

Mythology is ancient history or biography The oldest history still memorable becomes a mythus– It is the fruit which history at last bears– The fable so far from being false contains only the essential parts of the history– What is today a diffuse biography–was anciently before printing was discovered– –a short & pithy tradition   a century was equal to a thousand years. To day you have the story told at length with all its accompaniments In mythology you have the essential &

memorable parts alone–the you & I the here & there the
now & then being omitted– In how few words for
instance the Greeks would have told the story of Abelard
& Heloise   instead of a volume They would have made a
mythus of it among the fables of their gods and demigods
or mortals–and then have stuck up their names to
shine in some corner of the firmament– And who knows
what Greeks may come again at last to mythologize their
Love.– and our own deeds.

How many Vols folio must the life and labors of
Prometheus have filled if perchance it fell in days of
cheap printing!– What shape at length will assume the
fable of Columbus–to be confounded at last with that of
Jason–& the expedition of the Argonauts–and future
Homers quoted as authority. And Franklin there may be a
line for him in the future Classical dictionary recording
what that demigod did.– & referring him to some new
genealogy–

I see already the naked fables scattered up & down the
history of modern–Europe– A small volume of mythology
preparing in the press of time– The hero tell–with his
bow–Shakspeare–the new Apollo– –Cromwell–Napoleon.

The most comprehensive the most pithy & significant
book is the mythology

Few phenomena give me more delight in the spring of
the year than to observe the forms which thawing clay
and sand assume on flowing down the sides of a deep cut
on the rail road through which I walk.

The clay especially assumes an infinite variety of
forms–

There lie the sand and clay all winter on this shelving
surface an inert mass but when the spring sun comes to
thaw the ice which binds them they begin to flow down
the bank like lava–

These little streams & ripples of lava like clay over flow
& interlace one another like some mythological
vegetation–like the forms which I seem to have seen
imitated in bronze– What affects me is the presence of
the law–between the inert mass and the luxuriant
vegetation what interval is there? Here is an artist at
work–as it were not at work but–a-playing designing
– – It begins to flow & immediately it takes the forms of
vines–or of the feet & claws of animals–or of the human
brain or lungs or bowels– Now it is bluish clay now clay
mixed with reddish sand–now pure iron sand–and sand
and clay of every degree of fineness and every shade of
color– The whole bank for a quarter of a mile on both
sides is sometimes overlaid with a mass of plump & sappy
verdure of this kind– I am startled probably because it
grows so fast–it is produced in one spring day. The lobe
of these leaves–perchance of all leaves–is a thick–now
loitering drop like the ball of the finger larger or
smaller   so perchance the fingers & toes flow to their
extent from the thawing mass of the body–& then are
congealed for a night.

–Whither may the sun of new spring lead them
on– These roots of ours– In the mornings these resting
streams start again and branch & branch again into a
myriad others– Here it is coarse red sand & even
pebbles–there fine adhesive clay–

–And where the flowing mass reaches the drain at the
foot of the bank on either side it spreads out flatter in to
sands like those formed at the mouths of rivers–the
separate streams losing their semicilindrical form–and
gradually growing more and more flat–and running
together as it is more moist till they form an almost flat
sand–variously & beautifully shaded–& in which you can
still trace the forms of vegetation till at length in the
water itself they become the ripple marks on the bottom

The lobes are the fingers of the leaf as many lobes as it has in so many directions it inclines to flow—more genial heat or other influences in its springs might have caused it flow farther.

—So it seemed as if this one hill side contained an epitome of all the operations in nature.

So the stream is but a leaf What is the river with all its branches—but a leaf divested of its pulp— — but its pulp is intervening earth—forests & fields & town & cities— What is the river but a tree an oak or pine—& its leaves perchance are ponds & lakes & meadows innumerable as the springs which feed it.

I perceive that there is the same power that made me my brain my lungs my bowels my fingers & toes working in other clay this very day— I am in the studio of an artist.

This cut is about a quarter of a mile long—& 30 or 40 feet deep—and in several places clay occurs which rises to within a dozen feet of the surface.— Where there is sand only the slope is great & uniform—but the clay being more adhesive inclines to stand out longer from the sand as in boulders—which are continually washing & coming down.

Flowing down it of course runs together and forms masses and conglomerations but if flowed upward it would disperesed itself more—& grow more freely—& unimpeded

In the next 9 miles which completed the extent of the voyage for this day We rowed across several small lakes—poled up numerous rapids & thoroughfares, and carried over 4 portages— I will give the names and distances for the benefit of future tourists

1st after leaving Ambejijis lake—a a quarter of a mile of rapids to the Portage or carry of 90 rods around Ambejisjis Falls.

—

Then a mile & a half through Passamagamet lake, which is narrow & river like to the falls of the same name–Ambejisjis stream coming in on the right

—

Then 2 miles through Katepskonegan lake.– to the carry of 90 rods around Katepskonegan Falls–which name signifies "carrying place"–Passamagamet stream coming in on the left.

—

Then 3 miles through Pockwockomus lake–a slight expansion of the river to the carry of 40 rods around the falls of the same name Katepskonegan stream coming in on the left

—

Then 3/4 of a mile through Aboljacarmegus lake, similar to the last to the portage of 40 rods aroud the fall of the same name

—

Then 1/2 mile of rapid water to the Sowadnehunk dead water & the Aboljacknagesic stream.

This is generally the order of names as you ascend the river &c v 81

Appendix

Men of the French revolution   107   {221}
John Frost   82   {210}
Carlisle–wordsworth–Emerson &c   121-7   {222-226}

On back endpaper
1   beans   10 11 68   {158, 159, *missing*}
no 4 / 222-3-4 228   {129-131, 134}
No 2 / 1 47-8 50   {174, 175}
3   Field mouse   19   {162}
Pewee & Robin & {*illegible word(s)*} Jays
21   spring
4   Geese & ducks   no 2 / 91-2   {214}   no 2 / 1 {*missing*}
2   Walden place of eagles   232   {131}
7   Ground nuts   224   {131}
6   Bread   119   {222}
8   nuts   235   {140}
5   Racoon   Loon   89 no 2   {213}
9   Flints Goose Fair Haven ponds   235-6   {140-141}
10   John Field   1 / 52-3-4-5-6-7-8 61-2 /   {175-177, 179}
    no 2 / 82-3   {210-211}
11   savage life & c   1 / 56   {177}
13   Freezing of pond &c   10 inches of ice
14   winter sounds   233   {138-139}
15   Fox hunter   no 3 / 68 103   {*missing*, 190}
16   Foxes   86- 91-92   {188, 214}
18   chicadee   104– no 3 /   {190-191}   233   {138}
19   ice man   Fisherman   94   {215}
17   moles   100   {217-218}
12   old inhabitants   87-8-9-93–95–108   {212-213, 215, 221}
20   survey of Pond.
21   Spring

[Berg Journal]

On front endpaper
husbandry   3   {234-235}
bathing   5   {235}

hum of a mosquito 5 {235}
loneliness 5 {235-236}
morning 4-6-7-8 {235-237}
hawk 9 {*missing*}
wild-life 10 {*missing*}
commerce is brave 12 {237}
relation to others–15 {238-239}
struggle between philosophy & practical life 17 {240}
law of the pond applied to man 18-19 {240-241}
fishing 20 {241}
The fruit & flower of life intangible–24 {*missing*}
a fish in pond 24 {*missing*}
music in the air 25 {241-242}
I smile at my good fortune instead of singing
   25-6 {242}
sex 30 {244-245}
reality fabulous 34 {246}
delicious evening 35 {*missing*}
spring signs 37 {247}
Homer 38-39 {247-248}
I must mind my business let them say what they
   will 40-1 {248-249}
Chivin. 42-3 {249-250}
Varro on Agriculture 77-8 {269-270}
Turks camped in Europe 243 {349}
Chateaubriands comp. of Ind & Arabs 250 {352}
material things man's kindred 254 {354}
How to Cut nails–255 {*missing*}
Indians 256 {*missing*}
Goethe 266– {356-357}
steam engine 269 {358}

On MS page 242 {*349*}
1 (Passengers & water) 239 new
V p 253
88 {276-277} sailing over N Twin lake. 253
89 {277} perfectly wild country.–234

Annotations

THE ANNOTATIONS provide the following kinds of information: the sources of direct quotations; translations of passages in foreign languages; topical references; identification of persons and places not included in *Webster's Biographical Dictionary* (1943) and *Webster's Geographical Dictionary* (1962); identification of obscure or archaic terms not contained in *Webster's New Collegiate Dictionary* (1979); completion of references to authors and books; important biographical facts that pertain to the Journal. Place names mentioned in Thoreau's accounts of his trips on the Concord and Merrimack rivers and to Mt. Katahdin in Maine are not identified systematically in the Annotations; instead, maps of these regions are provided following the Annotations.

In general, information given in the text is not repeated in the annotation. Short-title references are expanded in the Bibliography, which follows the Annotations, and the edition Thoreau used is cited whenever possible. Where his edition is unknown, the Bibliography lists either his probable source (for example, the edition Emerson owned) or a currently available one. Translations are by the staff of the Thoreau Edition unless otherwise noted. Thoreau's errors or changes in the substantives of quotations are also indicated. Contextual punctuation appears outside of quotation marks when ambiguity would result from using the standard form. The following abbreviations and short titles are used throughout this section:

A Week	Henry D. Thoreau, *A Week on the Concord and Merrimack Rivers*, ed. Carl F. Hovde, William L. Howarth, and Elizabeth Hall Witherell (Princeton: Princeton University Press, 1980)
Days	Walter Harding, *The Days of Henry Thoreau* (New York: Alfred A. Knopf, 1965)

JMN	*The Journals and Miscellaneous Note-books of Ralph Waldo Emerson*, ed. William H. Gilman et al. (Cambridge: The Belknap Press of Harvard University Press, 1960-1982)
Journal 1	Henry D. Thoreau, *Journal 1: 1837-1844*, ed. John C. Broderick et al. (Princeton: Princeton University Press, 1981)
(Loeb)	Translation from the Loeb Classical Library
The Maine Woods	Henry D. Thoreau, *The Maine Woods*, ed. Joseph J. Moldenhauer (Princeton: Princeton University Press, 1972)
(OED)	*Oxford English Dictionary* (Compact Edition, 1971)
Reform Papers	Henry D. Thoreau, *Reform Papers*, ed. Wendell Glick (Princeton: Princeton University Press, 1973)
(T)	Thoreau's translation
Variorum Walden	Henry D. Thoreau, *The Variorum Walden*, annotated and with an introduction by Walter Harding (New York: Twayne Publishers, Inc., 1962)
Walden	Henry D. Thoreau, *Walden*, ed. J. Lyndon Shanley (Princeton: Princeton University Press, 1971)

Long Book

3.2 While . . . stream: This manuscript volume begins with material related to T's 1839 trip on the Concord and Merrimack rivers; many of the entries were transcribed and revised from earlier Journal volumes. See Historical Introduction, pp. 449-450.

4.7-8 "siluer . . . spring": "Another of the same Nature, Made Since" (anon.), in *England's Helicon*, p. 217.

4.15-16 "Pulsae . . . Olympo.": Virgil, *Eclogues*, VI, 84, 86; lines 84-86 translate "The re-echoing valleys fling them again to the stars, till Vesper gave the word to fold the flocks and tell their tale, as he set forth over an unwilling sky" (Loeb).

4.20 –"jam . . . gemmae,": Virgil, *Eclogues*, VII, 48; "now the buds swell on the joyful stem" (T).

4.22 "strata . . . poma.": *Eclogues*, VII, 54; "The apples lie scattered every where, each under its tree" (T).

7.13-14 "optic . . . Fesolé": Milton, *Paradise Lost*, I, 288-289, reads "Fesole".

13.13 Campton: Campton, N.H., which T mentions in the itinerary of his river trip (see *Journal 1*, p. 136), is located fifty miles northwest of Concord, N.H. The MS reads "Compton", but neither John Hayward's *New England Gazetteer* (Concord, N.H.: Israel S. Boyd and William White, 1839), which T owned, nor contemporary atlases lists a Compton, N.H.

13.15 "When . . . night": Campbell, "Hohenlinden," in *Poetical Works*, p. 102, l. 6.

15.1-2 "I . . . moon": *Julius Caesar*, IV, iii, 27.

15.25 Ball's hill: A small hill on the Concord River northeast of Concord, Mass.

15.25-26 St Anne's: Henry, *Travels and Adventures in Canada*, p. 16, comments: "we reached the rapids and carrying-place of Saint-Anne, two miles below the upper end of the island of Montréal; and it is not till after passing these, that the voyage may be properly said to be commenced."

16.11 mr. Mitchels: A Joseph Mitchell kept an inn in Hooksett at this time.

17.23 Crotched mountain: Crotched Mountain rises about fifteen miles west of Goffstown, N.H.

17.25-29 "Plato . . . Degerando: Gérando, *Histoire Comparée*, I, 84 (T).

22.10-13 "For . . . hue.": Morton, *New England's Memorial*, p. 35.

24.7-8 Hunters moon: "A name for the full moon next after the Harvest Moon" (OED).

24.20 annual Cattleshow: Agricultural exposition in Concord sponsored by the Society of Middlesex Husbandmen and Manufacturers.

26.8-14 Mount Sabér . . . conversation.": "Review of Botta's *Travels in Arabia*," p. 4.

26.23 sinker creels: A creel is "a contrivance made of wickerwork used as a trap for catching fish, lobsters, etc." (OED).

32.18 Iolchos: Iolcos, a town in Thessaly said to be the birthplace of Jason and starting point of his search for the Golden Fleece.

35.11-13 Thus . . . shell.: Articles commonly associated with pilgrims; a scrip is "a small bag, wallet, or satchel, esp., one carried by a pilgrim" (OED); the scallop shell was the emblem and proof of pilgrimage to St. James's shrine at Santiago de Compostela in Spain.

35.19-22 The mountains . . . bayonnette: The oppressive rule of the Pasha over the Egyptians was noted by many travelers; for example, see Edward Lane, *An Account of the Manners and Customs of the Modern Egyptians*, 2 vols. (London: C. Knight & Co., 1837), I, 176-179.

37.3 Barnsdale: Barnsdale Wood in Nottinghamshire, England, was associated with the legend of Robin Hood.

39.4-5 Stockbridge Indians: The Stockbridge Indians fought on the American side during the Revolutionary War. After the war, they were removed to New Stockbridge, Oneida County, N.Y.

40.5 Philip and Paugus: Principal figures in King Philip's War (1675-1676).

40.10-11 Veeshnoo Sarma: *The Hĕĕtŏpādēs of Vĕĕshnŏŏ-Sārmā* are instructive fables told by the aged Hindu priest Vĕĕshnŏŏ-Sārmā to educate the sons of a Hindu king. See Hitopadeśa.

40.20 Mourzuk to Darfour: The city of Mourzuk lay in the western Sahara and was a stop for caravans; Darfour was a large area that lay to the east of present-day Sudan.

42.6-7 "common sense and labor.": Unidentified.

43.24-28 I . . . true: When, in 1741, Alexander Pope declined to write an inscription for a monument recently erected to honor Shakespeare, the following lines from *The Tempest* (IV, i, 152-156) were used instead: "The cloud-capp'd towers, the gorgeous palaces, / The solemn temples, the great globe itself, / Yea all which it inherit, shall dissolve, / And, like this insubstantial pageant faded, / Leave not a rack behind." T's source is unknown.

46.23-24 like . . . picture: Unidentified.

46.25-26 Styria or Cayster: In the *Iliad*, II, 459 ff., Cayster is noted for its abundance of birds. It is unclear whether T meant Styria, a province in Austria, or Styra, a city mentioned in the *Iliad*, II, 539; neither place is particularly associated with birds.

47.5 'Skieg: Amoskeag Falls, N.H.

47.32 "The far blue mountain": Unidentified.

48.5 Wonolanset: Indian friend of white settlers during King Philip's War. See Gookin, *Historical Collections of the Indians in New England*, p. 187, where the name is spelled "Wannalancet."

50.6 The red election: A later version (*A Week*, p. 57) reads "red Election-bird". This is probably the scarlet tanager. T noted several times the contrast between the tanager's bright red plumage and the forest background: "It flies through the green foliage as if it would ignite the leaves" (May 20, 1853). Twice in T's Journal (on May 23, 1854, and June 24, 1857) the tanager is associated with election day.

53.26 Hunters moon: See Annotation 24.7-8.

56.6 "Her . . . night.": "Description of a Most Noble Lady, [Queen

Mary,] Advewed by John Heywoode," in Evans, *Old Ballads*, III, 121.

56.11 Ροδοδακτυλος εως: "rosy-fingered dawn."

58.9 shotted colt: Shotted means "weighted with 'shot' " (OED); a colt is "a piece of rope with something heavy fastened to the end, used as a weapon" (OED).

63.5 Lyndeboro': Lyndeborough, N.H., lies near the Piscataquog River in Hillsborough County.

63.21 Xanthus and Meander: According to Lempriere's *Classical Dictionary*, two rivers were called Xanthus, one in Troas and one in Lycia; the former was also called Scamander. Meander was a sinuous river in ancient Phrygia.

65.5 Diluvian ... shroud,": In a Greek myth similar to the biblical account of the Deluge, Deucalion, son of Prometheus, was one of the survivors of a great flood.

65.15-17 From ... Pigwacket.: Captain John Lovewell actually left Dunstable, Mass., for Pigwacket (present-day Fryeburgh, Me.) about April 16, 1725. In *A Week*, p. 119, T gives the date as April 18.

65.26 "The pale ... night": Quarles, *Emblems, Divine and Moral*, Book II, Emblem 2, p. 78.

71.1-2 Buonaparte ... rarest: T's source is unknown. Emerson copied a similar remark from Emmanuel de Las Cases, *Mémorial de Sainte Hélène*, 4 vols. (Boston: Wells and Lilly, 1823), I, ii, 10, in his Journal (*JMN*, V, 474).

71.5 I ... poems: T's referent is uncertain, but possibly Jones Very's *Essays and Poems* (Boston: Charles C. Little and James Brown, 1839) is intended.

73.26-74.2 According ... make.: *Confessio Amantis*, IV, 2427-2432, in Chalmers, ed., *The Works of the English Poets*, II, 113.

74.3-11 also ... roote;: "Poem Against Idleness and the History of Sardanapalus," ll. 125-127, 134-137, in *A Selection from the Minor Poems of Dan John Lydgate*, pp. 88-89.

76.2-9 "The Greeks ... Toplis: The original source is Topsell, *The Historie of Foure-footed Beastes and Serpents* (London, 1607). T's source, Rennie, *The Faculties of Birds*, pp. 206-207, gives the author as "Toplis."

80.35 "From ... plain.": Marlowe, *Hero and Leander*, I, 116.

81.6-7 "wise ... hurl'd.": Drummond, "A Pastoral Elegy on the Death of S.W.A. [Sir Antonye Alexander]," ll. 97-98, in *Poems*, p. 209.

81.22 Panathenaea: An Athenian festival in honor of Minerva, which included athletic and artistic competitions.

82.9-83.1   Epitaph . . . body.:   The names used in these burlesque epitaphs are probably fictitious.

83.22   "Went . . . festival.":   Marlowe, *Hero and Leander*, I, 96, reads "Came lovers".

85.21   Aye . . . sea: Chaucer, *Troilus and Criseyde*, IV, 1549; in Chalmers, ed., *The Works of the English Poets*, I, 277. The text reads, "And thou Simois, that, as an arowe, clere / Through Troy rennest, aie dounward to the see".

85.30   Thompson: James Thomson (1700-1748), Scottish poet and author of *The Seasons*.

86.4-8   "attemper'd . . . stand;–":   "Autumn," ll. 28, 30-32, in *The Seasons*, in Chalmers, ed., *The Works of the English Poets*, XII, 436.

86.11-20   her . . . world.:   "Autumn," ll. 1089-1090, 1092-1095, 1099-1100, in *The Seasons*, in Chalmers, ed., *The Works of the English Poets*, XII, 443, which reads "spotted dales".

89.4   Capt. Parry: See Parry, *Three Voyages*, II, 49.

90.30   Zoraster: Zoroaster or Zarathustra (fl. 1000 B.C.) established the Persian religion Zoroastrianism.

91.21-23   I . . . Nature"–:   Probably Robert Mudie's *A Popular Guide to the Observation of Nature; or, Hints of Inducement to the Study of Natural Productions and Appearances, in their Connexions and Relations* (New York: J. & J. Harper, 1833).

95.17-18   "vast uplandish country":   Marlowe, *Hero and Leander*, I, 80.

96.3-100.20   I . . . milking: T's stay with Captain Luke Rice occurred in midsummer 1844 on a walking trip from Concord to Saddleback Mountain in northwest Massachusetts; Rice lived near Florida, Mass., a town that he helped to found. See *Days*, p. 171.

100.21-24   "The . . . owner.":   "Extracts from the Heetopades of Veeshnoo Sarma," p. 83.

101.35-102.1   The . . . trader: See Henry, *Travels and Adventures in Canada*. Wawatam was a Canadian Indian who saved Henry's life.

102.11   *necessarius*:   "A relation, relative, kinsman, connection, friend, client, patron" (Ethan Andrews, *A Copious and Critical Latin-English Lexicon* [New York: Harper & Brothers, 1851]).

102.20-32   I . . . out.":   Possibly the papers of Judge Ephraim Wood (1733-1814).

103.8-10   "formed . . . 'grass-ground',":   Shattuck, *A History of the Town of Concord*, p. 5, reads "two Indian words". Shattuck quotes this passage from a letter of Samuel Davis.

103.20-104.4   "One . . . wide.":   Shattuck, *A History of the Town of Concord*, pp. 200-201.

105.1-2   in . . . dead: Unidentified.

106.7-15   Standing . . . epitome.–:   Charles Cotton, "The Tempest," ll. 1-2, 7-12, in Chalmers, ed., *The Works of the English Poets*, VI, 704.

106.27-28   But . . . blossom'–:   Storer, *Reports on the Fishes, Reptiles and Birds of Massachusetts*, p. 116.

109.21   chivin: See the text at 249.28-251.7 and Annotation 250.28.

115.3-4   Chinese Cliff swallows: Rennie, *Natural History of Birds*, p. 98, quotes a description of this bird: " 'On the seacoast . . . of the kingdom of China, a sort of small particoloured birds, in the shape of swallows, at a certain season of the year, namely, their breeding time, come out of the midland country to the rocks, and from the foam or froth of the seawater dashing and breaking against the bottom of the rocks, gather a certain clammy, glutinous matter, perchance the sperm of whales or other fishes, of which they build their nests, wherein they lay their eggs and hatch their young.' "

115.12-14   that . . . brain.":   Michael Drayton, "To My Dearly Loved Friend, Henry Reynolds, Esq. Of Poets and Poesy," ll. 109-110, reads "rightly should." T's source is probably the introduction to Marlowe's *Works*, I, iv.

116.20   Wooster: Worcester, Mass.

116.21   Nobscot: Perhaps a small stream near Nobscot Hill, southeast of Sudbury, Mass.

118.31   disjecta membra: From Horace's *disjecta membra poetae*, "limbs of a dismembered poet," signifying "scattered remains" (OED).

119.25   burr millstones: Millstones "of coarse silicious rock imported from France or quarried locally in the United States" (*A Dictionary of American English*, comp. Sir William A. Craigie and James R. Hulbert [Chicago: University of Chicago Press, 1938-1944]).

120.7   Alamo & Fanning!:   James Walker Fannin (1804-1836) fought in the Texas Revolution. He led the defense of Goliad, where he and his men were captured and executed by Santa Anna before the fall of the Alamo.

120.14-124.31   We . . . profit.:   The controversial abolitionist Wendell Phillips (1811-1884) spoke to the Concord Lyceum on March 11, 1845. T's letter defending Phillips was published in the March 28 issue of *The Liberator*. See *Days*, pp. 175-176, and the published text and Textual Introduction in *Reform Papers*, pp. 59-62 and 303-309.

124.11-15   As . . . journey–":   Bernáldez, "Extract From the

History of the Catholic Sovereigns, Ferdinand and Isabella," p. 43, reads "and may God speed him on his journey."

126.11-12   Shermans bridge and Talls Island: Both locations lie about four miles south of Concord.

126.29   Geo Melvin: George Melvin (b. 1813?) was a local hunter and trapper and a favorite acquaintance of T. In the Journal for Dec. 2, 1856, he is described as "Awkward, gawky, loose-hung, dragging his legs after him. He is my contemporary and neighbor."

127.22   quackled: "choked" (OED).

127.31-32   "the . . . endeavor":   Henry Wadsworth Longfellow, "Seaweed," l. 37. First published in *Graham's American Monthly Magazine* 26, no. 1 (January 1845): 12, where the line reads, "From the strong Will, and the Endeavor".

128.1-4   Of . . . smooth: Izaak Walton's description of caddis worms in *The Complete Angler* (London: John Major, 1823), pp. 226-227, is similar; T's source is unknown.

129.30   agricola laboriosus: "laboring farmer."

129.32   Mr Coleman's report: The Rev. Henry Colman published four reports on agriculture in Massachusetts, 1838-1841.

131.30   In C.:   Passages on Carlyle here and throughout were intended for T's lecture "Thomas Carlyle and His Works" given at the Concord Lyceum on Feb. 4, 1846. The lecture was later published in *Graham's American Monthly Magazine* 30, no. 3 (March 1847): 145-152, and no. 4 (April 1847): 238-245.

131.33   "exceeding . . . great":   Carlyle, *Oliver Cromwell's Letters and Speeches*, II, 53.

132.3-5   "And . . . reel.":   Carlyle, *Oliver Cromwell's Letters and Speeches*, II, 53.

132.6-7   At . . . him?":   Carlyle, *Oliver Cromwell's Letters and Speeches*, II, 64.

132.7   "crowning mercies":   Carlyle, *Oliver Cromwell's Letters and Speeches*, II, 69, reads "crowning-mercy".

132.7-8   "intercalated . . . Commentators":   Carlyle, *Oliver Cromwell's Letters and Speeches*, II, 88.

132.9-28   "Say . . . it?":   Carlyle, *Oliver Cromwell's Letters and Speeches*, II, 94.

133.20   tare & tret: "the two ordinary deductions in calculating the net weight of goods to be sold by retail" (OED).

134.34   James Collins: Collins was one of the many itinerant Irish laborers who worked on the Fitchburg Railroad.

140.32-141.1   Lincoln . . . Hill: Hills around the village of Lincoln, about two miles southeast of Concord.

142.9-12   When . . . tonight.:   T's earlier lecture, on Carlyle, was presented on Feb. 4, 1846. This draft is for his next lecture,

"History of Myself," describing his life at Walden, which he did not give until Feb. 10, 1847.

143.23-26   I . . . frost–:   See Cook, *The Three Voyages*, II, 214.

143.27-30   food . . . less: See Liebig, *Animal Chemistry*, pp. 20-21.

147.15   Five points: A busy section of downtown New York known for its poverty and crime.

150.10   I . . . man: Alek Therien (see 160.10-33).

[Walden 1]

155.6-18   I . . . aisles.:   In the summer of 1844, T traveled with William Ellery Channing down the Hudson and into the Catskill Mountains of New York; see *Days*, p. 172.

160.11-12   Paphlagonian . . . Therien: The Paphlagonians, who inhabited a heavily forested region of Asia Minor, were known for their heaviness and dullness.

160.23-28   "Why . . . grieve.":   Homer, *Iliad*, XVI, 7-16 (T). Patroclus was the son of Menoetius and grandson of Actor; Peleus was the father of Achilles. All fought on the Greek side during the Trojan War.

160.34   Lestrigones: In the *Odyssey* (X), the Lestrigons are a cannibal people of Italy.

164.11-12   No . . . expeditions.:   See Plutarch, *Lives*, V, 196.

165.13   Sopsinwine: "An apple of very deep red, by some called sopsy-wine, *quasi* sopped in wine" (OED).

166.24   Titmans: A titman is "The smallest pig, etc. of a litter; hence, a man who is stunted physically or mentally" (OED).

168.7-8   "The . . . Cross":   Eliot Warburton, *The Crescent and the Cross; or, Romance and Realities of Eastern Travel* (New York: Wiley and Putnam, 1845).

170.8   the evening train: The Fitchburg Railroad, constructed in the 1840s, ran near the eastern edge of Walden Pond.

172.25-173.32   "Thus . . . misfortune: Two versions of Homer, *Iliad*, XVI, 101-111.

173.33-34   Twenty . . . pond: T's family lived in Boston from 1821 to 1823; he probably visited Walden in 1822. In *Walden*, p. 155, T gives his age at the time of his first visit as four.

175.32-33   the thunder . . . of: "The Legend of Dido, Queene of Cartage," ll. 293-294, in *The Legend of Good Women*; in Chalmers, ed., *The Works of the English Poets*, I, 308. Chaucer's text reads, "Emong all this, to romblen gan the Heven, / The thunder rorod with a grisly steven."

176.4   John Field: The Vital Records of Lincoln, Mass., record that a Mary Field, daughter of "John, Irish laborer, and Mary" was born in May 1844 (*Variorum Walden*, p. 302). In a later journal passage, Field is called John Frost; see Annotation 210.21 and *Walden*, pp. 204-209.

178.6-7 "from . . . day.":   Milton, *Paradise Lost*, I, 742-744, reads "Sheer o'er the crystal battlements: from morn / To noon he fell, from noon to dewy eve, / A summer's day."

180.30-35 According . . . string.:   See Gookin, *Historical Collections of the Indians in New England*, pp. 149-150.

181.20 Rumford fire place: A nonsmoking stove invented by Benjamin Thompson, Count Rumford (1753-1814).

183.13-14 a new . . . Capta":   To commemorate the Roman subjugation of the Jews in A.D. 70, the Emperor Vespasian minted a coin on which the phrase "Iudaea Capta" appeared.

184.11-13 The . . . Admetus: When banished from Heaven, Apollo tended Admetus's flocks for nine years.

184.15-16 To . . . judged: Three sons of Jupiter; see Ross, *Mystagogus Poeticus*, pp. 8-9.

184.16-19 As . . . Judge.":   Ross, *Mystagogus Poeticus*, p. 8.

185.1-3 Music . . . Marsias: See Ross, *Mystagogus Poeticus*, pp. 17-18.

185.28 "a meadow . . . flowers":   Ross, *Mystagogus Poeticus*, p. 30.

186.23-26 Aristeus . . . wind.":   Ross, *Mystagogus Poeticus*, p. 29. Aristaeus, the son of Apollo and the shepherdess Cyrene, was killed by a serpent while pursuing Eurydice.

187.3-27 I . . . his: T presumably planned to lecture on his life at Walden and the idea of economy in the spring of 1846 but did not speak on this topic until Feb. 10, 1847. See Annotation 142.9-12 for information about another draft of the beginning of the lecture and *Walden*, p. 4, for the published version.

187.17 hampers: "Something that hampers, or prevents freedom of movement; a shackle" (OED).

187.30 "Letters & Speeches":   Thomas Carlyle's *Oliver Cromwell's Letters and Speeches*.

188.19 Hallam's Hist. of Literature: Henry Hallam's *Introduction to the Literature of Europe, in the Fifteenth, Sixteenth, and Seventeenth Centuries*.

188.21-23 Morgante . . . prose.":   Hallam, *Introduction to the Literature of Europe*, I, 272.

188.24-26 Lionardo . . . century.":   Hallam, *Introduction to the Literature of Europe*, I, 304.

188.27-30 Read . . . Regained: See Hallam, *Introduction to the Literature of Europe*, I, 313-315.

189.1-17 Landor's . . . Deer-stealing.":   T found this information in Richard Henry Horne, *A New Spirit of the Age*, I, 156-173, passim.

189.19 Vide . . . Abbot": See Landor, "Richard I and the Abbot of Boxley," in *Imaginary Conversations*, I, 3-16. "Richard's sail" is described on pp. 12-14.

189.20-22 Phocion's . . . Eubulides": See Landor, "Eschines and Phocion" and "Demosthenes and Eubulides," in *Imaginary Conversations*, I, 113-131 and 327-345. Phocion's final remarks, on death, are on pp. 130-131.

189.23-28 In Milton . . . round.": Landor, "Milton and Andrew Marvel," in *Imaginary Conversations*, II, 14-15, reads "There is, if I may express myself so, without pursuing a metaphor till it falls exhausted at my feet, a sort".

189.29 Pericles & Sophocles: See Landor, "Pericles and Sophocles," in *Imaginary Conversations*, II, 137-157.

189.30-31 Marcus . . . Death.: See Landor, "Marcus Tullius Cicero and His Brother Quinctus," in *Imaginary Conversations*, II, 553-632. Sleep and death are compared in a passage on pp. 589-590.

189.32 Johnson . . . words.: See Landor, "Samuel Johnson and Horne Tooke," in *Imaginary Conversations*, II, 177-182.

190.26 Brittons camp: Britton's Camp was about a mile from T's cabin, on the Lincoln road near Little Goose Pond.

191.12-16 "It . . . Ibid.: Morton, *New England's Memorial*, pp. 397-398.

[Walden 2]

201.30-32 Rabelais . . . all.: Probably a reference to the apocryphal deathbed utterance of François Rabelais (c. 1490-1553): "La farce est jouée."

204.30-205.1 Carlyle . . . last: Emerson had kept notes of his first visit to Carlyle in 1833, which he probably recounted to T. See Emerson, *English Traits* (Boston: Phillips, Sampson, and Co., 1856), p. 22.

205.1-2 his . . . quarreling: "Cruthers and Jonson; or, The Outskirts of Life," pp. 691-705.

206.25 "only . . . night.": Carlyle, *The French Revolution*, I, 2.

207.7 Hugh Quoil's: According to *Concord, Massachusetts, Births, Marriages, and Deaths: 1635-1850* (Boston: Beacon Press, 1894), Hugh Coyle died October 1, 1845, at the age of 61.

210.21 John Frost: *Concord, Massachusetts, Births, Marriages, and Deaths* records the marriage of a John N. Frost in 1841. However, in an earlier Journal passage, this person is called John Field. See Annotation 176.4 and *Walden*, pp. 204-209.

211.24   King . . . best: See Selden, *Table Talk*, in *The Library of the Old English Prose Writers*, II, 169.

212.18-21   Over . . . woods: Cato Ingraham (1751?-1805) was the slave of Duncan Ingraham (d. 1811), a wealthy sea captain and merchant.

212.22   Zilpha: See *Walden*, p. 257.

212.23-24   Bristow . . . hill: Brister Freeman (1754?-1822); see *Walden*, pp. 257-258.

212.26   Breed's location: John Breed (d. 1824) was a hard-drinking barber; see *Variorum Walden*, p. 308, n. 13, and *Walden*, p. 258.

212.27   Hilda: Unidentified.

212.28   Wyeman the potter: Thomas Wyman (1774?-1843); see *Walden*, p. 261.

214.35   actaeon: In Greek mythology, Actaeon was a famous hunter who, having seen Diana bathing, was changed into a stag and devoured by his own dogs.

215.23   "to . . . drink":   Unidentified.

216.3   Breeds: See Annotation 212.26.

216.10-33   From . . . oracle":   See Gilfillan, *Sketches of Modern Literature, and Eminent Literary Men*, pp. 175-177. The final quotation reads "listened to, when he goes, as an oracle."

217.2-4   "come . . . England.:   Carlyle, "Death of the Rev. Edward Irving," in *Critical and Miscellaneous Essays*, IV, 83.

217.6   "Brest Shipping":   See Carlyle, *The French Revolution*, II, 72.

219.1-2   It . . . revolution: Possibly an allusion to a remark by the Duke de Liancourt quoted in Carlyle, *The French Revolution*, I, 193: "Sire, . . . It is not a revolt, it is a revolution."

219.13-14   Simeon Stylites: St. Simeon Stylites (c. 390-459), the first of the "stylites" or pillar ascetics.

219.24-25   They . . . head.–:   T quotes from Lempriere's *Classical Dictionary*, s.v. "Hercules". Iolas (or Iolaus), a son of Iphiclus, king of Thessaly, was the friend of Hercules.

221.1   'a . . . that':   Burns, "For A' That and A' That," in *Poetical Works*, II, 25-26. This refrain also occurs in "The Jolly Beggars," *Poetical Works*, II, 214-215.

221.7-12   In . . . &c &c: Historical figures described in Carlyle, *The French Revolution*.

221.13   Nutting & Le Gros: See *Variorum Walden*, p. 309, n. 25, where Nutting is identified as the Sam Nutting mentioned in *Walden*, p. 279, and John Le Grosse as a farmer who lived on Westford Road.

221.13-15   The Stratten . . . hill: In his copy of *Walden*, T later added more information on the Stratton family. See *Variorum Walden*, p. 308, nn. 11-12.

221.16   Brister Freeman: See Annotation 212.23-24.

221.16-17   Squire Cummings?:   Possibly John Cummings (d. 1788), a local physician.

221.24   Cato: See Annotation 212.18-21.

224.21-22   His ... hah!":   Asides such as these appear frequently in Carlyle's *Oliver Cromwell's Letters and Speeches*.

224.26-28   "I ... it!]":   Carlyle, *Oliver Cromwell's Letters and Speeches*, II, 97.

224.31-225.1   "groans ... assent":   See Carlyle, *Oliver Cromwell's Letters and Speeches*, II, 111, 100, 285, for example.

225.6-8   "little ... interior.":   Carlyle, *Oliver Cromwell's Letters and Speeches*, II, 118, reads "you see the Speech getting ready in the interior of his Highness!"

225.15-16   "O ... friend!":   Carlyle, *Oliver Cromwell's Letters and Speeches*, II, 52.

225.19-20   "Poor ... Oliver!":   Carlyle, *Oliver Cromwell's Letters and Speeches*, II, 242.

225.20-21   "Look ... Highness!":   Carlyle, *Oliver Cromwell's Letters and Speeches*, II, 246.

225.22   "Courage ... one!":   Carlyle, *Oliver Cromwell's Letters and Speeches*, II, 248.

225.25   "breaks down":   See Carlyle, *Oliver Cromwell's Letters and Speeches*, II, 279, 291, for example.

226.13-21   and ... to: See Carlyle, *Oliver Cromwell's Letters and Speeches*, II, 184-185. The remainder of the interrupted paragraph reads: "a spectacle to the West of England and Posterity! Singing as above; answering no question except in song. From Bedminster to Ratcliff Gate, along the streets, to the High Cross of Bristol: at the High Cross they are laid hold of by the Authorities;– turn out to be James Nayler and Company. James Nayler, 'from Andersloe' or Ardsley 'in Yorkshire,' heretofore a Trooper under Lambert; now a Quaker and something more. Infatuated Nayler and Company; given up to Enthusiasm,–to Animal Magnetism, to Chaos and Bedlam in some shape or other! Who will need to be coerced by the Major-Generals, I think;–to be forwarded to London, and there sifted and cross-questioned. Is not the Spiritualism of England developing itself in strange forms? The Hydra, royalist and sansculottic, has many heads."

227.15   the Yeoman's ... Freeman: Concord newspapers. *The Freeman* was a Democratic newspaper; the *Gazette*, which changed its name to *The Republican* in 1840, was a Whig newspaper.

228.25-26   Anursnack ... Monadnoc: Annursnack is a hill in

Concord; Wachusett, Watatic, and Monadnock are mountains west and northwest of Concord.

[Berg Journal]

233.4-7   When . . . like–:   The book T was reading has not been identified; it may be the source of material from 233.7 to 234.14 and from 234.38 to 235.13.

233.12-14   Anacreon . . . dives.:   *Carminum Poetarum Nouem*, p. 63. This poem is not by Anacreon himself but is part of a group of poems known as the "Anacreontea," originally published in 1554 by Henricus Stephanus (Henri Estienne).

233.17-234.14   According . . . 60:   The Greek song is from Athenaeus, *Deipnosophistae*, VIII, 360. T's source is unknown; "Hare" may be Julius Charles Hare (1795-1855), an English philologist.

234.17   καλὰς . . . above: T translates these phrases, from lines 3 to 4 of the poem at 233.17-234.14, as "beautiful hours" and "Beautiful seasons". Loeb reads: "καλὰς ὥρας" and "καλοὺς ἐνιαυτούς."

234.22-32   In . . . strife.:   *Iliad*, III, 1-7 (T).

234.38-235.13   "According . . . institutions.":   Unidentified.

235.28   Θειον: Divine, godlike.

237.31   long-wharf: Long Wharf is a large wharf in Boston Harbor.

238.14   Thomaston lime: Thomaston, Me., produced much of the lime used in New England.

238.18-19   muslin de laines: "a dress material originally composed wholly of wool, but afterwards of wool and cotton" (OED).

238.25-26   John . . . Vt.:   Cuttingsville is a post office in Shrewsbury, Rutland County, Vermont. John Brown is probably a fictitious name; see *Walden*, p. 121, where the name is John Smith.

244.29   Scotland's burning: A popular children's round.

247.20-22   Capt. . . . creek: See Frémont, *Report of the Exploring Expedition to the Rocky Mountains*, p. 22.

248.9-26   Chapman . . . gracers.":   "To the High Borne Prince of Men, Henrie Thrice," ll. 29-47. T's source is unknown.

248.29-32   They . . . poesy.:   "To the Reader," ll. 57-60. T's source is unknown.

249.28   chivin: See Annotation 250.28.

250.9-11   P.V.A. fins . . . C: Standard abbreviations for posterior, ventral, anal, dorsal, and caudal.

250.28   Leuciscus pulchellus: See Storer, *Reports on the Fishes, Reptiles and Birds of Massachusetts*, p. 91; from his description, T's chivin is probably the American Roach or Golden Shiner, whose modern taxonomic designation is *Notemegonus crysoleucas*.

252.3 flection: Flexion is "The action of bending, curvature; bent condition" (OED).

253.13-16 In . . . lusts.": Mahābhārata, *Bhăgvăt-Gēētā*, p. 9.

253.23-26 "He . . . others.": Carlyle, *Oliver Cromwell's Letters and Speeches*, I, 458.

253.31-261.3 "The . . . birth.": *Bhăgvăt-Gēētā*, pp. 45 (253.31-254.4), 46 (254.5-6), 47 (254.6-11), 48 (254.11-12), 53 (254.21-24: source reads "a perfect performer" [254.21]), 53-54 (254.24-33), 55 (255.1-2), 55-56 (255.3-7), 56 (255.7-10), 57 (255.11-16), 57-59 (255.22-256.15: source reads "deeds of mankind" [256.13]), 59-60 (256.15-25), 62 (256.27-31), 62-63 (256.31-257.2), 63 (257.3-6), 64-65 (257.7-18), 65-66 (257.18-21).

257.24-29 "I . . . works": *Bhăgvăt-Gēētā*, p. 79.

257.30-34 "They . . . hatred.: *Bhăgvăt-Gēētā*, p. 81.

257.35-258.3 "And . . . still.": *Bhăgvăt-Gēētā*, p. 88.

258.8-10 "This . . . quality.": *Bhăgvăt-Gēētā*, p. 105.

258.12-14 "A . . . smoke.": *Bhăgvăt-Gēētā*, p. 131.

258.17-259.6 remarks . . . own.": *Bhăgvăt-Gēētā*, p. 9.

259.12-13 the three Goon: See *Bhăgvăt-Gēētā*, p. 107.

260.28-32 "This . . . mystery.": *Bhăgvăt-Gēētā*, p. 51.

261.1-3 "Know . . . birth.": *Bhăgvăt-Gēētā*, p. 75.

261.26-262.2 It . . . him.: T is referring to Henry, *Travels and Adventures in Canada*; see *A Week*, p. 219.

262.24-25 Dudleian lectures: Harvard lectures named for Paul Dudley (1675-1751); speakers often took conservative stands on religious issues.

265.22 "no . . . sound": Milton, "On the Morning of Christ's Nativity," l. 53; Chalmers, ed., *The Works of the English Poets*, VII, 507, reads "no war or battle's sound".

266.16-17 the peak . . . Kearsarge: Mountains in Grafton County, N.H.

266.26-28 From . . . way: The Old Man of the Mountain is the likeness of a human profile on Mt. Jackson near Franconia, N.H. The Notch is a nearby gap in the surrounding mountains, and the Flume is a deep chasm through which the Pemigewasset River flows.

267.12-13 Squam . . . Winnipiseogee: New Hampshire lakes whose outlets, the Squam, Pemigewasset, and Winnipesaukee rivers, respectively, join to form the Merrimack.

267.14-16 Smith's . . . Contoocook: New Hampshire rivers that empty into the Pemigewasset, which eventually becomes the Merrimack.

268.29 Thornton: A village in Grafton County, N.H.

269.2 no . . . points: Possibly Canterbury Street in southwest Boston. Four corners was the shopping district of Boston around the intersection of Washington, Winter, and Summer streets; Five Points was a section of downtown New York notorious for its crime.

269.16 Agiocochook: Indian name for the White Mountains.

269.19 adroscoggin: The Androscoggin River runs through New Hampshire and Maine.

269.19-20 "take . . . march–: Cf. *Reform Papers*, pp. 52, 296.

269.26-33 Varro . . . value": Varro, *The Three Books*, pp. 49-50.

270.1-5 I . . . herbage.": Varro, *The Three Books*, p. 52.

270.9-19 In . . . this?": Varro, *The Three Books*, pp. 128-130.

270.22-23 Vide . . . Eng.: See Cato, *M. Porcius Cato Concerning Agriculture*, Chapter 1 (pp. 40-42) and Chapter 3 (pp. 44-46).

271.32 Mt.: Mt. Katahdin; see *The Maine Woods*, p. 21.

274.18 Thatcher's Rips: T named these rapids for his cousin, George Thatcher, who accompanied him on the trip.

276.22-23 The . . . Maine.: See Williamson, *The History of the State of Maine*, I, 92-94.

276.24 Prof. . . . 1837.: Jacob W. Bailey climbed Katahdin in 1836 and published an account in *The American Journal of Science and Arts* 32 (July 1837): 20-34.

276.26 Jackson . . . 38: Charles T. Jackson climbed Katahdin on a geological expedition in 1837; see his *Second Annual Report on the Geology of the Public Lands*, pp. 6-20.

276.27 Hale . . . 1845: Edward Everett Hale and William Francis Channing climbed Katahdin during the summer of 1845. Hale recounted their trip in the *Boston Daily Advertiser*, August 15, 1845.

281.13 lucus a non lucendo: According to D. E. MacDonnell, *A Dictionary of Select and Popular Quotations* (Philadelphia: A. Finley, 1818), "The word '*lucus*' a *grove*, is derived from, '*lucere*,' to shine, because the rays of the sun are supposed rarely to penetrate through its foliage. The phrase is generally used to mark an absurd or discordant etymology."

283.7 Charlevoix: Pierre Charlevoix (1682-1761) recounted his travels in North America in *Histoire et Description Générale de la Nouvelle France* (1744).

284.17-18 domi . . . venatus: In *The Maine Woods*, p. 7, the passage reads, "their life is *domi aut militiae*, at home or at war, or now rather *venatus*, that is, a hunting, and most of the latter."

284.20 Abenakis: Abenaki was the inclusive name for several tribes of Maine Indians.

285.4 great freshet: During the previous spring (March 1846), there had been a major flood caused by melting ice.

285.27 Cilley: Possibly Jonathan Cilley (1802-1838), a Maine politician known for his eloquence.

287.20 Louis Neptune: A well-known Indian guide.

287.35 Pomolar: Traditionally, Pomola was the evil spirit who inhabited the summit of Mt. Katahdin.

289.19 canalés: Percussion caps for rifled or grooved bore guns.

291.13 Province Man: A Canadian.

292.29 Jonathan: "A generic name for the people of the United States" (OED).

293.7-12 Flash . . . stories: Popular fiction of little literary value written and marketed quickly. Joseph Holt Ingraham (1809-1860) wrote a number of popular adventures, although there is no record of "The Belle of the Penobscots" in the *National Union Catalog*.

293.14 The . . . Maine: Moses Greenleaf (1777-1834), map maker and author; a posthumous edition of his map of Maine was published in 1844.

294.24 whistler duck: Commonly known as the American Golden-Eye.

301.22-24 There . . . Geog: The Wandering Jew is probably Eugène Sue's *Le Juif Errant*, published in English in 1844; the Criminal Calendar may be either the well-known *Newgate Calendar* or *The Criminal Recorder*, both published in many editions. Elijah Parish published two geographies: *A Compendious System of Universal Geography* and *A New System of Modern Geography*, both in several editions.

303.22-24 Such . . . vitae.–: Anon., "The Dragon of Wantley," in Percy, ed., *Reliques of Ancient English Poetry*, III, 356-367; the quoted line is on page 362.

304.1-2 "disafforested his mind": Donne, "To Sir Edward Herbert," l. 10, in Chalmers, ed., *The Works of the English Poets*, V, 165. To disafforest means "to free from the operation of the forest laws; to reduce from the legal state of forest to that of ordinary land" (OED).

308.10 Argo: The ship that carried Jason in search of the Golden Fleece. The allusion is to the Argo's escape from the Symplegades, floating islands that were said to crush ships.

310.10-11 Emerson . . . Emancipation: Emerson's address, "Emancipation in the West Indies," delivered on August 1, 1844, and published soon thereafter.

310.13-14 a pamphlet . . . Holley: *History of the Erection of the Monument on the Grave of Myron Holley* (Utica, N.Y.: H. H. Curtis, 1844); Holley was an abolitionist from New York.

313.19-27 It . . . stream.: See Thomas Moore, "A Canadian

Boat-Song," available in many editions, and *The Maine Woods*, pp. 38-39.

313.25   Ste Annes: See Annotation 15.25-26.

315.29-316.2   Our . . . occasion.:   See Melville, *Typee*, pp. 118-119.

317.18   "superb head-dress":   Melville, *Typee*, p. 131, reads, "a superb and striking head-dress."

317.21   the author of Typee: Herman Melville (1819-1891), whose South Seas adventure, *Typee*, was published in 1846.

317.23   old Marheyo: Father of Kory-Kory; the narrator of *Typee* is taken into his household and attended by his son. See Melville, *Typee*, pp. 91-92.

325.11   Depskaneig: Some pages later in this draft and in *The Maine Woods*, T normalized the spelling to "Katepskonegan".

326.13   Umbedegis: Some pages later in this draft and in *The Maine Woods*, T normalized the spelling to "Ambejijis".

326.25   oak hall: A large Boston clothing store.

329.14   the famous freshet: See Annotation 285.4.

329.32-331.11   Instantly . . . log: What T calls alternatively the chivin, the roach, and the cousin trout is probably the modern fallfish (*Semotilus corporalis*), which, according to W. B. Scott, *Freshwater Fishes of Eastern Canada* (Toronto: University of Toronto Press, 1967), p. 54, inhabits "eddies at the foot of falls and rapids" and is "often caught by sportsmen when fishing for brook trout." See also Annotation 250.28.

332.4   ἐξ ἔρον ἕντο: *Iliad*, I, 469.

332.7   οὐδέ . . . ἐϊσης: *Iliad*, I, 468.

333.33-36   I . . . watering.":   Fletcher, *The Faithful Shepherdess*, III, 450-453, in Beaumont and Fletcher, *Dramatick Works*, III, 167-168.

334.11   the . . . Astraea: Discovered in December 1845, the asteroid was named for the Greek goddess of justice.

334.16   newly . . . planet: Neptune, discovered in September 1846.

340.14   Pomola: See Annotation 287.35.

345.3-4   Welland canals: The canal, constructed between 1824 and 1833, connects Lake Erie with Lake Ontario.

345.14   Oak hall: See Annotation 326.25.

349.14-15   Uncle . . . Henry–:   George McCauslin, George A. Thatcher (T's cousin), Charles Lowell, Thomas Fowler, T; "Raish" is unidentified.

349.16-26   Nor . . . Heywood.:   From *The Hierarchy of the Blessed Angels* (1635), as modernized by Lamb in *Specimens of English Dramatic Poets*, II, 190.

349.28-29 "The . . . Europe": Chateaubriand, *Travels*, p. 64.

349.33-350.6 Chateaubriand . . . beauty.": *Travels*, p. 114.

350.24-26 The . . . Athens: Chateaubriand, *Travels*, p. 142.

350.26-29 Thus . . . them.: See Chateaubriand, *Travels*, p. 142.

350.30-33 As . . . foliage.": Chateaubriand, *Travels*, p. 143.

351.27-29 As . . . out.": Lamb, "Specimens From the Writings of Fuller," in *Prose Works*, I, 174.

352.23-353.14 Chateaubriand . . . state.": *Travels*, pp. 274-275.

353.17 Tasso's poem: *La Gerusalemme liberata (Jerusalem Delivered)*, published in 1575.

354.5-6 Saint . . . airs.: Thomas Moore, "A Canadian Boat-Song"; see Annotation 313.19-27 and *The Maine Woods*, p. 39.

354.7-10 Sir Thomas Browne . . . belief.": *Religio Medici*, in *Works*, II, 14.

356.24-32 Indeed . . . reach.": Goethe, *Auto-Biography*, II, 6-7.

357.4 "The . . . art": Quarles, "To My Booke," in *Divine Fancies*, IV, 117.

357.5-10 He . . . rather.": Goethe, *Auto-Biography*, II, 7.

359.24-365.27 I . . . myself: Description of trip T made to the Berkshires in the summer of 1844; see *Days*, pp. 171-173.

[I]

365.11 South Adams: Adams, Mass., so called by T to distinguish it from nearby North Adams.

366.27-367.20 Ovid . . . heavens: Ovid, *Metamorphoseon*, I, 15-17 (366.28-32), 23 (366.34-35), 39-42 (367.2-8), 61-62 (367.10-13), 69-71 (367.15-20) (T).

367.21-369.28 The . . . hair.: Ovid, *Metamorphoseon*, II, 63-66 (367.21-28), 67-87 (367.32-368.31), 91-92 (368.33-34), 103-124 (368.37-369.28) (T).

369.29-30 And . . . palm: Possibly R. W. Emerson, whose *Poems* (1847) appeared in late 1846.

369.31-34 "Olympian . . . so.": Emerson, "Ode to Beauty," ll. 60-63, in *Poems*, p. 139.

370.4-5 "lips . . . oracle.": Emerson, "The Problem," ll. 11-12, in *Poems*, p. 17.

371.27-28 India . . . Alexander: Alexander the Great entered India in 327 B.C. T's source was probably Plutarch, *Lives*, V, 266-276.

372.3 little reading: The catalogue of the Concord Social Library for 1836 (Kenneth W. Cameron, *The Transcendentalists and Minerva*, 3 vols. [Hartford, Conn.: Transcendental Books, 1958], II,

496-506) lists a five-volume series, *Much Instruction From Little Reading*.

372.7   deliquium: "Failure of the vital powers; a swoon" (OED).

372.9-10   The . . . tan: In his essay "Walking," T speaks of "the child's rigmarole, *Iery wiery ichery van, tittle-tol-tan*."

377.16-19   Sweavens . . . still.":   Ritson, "Robin Hood and Guy of Gisborne," ll. 17-20, in *Robin Hood*, I, 116. T modernizes some spellings.

377.22-25   His . . . slaine.":   Ritson, "Robin Hood and Guy of Gisborne," ll. 73-76, in *Robin Hood*, I, 118. T modernizes some spellings.

Selected Later Revisions

262.11   "The . . . way.":   "The Lordling Peasant," ll. 61-64, in Evans, *Old Ballads*, IV, 136.

347.16   "This . . . fro:":   Chaucer, "The Knight's Tale," ll. 2849-2850, in Chalmers, ed., *The Works of the English Poets*, I, 24.

350.33   "stone . . . hue":   Chateaubriand, *Travels*, p. 143.

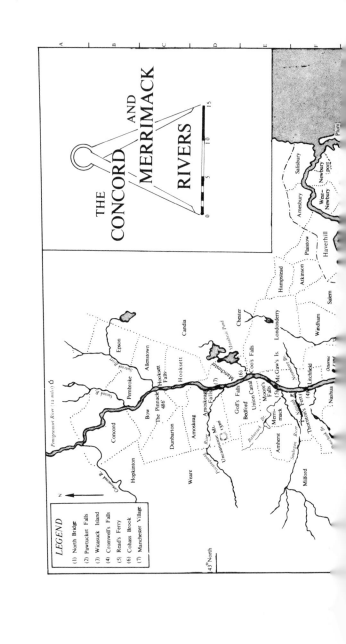

THE
CONCORD AND
MERRIMACK
RIVERS

0 5 10 15

Pemigewasset River (12 miles)

N

43° North

LEGEND

(1) North Bridge
(2) Pawtucket Falls
(3) Wicasuck Island
(4) Cromwell's Falls
(5) Read's Ferry
(6) Cohass Brook
(7) Manchester Village

Hopkinton
Weare
Concord
Bow
Dunbarton
The Pinnacle 486
Amoskeag
Uncannunuc Mt. 1390
Goff's Falls
Bedford
Milford
Amherst
Merrimack
Union Canal
Moore's Falls
Thornton's Ferry
Nashua
Pembroke
Allenstown
Hooksett
Falls
Hooksett
Manchester (7)
(6)
Goo's Falls
Mc Gaw's Is. (5)
Litchfield
Epson
Candia
Mandistic Pond
Chester
Londonderry
Windham
Salem
Atkinson
Hampstead
Plaistow
Haverhill
Salisbury
Amesbury
West-Newbury
Newbury port
Plum

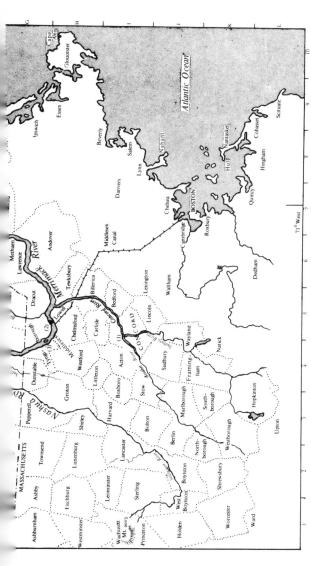

Reprinted from Map Three in Robert F. Stowell, *A Thoreau Gazetteer*, ed. William L. Howarth (Princeton: Princeton University Press, 1970)

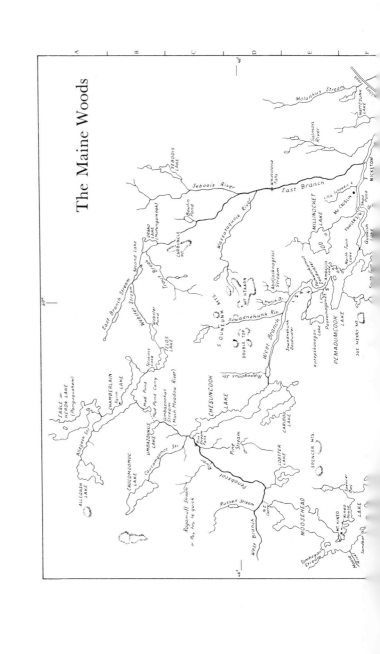

The Maine Woods

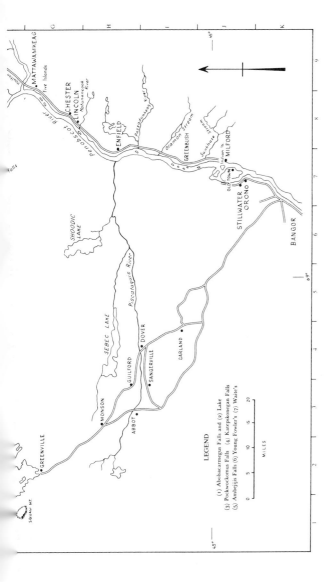

BIBLIOGRAPHY

Beaumont, Francis, and John Fletcher. *The Dramatick Works of Beaumont and Fletcher. . . .* 10 vols. London: T. Sherlock, 1778.

Bernáldez, Andrés. "Extract From the History of the Catholic Sovereigns, Ferdinand and Isabella." *Collections of the Massachusetts Historical Society,* ser. 3, vol. 8 (1843): 5-68.

Browne, Sir Thomas. *Sir Thomas Browne's Works, including His Life and Correspondence.* Ed. Simon Wilkin. 4 vols. London: W. Pickering, 1835-1836.

Burns, Robert. *The Poetical Works of Robert Burns: With a Sketch of His Life.* 2 vols. London: G. Jones & Co., 1830.

Campbell, Thomas. *Poetical Works, including Theodoric, and many other pieces not contained in any former edition.* Philadelphia: J. Crissy and J. Grigg, 1826.

Carlyle, Thomas. *Critical and Miscellaneous Essays.* 4 vols. Boston: James Munroe and Company, 1838-1839.

———. "Cruthers and Jonson; or, The Outskirts of Life." *Fraser's Magazine* 2, no. 12 (January 1831): 691-705.

———. *The French Revolution: A History.* 2 vols. Boston: Charles C. Little and James Brown, 1838.

———. *Oliver Cromwell's Letters and Speeches: With Elucidations.* 2 vols. New York: Wiley & Putnam, 1845.

Carminum Poetarum Nouem. In Pindarus. *Pindari Olympia, Pythia, Nemea, Isthmia. Græce & Latine . . .* and *Carminum Poetarum Nouem, Lyricæ Poeseωs Principum, Fragmenta.* 2 vols. in 1. [Heidelbergæ]: Apud Hieronymum Commelinum, Elect. Palat. typographum, 1598.

Cato, Marcus Porcius, *Censorius. M. Porcius Cato Concerning Agriculture.* Trans. T. Owen. London: J. White, 1803. Bound with Varro, Marcus Terentius. *The three books of M. Terentius Varro Concerning Agriculture.* 1800.

Chalmers, Alexander, ed. *The Works of the English Poets, from Chaucer to Cowper.* 21 vols. London: J. Johnson, 1810.

Charlevoix, Pierre. *Histoire et Description Générale de la Nouvelle France, avec le Journal Historique d'un Voyage fait par ordre du Roi dans l'Amérique Septentrionnale.* 6 vols. Paris: Rollin Fils; Didot, 1744.

Chateaubriand, François Auguste René, vicomte de. *Travels in Greece, Palestine, Egypt, and Barbary, During the Years 1806 and 1807.* Trans. F. Shoberl. New York: Van Winkle and Wiley, 1814.

Colman, Henry. *Report of the Agriculture of Massachusetts.* Boston: Dutton and Wentworth, 1838-1841.

Cook, James. *The Three Voyages of Captain James Cook Round the World.* 7 vols. London: Longman, Hurst, Rees, Orme, and Brown, 1821.

Drummond, William. *The Poems of William Drummond of Hawthornden.* London: J. Jeffery, 1790.

Emerson, Ralph Waldo. *Emancipation in the West Indies.* Boston: James Munroe and Company, 1844.

——. *Poems.* Boston: James Munroe and Company, 1847.

England's Helicon. In *The Paradise of Dainty Devices, reprinted from a transcript of the first edition ... and England's Helicon. A Collection of Pastoral and Lyric Poems ... To which is added a biographical and critical introduction.* 2 vols. in 1. London: T. Bensley, 1812.

Evans, Thomas. *Old Ballads, Historical and Narrative, with Some of Modern Date; Collected from Rare Copies and Manuscripts. New ed., rev. and ... enl. by R. H. Evans.* 4 vols. London: W. Bulmer, 1810.

"Extracts from the Heetopades of Veeshnoo Sarma." *The Dial* 3 (July 1842): 82-85.

Frémont, John Charles. *Report of the Exploring Expedition to the Rocky Mountains in the Year 1842, and to Oregon and North California in the Years 1843-'44.* Washington: Blair and Rives, 1845.

Gérando, Joseph Marie de, baron. *Histoire Comparée des Systèmes de Philosophie, Considérés Relativement aux Principes des Connaissances Humaines.* 2d ed., rev. and enl. 4 vols. Paris: A. Eymery, 1822-1823.

Gilfillan, George. *Sketches of Modern Literature, and Eminent Literary Men (Being a Gallery of Literary Portraits).* New York: D. Appleton & Co., 1846.

Goethe, Johann Wolfgang von. *The Auto-Biography of Goethe. Truth and Poetry: From my Life.* Ed. Parke Godwin. 4 vols. in 2. New York: Wiley and Putnam, 1846.

Gookin, Daniel. *Historical Collections of the Indians in New England. Collections of the Massachusetts Historical Society,* ser. 1, vol. 1 (1792; rpt. Boston: Munroe & Francis, 1806): 141-227.

Hallam, Henry. *Introduction to the Literature of Europe, in the Fifteenth, Sixteenth, and Seventeenth Centuries.* 4 vols. London: John Murray, 1837.

Henry, Alexander. *Travels and Adventures in Canada and the Indian Territories, Between the Years 1760 and 1776.* New York: I. Riley, 1809.

History of the Erection of the Monument on the Grave of Myron Holley. Utica, N.Y.: H. H. Curtis, 1844.

Hitopadeśa. *The Hĕĕtōpădēs of Vĕĕshnŏŏ-Sărmā, in a Series of Connected Fables, interspersed with Moral, Prudential, and Political Maxims.* Trans. Charles Wilkins. Bath: R. Cruttwell, 1787.

Homerus. *The Iliad of Homer, from the Text of Wolf. With English Notes.* Ed. C. C. Felton. Boston: Hilliard, Gray, and Company, 1833.

Horne, Richard Henry, ed. *A New Spirit of the Age.* 2d ed. 2 vols. London: Smith, Elder and Co., 1844.

Jackson, Charles Thomas. *Second Annual Report on the Geology of the Public Lands, Belonging to the Two States of Maine and Massachusetts.* Augusta: Luther Severance, 1838.

Lamb, Charles. *The Prose Works of Charles Lamb.* 3 vols. London: Edward Moxon, 1838.

————. *Specimens of English Dramatic Poets, Who Lived About the Time of Shakspeare.* 2 vols. London: Edward Moxon, 1835.

Landor, Walter Savage. *Imaginary Conversations of Literary Men and Statesmen.* 3 vols. London: Henry Colburn, 1826-1828.

Lempriere, John. *A Classical Dictionary; Containing a Copious Account of All the Proper Names Mentioned in Ancient Authors; with the Value of Coins, Weights, and Measures, Used among the Greeks and Romans; and a Chronological Table.* 6th ed., cor. London: T. Cadell and W. Davies, 1806.

Liebig, Justus, *Freiherr* von. *Animal Chemistry, or Organic Chemistry in its Applications to Physiology and Pathology.* Ed. William Gregory. New York: Wiley and Putnam, 1842.

Longfellow, Henry Wadsworth. "Seaweed." *Graham's American Monthly Magazine* 26 (January 1845): 12.

Lydgate, John. *A Selection from the Minor Poems of Dan John Lydgate.* Ed. James O. Halliwell. In vol. 2 of the Percy Society, *Early English Poetry, Ballads, and Popular Literature of the Middle Ages.* London: C. Richards, 1840.

Mahābhārata. *The Bhăgvăt-Gēētā, or Dialogues of Krĕĕshnă and Ărjŏŏn; in Eighteen Lectures, with Notes.* Trans. Charles Wilkins. London: C. Nourse, 1785.

Marlowe, Christopher. *The Works of Christopher Marlowe.* 3 vols. London: W. Pickering, 1826.

Melville, Herman. *Typee: A Peep at Polynesian Life. During a Four Months' Residence in A Valley of the Marquesas.* Rev. ed., with a sequel. New York: Wiley and Putnam, 1846.

Milton, John. *Paradise Lost: A Poem. In Twelve Books.* Philadelphia: Johnson & Warner, 1808.

Morton, Nathaniel. *New England's Memorial.* Ed. John Davis. 5th ed. Boston: Crocker and Brewster, 1826.

Mudie, Robert. *A Popular Guide to the Observation of Nature; or, Hints of Inducement to the Study of Natural Productions and Appearances, in their Connexions and Relations.* New York: J. & J. Harper, 1833.

Ovidius Naso, Publius. *Publii Ovidii Nasonis Metamorphoseon Libri XV*. Ed. Thomas S. Joy. Philadelphia: Long et al., 1823.

Parry, Sir William Edward. *Three Voyages for the Discovery of a Northwest Passage*. 2 vols. New York: Harper & Brothers, 1841.

Percy, Thomas, ed. *Reliques of Ancient English Poetry: consisting of Old Heroic Ballads, Songs, and Other Pieces of Our Earlier Poets. . . .* 3 vols. London: J. Dodsley, 1765.

Plutarchus. *Plutarch's Lives, Tr. from the Original Greek; with Notes Critical and Historical, and a Life of Plutarch. By John Langhorne, D.D. and William Langhorne, A.M. A New Ed., with Corrections and Additions, by The Rev. Francis Wrangham, M.A.F.R.S.* 8 vols. New York: Samuel Campbell et al., 1822.

Quarles, Francis. *Divine Fancies: Digested into Epigrammes, Meditations, and Observations*. London: M. F[lesher], 1638.

———. *Emblems, Divine and Moral*. Chiswick: C. & C. Whittingham, 1825.

Rennie, James. *The Faculties of Birds*. London: Charles Knight, 1835.

———. *Natural History of Birds. Their Architecture, Habits, and Faculties*. New York: Harper & Brothers, 1840.

"Review of Paul Émile Botta's *Travels in Arabia* [*Relation d'un Voyage dans l'Yémen, entrepris en 1837, pour le Museum d'Histoire Naturelle de Paris*]." *Athenæum*, January 1, 1842, pp. 3-5.

Ritson, Joseph, comp. *Robin Hood: A Collection of All the Ancient Poems, Songs, and Ballads. . . .* 2 vols. London: T. Egerton and J. Johnson, 1795.

Ross, Alexander. *Mystagogus Poeticus, or The Muses Interpreter*. 2d ed., enl. London: Thomas Whitaker, 1648.

Selden, John. *Table-Talk*. In *The Library of the Old English Prose Writers*. Cambridge: Hilliard and Brown, 1831.

Shakespeare, William. *The Dramatic Works of William Shakspeare*. Ed. George Stevens. 2 vols. Hartford, Conn.: Andrus & Judd, 1833.

Shattuck, Lemuel. *A History of the Town of Concord*. Boston: Russell, Odiorne and Company, 1835.

Storer, David Humphreys. *Reports on the Fishes, Reptiles and Birds of Massachusetts*. Boston: Dutton and Wentworth, 1839.

Topsell, Edward. *The Historie of Foure-footed Beastes and Serpents*. London: W. Iaggard, 1607.

Varro, Marcus Terentius. *The Three Books of M. Terentius Varro Concerning Agriculture*. 1800. Bound with Cato, Marcus Porcius, Censorius. *M. Porcius Cato Concerning Agriculture*, trans. T. Owen. London: J. White, 1803.

Vergilius Maro, Publius. *Opera ad usum Serenissimi Delphini. Juxta Editionem Novissimam Londoniensem.* Philadelphia: M. Carey & Son, 1817.

Very, Jones. *Essays and Poems.* Boston: Charles C. Little and James Brown, 1839.

Warburton, Eliot. *The Crescent and the Cross; or, Romance and Realities of Eastern Travel.* New York: Wiley and Putnam, 1845.

Williamson, William Durkee. *The History of the State of Maine. . . .* Hallowell, Me.: Glazier, Masters & Co., 1832.

Index

Abelard: and Heloise, 188, 382
Aboljacarmegus Lake, 329, 385
Aboljacarmegus [Aboljacareme-
 gus] Falls: letting bateau
 down, 344
Aboljacknagesic River, 278-279
Aboljacknagesic Stream, 385
account: old fisherman's, 105
Achilles, 172-173
action, 49; love of, versus love of
 contemplation, 240
actual: and ideal, 11
Adams [South Adams], MA, 365
Æacus, 184
Aeschylus (525-456 B.C.), 169,
 339
affinities: to nature, 158
air: effect of clarity of, on land-
 scape, 11-12; transparency of,
 70
Ajax: struggles of, 172-173
Alcott, Amos Bronson (1799-
 1888): characterized, 223-224
Ambejijis [Ambejisjis] Falls, 384
Ambejijis Lake, 384
Ambejijis [Ambejisjis] Stream,
 385
Ammonusuck River, 80
Amoskeag Falls, 48
Amphion, 185
Anacreontea: "Return of Spring,"
 quoted, 233
ancients: importance of, 366
"Another of the Same Nature,
 Made Since" [in *England's
 Helicon*], quoted, 4
Antaeus, 166, 185
antiquities: American, 351-352
anxiety, *see* care
Apollo: keeps sheep of King Ad-
 metus, 184; and Phaeton,
 Ovid's story of, 367-369
Apollodorus: *The Library*,
 quoted, 219
apples: fragrance of, 165-166;

not grafted in Maine, 286
apprentices: many skillful, 17
Arabia, 26
Arabs: and Indians [American],
 352-353
Aristeus, 186
Aristotle (384-322 B.C.), 17
arrow head flower, 11
arrowheads: making of, 58-59
ash, *see* brown ash
Assabet(h) [North] River, 104
asters, 50, 52, 84
Astraea [asteroid], 334
astronomy: answers to prophecy,
 359
Athenaeus (fl. ca. 200 A.D.):
 Deipnosophistae, quoted, 233-
 234
Autumn: signs of, 31; colors of,
 50; depth of, 51; tints of vegetation in, 52; atmosphere in,
 53

bait: digging for, 131, 379
bald eagles: and fish hawks, 304
Ball's Hill, 15
Bangor, ME, 281
Bare hill, 141
barrel: gnawed by bears, 321
bass wood, 72
bateau(x): making of, 282-283;
 method of carrying, 321-322;
 going down rapids, 343-344
beans, 192; raising at Walden,
 129-131, 134, 158-159, 373
bears, 321
Beaumont, Francis (1584-1616),
 333
beauty, 50, 55-56
Beaver River, 34
bed: made from cedar twigs,
 330-331
Bedford, NH, 16
beer: at Thomas Fowler's, 303

1882): characterized, 223, 224, 226; *Emancipation in the West Indies* in Maine, 310; *Essays*, 355; "Ode to Beauty," quoted, 369; "The Problem," quoted, 370

emotion: exhibition of, seems premature, 20

enthusiasm, 29

epithets: beauty of, 53

Esox reticulatus, see pickerel

essays: poems and, Thoreau praises a volume of, 71

evening, 43, 45-46

evergreens: beauty of, in Maine, 288

exaggeration, 204

fable: the Christian, 353

facts: and principles, 53

Fair Haven Lake, 141

Fair Haven Pond, 376

fall, *see* Autumn

family: more important than state, 374

fandango, *see* swing

farming: too tame, 22

fencing stuff, 318

ferry: peddler at, 283-284

Field, John, 176-177. *See also* Frost, John

field mice, 218

finch: purple, 50-51

fire: adding fuel to, 314-315; in Maine camps, 314; in savage and civilized states, 316

firs: on Katahdin, 337

fish: migratory, 89; of Concord River, 104-112; as contemporaries, 108; cooking in Maine, 335

fisherman(men), 84-85; on Merrimack River, 30; of Concord River, 104-105; in Winter, 141

fish-hawk(s), 170; and bald eagles, 304

fishing, 73; at Fair Haven Pond, 175-177, 179; Thoreau's am-

bivalence toward, 241; for trout in Maine, 278-279, 329-330, 331-332; at Depskaneig Falls, 325-326

Fletcher, Giles, the Younger (1588?-1623), 91

Fletcher, John (1579-1625): *The Faithful Shepherdess*, quoted, 333

flicker, 31

Flint's Pond, 140-141

flowers, 83-84; spiritual virtues of, 54-55; at the end of Summer, 84

fog, 33

forest: a sacred place, 37; on edge of towns, 64

Foster, Captain Jonathan, 82

Fowler, Thomas, 303; house of, 303; hired as guide, 304; climbs tree to get bearings, 342; discusses philosophy with Thoreau, 346-347

Fowler, Thomas [father], 300, 303, 304, 305

fox(es), 89, 188; skating after a, 89; hunting, 214

Frémont, John C. (1813-1890), 247

Franconia, NH, 269

Franklin, Benjamin (1706-1790), 382

Freeman, Brister [Bristow], 212-213, 215, 221

freight train: cargo of, 237-238

freshet: marks of great, 285; signs of, on Katahdin, 341

friend(s), 6, 7, 16, 19-20, 27, 29, 44-45, 57, 62, 69, 86-88; death of, 38; talk of old, 68; reproofs of, 248-249

friendship, 6, 12-13, 41, 49, 69, 87-88; incompatible with kindness, 54; reserve in, 101-102; never expressed, 380-381

frogs, *see* bull frogs

frost: kills Thoreau's garden, 249

Frost, John, 210-211. *See also* Field, John

Editorial Appendix

Notes on Illustrations

Pages 2-3 of Long Book following page 454

This manuscript volume begins with entries Thoreau transcribed and revised from earlier Journal volumes as part of his preliminary work on *A Week on the Concord and Merrimack Rivers*. He frequently left large spaces between entries so that he could expand them later. Here he continued such an expanded entry from the verso of one leaf to the bottom of the recto of the next. See Historical Introduction, p. 453.–Pierpont Morgan Library.

First page of [Walden 1]

Thoreau began a new Journal volume to record the details of his life at Walden Pond. This page contains his first Walden entry, made the day after he moved to the pond.–Pierpont Morgan Library.

Page of [Berg Journal]

This 275-page volume, kept from April 1846 to December 1846 or early 1847, is published for the first time in *Journal 2: 1842-1848*. It includes a first draft of the lecture and essay on "Ktaadn, and the Maine Woods." This page contains a portion of Thoreau's outline for the narrative, based on notes he took during his trip in September 1846.–Henry W. and Albert A. Berg Collection, New York Public Library, Astor, Lenox and Tilden Foundations.

Page of MS volume [I]

Manuscript volume [I] survives only in scattered and often fragmentary leaves. This page contains a portion of Thoreau's heavily revised draft for the "sand foliage" passage from "Spring" in *Walden* (pp. 304-309), probably composed in early spring 1848.–Henry E. Huntington Library.

Acknowledgments

FOR permission to refer to, copy, and publish manuscript material, the editor is indebted to the Pierpont Morgan Library, New York; the Huntington Library, San Marino, California; Henry W. and Albert A. Berg Collection, The New York Public Library, Astor, Lenox and Tilden Foundations; Houghton Library, Harvard University; John Hay Library, Brown University; William K. Bixby Collection, Special Collections, Washington University Libraries, Washington University; Robert H. Taylor Collection, Princeton, New Jersey; and Mr. W. Stephen Thomas, Rochester, New York.

Contributions of time, expertise, and good will were made by Elizabeth Ann Adams, Linda Allardt, Ray Angelo, Ruth H. Bennett, Susan Clarkin, J. Donald Crowley, Martin K. Doudna, John Foley, Anthony T. Grafton, Walter Harding, Edward A. Johnson, Richard M. Ludwig, David R. Miller, Marcia Moss, Glenn Most, Edward Naumberg, David Nordloh, Tom Quirk, Kenneth Rendell, Marilynne K. Roach, Anthony W. Shipps, Jeffrey Spear, Theodore Tarkow, Willard Thorp, and Kevin Van Anglen.

The staff of the Textual Center was generously assisted in preparing part of this volume for computer typesetting by Charles Cullen, Hannah Kaufman, Philip Leclerc, Anna Mitchell, Velga Stokes, and Catherine Thatcher.

Many present and former members of the Textual Center staff helped prepare *Journal* 2 (in addition to those mentioned in Editorial Contributions): Jennifer Abidari, Mary Jo Andersen, Mary Jane Bennett, Howard Blohm, William Brennan, Howard Curtis, Dalton Delan, John Holland, Susan McCloskey, Susan Mizruchi, and Jo Ann Pawlowski.

Material assistance was generously provided by Princeton University, the University of Texas of the Permian Basin, the American Council of Learned Societies, the University of Texas at Austin, and the National Endowment for the Humanities through both the Editing and Publication Programs and the Center for Editions of American Authors of the Modern Language Association. The editor is especially grateful to the Department of English and the Research Council of the University of Missouri-Columbia for generous grants of released time and financial support that helped bring this volume to completion.

Editorial Contributions

THE following people aided the editor in his work on this volume. Initial transcripts were prepared by Linck C. Johnson for Long Book, J. Lyndon Shanley for Walden 1 and Walden 2, John C. Broderick and Joseph J. Moldenhauer for the Berg Journal, and Thomas Blanding for "I". Leonard Neufeldt perfected the transcripts and prepared preliminary textual tables for the first four MS volumes; Elizabeth Hall Witherell and Mr. Sattelmeyer perfected "I" and Nancy Simmons prepared preliminary textual tables. Mr. Blanding, William L. Howarth, and Laraine Fergenson also helped establish the text. Mark R. Patterson compiled the table of Cross-References to Published Versions and, with Kristin Fossum, Wendell Glick, Mr. Johnson, and Martha Strom, wrote the Annotations. Carolyn Kappes prepared and reviewed copy throughout work on the volume. Mr. Sattelmeyer made final editorial decisions about the text and textual apparatus, wrote the introductions, and compiled the Index; his work was reviewed by Ms. Witherell and Mr. Broderick. The following shared the tasks of proofreading the text and tables: Louisa Dennis, Ms. Kappes, Christopher MacGowan, Lorna Carey Mack, Nora W. Mayo, Jody Millward, Susan Mizruchi, Kay Palmer, Mr. Patterson, Melissa Poole, Steven Quevedo, Susan Quevedo, George E. Ryan, Suzanne Sattelmeyer, Marsha Shankman, Jane E. Stimpson, Ms. Strom, and Ms. Witherell.

Historical Introduction

WHEN Henry Thoreau returned to Concord in December 1843, after an unsuccessful attempt to make a place for himself in the New York literary world, his barely nascent career as a writer was at a standstill. He had failed to find regular or remunerative outlets for his work during his seven-month stay on Staten Island, where he earned his keep by tutoring the son of Ralph Waldo Emerson's brother William. Upon his return, he found that *The Dial*, the Transcendental journal that had at least printed if not paid for his early work, was to end with the April 1844 issue. Thoreau had missed Concord and his family intensely during his New York sojourn, and now he re-entered his familiar domestic circle energetically, working long hours at the family pencil business and helping his father build a new house. Emerson, once confident of the literary promise of his protégé, now seemed resigned to Thoreau's displaced energies: "H[enry] will never be a writer," he confided in his Journal, "he is active as a shoemaker." No dated Journal entries after January 7 survive for 1844, and Thoreau published nothing that year after the last issue of *The Dial* went to press. He delivered no lectures, and even his correspondence waned: only three letters from the year are extant.

But Thoreau was not to confirm Emerson's fear that the young men who frequented his circle tended to promise bravely and then disappoint. After this interlude of physical labor (and perhaps of laying in stores for his "private business" at Walden), both his appetite for fronting life's essential facts and his literary aspirations reasserted themselves more strongly than before. The following winter found him at work on a new lecture on "Concord River" and an article on the Brahmin abolitionist Wendell Phillips's appearance before the Concord Lyceum. Early in 1845, his twenty-eighth year, he began his cabin at Walden Pond and by summer, having built on piles of his own driving at last, he was once more reporting to his Journal and simultaneously beginning an ambitious campaign of more public literary ventures. In his imaginative re-creation of the experience in *Walden*, Thoreau's stay at the pond is perhaps the most extended idyll in American literature, but to judge by the projects he began and completed there it was a period of sustained and concentrated literary work as well. At Walden, Thoreau wrote not only most of *A Week on the Concord and Merrimack Rivers* and the first draft of *Walden* but also a long essay on Thomas Carlyle and an even longer travel essay on his first trip to the Maine woods. Additionally, he wrote separate lecture versions of all these works, and some poetry. Although *Journal 2: 1842-1848* opens with a manuscript volume consisting mainly of transcription begun before Thoreau moved to the pond, it covers principally the Walden years and reflects the quickened pace of his literary activity during this time.

These years constitute the heart of the middle phase of Thoreau's Journal. Its earliest phase, 1837 to 1842, reflected the moral earnestness and high aspirations of a young man with no very sure sense of vocation. Having evolved alongside earlier commonplace books, it is stocked with quotations from his reading and his own highly polished if sometimes sententious pronouncements on such characteristic Transcendental themes as friendship, bravery, and truth. This earliest material survives only in a transcription of the original volumes that Thoreau made some time in 1841, and he may have revised and edited it deliberately to portray his apprenticeship in a light of aspirational high seriousness. Some time around 1850, when Thoreau realized that his works were destined for no very great popular success, he turned increasingly to the Journal to record both his thoughts and the details of his study of New England natural history, and gradually it became the major document of his imaginative life. This third stage of the Journal is the massive, detailed, dated, and regularly kept document with which most readers are familiar today. In between these stages of the Journal, however, lie the years of Thoreau's most intense devotion to the mastery of his craft, a period during which he still had hopes of gaining an audience and supporting himself by lecturing and writing. This second stage runs roughly from 1842, when he began to work with Emerson on the editing of *The Dial* and to write for other periodicals, to 1849, when the commercial failure of *A Week on the Concord and Merrimack Rivers* and his estrangement from Emerson caused Thoreau to reassess his literary goals and begin to reorder his life and career in light of the dismal but unmistakable fact that his writing would not pay. During these years, his Journal was primarily a literary workbook into which he copied and drafted passages intended for essays, lectures, and books. All the manuscript volumes of *Journal* 2 (as well as the concluding three volumes of *Journal* 1 and the first volume of the forthcoming *Journal* 3) belong to this middle phase of the Journal.

Accordingly, the physical characteristics and format of *Journal* 2 manuscripts differ from those of the earlier and later phases. Conventional dated entries, except during portions of the summer of 1845 and the spring of 1846, are rare; and only scattered dates appear elsewhere, mostly in brief entries noting seasonal phenomena Thoreau observed at the pond. The literary drafts, which make up the bulk of *Journal* 2, are often intermingled with one another and fragmentary, since Thoreau characteristically worked on several projects at once and later excised many leaves for use in subsequent versions. A number of these excised leaves have been located among the surviving manuscripts of literary works—especially of *A Week* and *Walden*—and restored in the present text to their original places in the manuscript volumes.

Because of the fragmentary character of these volumes, and also because of the nature of the material they contain, most of the Journal for the Walden years was not included in the 1906 Edition of the Journal that has heretofore been standard. Its editors, Bradford Torrey and Francis H. Allen, did not have access to the literary manuscripts containing missing Journal pages, and they were apparently unaware of the existence of two manuscript volumes from this period: the large volume Thoreau kept from April to December 1846 (pp. 233-361), currently in the Berg Collection of the New York Public Library, and the now fragmentary volume (pp. 365-385) that followed it.

Moreover, Torrey and Allen edited the Journal as the diary of a poet-naturalist rather than as the workbook of a busy writer, altering the punctuation and sometimes the syntax to give Thoreau's prose a more finished and polished surface than it has in manuscript. When they could do so without disrupting the context, they also omitted portions of the Journal that essentially duplicated passages in Thoreau's published writings. Since the bulk of the Journal for this period consists of precisely such duplication in the form of literary drafts, they printed a relatively small portion of the material to which they did have access. Consequently, in the 1906 Edition, the Journal for the Walden years seems quite meager.

In fact, however, a large amount of Journal material survives from this period, chiefly in the form of early versions of Thoreau's most famous literary works. When compared to these finished works, and when considered in the sequence and order of their composition, these Journal volumes constitute the raw material for a history of the first major flowering of Thoreau's art, and suggest the principles by which he conceived and began writing both *A Week on the Concord and Merrimack Rivers* and *Walden*. Previously, Thoreau's own natural reticence about the sources of his writing, together with the inadvertent distortion of his literary output conveyed by the abridged text available in the 1906 Edition of the Journal, have combined to make this most crucial phase of his career seem somewhat more mysterious than it actually is. The new material in this volume will by no means dispel the aura of enchantment that surrounds Thoreau's Walden years, but it will add substantially to what is known about the literary projects that he pursued there.

Long Book

Viewed in the light of his literary career, Thoreau's move to Walden Pond was one of a series of temporary living and working arrangements he tried during the 1840s in order to secure time to write. Earlier (1841 to 1843) he had lived with the Emersons, paying for his room and board by occasional work around the house, and while in New York in 1843 he had boarded with Emerson's brother William and tutored his son. When he left Walden in September 1847, he returned to the Emersons' in something like his former capacity as handyman. The immediate motivation for moving to Walden, while unrecorded, was probably Thoreau's need for time and solitude to write his first book, *A Week on the Concord and Merrimack Rivers*. He conceived *A Week* as a work that would be at once a memorial to his brother John, who had died in 1842, and a recapitulation of his early career, including within its narrative framework many of his early essays and poems. Some time before moving to Walden, Thoreau began collecting material for this project in the manuscript volume with which *Journal* 2 begins. Probably because its pages were considerably larger than those of his other Journal volumes, he referred to it in cross-references as "long book." A dated entry near the end of Long Book (p. 149) indicates that Thoreau finished filling it with drafts of other literary works at Walden in the spring of 1846. The date at which he began this volume is both more difficult and more important to determine, since it constitutes the principal evidence for dating Thoreau's earliest significant work on his first book.

The passages collected for *A Week* fill about the first 190 pages, or roughly three-fourths of the 250-page manuscript volume. They consist of entries copied from the earlier Journal—often combined or expanded—as well as original passages that either describe some incident of the 1839 boating trip or record some thought or reflection that Thoreau intended to develop in the book. For the most part, the order of these entries follows the order of the earlier Journal rather than the chronology of the trip itself. The first page, for example, contains an adaptation of a Journal passage from November 3, 1837 (*Journal 1*, p. 10), the third page contains an entry from November 9, 1837 (*Journal 1*, p. 10), and the next page one from November 20, 1837 (*Journal 1*, p. 14). (See Long Book, pp. 3-4.) With occasional minor variations, this pattern continues throughout the whole of that portion of Long Book devoted to transcriptions for *A Week*. Interspersed with these transcriptions are other passages, usually describing some event of the trip. They are presumed to be original because they have no source in the earlier Journal, although they were probably based on a log or other records of the 1839 excursion.

The only dated entries in this portion of Long Book (except for dates of the 1839 trip itself) describe seasonal phenomena from the late summer and early fall of 1842. These dates (see pp. 9-54 passim) range from July 28 to October 30, 1842, and are, with the exception of the first two, in chronological order. None of the dated entries has a source in the earlier extant Journal, while the passages that precede and follow them are for the most part transcriptions of Journal material from the summer of 1840. These dated entries are presumed, then, to be current, suggesting that Thoreau began to compile them for *A Week* in the latter part of 1842. In January of that year his brother John had died, and Henry had been stricken shortly afterwards with a sympathetic illness that left him weak and unable to do much work until well into spring. As his health and strength returned that summer, he may have thought of undertaking an extended literary work as a memorial to his brother, and an obvious subject for such a work would be the one long trip they took together on the Concord and Merrimack rivers in 1839. Thoreau was also just beginning, in the second half of 1842, to write travel narrative with a symbolic dimension: he composed his first such essay, "A Walk to Wachusett," during that summer and fall. A book that wove together travel narrative and reflective essays would be a natural extension of a kind of writing in which he was already engaged.

On the other hand, this portion of Long Book could have been filled any time before Thoreau began to write out a first draft of *A Week* in 1845. The fact that the dated entries have no extant source in the earlier Journal does not prove their currency, for the Journal of late 1842 (*Journal 1*, pp. 433-445) is fragmentary and incomplete and may even have been kept in part on loose sheets that have not survived. The dates attached to these entries, all of which deal with seasonal appearances such as the vegetation notable on a certain date and the migration of birds, may indicate only that Thoreau wished to record the time of year when he had observed these phenomena. And the fact that the first two of these entries, the ones for September 12 and July 28 (pp. 9, 10), are out of chronological order suggests the possibility that these passages were transcribed from another source some time after they were composed. Nevertheless, in the absence of any positive evidence to the contrary, these dated entries are presumed to be current, and thus the beginning both of this notebook and of Thoreau's work on *A Week* may be tentatively dated from the fall of 1842.

If Thoreau began filling Long Book in the fall of 1842, then the rest of the material for *A Week*–approximately ninety more manuscript pages of transcribed material that follows the last dated 1842 entry–was probably completed soon after the first hundred pages, for the ink and handwriting are similar throughout. In any case, some time between the fall of 1842 and early 1845 Thoreau filled the first 190 pages of Long Book with material destined for *A Week*. The *terminus ad quem* is established by the fact that the *Week* transcriptions are followed in Long Book by drafts of Thoreau's lecture on "Concord River" and his article on Wendell Phillips (pp. 106-128); the first was delivered and the second published in March 1845. He then used the remaining thirty manuscript pages of the volume for drafting portions of other literary works he was engaged upon during the following winter of 1845-1846. This last section is thus contemporary with the two Journal volumes that followed Long Book (see below, pp. 454-459).

The compilation of material in the first three-fourths of Long Book formed the basis of the first draft of *A Week*, and as such it demonstrates graphically how Thoreau initially conceptualized the complex process of writing a book. He seems to have found this task especially challenging, perhaps due to the circumstances of his early career and to his Transcendental bias in literary composition. He had not attempted a long work before, and the Transcendentalists, except perhaps for Margaret Fuller with her *Summer on the Lakes* (1844), offered him little in the way of models. They tended toward brief, private, or even ephemeral literary modes: the journal, the "fragment," the "conversation," the lyric poem, the essay. Although Emerson liked to call his essays "chapters," the only large-scale structural principle generally evident in his books, as opposed to his essays, is the thread of a common theme in such later works as *Representative Men* or *English Traits*. How to weave the often disparate and discrete thoughts he had been collecting in his Journal into the narrative of a boating excursion posed a formidable structural problem for Thoreau. The finished work, which he labored for many years to assemble, met censure from the first for its apparent lack of cohesion and the discordance of its narrative and reflective parts.

The seeds of this problem are evident in Thoreau's first stage of work on *A Week*, his collection of material in Long Book. He neither began with nor observed the chronology of the trip in his initial compilation; nor did he proceed according to any other discernible organizing principle. The only order apparent in these passages is the chronology of the earlier Journal. Some time after he had finished amassing all this material, Thoreau decided on a structure for his book, compressing the two weeks of the actual trip into one and assigning each chapter to a day of the week. Originally he planned two "Thursday" chapters, making a total of eight. He then went back over the collected passages and gave entries a number from one to eight in the margin to designate the chapter to which they would belong.

Another physical feature of Long Book is perhaps even more revealing of Thoreau's literary practice at this stage of his career. He characteristically left large blank spaces— sometimes more than half a page–above or below an entry. Often he returned to these entries and expanded them: some passages are increasingly cramped toward the bottom of the page, indicating that he had already written the material at the top of the following page, and on one occasion (see the first illustration, following p. 454) he carried such an expanded passage over to the bottom of the following page.

Thoreau had at first, then, a kind of "germ" theory of composition for *A Week*. He sowed small entries at intervals in Long Book, leaving room for them to grow by a process of creative accretion. The appearance itself of this manuscript thereby suggests the extent to which Thoreau cherished the integrity of the individual thought or moment of inspiration. He did not begin with an overarching structure to which these discrete passages would be subordinated but seems rather to have expected the completed work to evolve from the aggregation of these parts. Commenting in another manuscript volume of the Journal from the same period on the difficulties of this method of composition, and perhaps referring explicitly to the problem of writing *A Week*, Thoreau accurately anticipated the most persistent criticism directed against his book:

From all points of the compass from the earth beneath and the heavens above have come these inspirations and been entered duly in such order as they came in the Journal. Thereafter when the time arrived they were winnowed into Lectures–and again in due time from Lectures into Essays– And at last they stand like the cubes of Pythagoras firmly on either basis–like statues on their pedestals–but the statues rarely take hold of hands– There is only such connexion and series as is attainable in the galleries. And this affects their immediate practical & popular influence. (Pp. 205-206)

[Walden 1] and [Walden 2]

After an entry for January 7, 1844 (*Journal 1*, p. 493), no regular Journal assignable to 1844 or the first half of 1845 survives. However, the accretion of passages in Long Book apparently continued during this time, either by transcription and drafting or by the expansion of "germ" entries in the manner just described. When Thoreau actually took up residence at Walden Pond on July 4, 1845, however, he seems to have had a sense of the heightened significance of his experiment, for he began a new Journal volume to inaugurate this new stage in his life. This volume, perhaps the first he had kept regularly in eighteen months, is dated "Walden Sat. July 5th–45" and begins "Yesterday I came here to live" (see the second illustration, following p. 454). Thoreau later indexed this notebook as "1" among his Walden Journals (see Appendix, p. 388), and it is designated Walden 1 in the present volume.

He also brought with him to Walden another new Journal volume, physically identical to the first, which he seems to have viewed as complementary to it. He used the first, Walden 1, in the beginning as a "regular" Journal; it contains dated entries for the summer of 1845 describing his life at the pond. He used the second–"2" in his index (see Appendix, p. 388) and hence Walden 2 in the present volume– primarily as a draft book for current literary projects. Its first surviving page, for example (p. 197), contains a passage composed for *A Week*, and much of the rest of the now quite fragmentary volume consists of material for Thoreau's lecture and subsequent essay on Thomas Carlyle (*Early Essays*, pp. 219-267) and passages intended for his first lectures on life at Walden.

Most of the passages on the latter subject found their way

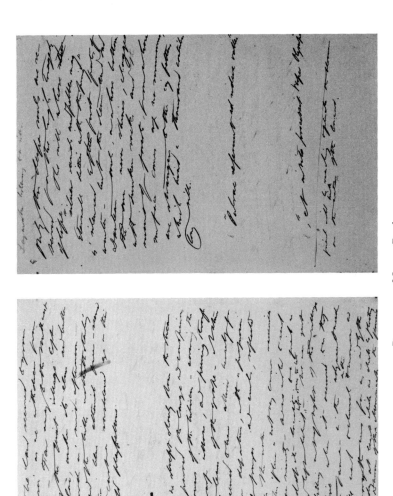

Pages 2-3 of Long Book

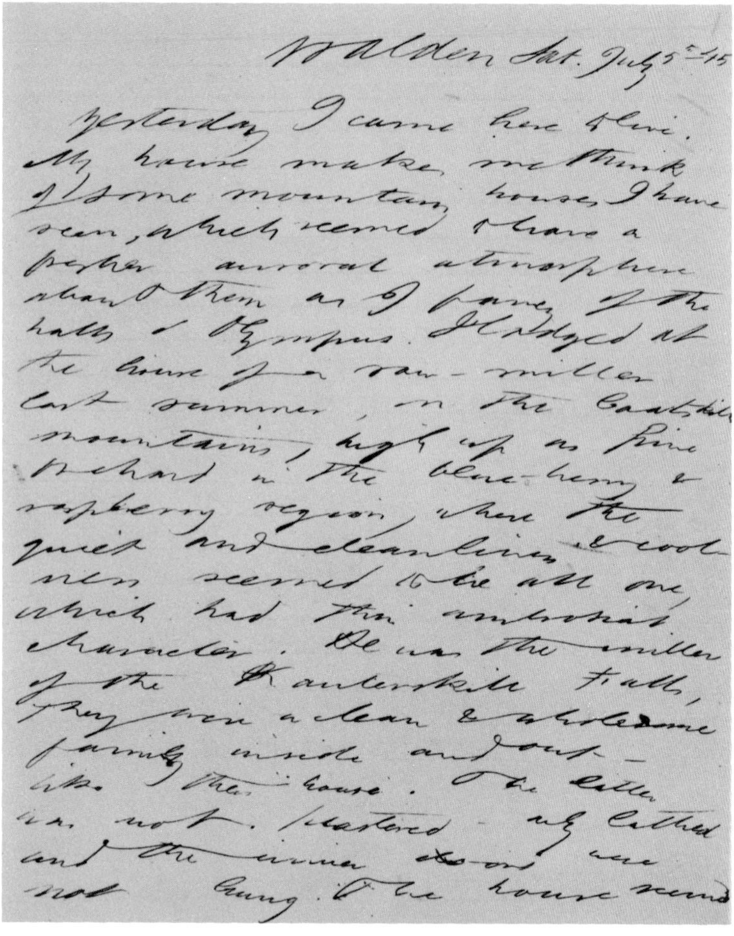

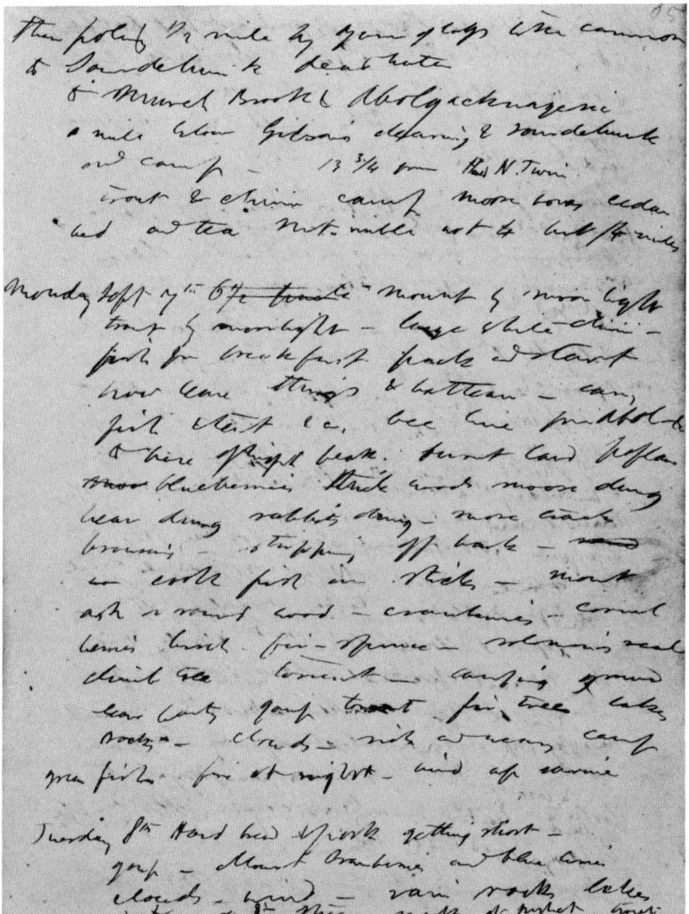

Page of [Berg Journal]

Page of MS volume [I]

eventually into "Economy" and "Where I Lived, and What I Lived For" in *Walden*. Their appearance in this notebook from the summer of 1845 demonstrates the close connection between Thoreau's journalizing and his literary activities at this time; it reveals also his early appreciation of the advantages that his mode of life offered in the way of stance and subject matter for his writing. Most of the passages dealing with life at the pond in both Walden 1 and Walden 2, in fact, are clearly "worked up" and given a literary treatment. The histories of early residents of his neighborhood, for example (pp. 207-221 passim), ultimately becoming "Former Inhabitants" in *Walden*, already have in this earliest version that chapter's elegiac tone. Perhaps the best example of this feature of the Walden notebooks–the virtually immediate transformation of personal experience into literary vignette– is Thoreau's description of his visit to the hut of the "lately dead" Irish ditcher Hugh Quoil in Walden 2 (pp. 207-210 and Selected Later Revision 207.7-210.19). Here Thoreau actually wrote the story twice, first sketching the principal details and then immediately recasting and elaborating the incident into an extended meditation on the man's death.

Such extensive revisions in the account of a recent event indicate that Thoreau intended from the beginning of his stay to make literary use of his Walden experiences. Seen in this light, the apparent distinction between the two Walden Journal notebooks–Walden 1 as a series of "regular" Journal entries and Walden 2 as literary draft–fades, overshadowed by the larger fact that Thoreau used both volumes to further his literary works, present and projected. At times, indeed, the two volumes were interchangeable. Thoreau's account of his visit to the Irishman John Field and their subsequent fishing expedition appears in a series of dated entries in late August 1846 in Walden 1 (pp. 175-179). He concludes the account in an entry in Walden 2 (pp. 210-211), where the Irishman is given the pseudonym "John Frost"–probably because Thoreau intended to use this anecdote in a Concord Lyceum lecture. Eventually the two portions were combined in the version of the story that appears in "Baker Farm" in *Walden*.

Finally, one of these volumes became essentially an extension of the other. Thoreau filled Walden 2 before he had finished Walden 1, and then turned back to Walden 1, which still had a number of blank leaves at the end, to continue drafting material for his lectures on Thomas Carlyle and life at the pond. He gave this last section of Walden 1 a different paging sequence, perhaps to correspond to the paging of a lecture draft that has not survived (see Textual Note 187.28). To make the relationship between them clear when he later indexed these volumes for an early version of *Walden*, Thoreau referred to the beginning section of Walden 1 as "1," to Walden 2 as "2," and to the final section of Walden 1 as "3." And, since he was also using the concluding portion of Long Book at the same time, and since it too contained *Walden* material he wished to use, he indexed this portion of Long Book as "4" (see Appendix, p. 388).

The most striking feature of Thoreau's Journal for the summer and fall of 1845 and the winter of 1845-1846 is the large amount of draft material for *Walden* it contains. Despite the fact that Thoreau was busy with both *A Week* and his Carlyle lecture, he still found time to write out detailed accounts of his activities at the pond and to draft long passages of social criticism and satire that would eventually go into the first two chapters of *Walden*. The Journal material for this year, even in its fragmentary state, contains more than half the passages that make up the first draft of *Walden* itself, written the following year. This material was not simply a straightforward account of Thoreau's life that he later modified for the book; rather, it was a careful examination of the conventions and assumed virtues of his contemporaries, written from the vantage point of his position outside society.

The inception of *Walden* itself is generally thought to date from the following year, 1846 to 1847. Thoreau delivered his first lecture on his life at the pond, "A History of Myself," before the Concord Lyceum on February 10, 1847, probably coinciding with his work on the first draft. In a Journal draft of the opening of this Walden lecture (p. 141), Thoreau himself implies that the particular inquiries of his townsmen about his mode of life, put to him after his Carlyle lecture in February 1846, prompted him to deliver a justification of his experiment. But initially he intended to give this lecture the same winter, shortly after the one on Carlyle, for he begins the draft of his talk on life at Walden by saying "When I lectured here before this winter." The Journal also demonstrates that many of the passages to be used in the Walden lecture clearly predate the Carlyle lecture (see, for example, p. 187). Thus Thoreau worked on them together during the fall of 1845 and the early winter of 1846, and intended to deliver them both that season. In reality, the questions of his neighbors about his way of life only afforded him a convenient rhetorical pretext for explaining the purpose of a lecture he had already begun to write.

In summary, the two Walden Journal volumes, together with the last thirty pages of Long Book, provide a fairly clear outline of Thoreau's literary projects during his first year at the pond. They reveal that he was at work simultaneously on the first draft of *A Week*, the Carlyle lecture, and, from the very beginning of his stay, an account of his own life that was counterpointed by his critique of the materialistic assumptions of contemporary American society.

Hence *Walden* did not, as has usually been assumed, follow *A Week* in its conception and early stages but rather proceeded in parallel with it. During his first year at the pond, Thoreau collected and began to organize material for *Walden* at the same time that he was writing the first draft of *A Week*. The two books are thus much closer together in origin than either their respective dates of publication (1849 and 1854) or the differences in their form and execution would suggest. *Walden* obviously benefited from the years of revision and expansion Thoreau devoted to it after the commercial failure of *A Week* in 1849 dashed his hopes of

publishing a second book soon after his first. But the distinctive character of *Walden* also owes a great deal to the
circumstances surrounding its inception. While the events
forming the biographical basis of *A Week* had occurred seven
years before the completion of the first draft, the experiences
upon which *Walden* was based were immediate and vividly
present at the time of writing. A still more important difference in the works is the rhetorical sharpness of stance and
purpose, the characteristically Thoreauvian voice, evident
even in the first draft passages for *Walden* in the Journal.
Whereas the tone and voice of *A Week* tend to be impersonal
and subdued (a quality arising in part from its elegiac purpose), the voice of *Walden* in its earliest drafts is already
personal, iconoclastic, confident. The reason for this rhetorical and stylistic verve may be as simple as Thoreau's own
new-found independence, but the Journal for 1845 to 1846
suggests a literary source as well.

These early drafts of *Walden* material are frequently mingled with passages for the lecture on Thomas Carlyle. Thoreau was working on the Carlyle and Walden lectures simultaneously, it will be recalled, and was using the same
notebooks for composing them. In Walden 2 especially, passages on Carlyle and material for the Walden lecture are
often found in close proximity. Although Thoreau occasionally expresses reservations about Carlyle, he praises both his
style—especially its virtues of exaggeration (p. 204)—and the
distinctive presence and personality of the narrator in his
work (pp. 224-225). Since these comments are interspersed
with hortatory passages for the Walden lecture, Thoreau's
notebooks suggest that he may have been trying to put into
practice those features of Carlyle's literary idiom that he
admired. The influence of Carlyle on subject matter is manifest in Thoreau's meditation on clothes (pp. 211-212), but
perhaps the more telling influence announces itself in tone,
voice, and sheer rhetorical exuberance. In writing his lecture, Thoreau necessarily considered carefully the features
of Carlyle's prose that had made his work so exemplary and

influential to a generation of English and American readers; he seemed to grasp instinctively certain of these stylistic features that lent themselves to his own work at hand. In Carlyle, Thoreau discovered first a distinctive voice–a narrative persona that could both vivify and unify discursive material–and then a calculated exaggeration–what he would refer to in *Walden* as "extra-vagant" speech–rhetorical strategies that lent themselves to his announced purpose of waking up his contemporaries. He seems to have learned through Carlyle at this time that, as he put it in the Journal, "you must speak loud to those who are hard of hearing" (p. 204).

[Berg Journal]

By the spring of 1846, Thoreau had filled Walden 1 and 2, for on March 26 and 27 he used the front endpapers of Walden 1–probably the last available space in these volumes–to note the arrival of ducks and geese at the pond. In April, he began a new Journal volume, similar in content and format to the notebooks of his first year at the pond: it contains dated entries, scattered literary drafts, and a long complete draft of his most important travel essay, "Ktaadn, and the Maine Woods." This volume, which was apparently unknown to the editors of the 1906 Edition, is now in the Henry W. and Albert A. Berg Collection of the New York Public Library; it has not heretofore appeared in print. Since Thoreau did not assign this volume a title or a number, it will be cited hereafter simply as the "Berg Journal." Dated and undated Journal entries occur irregularly throughout the notebook–even occasionally interpolated in the "Ktaadn" draft–but are concentrated in the first seventy-five pages, which were written during the spring and summer of 1846.

Although Thoreau typically spent more time on his literary projects during fall and winter than during spring and summer (a rhythm attuned as much to the New England lyceum lecture season as to the cycle of the year), during his second summer at Walden he worked steadily on the projects he had begun the previous year. (He did not repeat his experiment in raising beans this year, and perhaps the late frost that killed his vegetable garden on the twelfth of June [p. 249] gave him still more time to tend his growing crop of literary works.) Interspersed with the dated entries and the commentaries on his reading that make up the first section of the Berg Journal are passages of literary draft for "Thomas Carlyle and His Works," *A Week*, *Walden*, and the germ of his most famous essay, "Resistance to Civil Government." After delivering the Carlyle lecture before the Concord Lyceum on February 4, 1846, he revised it for periodical publication during the following spring and summer and sent the manuscript to Horace Greeley about the first of August. The busy editor of the New York *Tribune* was sympathetic to the young Transcendentalists–he had given Margaret Fuller and Ellery Channing jobs on his newspaper–and he undertook to act as Thoreau's unofficial literary agent and publicist. Greeley managed, although not without difficulty, to place the essay in *Graham's Magazine*, where it ran as the lead article in March and April 1847.

Thoreau also drafted in the Berg Journal passages for *A Week*, the first version of which was probably completed by mid-summer. He read portions of it to Emerson, whose description of the work (in a letter to Charles King Newcombe on July 16) as "a seven days voyage in as many chapters" suggests a complete manuscript. The most extensive material related to *A Week* in this volume describes Henry and John's hiking trip to the White Mountains during the second week of their excursion (pp. 265-269). Most of this narrative does not appear in the completed book, and hence it provides a biographical supplement to the literary record of the 1839 trip.

Thoreau also continued to write about life at the pond and to develop ideas suggested by his experiment for eventual use in *Walden*. These passages generally have a more introspective and personal cast to them than the *Walden* material of the preceding winter, as though, having questioned the presuppositions of his countrymen, Thoreau were now turning inward to scrutinize his own motives and assumptions. He faces the strongly conflicting impulses in himself between the love of contemplation and the love of action (p. 240), and he also ponders man's sexual nature, alternating between visions of apotheosizing love (pp. 244-246), and dismay that "a trivial tittillation [*sic*] of the vulgar sense should be the exciting cause that calls man into life" (p. 324). These anxieties and speculations are the source of his later essay on "Chastity & Sensuality" (*Early Essays*, pp. 274-278), and they manifest themselves as well in some of the tensions and ambiguities of "Higher Laws" in *Walden*.

On July 23 or 24, while he was in town to pick up a shoe he had had mended, Thoreau was arrested and spent one night in the Concord jail for several years' nonpayment of the poll tax. He had not chosen this moment to be arrested, to be sure. His civil disobedience had been deliberate, however, and upon his release he wrote out a brief invective against the oppressive tendencies of the state (pp. 262-264) that later blossomed into "Resistance to Civil Government" (*Reform Papers*, pp. 63-90). At this time, however, he confided to the Journal none of the details of his incarceration, but only the passionate moral indignation the government had aroused in him.

His thoughts, in fact, were not greatly occupied with the state just then. He had been at Walden a year, had finished a draft of his first book and the long essay on Carlyle, and was ready for a change of scenery and a break from literary labor. During the first two weeks of September, he made the first of his three wilderness boat trips to the interior of Maine, traveling up the West Branch of the Penobscot River and climbing Mt. Katahdin, the state's highest peak. Thoreau's experience on the mountain profoundly affected his conception of man's relation to primeval nature, a reorientation he would integrate into "Spring" in *Walden* and dramatize in "Ktaadn, and the Maine Woods." Immediately, however, the trip provided him with material for a potentially popular travel narrative. Accordingly, he kept careful notes during the trip. He even mentions at one point writing while in a bateau in the midst of rapids (p. 322). Perhaps he had learned from his labored, mosaic method of composition for *A Week* how important careful narrative exposition was to a work with a temporal structure. At any rate, soon after his return he set about outlining and drafting in the Berg Journal a lengthy, carefully sequential account of the excursion. This draft of what would eventually become a lecture and then an essay titled "Ktaadn, and the Maine Woods" fills 170 pages, most of the remaining space in the volume, and constitutes Thoreau's principal literary labor in the Journal during the fall of 1846.

Thoreau's detailed preliminary outline for the narrative (pp. 270-276; see the third illustration, following p. 454), compiled no doubt from field notes, along with the sustained and swiftly moving narrative itself, reveal how greatly his habits of composition had changed since his first tentative compilations for *A Week* a few years earlier. *A Week* was a far more ambitious and complex work, to be sure, but the "Ktaadn" draft nonetheless suggests the strides toward literary professionalism he had made since coming to Walden. Altogether, the outline for the draft, the draft itself, which is heavily revised in the manuscript, and the final version of the essay (*The Maine Woods*, pp. 3-83) constitute an unusually complete set of working papers for one of Thoreau's major essays.

[I]

Thoreau finished his first draft of "Ktaadn," which nearly filled the Berg Journal, before the second of December 1846 (p. 355). After this dated entry, however, the record of both his literary activities and his Journal keeping becomes more difficult to follow. As the remaining dozen or so manuscript pages in the Berg Journal testify, he continued to make conventional entries, interspersing them with literary draft for *A Week* and *Walden*. Doubtless he was occupied at this time with revising and expanding *A Week* and with finishing his first Walden lecture, delivered in February 1847. All that is now extant of his Journal, however, between the end of the Berg volume in late 1846 or very early 1847, and mid-1848, when the first post-Walden volume begins, is sixteen scattered leaves and partial leaves from Thoreau's next notebook, with which *Journal* 2 concludes. Conjecturally titled "I" in this edition (because the next surviving volume is titled "II" by Thoreau, beginning the sequence of roman numerals he would use for the Journal for the rest of his career), this fragmentary volume was probably devoted extensively, perhaps exclusively, to the composition of literary works in 1847 and 1848.

Thoreau almost certainly began this volume immediately after filling the Berg Journal: the narrative of his 1844 hiking trip to the Berkshires with which the Berg Journal concludes continues on the first surviving leaf of the fragmentary volume "I." He probably filled the first portion of the notebook fairly rapidly with such literary draft, for the leaf paged "97-[98]" (370.29-371.35) describes the activity of the commercial ice-cutters at Walden during this same winter of 1847; and regularly paged leaves from this volume end with the scrap of a leaf paged "159-[160]" (376.27-377.10), dated April 8, 1847. The paper of this fragmentary volume is identical to that of the Berg Journal, and, assuming both that it was the same length as the Berg Journal and that the April date is current, Thoreau would have filled a bit more than half the volume by the onset of spring. Both these assumptions are, however, open to question. The date, interlined in a smaller hand at the top of the leaf, may not be current. Any conjectures about the dating of this volume must necessarily be tentative.

Following this dated scrap in the present volume are six more leaves of the same kind of paper that are presumed to belong to this notebook despite the fact that they are paged anomalously. Their different paging sequences perhaps indicate their order in some literary draft, although it is possible that they may have belonged originally to some other notebook or set of papers. One group of three continuously paged leaves (381.18-385.23) contains material on mythology for *A Week*, Thoreau's first extensive draft of the famous sand foliage passage in "Spring" in *Walden* (see the fourth illustration, following p. 454), and some information on his route to the mountain that appeared in the essay version of "Ktaadn, and the Maine Woods." These three leaves could have been written in early 1847, for Thoreau had begun work on all three projects by then, but the available evidence points more strongly to the spring of 1848 as the time of composition. Since the sand foliage passage does not appear in the first draft of *Walden*, composed in 1846 and 1847, these extensive observations probably date from the following year. Also, the nature of the "Ktaadn" material on these leaves suggests that it was written for the essay version, which Thoreau sent to Horace Greeley on March 31, 1848 (having delivered the lecture the previous January 5). This list of place names and distances would be of little interest to a lecture audience but is the sort of information Thoreau would be likely to add in the process of preparing the lecture for periodical publication.

The other three leaves (377.14-381.16), containing a revision of "A Walk to Wachusett" for *A Week*, material used in Thoreau's essay on Friendship in *A Week*, and a partial draft of the Poet-Hermit colloquy from "Brute Neighbors" in *Walden*, are even more difficult to date with certainty, but they have been placed in the present text preceding the three leaves described above on the basis of Thoreau's having written his Friendship essay by January 1848—a fact that he reported in a letter to Emerson on the twelfth of that month. What the remainder of this volume contained is impossible to say, except that a part of it was almost certainly taken up with a second draft or perhaps the fair copy of "Ktaadn": an index at the end of the "Ktaadn" draft in the Berg Journal (Appendix, pp. 389-390) contains a series of cross-references to a new draft. In addition, a cross-reference in the draft itself refers to "next Book p. 47."

Like the first volume of the Journal in the Princeton Edition, *Journal 2: 1842-1848* ends with a fragmentary notebook that introduces a significant lapse in the Journal, for the extant record does not resume until after Thoreau left Emerson's house in July 1848 to return to his family home for good. This hiatus in the Journal, however, signals not a decline in creative energy but rather the reverse: the likelihood is that if any Journal was kept, it was spent so exclusively on literary material for *A Week* and *Walden* that it was consumed in the process. Thoreau prepared not only a final draft of *A Week* in 1848 but also a version of *Walden* that he judged finished enough to consider printing. Preparing two book-length manuscripts for the press (as he thought), as well as fair copy for "Ktaadn" and "Resistance to Civil Government," may well have prevented him from keeping a Journal regularly. Paradoxically, it was to be the commercial failure of this ambitious literary program, especially the disappointing reception of *A Week*, that would in part eventually lead to the resumption of regular Journal writing in 1850. Like Melville a few years later, Thoreau came to realize that the world would not reward him for what he considered his best work. So he altered his expectations, his way of life, and his primary medium of composition in order to be able to continue to write and to explore the issues that interested him.

Yet the Walden years had been years of dramatic professional as well as personal and spiritual growth for Thoreau. The Journal manuscripts that survive from this period, though fragmentary and often difficult to follow, chronicle the development of a major writer from the end of his apprenticeship to the attainment, in the early work on *Walden*, of his mature style and voice. These manuscripts, most of them printed here for the first time in their extant entirety, provide significant evidence for critical and biographical reconsiderations of Thoreau's career as a writer. They amply document the truth of Ellery Channing's observation that his friend's principal aim was "to bring his life into the shape of good and substantial literary expression," and they reveal the diligence with which he pursued that aim at Walden Pond.

SOURCES

The principal source of details about Thoreau's life and literary activities from 1842 to 1848 is Walter Harding, *The Days of Henry Thoreau* (New York: Alfred A. Knopf, 1965); the other biographical work quoted is Ellery Channing, *Thoreau: The Poet-Naturalist*, ed. F. B. Sanborn (Boston: Goodspeed, 1902). Other details about Thoreau's literary use of Journal material were provided by J. Lyndon Shanley's *The Making of Walden* (Chicago: University of Chicago Press, 1957) and by the introductions to *The Maine Woods*, ed. Joseph J. Moldenhauer (1972); *Reform Papers*, ed. Wendell Glick (1973); *Early Essays and Miscellanies*, ed. Joseph J. Moldenhauer et al. (1975); *A Week on the Concord and Merrimack Rivers*, ed. Carl F. Hovde et al. (1980; see especially the "Historical Introduction" by Linck C. Johnson); and *Journal 1: 1837-1844*, ed. Elizabeth Hall Witherell et al. (1981; see especially the "General Introduction" for a history of the publication of the Journal).

The following additional primary sources are organized chronologically, and may be consulted by reference to dates provided in the Historical Introduction: *The Correspondence of Henry David Thoreau*, ed. Walter Harding and Carl Bode (New York: New York University Press, 1958); *The Letters of Ralph Waldo Emerson*, ed. Ralph L. Rusk, 6 vols. (New York: Columbia University Press, 1939); *The Journals and Miscellaneous Notebooks of Ralph Waldo Emerson*, ed. William H. Gilman et al., 16 vols. (Cambridge, Mass.: The Belknap Press of Harvard University Press, 1960-1982).

Textual Introduction

Journal 2: 1842-1848, like other volumes in the Princeton Edition of Thoreau's Journal, is edited from the holograph manuscripts, conservatively emended and printed in clear text. The text is accompanied by Annotations, an Index, and an Editorial Appendix detailing relevant textual information. A special feature of this volume, which consists largely of early drafts of Thoreau's literary works, is a table of Cross-References to Published Versions (pp. 580-602) that provides cross-references between drafts in Journal and later versions in print. This Textual Introduction describes the pertinent characteristics of the manuscripts and the editorial procedures and principles followed in the preparation of the volume.[1]

THE JOURNAL TEXT, 1842-1848

The present volume provides the text of extant Journal volumes kept by Thoreau between 1842 and 1848. During these years, the Journal was neither a simple diary nor a straightforward literary notebook but a complex document whose original material was sometimes expanded, often revised, and frequently used as first drafts of literary works. The Journal is not just one "text," then, but through various kinds of revision a number of different texts all present in the same place and often difficult to separate one from another. The present edition has as its aim the publication in clear and readable form that layer of the Journal representing Thoreau's original stage of composition, with the least edi-

[1] A more comprehensive description of the editorial practices and policies of the Princeton Edition of the Journal may be found in the Textual Introduction to *Journal 1: 1837-1844* (Princeton: Princeton University Press, 1981), pp. 614-643; see also the General Introduction to the same volume, pp. 578-591. In the interest of simplicity, certain changes in the way in which emendations are defined and reported have been made in the present volume.

torial intrusion necessary to make its sometimes elliptical, disjunctive, or erroneous material intelligible.

Four intact manuscript volumes and scattered leaves from a fifth volume that is no longer intact comprise *Journal 2: 1842-1848*. The four bound volumes themselves lack many leaves that Thoreau removed for inclusion in drafts of literary works during these years. A number of these missing leaves have been located and are restored in the present edition to their original places in the Journal. Those leaves still missing were probably destroyed along with the early or intermediate drafts of which they were a part, although some may eventually be found. The restored leaves are identified below in the physical descriptions of individual manuscript volumes. The 1842 *terminus a quo* for the first volume and the 1848 *terminus ad quem* for the last volume are conjectural, and the evidence supporting these dates is detailed in the Historical Introduction. The five volumes are integrally related to one another, however, since they all contain dated entries from the period of Thoreau's residence at Walden Pond, 1845 to 1847, and thus furnish the principal documentary evidence of his life and literary labors there.

During these years, and especially during the Walden sojourn itself, Thoreau employed his Journal principally to draft passages for literary projects, especially *A Week on the Concord and Merrimack Rivers* and *Walden*, but also to write lecture and essay drafts for "Thomas Carlyle and His Works," "Wendell Phillips Before Concord Lyceum," and "Ktaadn, and the Maine Woods." (The relationship between the Journal and the genesis of these works is described in the Historical Introduction.) The first manuscript volume also contains about 190 manuscript pages of transcription from the earlier manuscript volumes of the Journal (often combined or expanded from the original) compiled for use in drafting *A Week*. And all the volumes contain in greater or lesser amounts conventional–that is, discrete and dated–Journal entries. Thus the Journal for this period consists of five diverse and often fragmentary manuscript volumes ranging in nature and appearance from carefully copied transcriptions to ordinary dated entries to hastily scrawled and heavily revised preliminary drafts of literary works. Considerably more than half of this material is published here for the first time.

From a textual standpoint, two other potentially relevant versions of the text exist: earlier Journal entries, upon which the transcribed material was based; and later versions–either manuscript drafts, printed works, or both. These earlier and later forms are of no significance as alternate or competing versions of the text, since they were composed at different times for different purposes, but they do provide sources for the emendation of obscurities in the Journal itself. Since Thoreau did not intend or prepare the Journal for publication, and since the first extensive selections of the Journal did not appear in print until nearly twenty years after his death,[2] no printed version has any textual authority.

PHYSICAL DESCRIPTIONS OF MANUSCRIPTS

The following descriptions observe the order of composition of the manuscript volumes. This is also their sequence in the present volume.[3]

---

[2] In H.G.O. Blake's *Early Spring in Massachusetts* (Boston: Houghton Mifflin, 1881), the first of his collection of seasonal extracts from the Journal. For the history of the Journal during the years following Thoreau's death, see the General Introduction in *Journal 1: 1837-1844*, pp. 578-591.

[3] Measurements of the manuscript volume leaves vary by approximately 0.2 cm., depending on positions in gatherings. Single leaves have greater variations because of torn or cut edges. In these descriptions paste-down endpapers are unnumbered unless otherwise noted. The following abbreviations are used in the physical descriptions:

HM	Manuscripts at the Henry E. Huntington Library, San Marino, California
MA	Manuscripts at the Pierpont Morgan Library
NNPM	Pierpont Morgan Library, New York

Long Book

A large-format notebook of 264 pages, now in the Pierpont Morgan Library (MA 1303), that Thoreau used primarily to compile material for *A Week on the Concord and Merrimack Rivers* and also to draft passages for other literary works. Near its end, it contains a currently dated entry from March 1846. The *Week* transcriptions make up the bulk of the first 200 pages and were probably compiled between 1842 and 1845. The rest of the notebook was filled early in 1845, and at Walden during the winter of 1845-1846. Twenty-six leaves or parts of leaves were removed for insertion in other literary drafts; all but three of these leaves have been located and restored in the present text.

Marbled green/brown/black/tan boards; brown spine. Originally 132 leaves bound [A-L¹²], with free endpapers and flyleaves; now 129 leaves, pp. [1-258], with front endpaper, back flyleaf, and back free endpaper, paged "1-201, 221-237" in pencil and "240-241" in ink. Front free endpaper, back flyleaf and endpaper, pages 202-212, 217-220, 238-239, 242-264 unnumbered; front flyleaf and pages 213-216, 251-252 missing, pages 253-264 blank. Leaf paged "175-[176]" has been cut out and laid in; twenty-two leaves and one-half leaf have been removed and are now in other collections:

Collection of W. Stephen Thomas

1	leaf "43-[44]"	{23.15-24.18}⁴
1	leaf "87-[88]"	{45.23-46.34}
2	leaves "101-[104]"	{53.25-56.11}
2	leaves "143-[146]"	{80.12-83.1}
½	leaf "147-[148]"	{83.2-83.22}
2	leaves "191-[194]"	{111.32 "time . . . -114.22 . . . and"}

Huntington Library
(HM 956)

1	leaf "91-[92]"	{48.2-49.5 . . . gradually"}
5	leaves "165-[174]"	{95.1-101.11}

⁴ Numbers in braces in the physical descriptions refer to page and line numbers in this volume.

(HM 13194)
   1 leaf "129-[130]"   {71.25-72.33}

(HM 13195)
   1 leaf "131-[132]"   {73.1-74.16 . . . dis[covered]"}

(HM 924)
   1 leaf "133-[134]"   {74.16 "[dis]covered . . .
                                  -75.16}
   1 leaf "231-[232]"   {136.25 "I . . . -138.14 . . .
                                  scar."}
   1 leaf "[243-244]"   {147.6-148.27}
   2 leaves "[247-250]"   {150.10-152.13}

(HM 13188)
   1 leaf "163-[164]"   {93.24-94.40}

Leaves are white wove paper 32 x 20 cm., unlined, with green edges. Three leaves of anomalous paper containing pencilled notes for *A Week on the Concord and Merrimack Rivers* are laid in between pages 252 and 253. Nonauthorial contents are: label, probably by H.G.O. Blake, in ink on front board; John Pierpont Morgan bookplate and NNPM title on front paste-down endpaper; NNPM accession and call numbers, "R-V/12/F" and "MA 1303," on front free endpaper; pencilled pagination on page "219"; pencilled note on page 251 identifying laid-in leaves.

[Walden 1]

A volume now in the Pierpont Morgan Library (MA 1302:8), begun at Walden Pond on July 5, 1845, and concluded with entries on March 26 and 27, 1846, on the front endpapers. Thoreau used it at first as a conventional Journal and later, with a different paging sequence, as a draft book for his lectures on Walden life and Thomas Carlyle. Thirty-three leaves were removed. Five of these have been located in the *Walden* MS at the Huntington Library (HM 924) and restored; the rest are unaccounted for.

Marbled brown/tan/red/black boards; dark blue spine embossed with horizontal gold rules. Originally seventy-two leaves, bound [A-F¹²], with two free endpapers; now forty-four leaves, pp. [1-88], with two free endpapers, irregularly paged in pencil "1-71" in one paging sequence and "45-100" in a second paging sequence (first front free endpaper paged "8" and first back free endpaper paged "101"). Second front free endpaper, pages 23-29, 31-32, 73-82, and second back free endpaper unnumbered; pages 83-88, 91-128, 131-142 missing. Text continues on front and back free endpapers and back paste-down endpaper. Leaves paged "15-18" and "[27]-30" have been repaired. The following leaves are located in another collection:

Huntington Library
   (HM 924)
      2 leaves "7-[10]"   {157.16-159.3 . . . look"}
      1 leaf "45-[46]"   {172.15-173.32}
      2 leaves "61-[64]"   {179.3-180.11 . . . Adam)"}

Leaves are white wove paper 19.1 x 16.6 cm., lined. Non-authorial contents are: Blake's label in ink on front board; "w/.50", probably by stationer, on front paste-down endpaper; library accession number "MA 1302-8" on first front free endpaper; pencilled "38" and "51" on back paste-down endpaper.

[Walden 2]

Companion volume to Walden 1, physically identical and concurrently kept, used primarily for literary drafts for *A Week* and the lectures on Walden life and Thomas Carlyle and also housed in the Pierpont Morgan Library (MA 1302:7). It was probably begun at the same time as, or slightly before, Walden 1, and finished somewhat earlier during the winter of 1845-1846. Thirty-nine leaves and the two front endpapers were removed; none of these leaves has been recovered.

Marbled brown/tan/red/black boards; dark blue spine embossed with horizontal gold rules. Originally seventy-two leaves, bound [A-F¹²], with two free front and back endpapers; now thirty-three leaves, pp. [1-66], with two free back endpapers, paged irregularly in pencil "7-140" on twenty-two pages (page "135" paged in ink); front free endpapers and pages 1-12, 19-26, 37-49, 43-70, 73-80, 105-106, 117-126, 137-142 missing. Text continues on back free and paste-down endpapers. Laid in is a scrap of paper containing designs created by folding paper over ink blots. Leaves are white wove paper 19.1 x 16.6 cm., lined. Nonauthorial contents are: Blake's label on front board in ink; pencilled "w/50", probably by stationer, on front paste-down endpaper; library accession number "MA 1302-7" on page 8.

[Berg Journal]

A large-format bound volume untitled by Thoreau, so named in the present text because it is housed in the Henry W. and Albert A. Berg Collection of the New York Public Library. It was kept at Walden from April 16 to shortly after December 2, 1846, and contains regular dated entries and a long draft of "Ktaadn, and the Maine Woods." Nineteen leaves were removed from the notebook; only one has been located, in a draft of *A Week* at the Huntington Library.

Marbled brown/tan/black/blue-green boards; brown spine. Originally 144 leaves, bound [A-M¹²], with no free endpapers or flyleaves; now 126 leaves, pp. [1-252], paged "1-275" in pencil, with seven leaves removed before paging and pages 9-12, 21-24, 35-36, 197-198, 247-248, 257-258, 261-266 missing. Leaf paged "[259-260]" {355.6-356.15} is at the Huntington Library (HM 13182). Text continues on back paste-down endpaper. Leaves are blue-green, faded partly to brown, 24.2 x 19.6 cm., unlined. Nonauthorial contents are: bookplate of Stephen H. Wakeman, and New York Public Library accession number "66B0514" and stamp "NYPL" on front paste-down endpaper; New York Public Library pagination in pencil on rectos and versos; small stamp "NYPL" irregularly throughout volume.

[I]

Sixteen scattered leaves and partial leaves survive from what was apparently Thoreau's next volume. The paper is identical to that of the Berg Journal, and the first surviving leaves continue the entry with which the Berg Journal concludes. The title is conjectural but is supported by the fact that Thoreau's next manuscript volume is titled "II". Surviving leaves chiefly contain literary drafts for *A Week*, *Walden*, and "Ktaadn, and the Maine Woods." There is one dated entry, for April 1847; the notebook was probably kept from early 1847 to early 1848.

Boards and binders' leaves are missing. Originally probably 144 leaves (assuming the volume to have been identical to the Berg Journal); fourteen leaves and two partial leaves survive, pp. [1-32]. Repositories, number of leaves, pagination, and order in the present text are as follows:

Huntington Library
   (HM 13182)
      ⅗ leaf "5-[6]"   {365.2-365.28}
      1 leaf "39-[40]"   {366.1-367.20}
      2 leaves "[65-68]"   {367.21-370.27}

Houghton Library, Harvard University
   (MS Am 278.5.15S)
      1 leaf "97-[98]"   {370.29-371.35}

Huntington Library
   (HM 924)
      1 leaf "105-[106]"   {372.2-373.18}
      2 leaves "141-[144]"   {373.20-375.35}
      ½ leaf "[145-146]"   {376.2-376.25}
      ⅕ leaf "159-[160]"   {376.27-377.10}

John Hay Library, Brown University
      1 leaf unpaged   {377.13-378.33}

Huntington Library
   (HM 924)

2 leaves "8'-9'",
  "160-[161]"   {379.1-381.16}
3 leaves unpaged {381.18-385.23}

Leaves are blue-green, faded partly to brown, 24.2 x 19.6 cm., unlined. Nonauthorial contents are: memoranda in ink, probably by F. B. Sanborn, on several leaves, identifying later versions of the text or conjectural dates.

LEVEL OF TEXT REPRESENTED

Characteristically, the extent and degree of revision in Thoreau's Journal volumes vary considerably. Original composition is invariably in ink, and some passages are relatively clean, with only such minor corrections and changes as a writer customarily makes in the process of composition. Other passages—those intended or adapted for use in a literary work—are heavily revised, in ink or pencil, or both. The ink used for revisions may appear identical to that used for the original composition or may vary in color; single or multiple stages of revision may be discernible; and revision may be confined to a sentence or two or extend over many pages. In a clear text edition such as the present one, in which only a single level of the text may be reproduced, the editor must choose and represent one stage of composition consistently, clearly identify that stage of composition to the reader, and report any necessary departures from the announced policy.[5]

There is no evidence in the manuscripts themselves to suggest that Thoreau made extensive revisions in the Journal as Journal. Occasionally he corrected an error, added a fact, or provided a cross-reference to a related entry, but he

[5] Bradford Torrey and Francis H. Allen, the editors of the 1906 Houghton Mifflin edition of the Journal, the only previous attempt at a comprehensive printing of the Journal, solved this problem by silently choosing whatever version of a revised passage seemed best to them on aesthetic grounds. In practice, they tended to choose the final revised version of most passages, the version that resembles most closely the printed version and that is most distant from the original.

did not significantly revise material unless he intended to use it in some literary project. Therefore the policy of this edition is to define as Journal and to reproduce only the first level of composition in the document. Minor corrections and revisions made in the act of writing (which are necessarily in the same ink and hand as the first level of text) are incorporated, but later revisions are not, except in rare cases where they correct an error that would be misleading to the reader (see Table of Emendations (1), p. 480). In practice, Thoreau's later revisions are actually preliminary versions of his literary works and are thus no longer related to the Journal itself. Substantial revisions that do not appear in the printed version of a later work, or that appear in a significantly different form, are reported in the Editorial Appendix as Selected Later Revisions.

The textual situation in *Journal 2: 1842-1848* is somewhat more complex than this preliminary overview would suggest. Unlike either the first volume in the edition, covering 1837 to 1844, or the volumes that will follow, this volume is made up primarily of literary drafts. A significant amount of this draft material (approximately 25 percent of the whole) consists of transcriptions from the earlier Journal. Conventional Journal entries make up a relatively small proportion of the volume. Many passages, however, are not easily classified: in transcribing entries from the earlier Journal, Thoreau often modified, combined, or expanded them; and he clearly composed some conventional dated entries with a literary product in mind. Such heterogeneity does not, however, affect the basic editorial policy of the Edition, which has, with one exception, been followed throughout.

Conventional dated Journal entries are of course treated as elsewhere in the Princeton Edition: the first level of composition, as currently revised or corrected, is reproduced. This same policy has been applied to the literary drafts that make up the bulk of the volume, since the earliest discrete version of a passage presents at once both an accurate representation of Thoreau's use of his Journal as a draft book and the single stage of composition of most value for the study of the genesis of his writings. Although a clear text edition is not the ideal format for presenting such material– to reproduce all the stages of revision would require a textual apparatus considerably longer than the text itself–a comparison of the first draft as reproduced here with the final printed version (identified in the table of Cross-References to Published Versions) permits the interested reader to examine the nature, the extent, and something of the course of revision within a passage.

For the material transcribed from the earlier Journal, however (confined to pp. 3-116 of this volume, representing that section of Long Book in which he collected passages for *A Week*), Thoreau's intention and method of compilation have dictated a modification of the basic policy. Since he often left large blank spaces surrounding individual transcribed entries, and since the appearance of the manuscript indicates that he went back on occasion and added to these passages (see Historical Introduction, p. 453, and the first illustration, following p. 454), it seems clear that he intended from the first some later expansion of his original entries. In this section of the present text, therefore, Thoreau's *additions* to his first level of composition are accepted. His *revisions* of these passages, however, are *not* incorporated. In other words, in that section of the Journal in which Thoreau was compiling material for *A Week*, all his compilation is reproduced. After he compiled the material, he reworked and revised much of it for the first draft of *A Week*. Such revisions, in keeping with the basic policy of the Edition, are excluded. Theoretical considerations of intent aside, practical considerations make this policy inevitable. It is often impossible to distinguish where an original entry ends and expansion begins: only the fact that the hand becomes progressively smaller and more cramped toward the bottom of one manuscript page indicates that Thoreau expanded the entry some time after writing the passage at the top of the following page. Revision within a paragraph, however, is easily discernible.

EDITORIAL PROCEDURES AND DECISIONS

The text of the Princeton Edition of Thoreau's Journal is based upon a typed literal transcript of photocopy of the original manuscript prepared by transcribers and editors at the Textual Center. The editorial staff reads the transcript and preliminary textual apparatus four times against photocopy and the transcript itself once against the original manuscript. Obscure elements and cruxes are rechecked against the original manuscript. Editors read printer's copy of the text and apparatus. They read galley, page, and revised page proof, and "blue lines"–photoprints of the film positives from which the text is printed–three times against the transcript; two more readings at each stage are provided at the Press. The text and apparatus thus receive multiple readings at every stage of transmission from manuscript to printed book.[6] In accordance with guidelines established by the Center for Editions of American Authors and continued by the Committee on Scholarly Editions, this volume has been examined by an independent textual expert, Douglas Emory Wilson, LTC, AUS-Retired.

Like all other volumes in *The Writings of Henry D. Thoreau, Journal 2: 1842-1848* is printed in clear text with editorial notation and commentary confined to a separate Editorial Appendix following the text. The only editorial interpolations in the text itself are references to physical gaps in the manuscript, which are set in italic type and enclosed in braces–e.g., *{Two leaves missing}* or *{MS torn}*–and Princeton Edition volume and page numbers, also enclosed

---

[6] While the text for this volume (pp. 3-385) was set by linotype, the front and back matter were photocomposed on a Linotron 202 from a magnetic tape produced in the main computer at Princeton University by Textual Center and Computer Center staff.

in braces, following Thoreau's internal page references to material in an earlier Journal volume (see Table of Emendations (4), p. 480). The text is printed with a ragged right-hand margin to avoid hyphenating compound words at the ends of lines and to simulate the informal character of the Journal. The editor has supplied running heads and conjectural titles (enclosed in square brackets) for some manuscript volumes. The line scale printed on the dust jacket and endpapers of this volume applies only to those pages with ordinary typography and no extra spacing between lines; for any page with smaller type or extra spacing, page and line references in the Editorial Appendix are based on a literal line count.

EDITORIAL APPENDIX

Each of the sections of apparatus in the Editorial Appendix is explained in a headnote that precedes it. The sections that report editorial decisions–Textual Notes and tables of Emendations, Alterations, and End-of-Line Hyphenation–are described in more detail below.

Textual Notes

The Textual Notes describe significant features of the text and editorial decisions that require more explanation than is provided by the Textual Introduction or tables. Entries marked with an asterisk in the tables are discussed in Textual Notes.

Table of Emendations

The Table of Emendations is a sequential list of all substantive editorial modifications of the text. It also lists possible alternative readings of words especially difficult to decipher in the manuscript. The general emendation policy is conservative, and the text has been changed only when the original form was judged to be misleading or distracting to the reader. Emended readings derive from one or more of the following levels of authority: identical or analogous forms in the text; earlier or later versions of the text in manuscript or in print; Thoreau's sources or reference works; and the editor's judgment. Types of emendation include:

(1) Thoreau's errors of fact, spelling, punctuation, and handwriting. When he corrected the error himself at a later time, in either pencil or ink, his correction is accepted and reported as an emendation; in other cases, the editor has emended only those errors that would confuse the sense of a passage. Thoreau's uncancelled false starts and ambiguous stray marks or flourishes have been removed without report.

(2) Indecipherable elements in the manuscript. Blotted, torn, or otherwise unreadable elements are emended from earlier or later versions of the text, or from Thoreau's source if found within a quotation. If no other version exists, the indecipherable element is reported in the text, e.g., {MS torn}, and described in a Textual Note.

(3) Ambiguous placement of text in the manuscript. Placement of text is revised only when retaining the original sequence would cause confusion, as, for example, in the case of a final notebook entry written on the front endpapers of a volume (191.18-193.12), or an entry continued on the bottom rather than the top of the following manuscript page (4.2).

(4) Thoreau's pagination in the manuscript. Thoreau's references to his manuscript page numbers contained in this volume are emended to those of the Princeton Edition text; page numbers that refer to manuscript volumes already printed in *Journal 1: 1837-1844* are cited in braces, e.g., {1:234}. In Thoreau's indexes (see Appendix, pp. 387-390), the manuscript page numbers have been retained, since they identify the length of lost entries, but Princeton Edition page numbers are also provided in braces.

(5) Unhyphenated end-of-line syllables in the manuscript. Words Thoreau neglected to hyphenate at the ends of lines are emended by closing up the space. For compound or

possibly compound words broken at the ends of lines, see the table of End-of-Line Hyphenation.

Since the Princeton Edition of the Journal is sparingly emended, the text preserves a great many of the anomalies inevitable in a handwritten document the author never prepared for publication. Errors of fact, spelling, and grammar; inconsistencies in spelling, capitalization, punctuation, and word division; and occasional *lacunae* in entries are all permitted to stand if they do not seriously affect the sense of a passage. Certain other recurring idiosyncrasies of Thoreau's handwriting and spacing in the manuscript that are not meaningful or not susceptible to typographic reproduction are normalized and not reported in the Table of Emendations. These include:

(1) Irregular spacing of dashes, hyphens, quotation marks, and apostrophes, owing either to the extreme right-hand slant of Thoreau's script or to his habits of punctuation. He used dashes, in particular, in several different ways, which have been normalized as follows:

(a) Dashes used as internal punctuation (comma, semicolon, colon, or parenthesis) are printed as a closed dash: *word–word.*

(b) Dashes used as end punctuation (period, question or exclamation mark) are printed as a half-closed dash: *word– Word.*

(c) Dashes used as a transition or to introduce a quotation are printed as a longer closed dash: *word—word.*

(d) Dashes used to separate entries are printed as a longer centered dash with space above and below.

(e) Dashes used as a paragraph sign are printed as a dash indented and closed to the first word of the paragraph: ¶*–Word.*

(f) Dashes used to indicate abridgement of a source text are printed as two open dashes: *word – – word.*

(2) Features of handwriting that elude exact reproduction

in typography. All words and letters Thoreau underlined are set in italic type. His superscript letters (*th, d, nd, rd, st*) in dates, numbers, and abbreviations are often imperfectly formed and underlined in the manuscript; except when he is quoting, they are normalized to on-line, roman type, with consistent spellings.

(3) Elements in the manuscript that are not meaningful or that relate only to Thoreau's later revisions for literary works. These are omitted. They include blots, flourishes, and stray marks; use marks drawn vertically through passages after Thoreau had revised or copied them; and cross-references (*v, V, vide,* with manuscript pagination) that key revised passages to other literary drafts. Textual Notes describe these cross-references when they help identify the contents of missing Journal pages.

(4) Irregular spacing of text on manuscript pages or in paragraphs and sentences. Blank space measuring one-fifth or more of a page is reported; anything less is normalized to a single line space. Thoreau's variable indentations for paragraphs, datelines, margins, and inset quotations are normalized to uniform indentations at page left, right, and center. In the manuscript, his paragraphs begin variably with an indentation from the margin, with a dash flush to the margin, or flush to the margin but preceded by a line space, or by a preceding sentence that ends short of the right margin. In all these cases, the printed paragraphs are normalized by indentation. His irregular spacing of sentence endings is normalized as follows: a single word space for the norm (*go. Now*); a double word space if the sentence ends with a dash (*go– Now*; *go– now*), if the sentence has another end mark but the first word of the next sentence is not capitalized (*go? now*), or if the sentence has no end mark but the next sentence begins with a capital (*go Now*); a quadruple word space if the sentence has no end mark and the first word of the next sentence is not capitalized (*go now*).

Table of Alterations

The Table of Alterations is a sequential list of Thoreau's current revisions in the manuscript, as defined above, pp. 475-476. Only alterations that affect meaning are reported, and the report of simple changes normally describes the alteration itself, not the means of revision. For example, "come]   comes" means that Thoreau first wrote "comes" and then altered it–either by cancellation or erasure–to "come". Small changes of this sort form a large percentage of the alterations. More complex changes are necessarily described more fully, with editorial notation italicized, e.g., "work] *interlined above cancelled* life". Insignificant alterations due to the intrinsic nature of a handwritten document are not reported. These include Thoreau's corrections of meaningless misspellings, cancelled false starts, and letters or words he reformed for greater clarity.

End-of-Line Hyphenation

When Thoreau's end-of-line hyphens in the manuscript divide compound words (*heart- / break*) the words must be emended to one of two possibly intended forms: closed (*heartbreak*) or hyphenated (*heart-break*). If the evidence from analogous contemporaneous forms, sources, and later versions is inconclusive, the hyphens are retained. All line-end hyphenated compounds have been resolved to the forms that appear in the table. Since the present text has a ragged right-hand margin, it introduces no new end-of-line hyphens.

Textual Notes

THE TEXTUAL NOTES report significant features of the manuscripts and sources for editorial emendations. Contextual punctuation appears outside of quotation marks when ambiguity would result from using the standard form. Those abbreviations and short titles in the Textual Notes not previously identified in the headnote to Annotations (p. 391) refer to the following:

CRS	"Concord River" and "Saturday", first-draft manuscript of *A Week on the Concord and Merrimack Rivers* at the New York Public Library
Early Essays	Henry D. Thoreau, *Early Essays and Miscellanies*, ed. Joseph J. Moldenhauer et al. (Princeton: Princeton University Press, 1975)
HM	Manuscript at the Henry E. Huntington Library, San Marino, California; followed by catalogue number
NjP Taylor	Taylor Collection, Firestone Library, Princeton University, Princeton, N.J.
Shanley	J. Lyndon Shanley, *The Making of Walden* (Chicago: University of Chicago Press, 1957)

Long Book

7.17 no 2 . . . 122}: When T refers to Journal passages outside the present volume, his numbers are retained in the text and volume and page numbers of the Princeton Edition are supplied in braces. When he cites passages in this volume, his numbers are emended to the printed page numbers.

10.10 Tansy . . . pipes: Interlined in smaller hand at top of MS page; probably a continuation of the preceding passage ("The snakehead . . . milkweed."), which is compressed at bottom of previous MS page.

13.13 Campton: "Compton" in MS; see Annotation 13.13.

15.16-21 The hounding ... invented.: Written in a smaller hand and followed by a horizontal line across MS page; possibly added later.

16.10 Hooksett: "se" blotted in MS; an earlier version (*Journal 1*, p. 136) reads "Hooksett".

19.3-14 music ... {40}: Index written horizontally in MS; rearranged in a vertical column to make cross-references to Princeton Edition page numbers clearer. The first entry, "music no 8-257-", almost certainly refers to T's MS volume 7, p. 257 (*Journal 1*, p. 446); T's "8" may have been altered, or he may have had another numbering sequence for his MS volumes at some time.

24.2 than: "tha{*MS torn*}" in MS; an earlier version (*Journal 1*, p. 330) reads "than".

25.25 of: Illegible in MS; a later version (HM 13195) reads "of".

26.21-29 He ... endure?: Added later in a smaller hand.

32.21-26 The waves ... sky: Verse and horizontal line separating it from preceding text are written at bottom of MS page in lighter ink.

34.20-21 were ... water: Added later in a smaller hand.

36.2 broke: "brook" in MS; a later version (*A Week*, p. 123) reads "broke".

36.26 late ... retrospective: Originally "late and retrospective"; T interlined "as it were defeated" above "and" but did not cancel "retrospective". He added "anticipated?" as an alternate reading.

38.2 leave: "lave" in MS; an earlier version (*Journal 1*, p. 369) reads "leave".

44.20 ordinance: T revised in pencil to read "ordnance"; an earlier version (Special Collections, Washington University Library, St. Louis, Missouri) also reads "ordinance".

48.16 impelled: MS torn; a later version (*A Week*, p. 258) reads "impelled".

51.14-27 I am ... relief.: Verse probably added later. T wrote the first six lines and "v next p" at the bottom of MS page "[96]," then completed the poem below a horizontal rule at the bottom of MS page "97."

56.3 a chaste: T originally wrote "a pure"; he cancelled "pure" and added "a chaste" without cancelling the "a" before "pure".

57.24-25 in to circles: "in to a circles" in MS; a later version (CRS) reads "into circles".

69.9 importunate: Possibly "unfortunate" in MS; an earlier version (*Journal 1*, p. 456) reads "uneasy", and a later version (HM 13195) reads "unhappy".

69.17   Marlowe . . . 8:   "397" was originally "197": an entry on Marlowe appears on page "197" in MS volume 8 (*Journal 1*, p. 457). T may have changed his page and volume numbers for the fragmentary Journal volumes 7, 8, and 9.

77.16   V p. 78:   "V n p but 2." in MS, referring to text two MS pages later, beginning "Where is the proper Herbarium" at 78.24.

79.18   V. n.p.:   Probably a reference to text appearing at 79.25-29 ("Waves . . . history.").

80.30   year: Illegible in MS; an earlier version (*Journal 1*, p. 477) reads "year".

80.35   plain.":   Compressed at inner edge of leaf with quotation mark written above.

83.17   broke: "brook" in MS; a later version (*A Week*, p. 337) reads "broke".

91.17   such thing as: "(such thing) as)" in MS; parentheses may indicate T's intention to cancel the phrase.

95.23   There is reason . . . :   Beginning with the extended narrative of T's encounter with Rice at 95.23, the make-up of Long Book changes from mainly transcribed and miscellaneous entries intended for *A Week* to draft composition for *A Week* and other literary works; see Historical Introduction, pp. 449-452.

101.13   gardener: "garden" in MS; a later version (HM 13195) reads "gardener".

103.34-104.2   mark? . . . Boston.:   No question mark in T's source (see Annotation 103.20-104.4); he also enclosed text at 103.35-104.2 ("Where . . . Boston.") in parentheses and placed a question mark in the margin opposite, querying these figures as well.

105.5-34   "Fisherman's . . . $8:82½: Number of dashes varies to close up space where necessary.

106.26   month–:   T's revision here (see Alterations) is current, but the extent of his cancellation is uncertain: his cancellation lines extend through "river during the whole of the month," (106.25-26), but context indicates that he intended to cancel only "According to Dr Storer–'on their greatest run."

107.19   And: "Am" in MS; a later version (CRS) reads "and".

109.7   schools: "shools" or possibly "shoals" in MS; a later MS version (CRS) reads "schools", but *A Week*, p. 28, reads "shoals".

111.4   time to time: "time time" in MS; a later version (CRS) reads "time to time".

111.29-31   at . . . taken: As in MS; T interlined "one" to agree with "is taken" but did not revise the rest of the phrase.

113.4-5   and . . . there.:   Written at bottom of MS page and marked for insertion; probably a slip in transcription rather than a later revision, since corrected reading follows order of original Journal passage (see *Journal 1*, p. 61).

113.30 we: Illegible in MS; a later version (*A Week*, p. 392) reads "we".

117.36 baby-houses: MS ambiguous; possibly "holy-houses" or "body-houses"; OED defines "baby-house" as "a doll's house, *also*, a toy house barometer or hygrometer from which little dolls issue to indicate changes of weather." Cf. "baby house" at 198.44.

119.24 an exhalation: "and exhalation" in MS; a later version (*A Week*, p. 103) reads "an exhalation".

120.14-124.31 We . . . profit.: Draft of "Wendell Phillips Before Concord Lyceum"; see *Reform Papers*, pp. 59-62 and 304-305, for the printed version and a description of this manuscript draft.

121.13 "the: " 'the" blotted in MS; a later version (*Reform Papers*, p. 60) reads "the".

121.36 v n p b 1: ("See next page but [or below] 1"). T cancelled the preceding phrase, "And make us a new one of course," and refers here to a continuation of this passage on Phillips' prayer and the case of Frederick Douglass at 122.35-123.19 ("While . . . v 1 p b 1"). See *Reform Papers*, pp. 60-61, for a later version.

122.18-19 and acuteness: Illegible in MS; a later version (*Reform Papers*, p. 61) reads "and acuteness".

123.12 and the: "and" illegible in MS; a later version (*Reform Papers*, p. 61) reads "and".

123.19 v 1 p b 1: See Textual Note 121.36.

123.24 hospitality: Illegible in MS; a later version (*Reform Papers*, p. 62) reads "hospitality".

124.11 Alfaetio: Originally "alfate"; T later corrected the spelling to that in his source, Bernáldez's "Extracts" (see Annotation 124.11-15).

126.4 *Two leaves missing*: A later version (*A Week*, p. 25) continues the text incomplete at 126.3.

128.31-129.7 There . . . heaven: Written at bottom of MS page below horizontal rule; possibly added later.

132.30 acquire: "enquire" in MS; a later version (HM 924) reads "acquire".

133.8 night & day: "nigh & day" in MS; a later version (HM 924) reads "night & day".

133.22 from time to time–: "from time–" in MS; a later version (HM 924) reads "from time to time".

139.5-6 Now up they go ding &c: The first line of a poem which, in the first version of *Walden*, follows T's description of the bells; see Shanley, pp. 161-162.

152.13-15 *One page . . . endpapers blank*: Blank page contains pencilled text used in *Walden*; paste-down endpaper contains partial index in pencil of contents of Long Book. See Appendix, p. 387.

[Walden 1]

153.1 [Walden 1]: Title supplied by editor; see Historical Introduction, p. 454, and Appendix, p. 388.

155.1 *Front . . . flyleaf*: Paste-down endpaper contains partial index and computations in pencil; see Appendix, p. 387. Free endpaper and flyleaf contain ink Journal text composed after volume was filled, printed at 191.18-193.12; see Textual Note 191.18-193.12.

155.11 Kaaterskill: Possibly "Kanterskill" or "Kauterskill". Richard Fisher's *A New and Complete Statistical Gazetteer of the United States of America . . .* (New York: J. H. Colton and Company, 1857), which is based on the 1850 census, gives "Kaaterskill" as the name of the falls.

156.3 where: As in MS.

158.25 7: Illegible in MS; a later version (HM 924) reads "7".

162.25 At: "It" in MS; a later version (HM 924) reads "At".

167.38-168.1 adjacent . . . laborious: T interlined "They are the pot-herbs of the gods" above this line (see Alterations). The interlineation may be current, but he did not indicate its position; for a later version of the passage, see *A Week*, p. 381.

169.5-12 And . . . sky: Written at top of following MS page and marked for insertion. Prose at 168.34-169.4 ("Behold . . . morn") becomes incorporated into poem in a later version; see *A Week*, p. 252.

169.11-12 Whose . . . sky: Originally "Whose propylaeum is the visible sky / And sculptured facade the system nigh"; T marked "the visible sky" with a "2" and "the system nigh" with a "1" to indicate transposition of these two phrases, and the appearance of the MS suggests that the revision was current.

169.28 and: "an" in MS; a later version (HM 924) reads "&".

170.9 her: "here" in MS; a later version (HM 924) reads "her".

170.11 mourning: "morning" in MS; a later version (HM 924) reads "mourning".

172.25-173.32 "Thus . . . misfortune: T's first rough translation of this passage from the *Iliad* (172.25-173.10) is heavily revised in the MS, and since a second draft follows immediately below (173.12-32), the revisions were probably current. However, since the second version incorporates almost all of these revisions, the first draft is printed here.

176.30 ever: "eve" in MS; a later version (*Walden*, p. 206) reads "ever".

177.4   country: Illegible in MS; a later version (*Walden*, p. 208) reads "country".

178.4   day light: "daylight" in MS, but context requires two words, and connecting stroke between two words is common in T's handwriting.

178.18   the divinity: "the" illegible in MS; a later version (HM 924) reads "the".

179.2   wholly: Below this entry T wrote later and in a different hand and ink "Left house on account of plastering Wed. Nov. 12 at night   returned Sat Dec 6th". This sentence also appears on the second of the two following MS leaves, which T removed from the volume and which are now in the *Walden* manuscript (HM 924); see 180.1-2.

179.11   thee: "the" in MS; a later version (*Walden*, p. 207) reads "thee".

179.21-22   yon the red: Possibly "you the red" in MS; in either case, T probably left out or forgot to cancel a word. The passage does not appear in either the *Walden* manuscripts or in the printed version.

179.24   rain: Possibly "ruin" in MS. Though a later version (HM 924) reads "ruin", the context here supports "rain". In addition, two alternate later revisions interlined above "rain"–"unseasonable" and "in season or not"–strengthen the case for "rain".

180.27   or even: "ore even" in MS; a later version (HM 924) reads "or even".

180.31   an Indian: "and Indian" in MS; a later version (HM 924) reads "an Indian".

181.26   at night: "at" illegible in MS; a later version (HM 924) reads "at night".

186.32-34   Tuesday . . . upon.:   Written in a different hand and ink; the following three leaves are missing. It is possible that this entry was originally on one of these leaves and that T copied it here when he removed them; see Textual Note 179.2 for another case of an entry copied from a removed leaf.

187.14-15   of you by: "of by" in MS; a later version (HM 924) reads "of you by".

187.28   *missing*:   Indecipherable ink and pencil marks on several of the stubs, indicating that T composed and revised text on these pages before removing them, probably for his lecture on Thomas Carlyle (February 1846) or an early version of his Walden lecture (February 1847); see *Walden*, p. 7, for continuation of text interrupted at 187.27.

187.29   *missing*:   Portion of leaf torn out; see "Thomas Carlyle and His Works," *Early Essays*, p. 259, for a later version of text incomplete at 187.30.

187.30   "Letters: MS torn; a later version (*Early Essays*, p. 259) reads "Letters".

188.19-191.16   Reading . . . Ibid.:   Written on back flyleaves and endpapers; verso of second flyleaf also contains pencilled text later used in *Walden*, and paste-down endpaper contains computations in ink and pencil.

190.20   here: Possibly "hre" or "he", in which case a word or words may have been omitted; another possibility is that the word may have been an uncancelled false start.

190.29-30   hear . . . axes.:   Interlined above "there dont you" at bottom of MS page.

191.18-193.12   March . . . ducks.:   Written on front free endpapers. The dates indicate that T wrote these entries after he filled the rest of the volume, and they are therefore printed in their chronological position.

191.19   danck: As in MS; a later version (HM 924) reads "dark".

192.28   a: Possibly "an" or "our"; a later version (HM 924) reads "a".

[Walden 2]

195.1   [Walden 2]:   Title supplied by editor; see Historical Introduction, p. 454, and Appendix, p. 388.

197.1   *Free . . . missing*:   Paste-down endpaper contains partial index in pencil (see Appendix, pp. 387-388). Missing leaves may have contained material for "Wednesday" of *A Week*; see *A Week*, p. 242, for a later version of text incomplete at 197.2.

197.17-200.20   What . . . out.:   T later supplied title, "The Hero", in pencil.

197.32   Health: "Heath" in MS; a later version (HM 924) reads "Health".

200.21   *missing*:   Indecipherable ink marks survive on verso of stub of first missing leaf. According to T's index, several of these MS pages (15, 18-21) contained material on "Indian"; see Appendix, p. 387.

200.36   good: "god" in MS; index on front paste-down endpaper lists this entry under the heading "a good old age".

202.25   This pleasant weather: Preceded by a cancelled line, "The vagabonds garb–"; the cancellation is probably current because there is no rhyme for "garb" in an adjacent line.

203.11   are: "ar" or "as" in MS; a later version (HM 924) reads "are".

203.18   And: "An" in MS; a later version (HM 924) reads "And".

203.22   they've: Illegible in MS; a later version (HM 924) reads "they've".

204.11-12   You . . . hearing: MS ambiguous; a later version (*Early Essays*, p. 265) reads "You must speak loud to those who are hard of hearing".

204.23   *missing*:   See *Early Essays*, p. 265, for continuation of text interrupted at 204.22.

204.24   {*MS torn*}:   The missing two-thirds page has been torn out, leaving only "different" and "ses." legible on this line.

205.17   {*MS torn*}:   See *Early Essays*, p. 249, for continuation of text interrupted at 205.17.

205.19   *missing*:   Several stubs contain ink and pencil marks. Missing text probably included continuation of draft of "Thomas Carlyle and His Works"; see Textual Notes 205.17, 205.20, and 206.21.

205.20   of Genius: See *Early Essays*, p. 264, for continuation of text interrupted at 205.20.

206.21   *missing*:   See *Early Essays*, p. 253, for continuation of text interrupted at 206.19; missing leaves probably contained more draft material for "Thomas Carlyle and His Works".

206.22   {*MS torn*}:   See *Early Essays*, p. 228, for a later version of interrupted text.

206.31   *missing*:   See *Early Essays*, p. 228, for continuation of text interrupted at 206.30.

207.7-210.19   I went . . . school.:   The story of Hugh Quoil is revised extensively in the manuscript, but T used only a small portion of it in *Walden*, pp. 261-262; see Selected Later Revisions for the revised manuscript version.

210.21-211.4   Poor . . . wings.:   This passage continues a narrative begun in Walden 1 (see 175.25-177.5). In the earlier version and in *Walden* (pp. 203-209), the man's name is John Field. T may have chosen a fictitious name because he planned to use the anecdote in a lecture, for he later interlined "I trust he is not here tonight" after "John Frost".

210.32   motes: "moats" in MS; a later version (HM 924) reads "motes".

212.14-15   not a deed of charity: "not deed charity" in MS; a later version (HM 924) reads "Not a deed of charity".

212.23   Bristow: As in MS; at 221.15 and in *Walden*, p. 257, T used the correct name, "Brister".

212.27   Hilda: T later cancelled "Hilda" and interlined "Nutting" above; see "Hildas" at 215.10 and "Nutting" at 221.13.

213.9   sweet-scented: "sweat-scented" in MS; a later version (HM 924) reads "sweet-scented".

214.7   sweep: T first wrote "scoure", then crossed it out and interlined "scour" below; he then wrote "sweep" following the cancelled "scoure".

215.9-11   And transmitted . . . posterity–:   Marked in margin to follow "the rose?" at 215.8.

216.10   Gilfillan's: "Glinfillan's" in MS; see Annotation 216.10-33.

217.5   *missing*:   Missing leaf contained draft material for "Thomas Carlyle and His Works"; for a later version of text incomplete at 217.5, see *Early Essays*, p. 247.

218.32   unheard of: "72" in pencil following this phrase, probably referring to a missing MS page preceding text at 206.23 that contained related Carlyle material. See *Early Essays*, p. 228, for a later version of this passage.

219.31   others.:   "v no 2 p 4" in pencil interlined below this paragraph, referring to related text in Walden 1, 156.19-25. T's reference to "no 2" is puzzling, since he usually refers to this volume as "no 1" (see Historical Introduction, p. 454, and Appendix, p. 388), but he may have used different numbers at different times for these concurrently kept volumes.

220.29-33   The man . . . self–:   T later cancelled these sentences in pencil and noted "v p 49" below "The man" at 220.29, referring to a MS page missing before text at 205.20, which probably contained related material.

222.9   Indian meal: "Indian" in MS; a later version (HM 924) reads "Indian meal".

224.21   His: Begins new MS page and refers to Carlyle and not Alcott; see *Early Essays*, p. 261.

226.12   *missing*:   Portion of page torn out, leaving several ink marks on stub.

226.21   it . . . spectacle: "{*MS torn*} their hose & breeches'. {*MS torn*} spectacle" in MS; T's source (see Annotation 226.13-21) reads "it at their hose & breeches:' a spectacle".

226.22   *Three-fifths page missing*:   Portion of page torn out, leaving several ink marks and three legible words, "as", "From", and "streets", on stub; see Annotation 226.13-21 for a continuation of quoted text interrupted at 226.21.

226.23   *Three leaves missing*:   See *Walden*, p. 17, for a later version of the text interrupted at 226.24.

227.16   intelligence.:   Followed by "v 138-9" in pencil, referring to text at 228.7-27, portions of which were shifted to this location in the first draft of *Walden*; see Shanley, p. 113.

227.27-229.16 So ... elsewhere–: Text on back flyleaf and free endpaper.

228.3-4 that ... business.: "v 138" in pencil in margin, referring to text at 228.15-18, which follows this phrase in the first draft of *Walden*; see Shanley, p. 114.

228.18 The white grape: "Thus I went on &c v p 137" follows in pencil; see Textual Note 228.3-4.

228.35-36 not done: Illegible in MS; a later version (HM 924) reads "not done".

229.17 *endpaper*: Contains partial index, related to composition of *Walden*, to contents of Walden 1, Walden 2, and Long Book (see Historical Introduction, p. 456, and Appendix, p. 388). The phrase "In Landor–Richard's sail in Richard 1st & The Abbot of &c / Phocion's remarks in conclusion of Eschines & Phocion." appears in ink and inverted at bottom of MS page.

[Berg Journal]

233.1 *Endpaper*: Contains partial index; see Appendix, pp. 388-389.

233.21-234.9 I ... off.: Written vertically in the margin opposite these lines, but not marked for insertion, is the following passage, possibly a revision of 234.15-17: "Only the Greeks could use this word beautiful with expression–it is a poem in itself–καλας ωρας–yet excluded from modern verse".

234.14 Athenaeus: "Atheaeus" in MS; see Annotation 233.27-234.14.

234.33 here: Preceded by a vertical line, possibly pointing to "air" at 234.31.

236.5 and the: Possibly "in the"; a later version (HM 924) reads "in the".

237.7 is it that: "is that" in MS; a later version (HM 924) reads "is it that".

237.22 *missing*: MS paging discontinuous, "8 [9-12] 13"; see *Walden*, p. 118, for a later version of text interrupted at 237.23. According to T's index, the missing MS pages contained entries on "hawk" (9) and "wild-life" (10); see Appendix, p. 389.

238.17-18 longer cried up: T originally wrote "longer, and". He cancelled the "and" and wrote "cried up", but neglected to cancel the comma.

239.35 am looking: Horizontal stroke below, probably inadvertent mark made in crossing the "t" in "education" on line below these words (239.35), but possibly underlining.

240.1   a love: "a a love" in MS; T first wrote "a tendency to", then cancelled "tendency to" and wrote "a love", neglecting to cancel the first "a".

241.5   and in each: "and each" in MS; a later version (HM 924) reads "in which".

241.28   *missing*:   MS paging discontinuous, "19-[20] [21-24] 25"; see Shanley, p. 190, for a continuation of text interrupted at 241.27; and see *Walden*, pp. 213-214, for a revised version of the passage. According to T's index, one of the missing MS pages (24) contained entries on "The fruit & flower of life intangible" and "a fish in pond"; see Appendix, p. 389.

246.19   any: "and" in MS; a later version (HM 924) reads "any".

250.27   19 or 22:   "19" later cancelled in ink.

253.18   timidly so: Originally "timidly."; T added "so." later in a different ink, without cancelling the period after "timidly".

253.20-25   The sincere . . . of the: "43 53 55 60 62 66 71 75 92 98-9 104-5 112 126 131" in pencil in a column opposite these lines; probably referring to page numbers for a draft of "Thomas Carlyle and His Works."

254.21   duty." – – :   Here and at several other places in his extracts from the *Bhăgvăt-Gēētă*, T indicated ellipses in his transcription with a variety of dashes and asterisks in the MS; the dashes (at 254.21, 254.24, 255.3, 255.7, 256.15, 256.25, 256.26, 258.11, 260.32, and 260.33) have been normalized to two dashes in the printed text. The asterisks have not been normalized.

255.20   *to continue*:   Underlined in MS; horizontal stroke beneath these words may be to separate entries rather than for emphasis.

255.27   restrained: "restained" in MS; T's source (*The Bhăgvăt-Gēētă*, tr. Charles Wilkins, p. 58) reads "restrained".

257.7   "The Yogee . . . :   Mark, possibly an asterisk, in margin opposite the beginning of the paragraph; see Textual Note 254.21.

258.12-14   "A . . . smoke.":   Written in a smaller hand at bottom of MS page; possibly added later.

258.19-20   a voluminous: "an voluminous" in MS. T wrote "an" and then began to write "ancient", then wrote "voluminous" over the beginning of "ancient" but did not cancel the "n" in "an".

262.11   v poetry: T later interlined the verse he had in mind; see Selected Later Revisions.

262.16   that: Illegible in MS; a later version (*A Week*, p. 130) reads "that".

262.24   Dudleian: Illegible in MS; a later version (*A Week*, p. 131) reads "*Dudleian*".

264.3   &:   Illegible in MS; a later version (*A Week*, p. 132) reads "and".

265.13-15   scrambled . . . rock–:   "leaping from rock–" originally followed "scrambled" at 265.13 and was followed by "which . . . parts". T then enclosed "leaping from rock–" in parentheses and indicated with a line and a caret that it was to follow "parts". He apparently neglected to complete the phrase "from rock to rock", as it appears in *A Week*, p. 233.

267.25   broke: "brook" in MS; a later version (*A Week*, p. 84) reads "broke".

269.8   size: Illegible in MS; a later version (*A Week*, p. 313) reads "size".

270.5-8   This . . . anecdote.:   Written in a smaller hand at bottom of MS page; possibly added later.

270.25-276.27   Aug 31st . . . 1845:   T's skeleton summary of his trip to Mt. Katahdin, preparatory to writing the lecture draft that follows; see the third illustration, following p. 454. Since he was gathering and organizing material here, his additions and interlineations are accepted and included as part of the text; in the ensuing draft of "Ktaadn," however, only the first level of composition is reproduced. See Textual Introduction, pp. 475-477. Where T provided no punctuation between subjects, the spacing has been determined by the sequence of incidents in the draft that follows.

270.32   Sept 1st: On the MS page, this date appears in the left margin beside "office" at 270.29. It has been moved to 270.32 to head the paragraph describing the events of September 1; see *The Maine Woods*, p. 4.

271.34   17:   MS ambiguous; T appears to have first written "17", written an "8" over the "7" to make "18", and then written "17" to the left. See 298.3 and *The Maine Woods*, p. 21, where the number is "18".

272.22   Pam: MS ambiguous; word written over illegible characters. The reference is probably to "Pamidumcook"; see 303.14.

274.3-4   beautiful . . . top–:   Interlined above "lake   to Rock & breakfast" without mark for position.

275.20   8 1/2:   Interlined above "down" without mark for position. The reference is probably to the hour at which the return began; see 341.14.

276.7   philosophy . . . lake: Interlined above "a . . . deep" without mark for position.

276.22-27   The . . . 1845:   Probably added later; ink resembles that of T's later revisions.

281.6   day night.:   "day. night." in MS; a later version (*The Maine Woods*, p. 4) reads "day night".

284.36-285.32   It was . . . –he: T inadvertently skipped MS pages "[106]-107" and wrote this text on the following pages "[108]-109"; he then turned back and filled "[106]-107" with the text at 285.32-286.32 ("having . . . after con /"). The printed text follows the order of composition.

295.15   an: "and" in MS; a later version (*The Maine Woods*, p. 17) reads "an".

296.10   cedar: Illegible in MS; a later version (*The Maine Woods*, p. 19) reads "cedar".

304.30   on: Illegible in MS; a later version (*The Maine Woods*, p. 29) reads "on".

308.34   the grindstone: "the" illegible in MS; a later version (*The Maine Woods*, p. 33) reads "the".

309.11   and we: "and" illegible in MS; a later version (*The Maine Woods*, p. 33) reads "and".

310.1   set: "sat" in MS; a later version (*The Maine Woods*, p. 34) reads "set".

311.34   and: Illegible in MS; a later version (*The Maine Woods*, p. 36) reads "and".

312.33   boat: "bat" in MS; a later version (*The Maine Woods*, p. 37) reads "boats".

313.12   common: Illegible in MS; a later version (*The Maine Woods*, p. 38) reads "common".

313.30   At last: "Ere last" in MS; a later version (*The Maine Woods*, p. 38) reads "At last".

314.11   dispersed: "disperused" in MS; a later version (*The Maine Woods*, p. 39) reads "dispersed".

318.30   fastened: "fasted" in MS; a later version (*The Maine Woods*, p. 42) reads "fastened".

319.6   across: "acrosses" in MS; a later version (*The Maine Woods*, p. 43) reads "across".

323.27   overshoot: "overshot" in MS; a later version (*The Maine Woods*, p. 49) reads "overshoot".

328.23   *missing*:   For a later version of the text interrupted at 328.24, see *The Maine Woods*, p. 52.

330.29   bed: "bead" in MS; a later version (*The Maine Woods*, p. 54) reads "bed".

331.1   bed: "bead" in MS; a later version (*The Maine Woods*, p. 54) reads "bed".

331.21   waked: "walked" in MS; a later version (*The Maine Woods*, p. 55) reads "awoke".

331.25   sleeping: "steeping" in MS; a later version (*The Maine Woods*, p. 55) reads "sleeping".

331.33 arc: "ark" in MS; a later version (*The Maine Woods*, p. 55) reads "arcs".

332.4 ἐξ: "ἐχ" in MS; T's source (*Iliad*, I, 469) reads "ἐξ".

332.14 as: "a" in MS; a later version (*The Maine Woods*, p. 56) reads "as".

333.6 stript: "striped" in MS; a later version (*The Maine Woods*, p. 57) reads "stript".

336.8 still: "sill" in MS; a later version (*The Maine Woods*, p. 59) reads "still".

338.27 bed: "bead" in MS; a later version (*The Maine Woods*, p. 62) reads "bed".

338.32 cloud: Followed by a period in MS; T first wrote "clouds.", then cancelled the "s" of "clouds" and added "or waterspout", but did not cancel the period.

339.6 smoother: "smother" in MS; a later version (*The Maine Woods*, p. 63) reads "smoother".

340.26 as the opposite: As in MS; T probably intended "as well as the opposite," for he later cancelled "as the opposite" and interlined "as well as S & W" as a substitute.

342.26 lose: "loose" in MS; a later version (*The Maine Woods*, p. 69) reads "lose".

342.34 as: "is" in MS; a later version (*The Maine Woods*, p. 69) reads "as".

345.32 and: "an" in MS; a later version (*The Maine Woods*, p. 76) reads "and".

348.14 while: Illegible in MS; a later version (*The Maine Woods*, p. 77) reads "while".

348.18 they: "thy" in MS; a later version (*The Maine Woods*, p. 78) reads "they".

349.27 *blank*: Contains a partial index of the preceding "Ktaadn" draft; see Appendix, pp. 389-390.

350.10 is: "i" in MS; a later version (*A Week*, p. 133) reads "is".

350.18 and: "ad" in MS; a later version (*A Week*, p. 133) reads "and".

353.5 words: MS ambiguous; this word may be "wood" or "woods", in which case the prepositional phrase of which it is the object would refer to "the American" and not introduce the quotation from Chateaubriand.

353.17-18 I . . . sweetly: Lower part of each word missing at torn edge of leaf; a later version (*A Week*, p. 67) reads "I trust some things are sweetly".

353.19 *missing*: Missing portion of leaf may have contained additional draft material for *A Week*; see *A Week*, p. 67, for later versions of the text at 353.16-18 and at 353.20-21.

354.29   *missing*: Missing portion of leaf may have contained additional draft material for *Walden*; see *Walden*, p. 10, for a later version of the text interrupted at 354.30. According to T's index, this MS page (255) contained an entry on "How to Cut nails", which probably refers to a passage later used in *Walden* (p. 10). See Appendix, p. 389.

355.2-3   The . . . 25th: Added in a different ink, probably later.

355.4   *missing*: According to T's index, this MS page (256) contained an entry on "Indians"; see Appendix, p. 389.

356.16   *missing*: See *A Week*, pp. 329 and 327, for later versions of the text interrupted at 356.15 and 356.17 respectively.

356.34   intercourse: "intercurse" in MS; a later version (*A Week*, p. 328) reads "intercourse".

360.17   a: Illegible in MS; a later version (*A Week*, p. 181) reads "a".

360.30   3 or 400:   "3 or 4000" in MS; the final zero must be inadvertent, for a later version (*A Week*, p. 181) describes these hills as "comparatively low".

361.1-21   There . . . distances.:   Written on back paste-down endpaper, with text at 361.20-21 ("in . . . distance.") written vertically in left margin.

[I]

363.1-2   [I] . . . 1848]:   Title and inclusive dates for this fragmentary volume are conjectural; see Historical Introduction, pp. 462-465.

365.1   *missing*: This first surviving leaf is paged "5"; see *A Week*, p. 182, for a later version of text interrupted at 365.2.

365.12-13   but . . . miles: "not more than 2 miles" originally followed "it was" at 365.11. After writing "I had left" at 365.12, T marked "not more than 2 miles" to follow and then continued the sentence "in a straight line–"; he later added "but" in pencil before "not more than 2 miles" to complete the sentence.

365.14   should: "sh{*MS torn*}" in MS; a later version (*A Week*, p. 183) reads "should".

365.26   {*MS torn*}:   Page torn horizontally at a slight angle so that the beginning of the last surviving line is missing.

365.29   *missing*: Missing pages may have contained more draft material for *A Week* and *Walden*; see *A Week*, p. 255, and *Walden*, p. 103, for later and much-revised versions of the text interrupted at 365.27 and 366.1 respectively.

366.28-369.28   "And . . . hair.:   In these translations from Ovid's *Metamorphoses*, T frequently interlined the original Latin word above his English rendering, and in many instances he interlined alternate English readings without indicating his final choice. The first level of his translation is printed here, and his uncancelled alternate readings are listed in the Table of Alterations.

367.7   plain: "plai{*MS torn*}" in MS; a later version (*A Week*, p. 4) reads "plain".

367.11   kingdom: "ki{*MS torn*}" in MS; a later version (*Walden*, p. 314) reads "kingdom".

367.13   morning rays: "morning {*MS torn*}" in MS; a later version (*Walden*, p. 314) reads "morning rays".

367.16   certain {*MS torn*}:   Missing portion of page must have contained T's translation of the Latin "limitibus" in Ovid's line "Vix ita limitibus disseperat omnia certes" (*Metamorphoseon*, I, 69); the Loeb translation is "Scarce had he thus parted off all things within their determined bounds".

368.19   Taurus, opposite: "Taurus," is interlined above "opposite" at the edge of the page; T wrote "1" before "Taurus," and "2" before "opposite" to indicate the order.

369.40   zones: "{*MS blotted*}es" in MS; a later version (*A Week*, p. 100) reads "zones".

370.1   writhe {*MS blotted*}:   A later version (*A Week*, p. 100) reads "writhe, and many a Nile".

370.2   back: "{*MS blotted*}ck" in MS; a later version (*A Week*, p. 100) reads "back".

370.6-15   I . . . reply: Some time after writing this passage, T revised it and divided it into lines of verse with virgules (/); a later version (NjP Taylor) was written as verse.

370.7   tort: As in MS; although the context would suggest that T intended "taut", a later version (NjP Taylor) also reads "tort".

370.9   crowed: "crowd" in MS; a later version (NjP Taylor) reads "crowed".

370.28   *missing*:   Missing pages may have contained additional draft material for "The Pond in Winter" in *Walden*; for a later version of the text interrupted at 370.29, see *Walden*, p. 296.

371.22   which: Lacking in MS; a later version (HM 924) reads "which".

372.1   *missing*:   Missing pages may have contained additional draft material for "Reading" in *Walden*; for a later and much-revised version of the text interrupted at 372.2, see *Walden*, p. 104.

372.13-24   There . . . letter–:   "v p. 145" in pencil in margin opposite this passage, referring to text at 376.2-8; see *Walden*, pp. 93-94, for later versions.

373.19 *missing*: At least some of the missing pages contained draft material for *Walden*; for later versions of the text interrupted at 373.18 and 373.20, see *Walden*, pp. 106-107 and 158, respectively.

373.29-30 trivial ... Or: "village (fishing at night–" interlined between these two paragraphs in ink, probably referring to an episode described in "The Ponds" in *Walden*, pp. 174-175.

374.28-29 {*MS torn*}: The upper left corner of the recto (the upper right corner of the verso) of this leaf has been torn off; several letters at the beginnings of lines here and at 375.16 are missing.

376.8 dreamed.: "v p 105" and "v 143" in pencil in margin beside "dreamed", referring to text at 372.13-24 and 374.30-375.35; see *Walden*, pp. 23-24 for later versions.

376.13 {*MS torn*}: This half leaf is torn at a slight angle from the horizontal so that text may be missing from the end of the first surviving line, " ... the".

376.15-22 In ... hole: "v p 129" in pencil written vertically in margin opposite this passage, probably referring to related text on a missing leaf paged "129".

376.24-25 In ... passed: "99" written in pencil in margin opposite these lines, probably referring to related text on a missing leaf paged "99".

376.26 *missing*: Missing pages may have contained additional draft for "House-Warming" and "Spring" in *Walden*; see *Walden*, p. 242, for a later version of the text interrupted at 376.25. See also Textual Note 376.27-377.2.

376.27-377.2 but ... of: These lines survive on the recto of a fragmentary leaf; for a later version of the text interrupted at 376.27 and 377.2, see *Walden*, p. 303.

377.4-6 Saw ... 1847: This notation of spring phenomena, containing the only dated entry in this MS volume, may have been added later, as it is written in a smaller hand at the top of the verso of a fragmentary leaf and is separated from the following entry by a horizontal line. The information is related to the passage on the recto of this fragment (376.27-377.2), for both passages were ultimately incorporated into "Spring" in *Walden*, p. 303.

377.11 *missing*: See *A Week*, pp. 320-321, for a later version of the text interrupted at 377.10.

377.12 *missing*: The text from 376.27 to 377.10 ("but ... the") is on the last extant regularly paged leaf, "159-[160]", of this MS volume. The leaves that follow are either unpaged or paged according to a numbering system different from that of the preceding leaves. The sequence of the remaining leaves in the present volume is conjectural and is based on the chronology of T's literary activities at this time; see Historical Introduction, pp. 463-465.

377.14-378.33   Robin Hood . . . fails.:   Text on unpaged leaf. Material from 377.13 to 378.17 is a revision of a portion of "A Walk to Wachusett" for inclusion in *A Week* (see p. 166).

378.8-12   Without . . . heavens: Added at bottom of MS page in a smaller hand, possibly later.

379.1-380.7   my sumachs . . . kind.:   This text is on a leaf anomalously paged "8'-9'"; see *Walden*, p. 223, for a later version of text interrupted at 379.1.

380.8-381.16   Poet . . . may: This text is on a leaf paged "160" on the recto, despite the fact that it continues the Poet/Hermit dialogue of the preceding leaf, paged "8'-9'"; some of the material on friendship at 380.16-381.16 appears in "Wednesday" of *A Week*, pp. 264-283 passim.

380.16   Friendship . . . peculiarity: "v p 93-& p 62-3" in ink above this line, probably referring to related material on friendship on leaves paged "62-63" and "93".

380.27   through: "though" in MS; a later version (*A Week*, p. 272) reads "through".

381.18-385.23   Yet . . . v 81:   Continuous text on three unpaged leaves that contain draft material for *A Week*, *Walden*, and "Ktaadn"; see Historical Introduction, p. 464.

381.18-22   Yet . . . themselves: For the context of this passage in a later version, see *A Week*, p. 282.

382.25-384.27   Few . . . unimpeded: This first extensive draft of the famous sand foliage passage from "Spring" in *Walden*, pp. 304-309, is heavily revised in ink and pencil; T's first level of composition is printed. His revised version appears in Selected Later Revisions. See Shanley, p. 204, for an earlier, much shorter version in the first draft of *Walden*.

385.22-23   This . . . v 81:   Notation for the placement of this addition to the "Ktaadn" draft; see *The Maine Woods*, p. 46.

Appendix

387.20   97   {191}:   Page "97" is missing from Walden 1; the only entry about a cicada is on the back paste-down endpaper (p. 191). T may have copied this passage from p. 97 when he removed the leaf.

388.5-31   I beans . . . Spring: This index was apparently constructed for an early version of the second half of *Walden* (see Shanley, pp. 100, 177-209). Passages indexed are from Walden 1, Walden 2, and Long Book.

388.24 91-92: "91-2" originally written at 388.23 for "Fox hunter" entry, then cancelled and added at 388.24 to entry on "Foxes".

389.33-390.17 1 . . . 242–: Page numbers that are not followed by numbers in braces in this index to the "Ktaadn" draft probably refer to a later version of the essay.

389.34 253: This number may refer either to the Berg Journal or to a later draft of "Ktaadn"; if it refers to the Berg Journal, it probably indexes text at 354.1-6.

390.12 201-2: This number may refer either to the Berg Journal or to a later draft of "Ktaadn"; if it refers to the Berg Journal, it indexes text at 329.21-330.15.

Table of Emendations

THIS table lists all changes made from the text other than normalized features described in the Textual Introduction (pp. 481-482), and it reports editorial resolutions of ambiguous manuscript features. Numbers at the left margin key the emendation to page and line, and if the number is marked with an asterisk, the emendation is discussed in a Textual Note. The emended reading appears to the left of the bracket, and the original reading appears to the right; editorial descriptions are italicized. A wavy dash (~) to the right of the bracket replaces the word to the left of the bracket in cases where only punctuation is emended. A virgule (/) indicates line-end division.

Long Book

4.3-4	friend . . . Concord.] *written at bottom of following MS page below horizontal rule drawn below* "et . . . Olympo" *at 4.16*
5.3	impulse] *possibly* ~,
5.5	guides] *possibly* guide
6.17	friendliness] friendlines *in MS*
6.22	hospitably,] *possibly* ~–
6.26	some] sone *in MS*
7.22	afternoon] *possibly* after noon
7.32	the] *possibly* this
8.8	still] *possibly* ~.
8.15	over] *possibly* ~–
9.4	hold.] *possibly* ~.–
9.8	water] wate *in MS*
9.24	sails] *possibly* ~- *or* ~–
10.18	nest] neest *in MS*
11.1	the narrow] *possibly* The narrow
11.24	revealed] *possibly* ~,
12.4	regularity,] *possibly* ~.,
12.9	Smith's] *possibly* smith's
* 13.13	Campton] Compton *in MS*
14.5	twilight] *possibly* ~,
14.6	the first] *possibly* The first
15.6	lull] *possibly* all

46.17-26	The . . . Cayster] *written on lower half of MS page*
	following river. *at 46.31 and marked for insertion*
47.15	these] *possibly* those
* 48.16	impelled] {*MS torn*}
48.29	middle] *possibly* ~–
49.1	Then] Th{*MS torn*}
50.8	fire] fir *in MS*
50.13	autumn] *possibly* Autumn
51.20-27	I . . . relief.] *written at bottom of following MS*
	page below horizontal rule drawn below and . . .
	health. *at 52.6 (see Textual Note 51.14-27)*
55.28	Those] *possibly* These
55.31	abode.] *possibly* ~
* 56.3	a chaste] a a chaste *in MS*
56.3	reserved] reseved *in MS*
56.24	desultoriness] desultorines *in MS*
56.25	noon] *possibly* moon
56.28	earthquake] eathquak *in MS*
57.25	circles] a circles *in MS (see Textual Note 57.24-*
	25)
58.6	groove] grove *in MS*
58.31	them] ~. *in MS*
59.14	blacksmith] blacks- / smith *in MS*
59.33	Rome–] *possibly* ~.–
60.2	Taunton] Tauton *in MS (see Annotation 60.2)*
60.13	admit] ad / mit *in MS*
60.31	position.] ~.. *in MS*
62.1	retain.] *possibly* ~:
62.3	kindness] *possibly* ~–
62.10	There] *possibly* Then
64.11	And] An *in MS*
65.5	spirit,] *possibly* ~;
66.28	mystery a] *possibly* mystery's
68.21	have] hae *in MS*
* 69.9	importunate] *possibly* unfortunate
70.19	kingfisher] *possibly* king fisher
70.26	corn fields] *possibly* cornfields
71.9	sure] *possibly* rare
72.26	wings–] ~.– *in MS*
74.20	lucky] luky *in MS*
74.24	without] withou{*MS torn*}
77.5	men] mean *in MS*
* 77.16	V p. 78] V n p but 2. *in MS*

77.21	the] (~ *in MS*
77.29	fibre–] ~.– *in MS*
79.5	right-perceiving] *possibly* sight-perceiving
79.16	us–] *possibly* ~–!
80.29	Cattle-shows] *possibly* Cattle shows
* 80.30	year] *illegible in MS*
* 80.35	plain."] "plain. *in MS*
81.28	today] to / day *in MS*
82.33	children.] *possibly* ~–
* 83.17	broke] brook *in MS*
83.20	neat] *possibly* meat
84.14	period] *possibly* periods
88.14	innocent] *possibly* ~,
88.15	it.] *followed by uncancelled caret*
88.21	nobleness–] *possibly second dash above dash*
88.32	irresponsible.] *possibly* ~.–
90.3	heard] *possibly* ~–
90.25	there] *possibly* these
* 91.17	such thing as] (~ ~) ~) *in MS*
91.27	Drying] *possibly* Dying
94.38	heaven] *interlined in pencil with a caret*
95.19	weather bleached] *possibly* weather-bleached
95.19	suntried] *possibly* sundried
96.31	house.] *possibly dash below period*
96.31	Some times] Som{*MS cut*} / times
97.21-22	mentioned–] *possibly* ~.
98.17	of,] *possibly* ~; *or* ~,–
99.12	could'nt] *possibly* could'not
99.17	much] muc{*MS cut*}
100.8	me–] ~.– *in MS*
*101.13	gardener] garden *in MS*
102.12	ever] *possibly* even
103.35-104.2	Where . . . Boston.] *enclosed in parentheses with question mark in margin opposite (see Textual Note 103.34-104.2)*
104.6	with] ~. *in MS*
104.27	extinct] ex / tinct *in MS*
*105.5-34	"Fisherman's . . . $8:82½] *lines of dashes normalized*
106.28	blossom'–] *second dash below dash*
107.9	meanwhile–] *possibly* ~
107.13	whole] whoole *in MS*
*107.19	And] Am *in MS*
107.25	man's] *possibly* Man's

139.4	and] *possibly* or
141.12	inhabits] *possibly* ~–
141.27	to him] *followed by* to him *cancelled in pencil*
141.33	it–] *possibly* ~–.
142.19	and] an *in MS*
142.21	behind] be / hind *in MS*
143.6	test–] *possibly* ~.–
143.18	particle] ~. *in MS*
144.17	themselves] them / selves *in MS*
145.31	its] *possibly* ~.
147.14	bar room] *possibly* bar-room
147.15	Beacon hill] *possibly* Beacon-hill
148.3	enquired] *possibly* inquired
149.17	get] *possibly* ~.
150.17	an] *corrected in pencil from* and
151.3	as] *interlined in pencil*
151.20	how] *possibly* from
151.33	they] thy *in MS*
152.5	conscientious] consinctious *in MS*

[Walden 1]

155.6	halls of] halls f *in MS*
*155.11	Kaaterskill] *possibly* Kanterskill *or* Kauterskill *in MS*
156.22	Self-emancipation] *possibly* Self emancipation
157.15	administered] ad / ministered *in MS*
157.25	dust] *possibly* duds
157.28	or] *possibly* as
157.31	firmament] firma / ment *in MS*
158.18	stand] stan *in MS*
158.20	which] *altered in pencil from* with
158.22	where] *possibly* when
*158.25	7] *illegible in MS*
159.26	rain] *possibly* ~.
159.35	once] onece *in MS*
160.8	New york] Ney- / york *in MS*
160.10	sang] *possibly* sung
160.28	grieve."] *quotation mark written below* grieve. *at outer edge*
160.29	white-oak] *possibly* white oak
161.7	there] *possibly* their
161.16	he,] *possibly* ~,.
*162.25	At] It *in MS*
162.28	piece] pice *in MS*

190.32	hopped] hoped *in MS*
*191.18-	
193.12	March . . . ducks.] *written on front free endpapers*
191.29	spring] *possibly* ~.
192.3	no where] *possibly* no-where
192.14	ornithologist] *possibly* Ornithologist
*192.28	a] *possibly* an *or* our
193.2	consolations] *possibly* consolation

[Walden 2]

*197.32	Health] Heath *in MS*
198.41	returns] *possibly* return
199.7	wintery] *possibly* wintering
200.7	man] *possibly* men
200.12	far] *possibly* afar
200.27	fate] *possibly* ~–
*200.36	good] god *in MS*
201.2	his] *possibly* lost
201.16	span] *possibly* spare
201.23	globe] *possibly* Globe
201.31	shade] hade *in MS*
202.12	yields] yilds *in MS*
202.33	hours] *possibly* hour
202.39	You'll] Youl'l *in MS*
203.8	some] *possibly* ~,
*203.11	are] ar *or* as *in MS*
203.11	wherewithal] *possibly* where withal
*203.18	And] An *in MS*
*203.22	they've] *illegible in MS*
204.3	exagggeration?] *possibly* ~?.
204.12	loud] *possibly* hard (*see Textual Note* 204.11-12)
204.12	hearing] heart *or* heard *in MS* (*see Textual Note* 204.11-12)
204.15	first] *possibly* ~–
204.18	an] *possibly* ~–
206.1	either] –~ *in MS*
206.24	countless] coutless *in MS*
206.24	French] *possibly* ~–
207.2	centre] *possibly* centres
207.3	health] heath *in MS*
207.17	stepping] steepping *in MS*
207.31	once] *possibly* even

207.31   an]   and *in MS*
208.17   ever]   *possibly* even
208.29   close]   lose *in MS*
*210.32   motes]   moats *in MS*
211.5   embargo]   *possibly* Embargo
*212.14-15 not . . . charity]   not deed charity *in MS*
213.5   ton]   *possibly* tun
*213.9   sweet-scented]   sweat-scented *in MS*
213.11   yard]   *possibly* yards
213.15   so–]   *possibly* ~–.
214.7   seen]   *possibly* ~–
214.14   black-duck]   *possibly* black duck
*216.10   Gilfillan's]   Glinfillan's *in MS*
216.14   dead]   deed *in MS*
217.21   feet]   ~. *in MS*
217.24   antiquity–]   *possibly* ~
218.10   & vines]   *possibly* berries
218.20   demonstrative]   demonstative *in MS*
219.7   especially]   espeially *in MS*
219.7   –and]   *possibly* – And
219.10   everywhere]   *possibly* every where
219.13   anything]   *possibly* any thing
220.25   spirit–]   *possibly* ~
221.7-12   (Mirabeau . . . judge)]   *parentheses added later in ink*
221.29   town]   *possibly* towns
222.5   lucky]   loucky *in MS*
*222.9   Indian meal]   Indian *in MS*
222.11   yeast–]   *possibly* ~
222.33   –not]   *possibly* – Not
225.10   My]   *possibly* .~
225.31   breed]   *possibly* ~–
226.1   young]   *altered in pencil from* yound
*226.21   it . . . spectacle]   {*MS torn*} their hose & breeches'. {*MS torn*} spectacle
227.2   a]   *possibly* to
227.15   Yeoman's]   *uncancelled apostrophe before* a
227.23   importance]   *preceded by uncancelled* f
227.25   foreborne]   *possibly* fore borne
227.25   foreborne]   freborne *in MS*
227.31   allowance]   *possibly* allowances
228.32   and]   ad *in MS*
*228.35-36 not done]   *illegible in MS*

[Berg Journal]

233.17	Hare] *possibly* ~.
*234.14	Athenaeus] Atheaeus *in MS*
234.18	this] *possibly* the
235.22	atmosphere] atmospher *in MS*
235.32	when] *possibly* When
236.4	prevailed– There] *possibly* prevailed–there
*236.5	and the] *possibly* in the
236.8	distinctly] *possibly* ~–
236.25	atmosphere–] *possibly* ~.–
236.26	are] *possibly* were
*237.7	is it that] is that *in MS*
237.32	me] *possibly* one
237.33	oceans] *possibly* Oceans
238.4	cocoanut] *possibly* cocoa nut
238.17	longer] ~, *in MS (see Textual Note 238.17-18)*
238.26	growers] *possibly* groves
239.10	demand] *possibly* demands
239.20	careless] *possibly* ~– *or* ~,
239.31	this.] *possibly* ~–
*239.35	am looking] *possibly underlined*
*240.1	a] a a *in MS*
*241.5	and in each] and each *in MS*
241.10	an] *possibly* and
244.10	ever] *possibly* even
244.16	that] *possibly* there
244.17	there] *preceded by* still *cancelled in pencil*
244.17	to,] *possibly* ~–
244.34	mankind] *interlined in pencil with a caret*
244.35	it–at] *possibly* it– At
245.5	silence] *possibly* Silence
245.12	woman] *possibly* women
245.15	silence] *possibly* Silence
245.19	forms] *interlined in pencil*
246.12	so] *possibly* as
*246.19	any] and *in MS*
246.20	fears] *possibly* ~–
246.24	everywhere–which] *possibly* everywhere– Which
246.33	1845] *corrected from* 1846 *in pencil*
247.2	Cove] *possibly* C on
247.19	15th] *possibly* 16th
248.35	not] *possibly* but
249.14	is] *possibly* in

249.19	To] *possibly* The
250.3	end.] *possibly* ~–
250.11	C] *possibly* G
250.12	bare] *possibly* base
250.20	gills.] *possibly* gills'.
252.3	all] *possibly* ~,
252.21	clouds] *possibly* ~–
253.11	receives] recives *in MS*
*253.18	timidly] ~. *in MS*
*253.18	so.] *added later in ink*
254.18	western] *possibly* Western
*255.27	restrained] restained *in MS*
257.23	They] The *in MS*
*258.19-20	a voluminous] an voluminous *in MS*
258.24	–"But] *possibly* –. "~
259.18	dynasties] dynas / ties *in MS*
259.29	Scripture] *possibly* scripture
259.31	Selections] *possibly* selections
260.1	edit.] *possibly* ~:
260.9	faith] *possibly* faiths
260.11	and] ad *in MS*
260.11	as] *possibly* at *or* and
260.13	no] *possibly* ~–
260.18	reader– To] *possibly* reader–to
260.28	"This] *quotation marks added in pencil*
261.1	"Know] *quotation marks added in pencil*
261.5	deeds] *possibly* deed
261.24	her] he *in MS*
261.33	as] *possibly* –~
262.3	life] *possibly* ~–
*262.16	that] *illegible in MS*
262.19	demanded] demand / ed *in MS*
*262.24	Dudleian] *illegible in MS*
262.30	my] *possibly* ~,
262.33	neighbor] *possibly* neighbors
263.1	its] *possibly* it's
263.25	father] *possibly* fathom
263.29	themselves] *possibly* them-selves *or* them selves
263.31	move] *possibly* ~–
*264.3	&] *illegible in MS*
*264.10	service] *possibly* awe
264.29	there] *possibly* then
265.4	strangers] *possibly* stranger
265.23	battle ground] *possibly* battleground

265.24	murmuring by] *possibly* murmuringly
265.26	some things] *possibly* somethings
266.7	Twice told Tale] *possibly* twice told tale
266.9	dark] *possibly* dank
266.26	where] *possibly* here
266.34	Such . . . distill] *follows on same line as* flavor of at 266.33
267.16	Piscataquoag] *possibly* Piscatauquoag
267.18	seaward] ~. *in MS*
267.19	then] *possibly* they
*267.25	broke] brook *in MS*
267.30	dews] ~. *in MS*
267.33	over] *possibly* on
268.2	the] *possibly* ~,
268.3	learning's] learning' *in MS*
268.13	Now] *possibly* ~–
268.17	a] *possibly* or
268.28	sheltered] shetered *in MS*
269.6	pigeon] *possibly* pigeons
*269.8	size] *illegible in MS*
269.11	late] lat *in MS*
269.13	bears] *possibly* beast
269.14	through] throught *in MS*
269.16	mountain] *possibly* Mountain
269.24	Norway] Noway *in MS*
270.7	be] *possibly* ~,
*270.32	Sept 1st] *written in left margin beside* office *at* 270.29
271.21	little] litte *in MS*
271.21	Ma'rm] *possibly* Ma'm
271.28	scent] *possibly* ~.
271.32	smoky] smooky *in MS*
272.14	shillings] *possibly* shilling
273.5	Camps] *possibly* camps
273.14	bread] *possibly* ~.
273.15	sweet] seet *in MS*
274.23	hall–] *possibly* ~.
274.24	isle–] *possibly* ~–,
274.24-25	track–] *second dash below dash*
275.6	&c.] *possibly* ~,
275.22	jumping–] *second dash below dash*
275.23	tree] *possibly* ~.
275.28	carry around] cary aroud *in MS*

288.26	luxuriantly] *possibly* luxuriously
288.29	ostler] *corrected later in ink from* osstler
289.1	wall,] *comma written over second* l
289.5	travellers] *possibly* traveller
289.10	has'nt] 'nt *interlined later in ink*
289.33	grooving] groving *in MS*
289.33	then] *added later in ink*
290.1	sleeps–] *second dash below dash*
290.5	houses] *second* s *added later in ink*
290.5	rank] k *added later in ink*
290.7	end] *interlined later in ink*
290.26	camping.] *possibly* ~:
291.2-3	dry shod] *possibly* dryshod
291.7	companions] compaions *in MS*
291.7	up] *interlined later in ink above cancelled* on *or* over
291.8	Houlton road] road *added later in ink*
291.10	woods] *added later in ink in margin*
291.17	water] *interlined later in ink*
291.24	them.] *added later in ink*
291.31	shop so] ~. ~ *in MS*
293.21	lakes.–] *possibly* ~– –
293.32	the few] *possibly* those few
294.5	left] lef *in MS*
294.17	log] *preceded by* log *cancelled in ink*
295.4	cabin–] *second dash above dash*
295.13	tucked] tucket *in MS*
*295.15	an] and *in MS*
295.22	Nickatow.] *possibly* ~:
295.26	dwelling–] *possibly period above dash*
295.27	woods–] *possibly* ~.
295.33	hay–] *possibly period below dash*
*296.10	cedar] *illegible in MS*
296.21	was] *illegible strokes altered later to* was *in ink*
297.5	loggers] *possibly* logger
297.5	loggers] *possibly* ~–
297.8	inhabitants–] *second dash below dash*
297.21	of] f *in MS*
298.4	my] *interlined in ink*
298.9	their] *altered later in ink from* there
298.17	we] *possibly* he
299.4	bank] *possibly* banks
299.21	afterward] *possibly* after ward

299.21	where] *possibly* when
300.5	nap.] *possibly* ~–
300.9	white cedar] *possibly* white-cedar
300.12	and] &nd *in MS*
300.17	penetrates] pentetrates *in MS*
300.26	a] *added later in ink in margin*
301.32	a] *inserted later in ink*
302.25	say–] *possibly period above dash*
302.28	Fowler,] *possibly* Fowler's
302.31	again] *possibly* ~,
303.12	is] *added later in ink*
303.22	better– Such] *possibly* better–such
303.24	vitae.] *possibly* ~:
303.26	and] *corrected later from* an *in ink*
303.30	one] *possibly* we
304.3	brought] brough *in MS*
304.9	bald-eagles] *possibly* bald-eagle
304.28	we] *altered later from* was *in ink*
304.29	better–] *possibly* ~.– *or* ~– –
304.30	making] *possibly* raking
*304.30	on] *illegible in MS*
305.14	meadows"] meadows' *in MS*
305.15	Fowlers,] *possibly* ~
305.17	south] outh *added later in ink*
306.11	bear] *possibly* ~.
307.3	horizontal] horizon / tal *in MS*
307.7	rocks–] *possibly* ~.
307.24	sleek] steek *in MS*
308.6	iron–and] *possibly* iron– And
308.18	uninhabited] uninhabed *in MS*
308.25	familiarity] famili / arity *in MS*
308.27	anywhere] *possibly* any where
*308.34	the grindstone] the *illegible in MS*
*309.11	and we] and *illegible in MS*
309.12	veiled] veilied *in MS*
*310.1	set] sat *in MS*
310.17	trade,] *possibly* trades
310.30	John] *followed by stray mark resembling* n
311.1	trail–] *possibly period above dash*
311.22	adventurers] *possibly* adventure
311.23	log-hut] *second hyphen above hyphen*
311.28	realized] relalized *in MS*
311.30	we] *interlined later in ink*

*311.34   and]   *illegible in MS*
*312.33   boat]   bat *in MS*
313.8   western]   *possibly* Western
*313.12   common]   *illegible in MS*
*313.30   At]   Ere *in MS*
313.31   landmark, and]   *possibly* landmark. And
*314.11   dispersed]   disperused *in MS*
314.12   felled]   feelled *in MS*
315.15   surface]   *possibly* ~–
315.22   until]   *possibly* Until
315.30   hills as]   *possibly* hills As
315.34   nuts–]   *possibly* ~ &
317.23   took]   too *in MS*
317.30   his]   *possibly* this
318.13   another]   a / nother *in MS*
318.27   spring]   ~. *in MS*
318.28   here.]   *possibly* ~–
*318.30   fastened]   fasted *in MS*
318.31   of this]   f this *in MS*
319.1   bark]   *possibly* hook
*319.6   across]   acrosses *in MS*
319.29   cook]   *inserted later in ink following cancelled* look
320.14   noticed]   notic *in MS*
320.14   rock–]   *second dash below dash*
320.20   man]   *possibly* ~.
322.13   walked]   *interlined later in ink*
322.17   assistance.]   *possibly* ~
322.33   something]   *possibly* some thing
323.25   instant]   ~. *in MS*
*323.27   overshoot]   overshot *in MS*
324.14   exciting]   *possibly* existing
324.29   maker–]   *second dash above dash*
324.31   your]   *possibly* you
325.8   gentleman]   *possibly* ~–
325.10   rot–]   *possibly* ~.–
325.12   Passamagummuck]   Passa / magummuck *in MS*
325.31   or]   *inserted later in ink*
326.18   George]   *interlined later in ink*
326.21   another]   a / nother *in MS*
327.16   portage– The]   *possibly* portage–the
327.19   Drivers]   *possibly* drivers
327.20   you've]   yove *in MS*
327.29   overhung]   *possibly* over hung

328.9	themselves] *possibly* them selves
328.19	gone and] *possibly* gone And
328.21	events] *written later in ink over* debts
329.26	Geo.] *possibly* ~
330.4	running] runing *in MS*
330.7	specimens] *followed by uncancelled* n
330.14	flowers,] *possibly* ~
*330.29	bed] bead *in MS*
330.34	skeleton] sketon *in MS*
330.34	bones] *interlined later in ink*
*331.1	bed] bead *in MS*
331.2	beginning] beging *in MS*
331.9	reserved] *possibly* rescued
331.13	obedience] obedinence *in MS*
331.18	swallows] sallows *in MS*
*331.21	waked] walked *in MS*
*331.25	sleeping] steeping *in MS*
331.27	moon-light] *possibly* moonlight
*331.33	arc] ark *in MS*
332.2	satiety] *possibly* ~.
332.3	companions] *possibly* companion
*332.4	ἐξ] ἐχ *in MS*
332.11	v 278] v 91 *in MS*
*332.14	as] a *in MS*
332.24	lead–so] *possibly* lead– So
332.26	keeping parallel] *interlined later in ink*
332.29	out] *possibly* ~.
333.2	rod] *possibly* ~.
333.5	scythe.] *second period after period*
*333.6	stript] striped *in MS*
334.8	truth–] *second dash above dash*
334.18	Leibnitz] *possibly* ~–
334.28	men] *possibly* man
334.34	without] with / out *in MS*
335.2	gone] goon *in MS*
335.25	prized] *possibly* priced
*336.8	still] sill *in MS*
336.18	Here] *possibly* ¶ ~
336.31	stair way] *possibly* stairway
337.13	erect] ereect *in MS*
337.25	any] *corrected later in ink from* and
337.30	firry] *possibly* furry *or* ferny
338.16	were] *interlined later in ink*

348.21	broad brimmed] *possibly* broadbrimmed
348.30	muskrat] *possibly* muskrats
349.1	kept] t *added later in ink*
349.6	are] *possibly* were
349.14	There were] *added later in ink*
349.34	years–] *second dash above dash*
*350.10	is] i *in MS*
*350.18	and] ad *in MS*
350.30	As] *possibly* ~–
351.4	autumnal] *possibly* Autumnal
351.8	atmosphere] *followed by* with them *cancelled in pencil*
351.20	(orderly)] *parentheses possibly later cancellation*
351.30	old–] *possibly* ~
352.10	masterpices] master / pices *in MS*
352.19	ever] *possibly* never *or* ~– *or* never–
352.20	dry] *possibly* sky
*353.5	words] *possibly* word *or* wood *or* woods
*353.17-18	I . . . sweetly] *lower part of each word missing at torn edge*
355.7	western] *possibly* winter
355.15	ever] *possibly* even
355.15	came] cam *in MS*
355.20	the] *possibly* that
355.24	shoe-strings] *possibly* shoe strings
356.5	health] l *added in pencil*
356.19	none] non *in MS*
356.27	youth] *possibly* ~.
*356.34	intercourse] intercurse *in MS*
358.29	harness] *possibly* ~–
359.24	alone] *possibly* ~,
360.5	Southwest] *possibly* South west
360.10	sloping] *possibly* Sloping
*360.17	a] *illegible in MS*
360.17-18	hay field] *possibly* hayfield
*360.30	3 or 400] 3 or 4000 *in MS*
360.33	southward] south / ward *in MS*
361.20-21	in a . . . distance.] *written vertically in margin* (*see Textual Note 361.1-21*)

[I]

| 365.3 | I] *possibly no* ¶ |
| 365.11 | that–] *possibly* ~ |

365.12   but]   *added in pencil (see Textual Note 365.12-*
                  13)
*365.14   should]   sh{*MS torn*}
365.19   once we go on]   *possibly* on we go now *or* once
                  we go soon
366.10   and]   an *in MS*
366.12   to]   *possibly* &
366.15   those]   *possibly* these
366.20   heavens.]   *possibly* ~'.
*367.7   plain]   plai{*MS torn*}
*367.11   kingdom]   ki{*MS torn*}
*367.13   morning rays]   morning {*MS torn*}
367.18   under]   unde{*MS torn*}
367.30   does not]   *possibly* does nt
368.9   rotating]   *possibly* rotatory
368.25   manage]   mange *in MS*
369.11   roses]   *possibly* ~.
369.35   coursed]   *possibly* crossed
369.39   eye]   –~ *in MS*
*369.40   zones]   {*MS blotted*}es
*370.2   back]   {*MS blotted*}ck
370.7   coaster]   coaste *in MS*
*370.9   crowed]   crowd *in MS*
370.24   ends]   *possibly* lusts
370.25   which]   *altered in pencil from* with
370.26   another]   onather *in MS*
*371.22   which]   *lacking in MS*
372.13   There]   Ther *in MS*
372.19   newspapers]   *possibly* newspaper
372.30   literature]   lierature *in MS*
373.28   they]   *possibly* They
373.30-31   shrub oaks]   *possibly* shruboaks
374.5   our]   ou *corrected to* our *in pencil*
374.6   to]   *possibly* by
374.7   country]   *possibly* county
374.7   life a]   *possibly* life or
374.10   inhabitants]   *corrected in pencil from* inhabitance
375.2   new–]   *possibly* ~.–
375.3   newspaper]   *possibly* news paper
375.6   need one]   *possibly* need we
375.11   a bore]   *possibly* alone
375.17   murmur]   mur{*MS torn*}
375.18   be]   b{*MS torn*}

375.26	with unrelaxed] *preceded by* No *cancelled in pencil*
375.35	notwithstanding] notwith / standing *in MS*
376.2	sympathy] {*MS torn*}ympathy
376.12	when] *possibly* unless
377.10	the] *possibly* these
378.5	equanimity] quanimity *in MS*
378.7	always] alays *in MS*
378.22	counterpart] *possibly* counterparts
379.12	meditation] medition *in MS*
379.31	to being] *possibly* being
380.13	lets] *possibly* let
*380.27	through] though *in MS*
381.4	man] *possibly* men
381.16	is] *possibly* ~–
381.20	flattered] *possibly* ~.
382.9	Love] *possibly* Loves
382.32	when] *possibly* When
383.18	larger] *possibly* longer
383.20	are] *possibly* be
384.2	more] mor *in MS*
384.30	thoroughfares] *possibly* Thoroughfares
385.8	place] *possibly* Place
385.21	stream] .~ *in MS*

Appendix

388.3	&c] *possibly flourish*
388.23	no 3] *possibly* no 2

Table of Alterations

THIS table reports Thoreau's substantive current alterations to the text. Several types of changes, discussed in the Textual Introduction, p. 483, are not reported. Numbers at the left margin key the alteration to page and line, and if the number is marked with an asterisk the alteration is discussed in a Textual Note. The revised reading appears to the left of the bracket, and the original reading appears to the right; editorial descriptions are italicized. A wavy dash (~) to the right of the bracket replaces the word to the left of the bracket in cases where only punctuation is altered.

Long Book

3.4	also] *inserted*
3.4	was] is
3.12	Brother] brother
3.27	before . . . late] *interlined with a caret*
3.30	on the morrow] tomorrow
4.3	water] *uncancelled* brink *interlined above*
4.6	whose] *followed by cancelled* siluer
4.18	nature] *interlined above cancelled* life
4.20	gemmae,] *written above cancelled* turgent.
4.30	Merrimack] merrimack
5.2	famous] *uncancelled* ancient *interlined above*
5.4	accompany its waters] *uncancelled* follow the current along the banks *interlined above*
5.8	exploration] *uncancelled* enterprise *interlined above*
5.14	current] *interlined above cancelled* stream
5.16	at the bottom] *interlined with a caret*
5.18	seeds] *preceded by cancelled* we
5.19	anon] *uncancelled* ere long *interlined above*
5.28	journeyed] *uncancelled* been moving *interlined above*
5.29	put] *uncancelled* trust *interlined above*
6.6	long] *interlined with a caret*
7.10	but they] but at *or* but as
8.11	conferred] *uncancelled* signed *interlined above*

8.26   has ... of life] *uncancelled* acquires an independent life *interlined above*

9.22   the nature of] *interlined with a caret*

9.31   blossom] *preceded by cancelled* flower

10.3   Proserpine] proserpine

12.11   Parthenon] parthenon

12.18   propitiate ... &] *interlined with a caret*

12.28   this] the

12.29   thus] this

13.5   For] for

13.20   thy] their

14.14   in] *followed by cancelled* nature for

14.14   the] that

14.24-25   each ... leaves] *interlined with a caret*

14.26   silence] *preceded by cancelled* stillness,

14.33   every night] *interlined with a caret*

14.34-35   and musically] *interlined with a caret*

14.35   barking] *preceded by cancelled* baying

15.1   line] *followed by cancelled* who would not

15.8   heard] the

15.9   the woods] a woods

15.12   less] *preceded by cancelled* not

15.14   shutting] *followed by cancelled* down

15.25-26   which ... voyageurs] *interlined with a caret*

16.13   Thursday] *interlined with a caret*

16.18-19   without ... us] *interlined with a caret*

16.26   clouds] *followed by cancelled* sailed

17.13   the] *interlined above cancelled* enough

17.26   toward] towards

18.4   and dimensions] *interlined with a caret*

18.5   our feet] *interlined with a caret*

18.5   to] *preceded by cancelled* many da

18.14-15   and grace] *interlined with a caret*

18.15   through] fro

18.23   seems respectable] *uncancelled* commends itself to us *interlined above*

19.14   B.] b.

19.16   reveal] reveals

20.13   Perhaps] perhaps

20.16   help] *interlined with a caret*

22.7   breaks ... clouds] *interlined above cancelled* rises and sets

22.15   farming] *preceded by cancelled* my

23.7   the]   *inserted*
23.8   Indian]   *followed by cancelled* we sho
23.25   whatever]   ever *inserted*
24.21   begin]   began
24.27   trees,]   ~–
24.29   over . . . over or]   *interlined with a caret*
24.31   ever]   *interlined above*
26.7   apology]   *followed by cancelled* for
26.15   along]   *interlined above cancelled* on
27.12   or a]   a *inserted*
27.16   children]   *preceded by cancelled* the
27.22-23   and people . . . us]   *interlined with a caret*
27.25   Tuesday]   *interlined at top of MS page*
27.31   Bursting]   *preceded by cancelled* Some of these
              springs are very pure and cold, and occur in pic-
              turesque places.
27.32   this]   their
28.7   perchance]   *preceded by cancelled* still
28.14   in]   *preceded by cancelled* like
28.14   the]   *interlined below cancelled* their *and can-*
              celled its
28.16   lives]   lifes
28.25   contemplation]   *preceded by cancelled* the
29.12   notice]   *followed by cancelled* to the
30.14   indefinite]   *preceded by cancelled* indifferent
30.22   He]   *preceded by cancelled* Ye an
30.22   He]   he
30.27   Friday]   *interlined at top of MS page*
31.11   Friday]   *interlined at top of MS page*
31.12   face]   *preceded by cancelled* scenery *or* scenes
32.11   under the heavens]   *uncancelled* instead of find-
              ing a ferry or a bridge *interlined above*
32.32   now]   no
32.32   rises]   *preceded by cancelled* longer reflects the day,
              But
33.10   There]   there
33.15   But]   *uncancelled* And *interlined above*
33.15   man]   *interlined above cancelled* sickles
33.15   severs]   sever
33.25   Carlisle]   Carlyle
34.17-18   and though . . . last.]   *interlined below*
34.20-21   were . . . water]   *inserted*
34.23   at]   of

35.3	willows of the] *interlined with a caret*
35.9	safely] *interlined with a caret*
35.11	Thus] The
35.14-15	the Nile . . . denied?] *interlined with a caret*
35.21	without fail] *interlined with a caret*
35.23-24	Consider . . . that] *interlined above*
35.31	instant–] ~.
36.7	was] were
36.15	in space] *interlined with a caret*
36.20	some unconscious] *uncancelled or interlined above* some
36.22	and wise] *interlined with a caret*
36.23	with averted face] *interlined with a caret*
* 36.26	as . . . defeated] *interlined with a caret*
* 36.26	defeated retrospective] *uncancelled* anticipated? *interlined below with a caret*
37.4	It] it
37.23	harp] *preceded by cancelled* unseen
38.1	much] *followed by cancelled* of
38.19	new] *followed by cancelled* world
38.20	country–] ~,
38.31	Indian] indian
39.21	ornaments] *followed by cancelled* of
39.22	implements] *followed by cancelled* for
39.29	plains] *preceded by cancelled* soils
39.29	plains] plain
39.33	crop] crops
40.17	instance, the] instance, in
40.24	as] is
40.24	stepping] *preceded by cancelled* from one
40.27	& even] & *interlined above cancelled* there may be
40.28	& wit] & *interlined above cancelled* there may be
41.1	exercise] *interlined above cancelled* life
41.18	laws] *interlined with a caret*
41.20	weather] *preceded by cancelled* hours.
42.19	an infant] *uncancelled* a babe *interlined above*
42.27	into the] the *interlined above cancelled* its
43.9	I] *inserted*
43.32	just,] ~.
44.5	uttered] *preceded by cancelled* abroad
44.22	gain.] ~?
45.10	suspicions] *followed by cancelled* for

45.25	where ... night] *interlined with a caret*
45.31-46.3	and surely ... them.] *interlined with a caret*
46.5-6	purer ... noon] *interlined with a caret*
46.8	objects] *preceded by cancelled* all th
46.9	familiar] *interlined below cancelled* subject
46.32-33	The sun ... mood.] *interlined at bottom of MS page*
47.9	When] We
47.10	with ... enthusiasm] *interlined with a caret*
47.26	nobleman's] noble *interlined above cancelled* gentle
47.28	Tuesday–] *interlined above*
47.31	left] *uncancelled* west *interlined above*
48.31	if] *preceded by cancelled* as
49.3	throw] *preceded by cancelled* take us in tow
49.22	stillness] *followed by cancelled* of
49.23	thought] *interlined above cancelled* thing
49.23	subside.] *followed by cancelled* or may be written.
49.27	Oh] I
50.19	the blue] the *altered from* this *or* their
50.25	While] We
50.28	Oct 7th –42] *interlined at top of MS page*
51.7	grain–] ~.
51.8	wholly] *preceded by cancelled* life
51.13	Father's] father's
52.22	directness] *uncancelled* in point *interlined above*
52.28	tints] hues
53.5	the other thinks] ~, ~ ~
53.16	true] *interlined with a caret*
53.27	Harvest] harvest
54.22-23	surely ... man's] *interlined with a caret*
54.26	to] *interlined above cancelled* which
54.26	heal] *followed by cancelled* the
54.28	thus] *followed by cancelled* are
55.30	an immortal] *preceded by cancelled* A true life shall not fail
* 56.3	a chaste] *preceded by cancelled* pure
56.21	scow] *added in margin*
56.22	and vastness] *interlined with a caret*
56.26-27	is echo, what] *interlined with a caret*
56.31	summers] *interlined above cancelled* years
57.10	under] *preceded by cancelled* by
57.25-26	they ... sucker] *interlined above*

72.18   the inner bark of] *interlined with a caret*
72.20   using] *preceded by cancelled* making
73.1   east or west] *interlined with a caret*
73.2-3   around . . . shadows] *interlined with a caret*
73.4   and in] *preceded by cancelled* who
73.13   russett &] *interlined with a caret*
73.15   threshed out] *uncancelled* like ripe grain *interlined above*
73.15   threshed out] *uncancelled* floating on the wind *interlined below with a caret*
73.17   but] *interlined above cancelled* and
73.18   do those] *preceded by cancelled* to to
73.26   According to Gower] *interlined*
73.28   toke.] ~,
74.6   Goddes] goddes
74.12   those] this
74.24   conveniences.] *preceded by cancelled* advantages
74.35   invented] *preceded by cancelled* first
74.35-36 portable cave] *followed by cancelled* And lo! the plains and Valleys too were populated
75.4   roof–] ~.
75.4   in course] *preceded by cancelled* lo! the
75.6   thereby] *interlined with a caret*
75.25   as a] *uncancelled* these *interlined above*
76.7   rest] *preceded by cancelled* parts
76.7   the eye] their eye
76.12   reminds] *followed by cancelled* of
76.19   its] is
76.23   there] then
76.28   between] *added in margin*
77.18   words] worlds
77.21   message] *interlined with a caret*
77.21   deliver] *interlined above cancelled* say
77.22   no] *preceded by cancelled* now
78.11   for the] *followed by cancelled* the
78.19   large–] ~.
79.2   who] *interlined above cancelled* because she
79.3   the] *interlined with a caret*
79.9-11   For . . . unlike] *inserted*
79.22   indigestion.] *followed by cancelled* V. n. p
80.20-22 The low . . . leaves.] *inserted*
80.29   amid] *uncancelled* among *interlined above*
80.32   not yet] *enclosed in parentheses and uncancelled* never *interlined above*

91.5	men's] man's
91.19	steps] *uncancelled* arches *and* industry *interlined below*
91.19	pass] *uncancelled* span. *and* bridge *interlined below*
92.9	dost] doth
92.11	walks] *preceded by cancelled* knows
93.36	he] *followed by cancelled* next to
94.13	speak] *followed by cancelled* In every beholder's eye / A sailing vessel doth descry
94.14	some] this
94.18	companions] *interlined above cancelled* beholder's
95.2	thoughts] *interlined with a caret*
95.11	again & again] *interlined with a caret*
95.12-13	It makes . . . real] *interlined above*
95.13-14	experience . . . of.] *interlined below*
95.15	New Hampshire] new hampshire
95.17	rude] *interlined above cancelled* rustic
95.30	accustomed] *uncancelled* wont *interlined above*
96.9-10	dwelt . . . themselves] *interlined with a caret*
96.20	and] but
96.22	my] *preceded by cancelled* Satyrus
96.33	And] I
96.36	There . . . post] *interlined with a caret*
97.1	it] *interlined and followed by cancelled* the front was
97.2	owner's] *uncancelled* Landlord's *and* Master's *interlined above*
97.18	It] it
97.20	find no] *interlined above cancelled* neither
98.5	breathing] *preceded by cancelled* and
98.10	that] it
98.20	neither the] the *inserted*
99.25	lamp] *followed by cancelled* and handed ⬥
99.34	half] *preceded by cancelled* over
100.1	country] *preceded by cancelled* fields and pastures of my hoste
100.6	answered] *interlined above cancelled* inquired
100.14	unjust,] *followed by cancelled* would not
100.23	of] on
102.13	ground] grounds
102.21	of this] *preceded by cancelled* of t

102.31	&] *preceded by cancelled* an
102.32	bare] *preceded by cancelled* bear
102.34	still] *interlined with a caret*
103.2-3	were . . . be] *interlined above cancelled* had promised
104.11	taken] *preceded by cancelled* weir by
104.17	elsewhere] *uncancelled* in other creeks *interlined above*
104.19	"grass-ground"] *preceded by cancelled* river
105.9	Brown] brown
105.12	rum &] rum *interlined with a caret*
105.21	First] first
105.23	5ᵈ] *preceded by cancelled virgule*
105.25	Qᵗˢ] *preceded by cancelled* 2 *or* Q
106.4	fluid] fluids
106.17	But] *preceded by cancelled* The shad make
106.18	are] is
*106.26	month–] *followed by cancelled* According to Dr Storer–"on their greatest run.
106.31	Lowell] lowel
106.32	patiently] *followed by cancelled* with
106.33	instinct] *interlined with a caret*
106.34	taught] *uncancelled* reasoned with *interlined below*
107.7	mouths] mouth
107.10	awaiting] *preceded by cancelled* till
107.12	tells] tell
107.13	instinct] *preceded by cancelled* faith
107.14	late] *uncancelled* backward *interlined above*
107.21	easy] *preceded by cancelled* easily
107.25	for man's] for *altered from* in
107.27	the God] the *inserted*
107.28	charities] *uncancelled* philanthropy *interlined above*
107.29	below] *preceded by cancelled* below
108.6	If] *inserted*
108.6	it were] twere
108.6	thou were] were *interlined below cancelled* poor
108.9	stiff] still
108.11	of various] *preceded by cancelled* we have
108.19	and if] *preceded by cancelled* or if
108.24	surely,] *uncancelled* as all things else *interlined above*

108.26	but what] but we
108.34	formed of] formed our
109.4	7 to] *preceded by cancelled* 7
109.8	once–] *followed by cancelled* of not one individual is
109.9	being commonly] not being more
109.10	only] *interlined with a caret*
109.16	loves] *uncancelled* delights *interlined above*
109.17	hang] hand
109.17	sunny] *uncancelled* shadowy *interlined above*
109.19	so] *preceded by cancelled* then
109.25	young] *uncancelled* minnows *interlined above*
109.26	Bream] bream
109.26	Ruff] *preceded by cancelled* Rough
109.29	shore] *preceded by cancelled* sandy
110.5	the birth] *enclosed in parentheses and uncancelled* regular fruit *interlined above*
110.12	prey] *uncancelled* victim *interlined above*
110.30	the tail] the *interlined above cancelled* his
110.32	line] in
111.22	The] *preceded by cancelled* This as indeed all fish
111.25	curious] *uncancelled* peculiar *interlined above*
111.30	one] *interlined with a caret (see Textual Note 111.29-31)*
112.4	set . . . dreaming] *uncancelled* realize our dreams of *interlined above*
114.9	Just] *followed by cancelled* as f
114.23	the book] *preceded by cancelled* he can
115.28	closed] *uncancelled* shut *interlined above*
115.29	fields of] fields were
116.2	keel] *preceded by cancelled* hull
116.7	tree] *interlined with a caret*
116.13	Nature] nature
116.18	And] *preceded by cancelled* A
117.11	not] *interlined with a caret*
117.19	have] *followed by cancelled* I
118.12	birds &] birds or
118.18	it] is
118.33	any] *preceded by cancelled* more
119.3	still–] still and *or* still at *(see Emendation 119.3)*
119.23	these] this *or* their
119.23	page] pad
119.31	slimy] *preceded by cancelled* slimly

120.14	our spirits] *interlined above cancelled* been
120.29	who] had
120.33	state &] *followed by cancelled* the Chu
121.2	themes] *preceded by cancelled* and pressing topics
121.9	He] he
121.17	who] *preceded by cancelled* to
121.21	audience,] *followed by cancelled* not for his
121.29	who] whom
122.3	one] *preceded by cancelled* man
122.5	will . . . vain] *interlined with a caret*
122.6	indirectly to] indirectly a
122.10	declared] declares
122.17	speakers] *preceded by cancelled* debaters
122.29	or the] *preceded by cancelled* and
122.30	when] *preceded by cancelled* and
122.33	an] *preceded by cancelled* right
123.1	Frederick] ~,
123.7	we] will
123.11-12	of writing] *preceded by cancelled* of begin
123.12	telling his] telling a
123.33	it's] *followed by cancelled* is
124.1	us] *inserted*
124.16	Pacifica] pacifica
125.25	tastes] taste
125.30	as in] as is
126.1	live] life
126.8	Wayland] wayland
126.11	bridge] *preceded by cancelled* breadth,
126.18	thousands] the
126.29	that] than
126.33	removed] *preceded by cancelled* dug along through the snow
127.3	fore-legs] fore-feet
127.3	legs] in
127.14	Such] such
127.32	has] *interlined with a caret*
128.7	running] *preceded by cancelled* compared
128.8	periods] *preceded by cancelled* time
129.5	Jove] Joves
129.5	Fates . . . Furies] fates . . . furies
129.6	a] an
129.17	hoe] how
130.7	round the] round in

131.23	is] *inserted*
131.25	ambrosial] *interlined with a caret*
131.33	a] *inserted*
131.33	psalm] "psalms"
132.7	mercies] mercy
132.25	Prophecy] Prophesy
133.22	are] were
133.23	Neva] neva
134.15	buy] by
134.19	round &] round–
134.21	will] if
134.25	sitting] *interlined above cancelled* standing on the
134.33	King] Kings
135.4	me] the
135.4	that the] that that
135.8	of] a
135.17	morn] *followed by cancelled* One large bundle
136.4	– And] & we
136.7	to] as
136.32	older] *followed by cancelled* than
137.30	Green] green
138.26	sent] set
138.29	out] *inserted*
138.30	fast] *preceded by cancelled* sprightly
139.2	windows] *interlined above cancelled* nest
139.3	Lincoln bell] Lincoln bells
139.12	like] *followed by cancelled* a
139.18	Here] here
139.29	the wit] *preceded by cancelled* wood to
140.5	shelving] *followed by cancelled* stone
140.18	crawled] *uncancelled* crept *interlined above*
140.22	when] whenever
140.27	ofttimes] oftimes
141.1	Bare Hill] bare hill
141.9	ground] *uncancelled* earth *interlined above*
141.10	Haven] haven
141.15	expect] *uncancelled* require *interlined above*
141.18	of other] of–
141.20	circumstance] *interlined above cancelled* position
142.5	incredible] *preceded by cancelled* strange & notori
142.6	a perverse] *preceded by cancelled* some s
142.7	nebulous] *preceded by cancelled* the fixed stars.
142.19	on] *preceded by cancelled* on veget

142.21   walking] *preceded by cancelled* looking
142.26   still–and]   still–any
142.30   he]   the
142.31   off]   of
143.13   twinkling] *preceded by cancelled* star
143.23   I] *preceded by cancelled* The *written over* I
143.27   Liebig is]   liebig–
143.31   then] *inserted*
144.2   is then] *preceded by cancelled* then the sun
144.8-9   the palatable . . . prairie] *uncancelled* a few inches
            of grass *interlined above*
144.12   even] *preceded by cancelled* many
144.14   ever] *inserted*
144.24   of . . . life] *uncancelled* of voluntary poverty *interlined above*
145.25   when] *preceded by cancelled* What
144.27   larger] *preceded by cancelled* & the like
144.29   As] *preceded by cancelled* And
145.10   of magnanimity]   of *inserted in margin*
145.26   ranked]   ranking
145.28   We]   we
146.17   be]   a
147.3   What]   Is
147.8   How] *preceded by cancelled* We a
147.9   dwell]   do
147.10   stars] *followed by cancelled* dwell whose
147.17   life]   lives
147.21   make] *interlined above cancelled* bear
147.25   It]   it
147.28   move] *preceded by cancelled* stay in
148.9   towns-man] *preceded by cancelled* horse m
148.12   getting] *preceded by cancelled* He too
148.19   wear . . . –]   are not better clothed nor
148.22   been cultivating]   cultivated
148.28   sum] *interlined with a caret*
148.31   How] *preceded by cancelled* With a hundred
148.35   this]   the
149.1   a] *inserted*
149.2   one] *inserted*
149.25   they]   there
149.25   not] *preceded by cancelled* be no coopera
150.3   it in my]   in my
150.18   If]   if

150.20	Shakspeare] shakspeare
151.2	than] *interlined with a caret*
151.10	me] my
151.13	live] life
151.14	him] *interlined above*
151.14	Along] On
151.31	Solitude] *followed by cancelled* and Sickness
152.5	Conscientious] *preceded by cancelled* Those who had lived

[*Walden 1*]

155.8	Pine] pine
155.11	Kaaterskill] Canterskill
155.23	loftier] lofty
156.10	week] *added in margin*
156.15	In] in
156.23	his] an
156.34	Grecian] grecian
156.35	?] !
157.5	to go] *interlined with a caret*
157.16	nourish] nourishes
157.27	one] *interlined with a caret*
158.4	with] to
158.10	daintiest] dainty
158.20	of] *preceded by cancelled* off
158.28	this small . . . labor] *interlined with a caret*
159.1	hoe] how
159.36	Jove] jove
160.7	if] If
160.11	boor] Boor
160.11	Paphlagonian] paphlagonian
160.12	Alek] Alex
160.12	now,] *followed by cancelled* who
160.16	Homer] homer
160.19	at Nicolet] *interlined with a caret*
160.31	no] nothing
160.34	5] *preceded by cancelled* 9 6
161.1-2	and legs] any legs
161.7	Only] *preceded by cancelled* I have
161.11	morning] *followed by cancelled* as h
162.26	it] I
162.29	paws] face *or* faces
163.22	Latins] latins

164.15	breathed and] *followed by cancelled* as it were
164.18	a revelation] revelations
165.16	of] *followed by cancelled* of
166.30	from] of
166.32	By] by
167.4	our] a
167.6	see] hear
167.10	traveller's] travellers
167.26	starry] stars.
*167.38-168.1	adjacent . . . laborious] *uncancelled* They are the pot-herbs of the gods *interlined above*
168.7	The] the
168.13	are needed] *interlined with a caret*
168.20-21	by line] *interlined with a caret*
168.24	and] any
168.32	shadowy] shallow
168.32	roofs] roof–
168.34	Time] time
168.35	ourselves] ourself
169.4	here . . . one] *uncancelled* This summer morn *interlined above with a caret*
169.5	sprightly . . . now] *interlined above cancelled* with unwrinkled brow
169.9	Carnac] *followed by cancelled* neath
169.10	Shelters] *preceded by cancelled* Was born
*169.11-12	Whose . . . sky] the system nigh *and* the visible sky *transposed*
169.21	for] to
169.26	word] *preceded by cancelled* line &
169.34	Isis] isis
170.8	has] hast
170.35	comes] *preceded by cancelled* is
171.33	invites] *preceded by cancelled* up
172.17	seem] are
172.32	Had] *interlined above cancelled* Gave ou
172.34	armor.] *interlined above cancelled* trappings;
173.9-10	misfortune] misfortunes
173.10	succeeded . . . misfortune.] *uncancelled* was riveted or welded to misfortune *interlined below*
173.27	constantly he] *interlined below cancelled* all the while
173.38	many] may
174.7	scene] scenes

212.19	Esqr] esqr
212.31	dent] dint
213.15	live] *preceded by cancelled* life *corrected to* live
213.21	still] *followed by cancelled* still
213.22	road] *interlined with a caret*
213.30	hollow] tree
213.32	making] *preceded by cancelled* laugh
213.33	wild] *preceded by cancelled* loud
214.7	ruffling] *uncancelled* rippling *interlined above*
*214.7	sweep] *preceded by cancelled* scoure
214.25	pond] ponds
215.4-5	alas . . . men] *uncancelled* to drink long healthy pure draughts *interlined above*
215.7	thrived here] thrived–
215.12	with me] *preceded by cancelled* and my house
215.18	lie] lies
215.18-19	prudent . . . land lord] *uncancelled* anticipating thirst *interlined above*
215.23	summer] *preceded by cancelled quotation mark*
216.2	hearth] *uncancelled* doorstone *interlined above*
216.11	Anandale] *followed by cancelled quotation mark and cancelled period*
216.16	till] *inserted*
216.18	tuition] *followed by two cancelled quotation marks*
216.18	translations] *preceded by cancelled quotation mark*
216.21	in] *interlined above cancelled* at
216.21	Dysart,] *followed by cancelled quotation mark*
216.21	at the same] *inserted*
216.21-22	time . . . Kirkaldy"] *interlined below*
216.24	Craigenputtock,] *followed by cancelled quotation mark*
216.24-25	a . . . Dumfriesshire"] *interlined above*
216.26-27	here . . . him.] *interlined with a caret*
216.27	His] his
217.6	Brest] brest
217.8-9	I . . . surprised] *uncancelled* the R. feels a queer surprise *interlined above*
217.10	coffee?] ~!
217.14	markets"] marts'
217.20-21	a ground . . . feet] *uncancelled* an underground *interlined above*
217.26	brought] *preceded by cancelled* send
218.2	Monsieur] monsieur
218.10	& vines] *interlined with a caret*

227.19	Surveyor] *followed by cancelled* of
227.21	keeping] *preceded by cancelled* not only without charge
227.21	ravines] *preceded by cancelled* and passable
227.35	counted] *followed by cancelled* all
228.2	always] *preceded by cancelled* know
228.9	manna-wise–] manna-wise,
228.22	or living] *preceded by cancelled* of

[Berg Journal]

233.11	note of] note and
233.25	Bringing] Bring
234.1	even] *followed by cancelled* the yold
234.6	the door] the *interlined above cancelled* thy
234.6-7	the lintel] thy lintel
234.8	Or the] or thy
234.10	But if] If
234.13	For] for
234.28	rain] *uncancelled* storm *interlined above*
234.29	Ocean] ocean
234.31	Passing . . . air] *uncancelled* high in the air *interlined above*
235.9	slayer of] slayer ox
236.8	insignificant] *preceded by cancelled* trivial
236.17	all] *preceded by cancelled* at
236.20	Genius] genius
236.32	carve &] *interlined with a caret*
237.15	to be] to live
237.19	even] *inserted in margin*
238.8	Maine] main
238.18	cried] *preceded by cancelled* and (*see Textual Note 238.17-18*)
238.29	coast] *preceded by cancelled* of
238.32	Times] times
239.24	this] *preceded by cancelled* there
*240.1	a] *preceded by cancelled* tendency to
240.2	action] *preceded by cancelled* her
240.13	base] bases
240.14	at] of
240.19	of] or
240.31	friction] action
240.34	where] *preceded by cancelled* you
242.11	!] *inserted*
242.13	Yet] yet

253.31	–"The] –"the
254.20-21	affirm . . . employed] *uncancelled* give their preference to a wise inaction–not mixing in affairs so as to be bound or dragged down by them *interlined above*
254.25	action.] *followed by cancelled quotation marks*
254.29	nothing.] *followed by cancelled quotation marks*
255.11	Yet] *interlined above cancelled* –"That man seeth, who seeth that the speculative doctrines and the practical are but one,"
255.15	that the] that that
255.25	employed] *followed by cancelled* , employed
257.27	power.] *followed by cancelled quotation marks*
257.30	Gods] gods
258.19	the Mahabharat] *preceded by cancelled* an voluminous ancient poem called
258.23	Brahmans] Brahmas
259.13	Goon] goon
259.17	adventure] adventures
259.17	they] their
259.30	several] *preceded by cancelled* Chinese
260.4	God] *preceded by cancelled* gold
260.12	day] *inserted*
260.28	This] this
261.4	thus] is
261.9	newest] newer
261.26	to a] of a
262.1	reader] ready
262.1	it lies] *preceded by cancelled* all na
262.8	the] *inserted*
262.16	not] *interlined with a caret*
262.16	foreseen] no
262.20	me] *inserted*
262.24	are] have
262.29	that] *preceded by cancelled* but
263.1	that] the
263.9	instance] instances
263.15	voluntarily] voluntary
263.21	were] *followed by cancelled* since
263.26	an] a
263.29	to] *preceded by cancelled* of an
263.35	majorities] *uncancelled* numbers *interlined above*
264.6	custom] *uncancelled* habit *interlined above*
264.13	they who] who *added in margin*

271.10	trees] *followed by cancelled* marks of freshet–
271.11	hemlock] *interlined with a caret*
271.14	Potatoes & turnips] *interlined above*
271.20-21	Pattagumpus sp–] *interlined with a caret and preceded by cancelled* till
271.21	Pt.] pt.
271.21	little Books] *added in margin*
271.22	books] *interlined with a caret*
271.22	potatoes &] potatoes–
271.31	Waites'] waites'
271.31	13] *preceded by cancelled* view
271.33	Little] little
*271.34	17] 18
272.4	logging roads] *interlined with a caret*
272.12	&] *interlined above*
272.19	Tho] *interlined above*
272.21	4 from Mc C:] *interlined above*
272.32	Salmon] *preceded by cancelled* shad &
272.33	2 miles] *interlined above*
272.35	to 4] *inserted*
273.2	mild . . . Melvin] *interlined with a caret*
273.3	entrance to] *added in margin*
273.4	Grand] *preceded by cancelled* Thunder s
273.6	Ind. . . . ways] *interlined with a caret*
273.8	N of W] *interlined with a caret*
273.8	clear] *interlined above*
273.10	double] *interlined with a caret*
273.11-12	take . . . baggage] *interlined with a caret*
273.22	S . . . inlet] *interlined with a caret*
273.32	Sept 6th] *inserted*
273.36-274.1	thoroughfare &] *interlined with a caret*
274.2	N E] *interlined with a caret*
*274.3-4	beautiful . . . top–] *interlined above*
274.5	pond lilies] *interlined above*
274.10	stream] *preceded by cancelled* Pork
274.14	river] *preceded by cancelled* Pass
274.15-16	a . . . falls] *interlined with a caret*
274.24	rush & cut] *interlined with a caret*
274.26	from Con. isle] *interlined above in pencil*
274.28	pikes] *uncancelled* spikes *interlined above*
274.30	poling] *followed by cancelled* 3/4
275.4	mount] *preceded by cancelled* 6 1/2 track
275.10	cook] *preceded by cancelled* sand no
275.15	green] *added in margin*
*275.20	8 1/2] *interlined above*

275.21   the]   &
275.22   brook . . . S W]   *interlined with a caret*
275.24   Moose]   *preceded by cancelled* burnt la
275.27   return]   *followed by cancelled* about
275.28-29   carry . . . Falls]   *interlined with a caret*
275.29   Oak hall]   *enclosed in parentheses and uncan-*
                celled Depskaneig *interlined above*
275.30   goes]   *interlined above cancelled* clears off
276.2   run]   *interlined above cancelled* the dropped
*276.7   philosophy . . . lake]   *interlined above*
276.8   NE]   *interlined above*
276.14   Indians]   *preceded by cancelled* moose track at
276.17   7]   8
276.17   7 miles]   *interlined above*
276.17   10 miles]   *interlined above*
277.32-33   whether . . . or]   *interlined above cancelled* for to
                be vast though
278.11   but]   *preceded by cancelled* here
278.22   The]   This
278.24   describe]   *preceded by cancelled* relate
278.26   frying]   flying
279.6   seeking]   *preceded by cancelled* had
279.16   roach]   *followed by cancelled* of large
279.18   red]   *followed by cancelled* swam here
279.19   at]   in *or* on
279.30   how we]   however
280.11   rightfully]   rightly
280.16   fareing]   farer
280.16   at]   *preceded by cancelled* in the morning
281.19   decide]   decides
281.21   over]   *preceded by cancelled* this
281.21   come]   came
281.31   think]   thing
282.2   Boston]   boston
282.11   still]   on
282.26   slightly]   slight
283.1   The]   This
283.17   wood]   *followed by cancelled* wood
283.22   logs]   *preceded by cancelled* timber *or* lumber
283.26   boat]   *followed by cancelled* with
283.31   amusement–]   *followed by cancelled* especially wh
284.7   shore]   *preceded by cancelled* the
284.17   home]   *followed by cancelled* of
284.24   amusement]   amuse

284.26	with] *preceded by cancelled* not
285.2	as well] as *interlined with a caret*
285.6	water-logged] water *altered from* with
285.10	at] in
285.16	earnestness] earnestly
285.19	they see] –and
285.26	yonder] the
285.28	step] *interlined with a caret*
286.1	river] *followed by cancelled* and the military ro
286.2	for] at
286.6	apple] *added in margin*
286.14-16	Here . . . harm.] *interlined above cancelled* We observed the next
286.28	there] *interlined with a caret*
286.31	woods] *preceded by cancelled* hay *or* wag *or* way
287.6	Near] *preceded by cancelled* We walked up to the
287.12	from] *preceded by cancelled* of
287.17	He] he
287.31	tomorrow–] *followed by cancelled* we
288.6	Mattawamkeag] Mattawamkead
288.8-9	coming . . . bank] *interlined with a caret*
288.11	if] is
288.13	left the] left them
288.15	lightly] *preceded by cancelled* half
288.23	by] on
288.25	balsam–] *followed by cancelled* beach
289.3	some] *preceded by cancelled* perchance
289.7	there] *followed by cancelled* and
289.7	and soon] *preceded by cancelled* while
289.21-22	to satisfy] *preceded by cancelled* for
289.33	way] *preceded by cancelled* man
289.35	Matawamkeag] matawamkeag
289.35	and] at
290.5	supper–] *followed by cancelled* the fron
290.9	here] –
290.9	here] *followed by cancelled* I say
290.19	insinuate] *preceded by cancelled* sleep
290.20	demand] *followed by cancelled* for veni
290.25	much] as
290.26	in] *preceded by cancelled* among
290.28	colored] *preceded by cancelled* beads
290.28	one] *interlined above cancelled* some
290.35	a] –
291.7	road] *followed by cancelled* at

291.8	Houlton] houlton
291.11	Libbey] libbey
291.19	is] was
291.19	track well-worn] well-worn track
291.26	who] *preceded by cancelled* with
291.35	may] *preceded by cancelled* are
292.1	an errand] *interlined with a caret*
292.6	fell] *preceded by cancelled* cut
292.7	cut] cup
292.7	rolled] *followed by cancelled* roll
292.13	got] *preceded by cancelled* went
292.15	growing] *preceded by cancelled* & tur
292.18	cities] *followed by cancelled* who will
292.18	immigrant] emmigrant
292.19	N Y.] *followed by cancelled* pay
292.19	5 dollars] *preceded by cancelled* 3 dolls
293.9	all] *preceded by cancelled* The be
293.13	rep. at] rep."
293.30	daughter] *followed by cancelled* proved
294.7	Penobscot] penobscot
294.28	crossed] *preceded by cancelled* pass
295.5	with] *preceded by cancelled* and a
295.6	boards] *preceded by cancelled* logs
295.10	John–] *followed by cancelled* who
295.18	was] too
295.21	Fisks] fisks
295.23	Our] *preceded by cancelled* We
295.29	were] *interlined with a caret*
295.31	which] was
296.10	rifted] *preceded by cancelled* made cut
296.10	a sledge] *preceded by cancelled* the axe
296.17	extend] extended
296.17	roofs] roof
297.7	the only] are only
297.12	an] a
297.20	whose] *preceded by cancelled* which we
297.28	dessert] desert
298.3	18] *preceded by cancelled* Soon we were in
298.10	as] by us
298.14	his] our
298.20	intervale] interval
298.34	As] *preceded by cancelled* The house was built of lu

299.4   But] *preceded by cancelled* a man
299.17   sweet cakes] *followed by cancelled* to wind
299.20   used] *followed by cancelled* to both
299.26   Mc Causlin] MacCauslin
299.34   minds] *followed by cancelled* to wa
300.2   drizzled] drib *or* drip
300.20   farm–] farms
300.21   Mc C.] Mc c.
300.26   with] the
300.33   for] it
301.1   neighbors] *followed by cancelled* nor ro
301.12   over] o'er
301.12   alight] light
301.21   rained] *preceded by cancelled* returned
301.24   Flash] flash
301.32   Cedar] *followed by cancelled* and
301.32   to] a
302.25   cotton] *preceded by cancelled* strip
302.28   Fowler] Tom
302.33   stretching] *preceded by cancelled* where
302.34   9] *preceded by cancelled* where
303.3   Great] great
303.12   of] *interlined with a caret*
303.14   Ktadn] *preceded by cancelled* the
303.22   Such] *preceded by cancelled* strong and mi
303.22   may] make
303.27   invigorating] invigoration
303.33   A] *preceded by cancelled* And if
304.9   bald-eagles] *followed by cancelled* nest
305.4   Uncle] *preceded by cancelled* The
305.10   on] *preceded by cancelled* On the meadows
305.10   meadows &] *interlined with a caret*
305.11   had] was
305.12   where] *interlined above cancelled* which
305.16   inhabitant] *preceded by cancelled* settler
305.17   formerly] *preceded by cancelled* once
305.24   One] A
305.35   out] *preceded by cancelled* of
306.4   said] *followed by cancelled* she sheared
306.4   they] are *or* one
306.4   were] *preceded by cancelled* of
306.5   She] The
306.10   steel] *preceded by cancelled* various

306.12	wolves] *interlined with a caret above cancelled* deer
306.12	are] *followed by cancelled* are
306.18	before] *preceded by cancelled* while
306.20	Hot cakes] Hot bread
306.23	length] *followed by cancelled* we
306.25	was] *followed by cancelled* over rocky hills a
306.26	where] *preceded by cancelled* at
306.34	woods] *followed by cancelled* follow
307.2	to time] were
307.10	pine] *followed by cancelled* which had f
307.14	a] an
307.25-26	while deluge] deluge *interlined above cancelled* shower
307.29	west] *preceded by cancelled* axe
307.35	bows] bow
308.7	the water] the *preceded by cancelled* grazing *and followed by cancelled* rush
308.8	eye] *interlined with a caret*
308.14	we] *preceded by cancelled* then we ha
308.16	with] without
308.29	practised] practiced
308.31	think] thinking
309.1	winter] *followed by cancelled* the ice is the great
309.3	logging] *preceded by cancelled* lumber
309.8	up] *followed by cancelled* the
309.10	were] *followed by cancelled* seen *or incomplete word*
309.12	Ktadn] *followed by cancelled* veiled
309.17	Here we] We
309.25	as it] *interlined above cancelled* for
309.26	It] *preceded by cancelled* The dam
310.6	&] *interlined above cancelled* & rain
310.8	bible] *followed by cancelled* containing a list of names
310.13	1834] 1844
310.13	Hist.] hist.
310.13	Erection] erection
310.14	these] *followed by cancelled* things things
310.16	The] These
310.19	of] and
310.24	in] *preceded by cancelled* from
311.3	though] *preceded by cancelled* but much less in a straight line

311.3	though] –
311.7	For] for
311.14	so–] *followed by cancelled* here
311.16	by moon light] *preceded by cancelled* at twilight
311.18	a] in
311.31	where] *preceded by cancelled* where the
312.15	Moose] *preceded by cancelled* the other
312.18	pilot] *preceded by cancelled* guide
312.19	on these] in this
312.23	in] a
312.27	irregularity] irregular
312.32	They] they
313.11	if] the
313.15	nor] no
313.23	For] for
313.25	Ste] St
314.3	an operation] *interlined below cancelled* for cheerf
314.14	by] an
314.23	drew] *preceded by cancelled* packed it away as
315.6	while] which
315.13	3] 2
315.23	our] we
316.4	of some] on some
316.5	white] *uncancelled* civilized *interlined above*
316.9	this] the *or* their
316.19	duskiest] *preceded by cancelled* most
316.24	steam] *followed by cancelled* nature's
316.25	lightning] light
317.17-18	and is] and *interlined above cancelled* letting the sides
317.23	Marheyo] marheyo
317.23	hastily] *interlined above cancelled* seize his
317.23	polish] polished
317.27	doff] *interlined above cancelled* calm
317.31	latitudes] *followed by cancelled* where
318.21	again] it
318.22	Penobscot] penobscot
319.4	surrounded] surround
319.15	driving] *preceded by cancelled* the
319.30	Uncle] uncle
319.31	former] *preceded by cancelled* a
320.29	this] the
320.34	Kennebeck] kennebeck
321.13	By] *preceded by cancelled* By the We fir

328.29	Leaping] leaping
329.4	some of] *interlined above cancelled* a part r
329.9	carry . . . around] *interlined with a caret*
329.22	Here] here
329.22	at] we
329.22	Murch] *preceded by cancelled* Mouth
329.30	our hooks] our *preceded by cancelled* them
329.32	white] *preceded by cancelled* red ro
330.7	as we] we we
330.14	their] they
330.14	they] *followed by cancelled* were
330.16	swum] swam
330.25	not] *preceded by cancelled* while
330.32	it] *interlined above cancelled* the had be
331.1	Our] *preceded by cancelled* A
331.2	foot] *interlined above cancelled* head
331.4	a] the
331.7	while] *preceded by cancelled* I studied one After supper
331.9	pan] *followed by cancelled* by the
331.10	upon] by
331.19	resembled] resembles
331.32	sped] speed
332.8	nor] *preceded by cancelled* in other
332.25	for] *followed by cancelled* the
332.30	for] *interlined above cancelled* we took
332.33	bunch] the
333.1	the tracks] *preceded by cancelled* the literally
333.1	of the latter] *interlined with a caret*
333.5	clipt] as
333.27	considerable] considerably
334.9	dullest] dull
334.13	at] in
334.14	local] *preceded by cancelled* go
334.21	antiquity,] *followed by cancelled* and
334.34	summits] *preceded by cancelled* mount the
335.7	with] which
335.31	Such] such
336.2	course] *followed by cancelled* lay not parallel with it.
336.11	not] a
336.15	if] it
336.21	at] *preceded by cancelled* before
336.29	walking] walked

336.35	width] *followed by cancelled* and
337.17	stood] *followed by cancelled* at
337.21	then] there
337.29	Having] *preceded by cancelled* Passing over this firry country
337.29	& walked] *interlined with a caret*
337.30-31	where rocks] rocks *followed by cancelled* we
338.3	earthyness] earth or
338.8	We] I
338.15	had] *preceded by cancelled* a *or* w
338.21	bed fellow] *preceded by cancelled* neighbor
*338.32	cloud] clouds
338.32	waterspout,] ~.
339.6	rarely] *preceded by cancelled* No soil
339.19	This] *preceded by cancelled* It was a smook factory
339.21	columnes] columned
339.25	dramatic] dramatics
340.2	never] *preceded by cancelled* not
340.4	rocks] *preceded by cancelled* breathing
340.14	whom] the
341.2	palates] palets
341.4	that] the
341.8	the P.] *preceded by cancelled* our cour
341.8	P.] p.
341.9	beneath] *preceded by cancelled* at
341.14	followed] *preceded by cancelled* trace
341.28	For] for
341.30	often] to their
341.35	high] in
342.1	This] The
342.9	turned] *preceded by cancelled* stared eyed *or* turned eyed
342.14	unstrap] *preceded by cancelled* drink with his
342.20	had] *interlined above cancelled* long since had since had
342.24	"throw] *preceded by cancelled* to fel
343.20	there] in
343.33	current] *preceded by cancelled* force of the stream
344.7	only] *preceded by cancelled* but was
344.11	a circuitous] an circuitous
344.24	Jumping] *preceded by cancelled* Wading out
344.27	The boatmen] *preceded by cancelled* the bow at first is run out ten or twelve feet into the air. Then

while one holds by the painter the other jumps in
again and they proceed to the next fall.

344.27 shelf of] shelf or
344.29 from] *preceded by cancelled* one & a h
344.30 holds] takes
344.35-36 to the unskilful] *interlined with a caret*
344.36 itself] *preceded by cancelled* to
345.7 their sublimity] there sublimity
345.8 Familiarity] familiarity
345.17 red] *preceded by cancelled* large raw
345.19 since] as
345.32 clothes] *followed by cancelled* before he
346.7 Uncle] *preceded by cancelled* had
346.15 In] We
346.20 of] on
346.23 rose] *preceded by cancelled* was
346.27 Tom] He
346.33 But] *interlined above cancelled* that
347.2 who made it?–] who made it–
347.4 Why] Its
347.9 hereafter?] ~–
347.9 Boys] boys
347.10 But] but
347.12 stranger] *preceded by cancelled* after
347.14 during] *preceded by cancelled* after
347.21 Deep] *preceded by cancelled* the fo
347.28 Uncle] Tom
347.29 4] *preceded by cancelled* three or four
347.31 longest] largest
348.6 this] there *or* the
348.8 Millinocket] millinocket
348.9 we had] who had
348.10 House] house
348.27 me go] we go
348.36 passed] *preceded by cancelled* rested and b
349.1 Geo.] geo.
349.5 whither] where
349.8 middle] midnight
349.8 night] *preceded by cancelled* day
349.10 the clink] a clink
349.11 one of the party] *interlined with a caret*
349.14 Geo.] geo.
349.24 come:] ~;
350.15 prospect of the] *interlined with a caret*

360.12	at] *followed by cancelled* at
360.13	prospect] prospects
360.22	And] *preceded by cancelled* At length I rea
360.24	than] *followed by cancelled* in
360.24	afforded] afford
360.25	head,] *followed by cancelled* wit *or* out
360.31	centre] *uncancelled* middle *interlined above*
360.34	Sandy] *preceded by cancelled* the lan
361.4	settlers] *followed by cancelled* of the
361.6	distant] *preceded by cancelled* mile
361.14	shore,] *followed by cancelled* when s were there
361.17	Dutch] dutch
361.18	ship] *preceded by cancelled* full

[I]

365.9	who] *interlined with a caret*
365.11	4] *preceded by cancelled* to the summit–in a straight, but
365.11-12	miles . . . summit] *interlined above*
*365.12-13	but . . . miles] *marked for insertion*
365.16	when] *preceded by cancelled* where
365.19	stream] *preceded by cancelled* river *or* run
366.17	where] *preceded by cancelled* and the
366.24	them] these
366.24	by] in
367.24	Fresh] First
367.24	strive] *enclosed in parentheses and uncancelled* may climb up *interlined above*
367.26	earth] *uncancelled* lands *interlined above*
367.27	trembles] *uncancelled* shudders *interlined above*
367.32	descending] *uncancelled* down hill *interlined above*
367.32	descending;] ~.
367.33	management] *uncancelled* conduct and guidance *interlined above*
367.36	with] will
367.36	underneath] neath *interlined with a caret*
368.5	me;] ~:
368.7	canst thou do?] *interlined above cancelled* can y
368.9	that] *uncancelled* lest *interlined above*
368.11	you] *uncancelled* thou mayest *interlined above*
368.11	your] *uncancelled* thy *interlined above*
368.13	shrines] *uncancelled* temples *interlined above*
368.16	You] *uncancelled* thou *interlined above*
368.16	should] *uncancelled* st *interlined above*

End-of-Line Hyphenation

THIS table lists all compound or possibly compound words that are hyphenated at end-line in manuscript and must therefore be resolved as hyphenated or closed. The table derives from a master list of all end-line hyphens in manuscript. The editor identified as a "compound" any word containing two or more words of standard English: *keystone, highways, child-like*. Words formed with prefixes and suffixes, such as *unguarded* or *forward*, and words inadvertently resembling compounds, such as *seasons* or *handsome*, are excluded. For a discussion of the rationale affecting resolution of compound words as hyphenated or closed, see Textual Introduction, p. 483.

Numbers at the left margin key the entry to page and line numbers, and if the number is marked with an asterisk the item is discussed in a Textual Note.

Because this text is printed with a ragged right margin, it introduces no unauthorized end-of-line hyphens. Subsequent reprintings or quotations of the Princeton Edition text should therefore consider its hyphenation to be authorial.

Long Book

5.4	lowlands	41.24	highway
8.2	muskmelons	42.32	pulse-beat
8.19	fishermen	47.26	nobleman's
11.7	themselves	52.11	pen-craft
12.5	lawn-like	52.16	elsewhere
20.9	themselves	54.23	hillside
22.18	woodpecker	57.27	somewhat
23.27	Whatever	59.8	myself
25.26	home-staying	59.14	blacksmith
26.21	haymaker	61.33	cannot
28.30	boatman	64.9	sand-heaps
30.31	school-boys	68.15	sometimes
32.12	out-door	69.6	packthread
32.31	Scotchman	75.15	fair-complexioned
38.11	overhanging	76.26	cobwebs
41.10	cannot	77.16	outside
		80.26	pea-jacket

80.27	outstanding	181.12	outside
80.28	kersymere	181.25	noblemen
85.4	sunset	182.5	wigwam
88.18	godlike	187.11	something
90.28	himself	189.17	Deer-stealing
101.14	something	190.25	somewhere
104.31	fishermen	192.7	landscape
110.20	Brook-minnow	192.9	oneanother
110.29	himself		
112.26	himself	*[Walden 2]*	
117.36	baby-houses		
118.17	white-washed	208.1	broad-cloth
120.19	gentleman	208.9	Straight-bodied
124.12	easternmost	209.15	snuff-colored
126.19	honeysuckle	213.26	woodmans
127.3	fore-legs	215.20	summer-drink
135.13	looking-glass	215.33	raspberries
140.22	outline	218.28	workmanlike
148.23	something	219.1	able-bodied
151.3	archangel	220.3	birth-right
		228.15	huckleberry
[Walden 1]			
		[Berg Journal]	
157.7	somewhat		
157.28	something	242.34	themselves
159.11	woodchucks	244.6	booksellers
160.8	New-york	244.8	journeyman
162.2	themselves	244.27	whippoorwill
163.36	stand-point	245.16	somewhat
165.23	likewise	245.35	themselves
165.24	sideboard	246.6	oneanother
168.4	rainbow's	246.9	human-being
170.6	rail-road	246.16	themselves
170.9	Whippoorwill	246.24	everywhere
170.12	Ben-Jonsonian	247.12	hillsides
170.15	graveyard	247.14	Whippoorwill
171.10	waterlogged	271.27	pork-barrel
172.12	oak-leaves	272.5	clapboards
176.7	crone-like	276.30	moonlight
176.21	anywhere	277.11	Double-top
177.16	long-missed	281.13	Stillwater
179.11	hearth-sides	285.4	Everywhere
180.31	wigwam	287.5	somewhat
181.8	woodchucks	291.14	landlord

293.19	oil-cloth	339.3	sometime
298.21	beaver-stream	344.21	boatmen
299.17	hot-cakes	346.13	day-light
299.29	tea-kettle	356.29	whenever
302.8	long-handled	360.26	overlooking
311.17	thorough-fare	360.28	homesteads
312.21	up-stream	*[I]*	
316.18	sometimes		
325.8	gentleman	370.11	Dutchman
329.7	ourselves	376.18	blackbirds
337.22	fir-trees	383.14	overlaid

Selected Later Revisions

THIS table is a selective list of Thoreau's revisions and additions to his Journal. It does not include revisions of passages that appear in later printed works.

Long Book

40.7 legislature.: And yet they did not always retreat before the ravages of time–nor the arrows of their foes– *added in pencil*

44.9 times: Knowing this, we may read those sonnets said to be *addressed* to particular persons or to a mistress' eyebrow *added in pencil*

67.21 Talking ... singular–: *revised in pencil to read* What is called talking is a remarkable though I believe universal phenomenon of human society

68.12 speech!: They cannot stand it nor sit against it *added in pencil*

74.17-19 The potatoe ... bestowed.: *revised in ink to read* The gifts of Ceres and Minerva have been long known & prized by men–but the potatoe which sprang from a goodwill as ancient and divine as this is a recent discovery

127.29 souls–: aye and the souls of brutes, for they must have souls as well as teeth *interlined in pencil*

135.35 spectatordom.: jingling his pockets lowly– A transaction of singular quietness noiseless unruffled as the sun on chips. The thrush sung a few notes as I drove along the woodland path. *added in ink*

145.5 it–: I have heard that in France and Germany Some even receive a considerable salary for being philosophers *interlined in ink*

148.20 neighbors–: I think that in the winter the poor man who wears cow-hide is better shod than the rich–with India rubbers over calf-skin *interlined in ink*

152.4 good.: All good men were they of course– I mean nothing against them. *added in pencil*

[Walden 1]

182.24 It ... dignity: Ah. These Greeks and Romans who will succeed them The young have thier Yankees what will they perform. *interlined in pencil*

183.30-184.10 He ... poetry–: Yet the former is unquestionably the most respectable to us & better suited to the general people *added in pencil*

[*Walden 2*]

199.11 On ... fell: The bridegroom cometh *added in ink in right margin*

207.7-210.19 I went ... school.: *revised in pencil to read* I had one neighbor within a half a mile for a short time when I first went to the woods Hugh Quoil Irishman who had been a soldier at waterloo–Colonel Quoil as he was called I believe that he had killed a col. & rode off his horse who lived from hand–sometimes to mouth– though it was commonly a glass of rum that the hand carried.

He and his wife awaited their fate together in an old ruin in Walden woods. Now that Irishmen with jugs avoided the old house I visited it–an "unlucky castle now" said they There lay old clothes &c by habit as if it were himself upon his raised plank bed. & scattered about were soiled cards king of diamonds hearts spades on the floor his pipe lay broken on the hearth. One black chicken which they could not catch still went to roost in the next apartment– stepping silent over the floor–frightened by the sound of its own wings–never–croaking–black as night and as silent too, not even croaking awaiting reynard–its God actually dead.

There was the dim outline of a garden which had been planted– but had never received its first hoeing. now with burrs and cockles which stick to your clothes overrun with weeds–as if in the spring he had contemplated a harvest of corn & beans before that strange trembling of the limbs overtook him.

I never was much acquainted with Hugh Quoil though sometimes I met him in the path, and now do believe that a solid shank bone or skull which no longer aches lie somewhere and can still be pro- duced which once with garment of flesh and broadcloth were called and hired to do work as Hugh Quoil. What life he got–or what means of Death–he got by ditching.

He was a man of manners & gentleman like as one who had seen this world–and was capable of more civil speech than you could well attend to.

At a distance he had seemingly a ruddy face as of biting January– but nearer at hand it was bright carmine It would have burnt your finger to touch his cheek– He wore a straight-bodied snuff colored coat which had long been familiar with him, & carried a turf knife in his hand instead of a sword– He had fought on the English side before–but he fought on the Napoleon side now– Nap went to st Helena–Hugh Quoil came to Walden Pond I heard that he used to tell travellers who enquired about myself–that   & Thoreau owned the farm together but Thoreau lived on the place & carried it on.

He was thirstier than I & drank more–probably–but not out of the pond– That was never the lower for him–perhaps I ate more than he. The last time I met him the only time I spoke with him was at the foot of the hill on the highway as I was crossing to the spring one summer afternoon–the pond water being too warm for me– I was crossing the road with a pail in my hand–when Quoil came down the hill wearing his snuff colored coat as if it were winter–& shaking with delerium tremens– I hailed him and told him that my errand was to get water at a spring close by at the foot of the hill over the fence– he answered with stuttering & parched lips–bloodshot eye–& staggering gesture–he'd like to see it– Follow me there then. But I had got my pail full and back before he scaled the fence– And he drawing his coat about him to warm him or to cool him answered in delerium tremens–hydrophobia dialect which is not easy to be written here he'd heard of it but had never seen it–and so shivered his way along to town–to liquor & to oblivion. On Sundays–Brother Irishman & others who had gone far astray from steady habits & the village crossed my bean field with empty jugs–toward Quoils– But what for?–did they sell rum there? I asked "Respectable people they" know no harm of them" "never heard that they drank too much" was the answer of all wayfarers

They went by sober stealthy silent–skulking–(no harm to get elm bark sundays)–returned loquacious sociable, having long intended to call on you.

At length one afternoon Hugh Quoil, feeling better perchance with snuff-colored coat–as usual paced solitary & soldier look thinking waterloo along the woodland road to the foot of the hill by the spring–and there the fates meet him–and threw him down in his snuff-colored coat on the gravel–and got ready to cut his thread–but not till travellers passed–who would raise him up–get him perpendicular–then settle quick but legs what are they?– "lay me down" says Hugh hoarsely– House locked up–key–in pocket–wife in town"–and the fates cut–and there he lay by the way side–5 feet 10–looking taller than in life–.

–Skin of wood chuck just stretched never to be cured–met once in beanfield by the Waterloo man with uplifted hoe–no cap no mittens wanted. Pipe on hearth no more to be lighted–best buried with him   & now that he was gone & his wife was gone too–for she could not support the solitude–before it was too late & the house was torn down I went once to make a call.

What kind of fighting or ditching work he finds to do now how it fares with him whether his thirst is quenched–whether there is still some semblance of the carmine cheek–struggles still with some liquid demon–perchance on more equal terms–till he swallow him completely I cannot by any means learn.

210.21   Poor John Frost: *revised in ink to read* Poor John Frost I trust he is not here tonight (*see Textual Note 210.21*)

212.21   woods–:   for which let him be thanked first & God afterwards *added in ink*

223.8   task: but his field is still higher–his task more arduous *added in ink*

223.31   His . . . faith: God will find it hard to astonish him. *interlined in pencil*

228.23   myself: I must furnish myself with the necessaries of life *added in ink*

228.25-26   to see . . . nearer.:   *revised in pencil to read* if Watchusett Watatic or Monadnoc had got an inch nearer or farther off you would have heard of it.

[Berg Journal]

233.21-234.9   I . . . off.:   Only the Greeks could use this word beautiful with expression–it is a poem in itself–καλας ωρας–yet excluded from modern verse *written vertically in margin opposite these lines in ink but not marked for insertion*

234.17   above–:   To me the whole charm of some lines is in the word Kalia *added in pencil*

236.26-29   And . . . difference: when I am present at either *and* his note does not suggest which way the sun is rising–there is no vaunt & no weariness in it. *interlined but not marked for insertion*

245.22   variety–:   The poets are but singing birds–& with them it is always the pairing season *interlined in pencil*

252.28   moral: It perhaps exaggerates some of the sentiments *interlined in ink*

261.19   Lyceum: where all that heard sat judges. *interlined in ink*

262.11   v poetry: "The early pilgrim blithe he hailed / That o'er the hills did stray; / And many an early husbandman, / That he met on his way." & for aught he knew they were all highwaymen *interlined in ink* (*see Annotations, p. 410*)

262.21   me.:   While the town holds fast the thief and murders for my protection it lets itself go loose *interlined in pencil*

267.3   Of Helicon again.:   i.e presuming I have already tasted it *interlined in pencil*

280.15-16 not . . . are–: *cancelled* We can never be foreigners anywhere and we are astonished to see him eat drink & sleep & yawn & not come to pieces with every movement *interlined in pencil*

280.35-281.2 down . . . leisure: *revised in pencil to read* to more aristocratic quarters seeming to the risen heads as if they had come upraised upon the business of the boat–or were going down town at their leisure sauntering with an assured air of familiarity

Though ready to pay the balance of their account with Neptune any moment by the way. At length we discerned the limekiln fires at Thomaston & the day did really begin to break a little and let in a ray of grey light on the waves–and the morning found us standing up Penobscot Bay–turning into the beautiful harbor of Camden & the deep bay of Belfast–and after we had fairly entered the river breakers we came by the wharves of Bucksport.

283.29 woods.–: I was greatly astonished by this apparition for I expected momentarily to reach the end of the civilized world–and could not imagine why one should be carting a load of tinware of this sort I despaired of ever reaching the wilderness with him in company *interlined in ink*

287.9 strain–: She was altogether a bleak dark ? looking object–dirty & all seemingly happy *interlined in ink*

288.11 upriver: for that is the way they get the truth out of Indians *interlined in ink*

288.32 use–: as usual we found the bar room just in the state in which it had been left by the last traveller like a room at Pompeii– and yet as if freshly sanded for us *written vertically in ink in margin and marked for insertion after* use–

293.3 hours.: not coveting such tenderness as sleep but hardily enduring the useless night hours with patience *interlined in ink*

295.2 way.: As often as we came out upon the bank we looked up & down the river–though in vain, for traces of the Indians. *written vertically in margin in ink and marked for insertion after* way

295.33 Ebeeme–: The water is comparatively smooth below Nickatow–though rough enough to daunt an inexperienced boatman, but above this the serious difficulties commence. *interlined in ink*

299.25 not.: but dry and smoke their meats merely to preserve them. When afterwards on the lakes I asked uncle George how the Indians saved the meat of a moose killed in warm weather far in the woods–he answered that they hung it up till it was tainted then successively buried & unearthed it–till it was dried or consumed.

interlined and written vertically in margin in ink and marked for insertion after not.

300.14-16 summer ... paths.: I asked Jim if he ever walked off into the untrodden woods of an afternoon to see what there was to be found—but no that was an unexplored region to him—and he only knew that The wolves came to the edge of the clearing & serenaded them at night *interlined in ink*

303.3 Gut—: and both of which cut off an island from the shore and at high water was passable by batteaux though now nearly dry & there *interlined in ink*

304.29 better—: Fowler said that it was smooth water til you reached rapids at the outlet from the lake Those who go to the Mt by way of Millinocket lake see comparatively little of the rapids. *interlined in ink*

305.4 affirmed: though I dont know with how much truth what I had long before pleased myself with conjecturing *interlined in ink*

305.32 mink.: But there being none others to compare them with we could'nt decide this question. *interlined below in ink*

309.33 One ... filed: Climbing up a narrow foot through the bushes from which the path to the spring was seen to diverge *interlined in ink without mark for positioning*

316.11 demigod: what more startling news can the whalers ever bring from the P. than that savages still dwell there? *interlined below in pencil*

331.6 breadth: There we lay where Indians once and since adventurous loggers seeking the white pine had camped before and caught trout like us *interlined below in ink and marked for insertion*

347.16 falls.: "This world 'nis but a thurgfare full of wo, / And we ben pilgrimes, passing to and fro:" *interlined below in ink (see Annotations, p. 410)*

350.33 foliage.": while in other climates "stone of the purest white soon turns black, or of a greenish hue" *interlined below in ink (see Annotations, p. 410)*

354.11-25 All ... relations.: *revised in ink to read* material things are in one sense man's kindred, and subject to the same laws with him. He & They have but one destiny follow one fate Even a taper is his relative—and burns not eternally, as some think lamps said to be found burning in ancient sepulchres—but only in certain number of his hours. He sleeps and ere he wakes a taper is extinguished.

such things belong to the same sphere or natural dynasty with himself. He witnesses their birth and their decay What mans life

stationary and eternal does not thus embrace he sees from one side
& it thrills him to behold

He sees the former objects at a very near and wide angle. They
have a very large parallax to him–but not so those tapers the fixed
stars which are not both lit and burnt out in the life of a man–yet
they too are his distant relations.

355.14   on?:   If there were any there would be no quarrel. There
is never a square inch in common. *interlined in ink*

[I]

365.24   fences: and sometimes a patch of tobacco or of buck
wheat or millet, which I had never seen before *interlined in ink*

374.16-28   and importance . . . flock: And so the family should
consist of individuals *written vertically in margin in pencil opposite
these lines*

374.20   family.:   Nor can wealth   Indeed those beasts & birds
which are gregarious & polygamous interest me the least of any.
interlined below in pencil

374.28   A flock: what is a flock of a hundred robins then compared with (a single robin) calling to its mate in the {*MS illegible*}
interlined below in pencil

378.28-29   Yet . . . unchanged: *revised in ink to read* Yet where
is the pregnant circumstance that has produced this revolution?

381.2   meant.:   A procession has passed through the streets &
none saw it. *added in ink*

382.25-384.27   Few . . . unimpeded.:   *revised in ink and pencil,
as follows: marginal numbers are T's, indicating his intended order
of passages; words in square brackets are uncancelled alternative
readings*

 2   This phenomenon must have been rare before railroads were
built since it is not often even now that you meet with a freshly
exposed bank of the right materials

———

 1   Few phenomena give me more delight than to observe the
forms in the spring of the year which thawing clay and sand
assume on flowing down the sides of a deep cut on the rail road
through which I pass on my way to the village

———

 5   The clay especially as it contains most moisture & so solidly
frozen & longest thawing assumes an infinite variety of forms–

———

 4   There lie the sand and clay all winter on this shelving surface
an inert mass but when the spring sun comes to thaw the ice

which binds them they begin to flow down the slope a distance
of 50 feet like lava–

―――

6   little streams & ripples like lava over flow & interlace [inter-
weave] one with another like vines–a sort of Hybrid product–
obeying half way the law of currents & half way the law of
vegetation. as it were mythological vegetation or like the forms
which I have seen imitated in bronze–

―――

10   I am affected as it were by the presentness of the eternal
law– between that inert mass and this luxuriant vegetation what
interval is there? but God Here is that God who is reputed to
have built this world 6000 years ago still at his work.–freshly
this spring day sporting on this bank–

―――

8   It no sooner begins to flow than it takes the forms of vines–
or of the feet & claws of animals–or of the human brain or lungs
or bowels & excrement of all kinds clusters of graceful sprays
sometimes overlying each other a foot or more in depth destined
perchance to be the subject of admiration to future geologists

―――

7   Now the material is bluish clay now clay mixed with reddish
sand–now pure iron colored sand–and sand and clay of every
degree of fineness and every shade of color–

―――

9'   The whole bank for a quarter of a mile on both sides of this cut
is sometimes over-laid with a mass of plump & sappy foliage
of this kind–the produce of one spring day It would not be so
remarkable if it did not spring into existence thus suddenly &
as it were by magic–while to the eye it has all the perfectness
which belongs to the slowly formed works of nature & art.

―――

13   Each rounded lobe of these earth leaves–perchance of all leaves–
is a thick–now loitering drop larger or smaller

―――

14" so perchance the ball of the finger is a drop congealed and the
fingers & toes flow to the extent from the thawing mass of the
body–& then are congealed for a night. [may the sun of new
spring lead] who knows what the human body would expand
and flow out to under a more genial sky?

―――

14'   In the mornings as the sun's rays fall on them these resting streams start again and branch & branch again into a myriad others–

9   –And where the flowing mass reaches the drain at the foot of the bank on either side it spreads out flatter in to sands like those formed at the mouths of rivers–the separate streams losing their semicilindrical form–and gradually growing more and more flat–and running together as it is more moist till they form an almost flat sand–variously & beautifully shaded–& in which you can still trace the original forms of vegetation till at length in the water itself they become the mere ripple marks on the bottom

14   The lobes are the fingers of the leaf   as many lobes as it has in so many directions it inclines to flow–more genial heat or other influences in its springs might have caused it flow farther.

17   –Thus it seemed as if this one hill side contained an epitome of all the operations in nature.

16   So too we may ask What is the river with all its branches–but a leaf divested of its pulp–unless its pulp is intervening earth– forests & fields & town & cities– What is the river but a tree an oak or pine–& its leaves perchance are ponds & lakes & meadows innumerable as the springs which feed it.

11   I perceive that there is the same power that made me my brain my lungs my bowels my fingers & toes working in other clay this very day– I am in the studio of an artist. Who is even now at work–or rather play–forming fresh designs.

3   This cut is about a quarter of a mile long–running north & south & 30 or 40 feet deep–and in several places clay occurs commencing about a dozen feet below the surface.– Where there is sand only the slope is greater & more uniform–but the clay being more adhesive now stands out from the sand as in threatening masses–which are continually washing & coming down.

15   The material Flowing downward it of course runs together and forms masses and conglomerations but if flowed upward as it in trees it would disperesed itself more finely–& grow more freely– & unimpeded open & airy

12   Here you may see how blood vessels are formed–first there
pushes forward from [But there lies the blood vessels forming
& the lungs] a little silvery stream glancing like lightning, and
swallowed up in the sands– It seemed so artful

The thawing mass a stream of softened clay or sand with a
drop-like point like the lobe of a finger feeling its way–till with
more heat and the moisture the water which is the blood in this
finger and is in most haste–rushing from above separates itself
from the solid parts and forms for itself a channel or artery
within–and as the sun dries the uper side it falls in & reveals
a little silvery stream glancing like lightning and anon swallowed
up in the sand–coursing through this whole system of So are
rivers but arteries whose uper halves have fallen in and they are
left open channels Those parts which are most inclined to flow–
whose particles perchance are the soundest in their efforts to
obey the law to which the most solid and inert also yield–form
for themselves channels through the latter. What is man but a
mass of thawing–dissolving clay? In the siliacious matter which
is deposited you see the boney system & in the still finer sand
& mould the flesh.

Cross-References to Published Versions

THE following table provides cross-references between literary drafts in *Journal* 2 and their published versions. The first two columns furnish page, line, and keyword references to draft Journal versions; the third provides abbreviated title and page references to the corresponding published versions. Abbreviated titles, with one exception, refer to volumes in the Princeton Edition of *The Writings of Henry D. Thoreau*:

AW	*A Week on the Concord and Merrimack Rivers*	
Wa	*Walden*	
EE	*Early Essays and Miscellanies*	
RP	*Reform Papers*	
MW	*The Maine Woods*	
Ex	*Excursions* (Boston and New York: Houghton Mifflin and Company, 1906)	

Long Book

Library of Congress Cataloging in Publication Data
(Revised for volume 2)

Thoreau, Henry David, 1817-1862.
  Journal.

  (The writings of Henry D. Thoreau)
  "The complete Journal as Thoreau originally wrote it."
  Includes index.
  Contents: v. 1. 1837-1844 — v. 2. 1842-1848.
  1. Thoreau, Henry David, 1817-1862—Diaries.
2. Authors, American—19th century—Biography.
I. Broderick, John C.   II. Series: Thoreau, Henry David,
1817-1862.   Works.   1973.
PS3053.A25   1981   818'.303   78-70325

ISBN 0-691-06361-3 (v. 1)
ISBN 0-691-06186-6 (v. 2)